PENGUIN BOOKS
BUSINESS MAHARAJAS

A freelance journalist with a Ph.D. in business history, Gita Piramal is the author of the best-selling *Business Legends* and the co-author of a pioneering work on business history, *India's Industrialists*. She has also contributed to the seminal volume *Business and Politics in India—A Historical Perspective*, edited by Dr Dwijendra Tripathi and published by the Indian Institute of Management, Ahmedabad. She has been writing and commenting on the corporate sector for over eighteen years for leading Indian and international newspapers such as the UK's *Financial Times* and *Economic Times*.

Piramal has been involved in the making of television programmes on Indian business for the BBC and for Plus Channel.

She is married to industrialist Dilip G. Piramal and they have two daughters, Aparna and Radhika. Piramal divides her time between Mumbai and London.

GITA PIRAMAL

BUSINESS MAHARAJAS

PENGUIN BOOKS

Penguin Books India (P) Ltd., 11 Community Centre, Panchsheel Park, New Delhi 110 017, India
Penguin Books Ltd., 80 Strand, London WC2R 0RL, UK
Penguin Group Inc., 375 Hudson Street, New York, NY 10014, USA
Penguin Books Australia Ltd., 250 Camberwell Road, Camberwell, Victoria 3124, Australia
Penguin Books Canada Ltd., 10 Alcorn Avenue, Suite 300, Toronto, Ontario M4V 3B2, Canada
Penguin Books (NZ) Ltd., Cnr Rosedale and Airborne Roads, Albany, Auckland, New Zealand
Penguin Books (South Africa) (Pty) Ltd., 24 Sturdee Avenue, Rosebank 2196, South Africa

First published in Viking by Penguin Books India 1996
First published by Penguin Books India 1997

Typeset in Times by Digital Technologies and Printing Solutions, New Delhi

Printed at Basu Mudran, Kolkata

For
Aparna and Radhika
my two little gurus

Acknowledgements

The maharajas for their time
Dilip for his confidence in me
Khozem Merchant, Nishit Kotecha, Subniv Babuta
and Sailesh Kottary for their suggestions
David Davidar for his encouragement
Krishan Chopra for his constructive criticism
Sindhu Sabale for my data bank
my parents for their support
Harsh Goenka for the title

Contents

Contents

Introduction

Like the territorial rajas of the past, businessmen today rule vast empires, maintain a watchful eye inside and outside their boundaries, and protect their turf against invaders. The eight featured here are among India's most powerful men. Between them, they control sales of roughly Rs 550bn* through over 500 companies and directly employ at least 650,000 people. Switch on a light, sip a cup of tea, have a shave, listen to music, drive to work, see a movie, snuggle into a pillow—and you'll find yourself using their products through the day and into the night.

They are a study in contrasts. Their businesses are distinct and varied. Some are highly educated, others are college drop-outs. Some are inheritors, others self-made. Some topped their chosen field in their thirties, others didn't approach the starting line until their fifties. Some dominate a particular business, others control more than one industry. What they do, what they think, how they react impacts the entire economy, not just their customers, shareholders, employees, and bank managers. So how *do* they think? How *do* they conduct their businesses, arrive at complex investment decisions involving

---

* Sums have mostly been expressed in million/billion. The equivalents in terms of lakh/crore are: ten lakhs: one million; ten million: one crore; 100 crores: one billion (1,000 million).

billions of rupees, or hire and fire the executives who manage their dominions?

For me, the challenge has always been to find out why a company behaves the way it does, to understand the people and the compulsions behind business events. Inevitably, therefore, this is a book about business personalities. Management gurus love to talk about strategy and strategic decisions, but the more I learn about business, the more I'm convinced that management decisions are based on the personal experiences, aims and vision of one person. Usually it's the head of a business house or the chairman of a company, but sometimes crucial decisions can be taken by unexpected people, as I found to my surprise while researching this book.

I learnt, for example, that the Williamson Magor group's Rs 2.9bn decision to acquire Union Carbide India was not taken by blue-ribboned directors in its boardroom at 4 Mangoe Lane but in the tranquil drawing room of Shanti Khaitan. In 1994, every financial journal covered the sale, billed as the biggest takeover in Indian corporate history. Discussing the deal with the Khaitans, I found that their bid was based not so much on the advice of bean counters but on human factors. Worried that their son Deepak was spending too much time in their stable of three hundred horses and not enough in his garage of engineering companies, Shanti persuaded her husband, Brij Mohan, to make an offer for the famous battery maker. Deepak needed to settle down, and she was convinced that a big company like Union Carbide would be just the right ticket.

At one time, Bhiki Shah was a far more worried mother than Shanti. In the late '70s, her younger son Vijay had established a tiny office and a state-of-the-art factory at Saphadz, outside Tel Aviv. It did so well that in 1981 it received the Israeli government's highest export award and the next year, sales surged from $2m to $21m. Persuaded that the future for him lay in Israel, Vijay—who speaks fluent Hebrew—wanted to settle there but Bhiki protested. 'My mother used to hear about bomb scares and all those things on television. So we thought we had better settle down in Antwerp,' says Vijay. Thereby he altered the course of B. Vijaykumar & Company.

I doubt if there's a more fascinating businessman than Dhirubhai Ambani. As a petrol station attendant, he used to dream of heading a huge company, maybe a global multinational like his first and only employer, Burmah Shell. All teenagers dream but how many have the ability and doggedness to turn fantasy into reality? Ambani founded a brash, upstart company which challenged the established business houses and their way of conducting business. He fought for and seized paper licences, converting them into large textile mills and huge petrochemical complexes.

Through the process of building Reliance Industries into a corporate behemoth, he rewrote management theories, fought with India's most fearsome newspaper, made friends with prime ministers, became the only businessman to be lampooned as often as Rajiv Gandhi. He nailed his nameplate onto an office door in 1966. From next to nothing, within two decades, sales had ballooned to Rs 9bn, making Reliance one of India's top ten companies, but Ambani wasn't satisfied. Sitting at his desk one day in 1984, he drew up a flow chart. If he built such-and-such factory, added a division here and a unit there, ten years down the road, Reliance could become a Rs 80bn company. Sceptics laughed when he announced his plans, but he proved them wrong. In 1995, sales nudged Rs 78bn. Some say Ambani is an acronym for ambition and money. It's probably true.

In the '80s, Reliance grew at an astonishing 1,100 per cent, with sales moving up from Rs 2bn to Rs 18.4bn, but it wasn't India's fastest growing company. Its expansion trailed behind Bajaj Auto's incredible growth rate of 1,852 per cent. Under Rahul Bajaj, the Pune-based scooter company's sales swelled from Rs 519m to Rs 18.5bn during the same decade. Both Reliance and Bajaj Auto are lean and owner-driven corporations, yet in terms of character, style, background—every parameter that counts—there couldn't be two more dissimilar chairmen than Dhirubhai Ambani and Rahul Bajaj.

Ambani is a first generation entrepreneur, the Bajajs were rich long before Ambani was born. Ambani hustled in Bombay's teeming markets selling yarn and later fabrics. Bajaj didn't have to hustle—there were long queues of people outside his air-conditioned office patiently waiting to be allotted scooters. Ambani cultivated political contacts, Bajaj was born into a family of patriots. Mahatma Gandhi referred to Rahul's grandfather as his fifth son; Rahul's father was a Congress member of Parliament. Yet the government raided Rahul Bajaj twice, stalled his repeated applications to build new factories and expand production, and wouldn't let him diversify. In 1987 he wanted to buy into Ashok Leyland, a truck maker, but to clinch the deal, he needed dollars. The government wouldn't exchange his rupees and he lost the opportunity. Despite the difficult conditions he worked under, Bajaj established Bajaj Auto as one of India's rare world-class organizations.

The late Aditya Birla came from a family with as rich a political legacy as Rahul Bajaj. Birla had an appetite as voracious or more—if that's possible—for empire-building as Dhirubhai Ambani. To feed it, Birla built 2.3 factories annually, on time and within budget, for thirty consecutive years. His corporate feats were so awesome that every entrepreneur worth his red ledger and Excel spreadsheet wanted to know how Aditya Birla ran his operations. How could he pack in so much in such a short time? Could Birla's trade secrets be taught and replicated? Yet at the end of the day, his wife of thirty years wondered: 'He used to say "I do this for getting more power", but I don't think that was the case because he never made use of that power. So what good was it?'

Like Ambani and Bajaj, Aditya Birla was a greenfield man, preferring to build his own companies rather than buy what others had erected. Once they were up and running, he would guard them jealously, fending off marauders. Some of the attackers were his own cousins, which made the battles within the Birla clan even more exciting for those watching from the sidelines.

In terms of sheer drama, there's little to beat takeovers and buy-outs. That's why acquisition stories are couched in military terminology. Cloak-and-dagger secrecy is what makes Rama Prasad Goenka, India's buy-out specialist, so interesting. Who's selling and at what price, who's buying and at what price? Much can go wrong in deals where political strings have to be pulled and mega bucks change hands, but Goenka usually gets what he wants without too many glitches. There were only a few ripples when he silently picked up Ceat, a tyre maker, and later CESC, a power generator and distributor. In contrast, reams of newsprint forced Dhirubhai Ambani to abort his bid for Larsen & Toubro.

The first company Goenka bought was the Calcutta-based Duncan Brothers. His father had managed to wrangle him a job in the prestigious managing agency firm as a covenanted assistant on the princely salary of Rs 350 per month, but within a week RP tendered his resignation in protest against the racism rampant in the Scottish firm. The Raj was at its pinnacle, it was

RP's first job, and his father was furious. RP was forced to swallow his pride and return—which made the acquisition all the sweeter when it came through in 1963. A dozen buy-outs later, Goenka entered the top twenty league but he would become a cover boy only in 1989 when he shot up the corporate ladder to fourth place from thirteenth.

One of Goenka's closest friends is Briju Babu, the tea baron. Once, when he was shopping in London, a bomb hurled Khaitan twenty yards from the doorway of Harrods. Nineteen people died. He survived. Brij Mohan Khaitan survived also the riots of pre-Independence Calcutta when Mahatma Gandhi prayed nightly for peace in the *bastis* of a city described as a 'hell-hole'. He survived too the Naxalite movement, staying on in Calcutta when other Marwaris abandoned the city for New Delhi and Bombay. Khaitan is the only businessman in this book who employs a private army. It patrols his tea gardens day and night.

Bodyguards and guns are a way of life for this intensely private and deeply religious man. He doesn't like them, but he doesn't have a choice. How else will he deal with terrorist groups such as ULFA and Bodo militants in Assam? After every murder, Khaitan has to keep high not only his own morale but also that of those who depend on him. The life of this tea maharaja provides an insight into a shadowy world far removed from glossily printed profit and loss statements, the Calcutta Stock Exchange and high profile tea auctions.

The world of diamonds is almost as shadowy and dangerous as that of the tea gardens. Security cameras unblinkingly eye visitors to the offices of Bharat and Vijay Shah, and armed guards swing their firearms warningly in front of massive vaults housing millions of rupees worth of glittering carbon. It's a far cry from the clever videos of gorgeous women clad in little more than a necklace and earrings.

Bharat and Vijay, both college drop-outs, started from scratch like Dhirubhai Ambani, a fellow Gujarati. In ten years, the brothers built a Rs 35bn international empire selling an Indian product which is globally competitive. To get to where they are they had to break the hold of a group of Hasidic Jews, identifiable in diamond markets by their long flapping black overcoats, curly forelocks and wide-brimmed dark wool hats. The tentacles of this trade used to stretch from De Beers' legendary mines in South Africa and Australia to the auction rooms of New York and Tel Aviv, Antwerp and London. The Shahs and other Palanpuri Jains brought the business to Surat and Bombay, where nimble diamond cutters cut and polish tiny brown stones, turning dross into gold. How did they do it?

To make the Tata group globally competitive is one of the priorities Ratan Tata, the head of India's biggest business house, has set for himself. The group is at a watershed in its 125-year-old history and Tata knows he has to take urgent steps to prevent the group from plummeting into terminal decline. It's hard being a Tata. The surname doesn't permit failure and the early years of his business career were distinguished more by losses than profits. In the five years since he's been in the saddle, Tata has come a long way. Under his leadership, Telco and Tisco, the group's two biggest companies which between them contribute over half the group's sales and profits, are performing better than they have ever done before. The other eighty-two companies are being spruced up and with every little improvement, Tata brings the group closer to his goal of 'living in today's world'.

Restructuring, in fact, is a recurring theme in all seven of this book's chapters, reflecting the concern of these businessmen about the future. The end of the Licence Raj with its corollary of greater industrial opportunity, stiffer competition from domestic and international rivals, the financial revolution, the lure of foreign markets, the shaky promise of globalization, and various aspects of the liberalization programme have generated considerable debate about the direction of change and how Indian industry should rise to meet these challenges. Virtually all eight businessmen profiled here have either already initiated or are about to initiate far-reaching changes in their organizations, and an attempt has been made to outline their strategies and to explain the rationale behind the individual responses.

Business Maharajas doesn't limit itself to the top five or ten business houses but profiles India's most fascinating tycoons. How were they chosen? One guiding principle used was to look both into the past and the future in order to make a selection. They had to be men who controlled business empires which were established in the twentieth century and which will flourish in the twenty-first century. There's no point picking shooting stars: yesterday's heroes shouldn't turn out to be tomorrow's nonentities.

There are many superstars who are equally—if not more—interesting, such as Vijay Mallya, the jet-setting liquor king, or Subhash Chandra of Zee TV. There's a whole new crop of steel tycoons such as the Ruias, the Mittals and the Jindals, besides a band of electronic products magnates led by Venugopal Dhoot of Videocon, the Mirchandani brothers of Onida and T.P.G. Nambiar of BPL. India is becoming a major pharmaceutical player in world markets because of the efforts of men like Bhai Mohan Singh of Ranbaxy. These men require a book to themselves, a book which doesn't look both at the past and the future as does this one.

Another guiding principle used in the selection was the concept of territorial dominance. The profiled businessmen had to be leaders in their chosen area of activity. B.M. Khaitan grows 65m kg of tea annually, which translates into roughly

50 per cent of the Indian market and five per cent of global tea production. According to De Beers, the South African diamond giant, Bharat and Vijay Shah are the world's biggest diamantaires, annually cutting, polishing and marketing several billion diamonds. Producing over a million vehicles a year, Rahul Bajaj has built the world's fourth largest two-wheeler company in western India. For a moment in history, R.P. Goenka controlled a massive 35 per cent of India's total tyre production, though he lost this position and is now in the process of carving out a place for himself in the power sector. Before his tragic death at an early age, Aditya Birla had established himself as the world's leading producer of viscose staple fibre and palm oil, the third largest producer of insulators and the sixth largest of carbon black. Within India, he was the largest producer of cement, rayon filament yarn, flax and caustic soda. From his high-rise office in Bombay, Dhirubhai Ambani dominates textiles and petrochemicals and dreams of becoming India's Arco, while Ratan Tata heads India's biggest business house and is the number one truck and private sector steel maker.

And what about men like Kishan L. Chugh of ITC or Sushim M. Datta of Unilever? Surely their lives and achievements are quite as extraordinary as those of Ratan Tata or Aditya Birla? Don't these outstanding chieftains rule huge corporate empires? Yes, but the third guiding principle of this volume is a focus not on the ranks of professional managers but on picking the best talent from family businesses.

After so many years of research on entrepreneurship, many ask whether I have gleaned any ideas on why some people are winners and others are losers. Can the elements of success be identified? I'm as puzzled today as the day I started out fifteen years ago.

Of the seven profiles drawn in these pages, three are

rags-to-riches stories (Ambani, Khaitan, and the two Shah brothers) and three are about inheritors who have added to their legacies (Birla, Bajaj, and Goenka). As a chairman who's been less than five years in the hot seat, the jury's still out where Tata is concerned.

Only two hold postgraduate degrees: Bajaj is an MBA from the Harvard Business School and Goenka is an MA from Calcutta University. Birla studied at Boston's prestigious MIT and Tata graduated from the equally famous Cornell, but the matriculate Ambani rolled up his sleeves and got a job at seventeen, Vijay Shah dropped out of the London School of Economics when his father died, and Khaitan completed his undergraduate studies in an undistinguished morning college.

In building their *jagirs,* each has developed a unique set of tenets which stems from his character, background and experiences. Inevitably the corporate culture of the companies they head is grounded in these tenets and reflects the personalities of their chiefs.

Take, for example, the measured growth of Grasim and Hindalco. In his twenties, soon after taking over the reins of Indian Rayon, the young Birla discovered that profitability improved dramatically if he ensured that the small spinning mill ran to rated capacity and if he kept adding new machinery in driblets. This strategy would become the essence of Birla's corporate philosophy. 'To keep on modernizing, updating, debottlenecking, cost cutting, increasing production (including capacities) by technological improvements, this is what we enjoy. Running a plant day in and day out in the same manner gives one no joy. The basic aim of technological advance should be to reduce the cost of production—not technology for technology's sake,' he once explained. Today his factories are the cheapest per unit manufacturers of their given products.

Ambani's corporate attitude is radically different from that of Birla. Instead of creating a 'safe' capacity based on conservative demand projections, Ambani planned huge factories which from the beginning would be world-scale in capacity, cost and quality standards—even if local demand didn't match or hadn't yet reached such volumes. Thus, for example, when he decided to manufacture polyester staple fibre in 1984, he didn't plan a medium size unit with the option to expand if the company did well. On the contrary, when local PSF production was 37,000 tpa and another 10,000 tonnes was being imported, Reliance applied for a licence of 45,000 tonnes, i.e. the total current production or 4.5 times the current import, knowing full well that half a dozen PSF licences, albeit smaller ones, had been awarded to other industrialists. Dhirubhai once said, 'I consider myself a pathfinder. I have been excavating the jungle and making the road for others to walk. I like to be the first in everything I do. Making money does not excite me, though I have to make it for my shareholders. What excites me is achievement. I could never do a normal job. In this room, extraordinary things must happen.' Birla was cut from quite a different cloth.

If there's little in common between Ambani and Birla about the road to success, the viewpoints of Bajaj and Tata are even more divergent. Both like to be hands-on managers, well-informed about nitty-gritty details of their companies, but the similarities end there. Their attitude towards partners and strategic alliances symbolizes the polarity between the two tall, sophisticated, American-educated heads of giant engineering concerns. Bajaj is a loner but Tata has over half a dozen joint ventures.

Defending his position, Bajaj once said, 'I do not want in my own country to share power, authority making and ownership with a foreigner. I have nothing against foreigners.

That is not the point. But General Motors does not have foreign equity. Nor does Sony or IBM. The weak do.' Tata, on the other hand, feels that there's nothing to be lost and much to be gained by joining up with others. 'We're too concerned about our individual sovereignty whereas we should be looking at alliances and aggregation of companies as it so often happens abroad. Where partnerships are based on human chemistry and there is a business case, then the two partners really begin to work as one.'

Each of the eight businessmen featured in *Business Maharajas* has hacked an individual path to his personal throne. As the profiles reveal, no two routes resemble each other. Yet, tangled in the disparities, are a few skeins which are common to each.

All eight follow two fundamental and simple management rules. Hire good people, treat them well and delegate responsibility. Secondly, when building factories, try to get them up and running as quickly as possible.

All eight share three common characteristics: they are highly focused, they possess a high level of energy, and they are obsessed. Totally committed to their ambitions, they work relentless hours. You could call them stubborn, even bullheaded, and once an idea has germinated in their mind, they won't give it up easily.

Indubitably, all eight are bright and talented. As such, one would expect them to shine in virtually any economy. A suitable background and appropriate training are clearly major advantages, but high achievers are usually good at most tasks they take up, even those unrelated to business. However, all eight partly owe their remarkable success to two external factors, two elements totally outside their control, and completely unconnected to their personal abilities. However talented, a businessman may still not achieve his individual pinnacle unless these two outside forces come to his aid. As far as these men are concerned, each at some point had a mentor who helped kick him upstairs. And at the first turning point in each of their careers, a piece of luck has come their way. In hindsight, often the lucky event seems trifling, of no major significance, but had it not been there, had they missed seeing opportunity and building on it, none of them would have got the jump-start enabling them to draw ahead of the crowd.

Without J.R.D. Tata's help, Ratan couldn't have become head of the Tata Group, and if his chief rival to the post, Russi Mody, had not given an unguarded interview to the *Hindu,* Mody and not Ratan might today be restructuring the Rs 240bn group. While strolling through Antwerp's Kring, had Monty Charles, a director of the London-based Diamond Trading Company, not spotted the potential in young Vijay Shah, the young Shah brothers might not today be the world's carat czars, and if the Shahs hadn't been offered diamond cutting factories in Surat at fire-sale prices in the '70s, they might not have been able to establish India's biggest privately held empire. In Calcutta, soon after the collapse of the British Raj, there were hundreds of budding tea planters but it was his friendship with Richard Magor which allowed Khaitan to become a *burra sahib* while other Marwari banias remained small-time suppliers. And it was a fluke that a slight connection with John Guthrie led to Khaitan's acquisition of McLeod Russel, a purchase which overnight made him India's leading tea producer.

While writing this book, have I been subjective? Yes, I have. I don't see how any biography can be objective. Objectivity can, in fact, be counterproductive. For one, it's impossible to be totally detached, impartial and completely well-informed. Secondly, how much detail should be included? How big should a biography be before it becomes useful? Is it thirty pages or three hundred? *Business Maharajas* tries to capture snapshots of critical or illustrative episodes in the action-packed careers of eight extremely busy people. It doesn't claim to be definitive or a Ph.D. thesis.

G.D. Birla, no mean writer himself, used to say that no Indian can write biography. Be that as it may, there is so much that is of interest in the lives of these 'maharajas' that one was still tempted to try.

Chapter 1

Dhirubhai Ambani

THE AMBANI FAMILY TREE

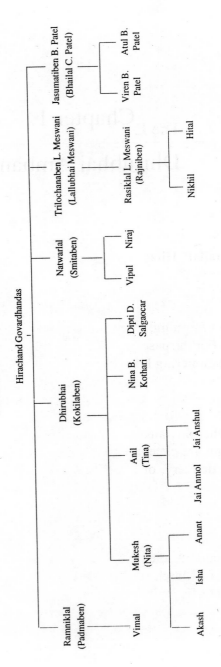

The Bombay Stock Exchange
April 30, 1982

Dhirajlal Hirachand Ambani became famous on the afternoon of April 30, 1982. He had no inkling when he woke up that morning that in the future he would be known as India's stock market messiah. The only emotion he felt that hot summer morning, as the mercury crossed the 33°C mark, was wrath. For the past six weeks, a syndicate of stockbrokers had been hammering his company's shares on the Bombay Stock Exchange, and he didn't like it.

April 30 was a Friday, the day he could vent his anger, take his revenge. On the BSE, alternate Fridays are settlement days when all transactions which have taken place the previous fortnight are cleared. Sellers deliver shares to buyers, buyers accept delivery, or either party asks for the transaction to be postponed to the next clearance day after paying *badla* or compensation for the delay. This was one of the settlement Fridays. It would go down in the BSE's history as a day of total chaos.

Actually, the stage for this drama was set a few days earlier, on March 18, when a selling hysteria shocked the BSE. In twenty-five minutes of panic, starting at 1.35 p.m., the price of blue-chips like Century and Tisco crashed by ten per cent. They fell like dominoes on the back of Ambani's Reliance

Textile Industries which fell from Rs 131 to Rs 121 as 350,000 of its shares hit the market.

The freefall had been engineered by a Calcutta-based bear syndicate led by a Marwari industrialist, perhaps a member of the powerful Birla clan. Using the technique of short selling—where a speculator believes that prices will fall, sells shares he doesn't have, and covers the sale by buying them at lower prices later—the bear syndicate sold 1.1 million Reliance shares worth over Rs 160m. They planned to later pick up these same shares very cheaply and thereby make a tidy profit on the difference. For the plan to succeed, it was important that there should be no big buyers mopping up the stock as it was being sold. The rich bears discounted the promoter of the company they were targeting. It was unlikely that Ambani, then a modest yarn trader and budding industrialist, would have the cash to beat off the attack.

The Marwari and his syndicate badly misjudged their victim. The moment they unloaded Reliance's shares on March 18, Ambani brokers stepped into action, collared every share in sight and pushed the price to Rs 125 before the day was out. They continued buying the next day, and the next, forcing the scrip to rise giddily. In India, technically managements cannot buy their own companies' shares, so a brand new organization, the 'Friends of Reliance Association', emerged which bought 857,000 of the bears' 1.1 million shares.

Instead of being pushed around, Ambani neatly turned the tables on the Marwari. In an obvious attempt to teach the bear syndicate a lesson for battering at his share price, Ambani delivered the *coup de grace* on that fateful Friday by demanding delivery. Meticulously knowledgeable about every aspect of his business, Ambani knew that the sellers couldn't possibly have the shares they had sold. Caught with their pants down, the panic-stricken bears bid for every Reliance share in sight in order to fulfil their commitments. It wasn't enough and the bear syndicate was forced to ask for time to deliver the elusive shares. Ambani's brokers refused any postponement of the deal except at a staggering Rs 50 *badla* charge.

In the bedlam that followed, the BSE had to be shut down for three days while the exchange authorities tried to bring about a compromise between the unyielding bull (Ambani) and the flustered bears. Once it became clear that no understanding could be reached, the panic buying began in earnest. The Reliance price skyrocketed as the syndicate scoured stock markets across the country. By May 10, the gap between sales and availability was almost covered and the crisis was over.

The crisis created a legend out of Ambani but he did not become a stockmarket messiah because the BSE had to be closed on his account nor because he had humbled the bears. Undoubtedly these feats of corporate valour were awesome, but he would in time become a cult figure not for what he did, but because of what he stood for—the ordinary shareholder.

Ambani, known better as Dhirubhai, was the first Indian industrialist to appreciate the ordinary investor and his needs. Asked once what was the secret of his success, he answered: 'One must have ambition and one must understand the minds of men.' His support for the small shareholder stemmed from personal experience. One, he knew what it was like to be poor. And secondly, banks had often turned him away when he badly needed money to build his factories. So he turned for support to the only other option he had: the public. Mobilizing funds directly from small investors was a major departure from normal practice at the time. Most businesses raise resources for capital investment from state-owned financial institutions such as the IDBI or ICICI.

Ambani realized that in order to seduce the public into investing in his schemes, he had to offer them something above and beyond what they were already used to getting. And this was the steady appreciation of their shareholding. Until he came on the scene, managements rarely bothered about the price of their company's shares. The business of a company was to earn profit and declare dividends, not to dabble on the stock markets, keeping track of share prices and supporting a scrip whenever it wobbled. In contrast, Ambani believed that management had a responsibility towards its shareholders and should play an active role in looking after their interest. The most generous of dividends could not make a shareholder rich, but capital appreciation of his shares could, he propounded.

This was an alien concept, an idea Ambani picked up from the West. It took him almost half a decade to propagate this philosophy but once it took root, it changed the entire mindset of corporate India and its way of doing business.

At the time, Ambani didn't realize that he had mounted a treadmill from which he would never be able to step off. Over the next few years, this treadmill sped ever faster, constantly threatening to whirl out of control. In order to retain the public's support, Dhirubhai had to ensure that the price of Reliance shares kept appreciating, month after month, year after year. As long as he kept moving, money poured in. He found he could tap the capital markets for bigger and bigger amounts. His popularity became so great that people rushed to hand their savings over to him. Other businessmen's issues might flop, but not his.

Ambani coined the term 'the mega issue'. Each year he beat his own record. With the exception of 1977 (when Reliance went public), traditionally the honour of the year's largest issue goes to Reliance. Up to 1995, Ambani has mobilized Rs 64.23bn from the public.

In the process, Ambani made Reliance India's most popular company. British Gas acquired 3.1 million shareholders after its 1988 floatation. Reliance Petrochemicals, which went public around the same time, attracted the world's second largest shareholder population of 1.6 million. In 1977, Reliance Industries had 58,000 investors. Today it has over 3.7 million.

Size brought its own problems and solutions. Traditional venues for company annual general meetings were too small to accommodate the army of shareholders who wanted to see their king, and Reliance started hiring huge football stadia to host its AGMs. India's creaky postal department couldn't cope with the number of share certificates, annual reports and other correspondence which Reliance entered into with its family of investors. The company had to fly executives to smaller cities with mail as personal luggage which was then posted locally.

Perhaps Dhirubhai's most outstanding achievement has been to introduce the equity cult to every small town in India. Fanning out to tap rural stock exchanges, he taught people who would never have thought of investing in shares how to buy them, to track the price movements of scrips, to deal with stockbrokers, and to develop the habit of reading financial dailies and stock market newsletters. An overwhelming majority of Reliance shareholders hold less than 100 shares, and one in four Indian investors owns shares in Reliance.

Dhirubhai single-handedly energized the Indian capital market. Before the huge Reliance Petrochemicals issue, rough rule of thumb calculations suggested there were three million shareholders in the country. In 1988, the government reckoned there were ten million. To arrive at this key statistic, it didn't use sophisticated tools of calculation or market research but simply multiplied the number of Reliance debenture holders by three. Ambani was more thorough. He painstakingly garnered information on present and potential investors, and the quality of his data surpassed that of the biggest and best merchant banks.

Ambani's relentless drive to keep Reliance's price at very high levels booted the BSE's market capitalization. A sleepy Rs 54bn in 1980, it had risen to Rs 510bn in 1990, and shot up to Rs 4,355bn in 1995. In tandem with the trend, Reliance's market cap exploded from Rs 1.2bn in 1980 to Rs 9.96bn in 1990 and Rs 96.2bn in 1995, making Ambani one of the richest men in the world.

Dhirubhai's modern way of thinking brought into play his second achievement: the idea that Indian manufacturing could and should be world class. He was the first industrialist in India to build facilities which could be compared to the best internationally, both in terms of volume of production and quality of output. 'My commitment is to produce at the cheapest price and the best quality,' he insisted time and time again. 'Think big, think fast, think ahead,' he would exhort colleagues.

Before Dhirubhai, most Indian plants were pigmy-sized, partly because of their promoters' blinkered horizon. 'The size of Reliance's facility represented a major departure from the "normal" Indian business practice of the time. Instead of creating a "safe" capacity based on reasonable projection of demand, Ambani applied for world scale capacity that could meet the cost and quality standards on a global basis,' says Sumantra Ghoshal, head of strategic planning at the London Business School and author of a major case study on Reliance.

According to S. P. Sapra, president of Reliance's polyester staple fibre division, who joined Ambani after a twenty-year career with ICI India: 'The fundamental difference between Reliance's approach and that of other companies was that

Dhirubhai saw things that were hidden to other companies. The user industry was held back by non-availability of supplies. Other companies would typically do a market survey that would show the current usage at, say, 2,000 tpa. They would project that usage into the future and arrive at a demand of, say, 5,000 tpa. They would then set up a 2,000 or 3,000 tpa facility, depending on their projections of their market share. Dhirubhai threw away that incrementalist mindset. He created capacity ahead of actual demand and on the basis of latent demand.'

Before he could build his world size plants, he had to get hundreds of licences. And for that, Ambani had to change the bureaucracy's mindset and force it to review the licensing system. Some industrialists—Rahul Bajaj, the scooter manufacturer, for example—shared Ambani's world vision, but lacked the latter's knack or clout of making bureaucrats listen. According to Ambani, convincing the government meant adopting a flexible approach. 'The most important external environment is the government of India. You have to sell your ideas to the government. Selling the idea is the most important thing, and for that I'll meet anybody in the government. I am willing to *salaam* anyone. One thing you won't find in me and that is an ego,' he once said. His use of the word *salaam* infuriated the older, established industrialists.

According to B. N. Uniyal, a one-time left-wing journalist friend of Dhirubhai whom he invited to run his two publications, the *Sunday Observer* and the *Business and Political Observer,* Ambani would spend hours educating the guardians of the Licence Raj. 'Bureaucrats needed to be convinced by numbers and details. Ambani and his team never went to Delhi without these,' says Uniyal. 'They would gather the latest status reports on what was happening in different parts of the world in their area of interest and distribute copies of these among influential politicians and bureaucrats. We cannot change our rulers, but we can at least help them learn how to rule us better, he used to tell his executives.'

Through his promotion of the equity cult and his world vision in manufacturing, Ambani impacted the economy and polity as no businessman has done, not even Jamsetji Tata (1839-1904), the man who brought steel and electricity to India. Dhirubhai boldly infringed on the turf of politicians and bureaucrats, saying, 'I consider myself a pathfinder. I have been excavating the jungle and making the road for others to walk. I like to be the first in everything I do. Making money does not excite me, though I have to make it for my shareholders. What excites me is achievement. I could never do a normal job. In this room, extraordinary things must happen.'

Yet in the same breath Dhirubhai says: 'I give least importance to being Number One. You know, I was nothing—just a small merchant—and now I have reached this level. I consider myself fortunate to be in this position . . . but I have no pride. I am as I was.'

Inevitably, his rise has been accompanied by controversy. The corporate world is sharply divided between those who feel he is a visionary and those who consider him to be a manipulator and a crook. A legion of critics accuse Ambani of leapfrogging the queue in obtaining licences, of getting faster-than-normal approvals for his public issues and capital goods imports, and of getting policies formulated favouring Reliance (or disadvantaging its rivals or both).

Many attribute Dhirubhai's success to political patronage rather than proficient management and claim that he will go to any lengths to achieve his motto: 'Where growth is a way of life.' Prior to the 1991 New Economic Policy which more or less ended the Licence Raj, Reliance was criticized for manipulating tariffs to suit its ends at the expense of its rivals.

To some, he became a symbol of all that is wrong in the Indian economy. Another set of businessmen felt that Reliance was an out-of-control monster, a bubble that would burst at any moment.

Outwardly, Ambani appeared unfazed by these allegations. 'Controversy is the price to be paid for success. You must understand human psychology. Because, not so long ago, I was just a riffraff boy and people would say: "Who is this Dhirubhai? He was merely a hawker who used to wait outside our cabins." This is the truth and I am not ashamed of that. My skin, fortunately, is very thick! However, the fact remains that when an elephant walks, dogs tend to bark.'

'Reliance would not have reached this level if any of the charges were true,' he continues. 'Look at the past. I wasn't the only one to get licences. But just because the government gives you a piece of paper, it doesn't automatically mean that you can raise money from the capital markets, or put up plants in record time. And give sensible returns to shareholders. That's 98 per cent of the work. The paper work is only 2 per cent.' He does, however, agree that Reliance has often been granted favourable licences, but claims that there were rejections as well.

In many ways, Ambani bridged the old and the new. The first time I interviewed Ambani, in April 1984, Reliance had just declared its intention of turning non-convertible debentures into convertible ones, a move which was being widely criticized. Smiling at my discomfort, he floored me. 'Why don't you just come out and tell me I am a crook to my face? I know some people think that what I am doing is a fraud, but before you journalists come to interview me, study what is happening in the international financial markets. And then come to me.' That year, in a tribute to Ambani's entrepreneurship, *Imprint*, a magazine which would later hound him, lauded Dhirubhai as 'the best of a new breed of Indian industrialists—a creation of the '60s when the politico-bureaucratic axis that was to determine the future of the Indian economy had emerged'.

Like the elephant he compares himself to, Reliance dominates the corporate jungle. The Ambani empire is smaller than those of Ratan Tata and Basant Kumar 'BK' Birla, but then, he didn't have the same head start. The Birla group has been around for a century, the Tatas for a century and a quarter. Like the vigorous pioneer-founders of these groups, Dhirubhai has never recognized barriers. As an attendant manning a Shell gas station, Dhirubhai swore he would one day head a company like Shell, hunt for oil and refine it. Sceptics laughed, but he made his dream come true within one lifetime. In 1986, he declared that Reliance, then a Rs 9bn company, would in ten years be a Rs 80bn company. Sales in 1995 were Rs 78bn. The sceptics were silenced: today, he believes Reliance can be a Rs 300bn company by the end of the century.

In 1995, the petrochemical, oil and textile manufacturer was India's biggest non-government company by almost every yardstick including sales, profits, net worth, and asset base. Its market capitalization that year was Rs 96bn. The previous year, it was the only Indian entrant in *Business Week's* list of the fifty largest companies headquartered in developing countries. From 1977 to March 1996, its sales have increased from Rs 1.2bn to Rs 78bn, operating profit from Rs 150m to Rs 17.5bn, net profit from Rs 25m to Rs 13 bn, net worth from Rs 140m to Rs 84bn, and asset base from Rs 310m to Rs 150bn. It is an incredible accomplishment. There is no doubt that Ambani was helped by political and bureaucratic decisions that went in his favour, but despite this his achievements are out of the ordinary—a testimonial to a man with extraordinary business acumen and vision.

One could be forgiven for thinking there's a sense of satisfaction at Maker Chamber IV, 222 Nariman Point, one of Bombay's most famous addresses and the headquarters of the nation's third largest private sector company. Curiously, there isn't. On the contrary, inside Reliance and within the family there is a feeling of being constantly under siege. Reliance could have gone further, could have done far more, had its enemies not put up roadblocks. 'The so-called torch-bearers of truth have always been trying to poison the minds of politicians and civil servants on behalf of our business rivals,' says Ambani.

Ambani is not the only overachiever to experience feelings of persecution. 'Success is a lousy teacher,' writes Bill Gates in his book *The Road Ahead.* Gates, founder of Microsoft, is one of the richest men in the world and in 1995 Microsoft's market cap was the tenth highest among US corporations, according to *Fortune.* Given the sheer number of records Microsoft and *Windows,* a computer operating system, have broken, complacency could have taken over. Instead, Gates says, 'The outside perception and the inside perception of Microsoft are so different. The view of Microsoft is always kind of an underdog thing. In the early years that underdog, almost paranoid attitude, was a matter of survival.'

At Reliance too an edginess, a sense of anxiety pervades the organization. This edginess has given birth to all kinds of odd and dangerous rumours. Cumulatively, they spread the message—play with Reliance and you play with fire.

Face to face with the legend, it's hard to believe that there's a dark side to Ambani. When he smiles, it's a cheek-splitting ear-to-ear grin. Genuine. Affable. Genial. He's quick to break into infectious, uninhibited laughter, to rub his hands in glee, or slap his knee to emphasize a point. Whether in a white half-sleeved safari or one of his conservative dark suits and crisp white shirts with his trademark flamboyant red silk tie, there's nothing half-hearted about the most talked about businessman in India.

Legs planted squarely on the ground, his head cocked slightly, his thinning hair cropped shorter than a marine's, eyebrows flying over a broad forehead, Ambani looks relaxed. It's a habit. He's at his coolest when the going is tough. At sixty-three a few years younger than Rama Prasad Goenka and a little older than Ratan Tata, Ambani's level of personal motivation is amazingly high, his drive, if that is possible, even more insatiable than before.

He freed himself from day-to-day operational management of the group's manufacturing facilities the moment his sons, Mukesh and Anil, joined the family firm in the mid-'80s. At the beginning of the '90s, he moved away from the chief executive's post (though technically he still holds that position) to conceptualize the company's long term goals as also to spend a little more time with the family.

Dhirubhai no longer puts in the long hours in the office he used to—he comes in at noon and leaves three hours later—and spends more time dandling his grandchildren on his knees than poring over financial reports. Despite the shorter hours and the inevitable distancing, his is a crucial role, beyond that of a visionary and strategist. Fiercely protective about the company he founded, he often steps in to smooth its working through a quiet word with a recalcitrant customer, a judicious telephone call to a political bigwig, or the occasional discreet meeting with a competitor at a lawyer's flat. Asked if he had ever thought of retirement, Dhirubhai riposted instantly: 'Never. Till my last breath I will work. To retire there is only one place—the cremation ground.'

The hectic pace he has always set for himself and the rapid tumble of hair-raising events have left their mark. In February

1986, when he was fifty-four, he suffered a paralytic stroke from which he never fully recovered. At the time, people whispered he would never be able to walk again. Undeterred, Ambani built himself a well-equipped gymnasium and got to work, teaching his body to respond to his mind's demands. Within months, he was at the mike, addressing his loyal shareholders, who cheered him as if he were movie hero Amitabh Bachchan himself.

In the autumn of his life, there are few regrets over the twists and turns it has taken. But when asked on his sixtieth birthday whether there was anything lacking in his life, Dhirubhai surprisingly replied: 'Yes. Business and its expansion takes up all my energy. I have not been able to devote enough time for social work and I feel sad about it. But, in another sense, 23 lakh shareholders plus countless others have benefited directly or indirectly from Reliance's success. Still, in the area of social work a lot needs to be done.'

The admission was a major turnaround for the man who earlier had stoutly attacked the idea of corporate charity. 'What is our social commitment? Helping the blind or doing charity or something like that? No,' he was fond of declaring. 'As an industrialist my job is to produce goods to satisfy the demand. Let's be very clear about it. Everyone has to do his job. My commitment is to produce at the cheapest price and the best quality. If you dabble in everything then you make a mess of things. If we can't take care of our shareholders and employees and start worrying about the world, then that is hypocrisy.'

Ambani's single-mindedness is legendary, and he's proud of it. 'I do not give attention to anything except Reliance. I am not a director in other companies. I am not actively participating in any associations or in anything else. My whole thinking, one hundred per cent of my time, from morning till evening, is about how to do better and better at Reliance.' No art previews, no theatre, no films and he rarely switches on his CD player.

What has sustained this single-minded commitment? *Nasha*, says K. K. Malhotra, head of Reliance's manufacturing operations and a former managing director of Indian Oil Corporation. 'One day, Dhirubhai and I were having lunch together at Patalganga. He ordered soup and a papad. I ordered a one-egg omelette. Then he said, "This is all we need, right! This is all we can consume . . . but the excitement is to build . . . *Usme nasha hai*."'

In shaping Reliance into a colossus, the largely self-taught Dhirubhai used his own brand of earthy, practical, bania brain aided by an inexhaustible desire for information. It's unlikely that he read Tom '*In Search of Excellence*' Peters and his 'sticking to the knitting' mantra. According to Anil, his father's reading habits don't include management texts. 'He won't read Arthur Steel and Ayn Rand but he will read *Time, Newsweek,* the *Economist* to appease his hunger for news. Though he won't read the *Harvard Business Review,* he will say: "Let my management chaps read that." He's still an avid reader. If you give him a world food market report, he would like to read it, but if you tell him here is a lesson on organization design, he will say: "Sorry, not my cup of tea."'

At Reliance, this habit developed into an almost obsessive interest in the economy and its strengths and weaknesses. A full-time brains trust is continually preparing position papers on subjects as diverse as IMF loans or the shortfall in the Sixth Plan. Information gathering has become as sophisticated as its other operations. According to R. Ramamurthy, who joined Reliance from Chemplast, the Ambanis 'are enormously bold but their actions are influenced by their unmatched access to information. They know what is happening in every single corridor of the government ministries. They know about their customers. They know more about their competitors—even about their day-to-day operations—than the top managers of those companies . . . they can judge where the money will flow . . . and it is not just about their immediate business. They suck up knowledge about everything, constantly. Their magic is not just ambition but ambition with information.'

It is traits such as these which make Dhirubhai stand out from the crowd. At the same time, if you're looking for sophistication in this self-made industrialist, you won't find it. He's never been one for ceremony—it's quicker to open the car door yourself than wait for the chauffeur to come round!—and if you're expecting management jargon, you won't hear it. 'Dhirubhai can talk shop non-stop, mostly in Bombay Hindi,' says a family friend. 'And he can compel the most reticent men to open up and contribute dozens of sentences. He provokes and lures you into talking. And when he talks, he doesn't bother about mundane things like correct sentences, grammar, etc. The meaning is conveyed in the quickest possible manner, his Hindi phrases filling up the gaps. If you are used to listening to English with a Gujarati accent like I am, then you're on a good wicket.'

THE ZERO CLUB

In the days before he became the typical reclusive billionaire, Dhirubhai would often ask journalists to write about his rags-to-riches background. 'Please mention this in your magazine because I am proud of it and people should get inspiration from this.' Or he would say, 'I am only a matriculate and I would like you to particularly mention this fact. People will have hope that they too can become successful.' Says Udayan Bose, founder of CreditCapital, a merchant bank, 'He's not in the old-fashioned mould and always jokes that he belongs to the Zero Club because he started with nothing.'

His lack of higher education seems to have bothered Dhirubhai. When his sons were old enough, he would send his sons to Stanford (Mukesh) and Wharton (Anil). 'It [further education] is most essential, otherwise I would not have educated my sons. I learnt the hard way. Maybe if I had some education my success and growth would have been quicker.'

Despite his self-evident achievements, Dhirubhai's tarnished image in the early years of his success denied him public recognition. *Business India*, a champion of capitalists, couldn't bring itself to bestow its prestigious Businessman of the Year award on Dhirubhai until twelve years after the citation had been instituted. Three Tata men (Russi Mody, S. Moolgaokar and Ratan Tata) got it before Ambani. H.P. Nanda, Rahul Bajaj and Keshub Mahindra were crowned before him. Ambani finally received it in 1993. The citation hailed him as the 'symbol of the new Indian dream' but the delay rankled.

Dhirubhai was born on December 28, 1932 to Jamna and Hirachand (d.1951) Ambani, the middle of five children, three boys and two girls. Hirachand was the local schoolteacher in a village called Chorwad, in Junagadh district, Gujarat. Nearby was Porbander, the birthplace of Mahatma Gandhi.

According to Ramniklal, the eldest son, his younger brother was always thinking up money-making schemes. 'During the Mahashivratri fair, Dhirubhai got together with some friends and sold *ganthia,* a Gujarati savoury,' he recalled. Adds a Chorwad contemporary, 'Dhirubhai was a familiar sight here, cycling from village to village. All he needed was the whiff of a business opportunity and he was off to book the orders.'

Schoolteachers aren't paid much. The salaries are a little better in cities, but village teachers can't afford higher education for their own children. Like his elder brother before him, as soon as Dhirubhai had matriculated, it was time to shut his books and get to work. Ramniklal was in Aden, a port city now part of Yemen but then a British crown colony, and he sent a message back that jobs were available. Dhirubhai joined him there.

Only Natwarlal, the youngest son, would get a college education. Once the two elder sons had started sending money home regularly, Hirachand felt they could afford to send Natwarlal to a smart Bombay college. It was hoped that the youngest son, if he could become a graduate, would lift the family from poverty to a middle-class lifestyle, but it would be Dhirubhai who would achieve this and more, his activities becoming important enough for *Forbes* and *Fortune,* the *Financial Times* and the *Far Eastern Economic Review* to report them.

At seventeen, Dhirubhai reached Aden. 'I wanted to earn a living. I wanted to start earning as quickly as possible. I was not looking at life from any other angle but the angle of how to earn. I wanted to make a success of whatever I did. That was the paramount thing in my life,' he would recall several years later.

Shell, who had set up a refinery in Aden in 1953, paid his first salary of Rs 300 a month. 'He learnt a lot about the oil business,' says Anil Ambani. 'He worked in a petrol station, filling gas, collecting money. Then he rose to become a sales manager.' Soon he graduated to clerkdom in a general merchandizing firm, A. Beese & Co (an affiliate of Burmah Shell), where he worked for the next five years, all the while improving his Arabic. By the time he left Aden, his salary had risen to Rs 1,100.

As a tiny cog in an insignificant subsidiary of Burmah Shell, the teenager from Chorwad watched the global giant's workings with growing fascination. 'Our backgrounds were so different. At that time we were worried about spending even ten rupees and here this company would not hesitate to send a telegram worth five thousand rupees. They didn't care. Whatever information must come, must come. In those days there were no telexes. So they used to send telegrams of five thousand words, even twenty thousand words. It wasn't an extravagance. It was the need for doing the right thing at the right time.' Dhirubhai's fertile mind soaked up the lessons. 'I had dreams of starting a company like Burmah Shell.'

Dhirubhai lived and worked in Aden for almost eight years before calling it a day. 'I was very happy there. I had my own car and flat, but a time came when I wanted to do something on my own. Yes, I could have done some business in Aden itself but I wanted to do something in my own country. So on December 31, 1958, I landed in Bombay to start my own business with a few thousand rupees.'

When Dhirubhai left Aden, he wasn't alone: he had a son and a pregnant wife. Kokila R. Patel and Dhirubhai were married in March 1954 at Chorwad. Mukesh was born in Aden three years later. Anil was born in Bombay's Cumballa Hill Hospital in June 1959. Dipti Dattaraj Salgaonkar was born in January 1961, and Nina Shyam Kothari in July the next year.

Jamna had chosen Kokila for Dhirubhai and her judgement turned out to be faultless. Now very much the family matriarch, Kokila rules over a luxurious household which needs a foods and beverage manager brought in from the Taj Mahal Hotel; takes the brood of Ambani, Salgaonkar and Kothari grandchildren on five-star holidays together; and sits in the front row at Reliance's mammoth annual general meetings with the other women of the family. At sixty, there are traces still of the slim and fair village belle Dhirubhai had married in a simple ceremony in Chorwad. In the early days, with her husband shuttling between the group's plants and

Delhi, Kokila quietly took over the job of rearing their children and looking after the extended family, cooking, cleaning and ironing the crisp white shirts Dhirubhai favoured, making ends meet.

The young couple decided to settle in Bombay. Hirachand had died in 1951 when Dhirubhai was nineteen and still unmarried, and there was little to draw them back to Chorwad. The entire family uprooted itself, from Jamna downwards, and rented a flat at Kabutarkhana.

'Do you know where Kabutarkhana is? Do you know where Bhuleshwar is?' asked Anil. 'That's where Maganlal Dresswalla is. That's where the *doodhwallas* are. We used to stay in a place called Jai Hind Estate on the fifth floor. It's a big chawl with 500 families staying in it. It was cheap. What was it? It was a one-bedroom house. My dad, my mother, my grandmother, my uncle, my brother and myself lived in one room.

'We used to play in the chawl. There used to be this big corridor running alongside twenty pigeonhole type flats on one floor. We used to be there, looking at the activity in the street below. Why is it called Kabutarkhana? It's a huge place where all the pigeons descend and people feed them *chana*. Next door there's a temple. So everybody goes into the temple, prays, comes out and throws *chana* to the pigeons. There's a milk market in a locality called Panjrapole. The embroidery business is right there. Oh, there's a lot of hustle and bustle in Kabutarkhana.'

Dhirubhai took a loan and started the Reliance Commercial Corporation, a trading firm, with a capital of Rs 15,000, operating out of a corner in a borrowed office in Bhaat Bazaar. 'I was primarily involved in general merchandizing,' recalls Dhirubhai. 'Reliance Commercial Corporation was an export house which dealt basically in commodities like ginger, cardamom, pepper, turmeric, cashewnut, etc. We had a lot of connections in Aden and we exploited these connections to export a wide range of commodities. Aden being a free port had tremendous demand for a range of commodities.'

'My father was not only exporting spices, he was also exporting sugar, ghee, sand, soil, anything that had the potential,' said Anil. Soil? Apparently an Arab had asked Dhirubhai to send him a consignment of Indian soil in which to grow roses in the desert. Was this a legitimate business deal or one of Dhirubhai's creative schemes? 'That was a one-time thing. The Arab sheikh opened the letter of credit and we got the money. Now if the sheikh dumps the soil into the sea or drinks it up, who cares? See the opportunity and strike.'

As the money started flowing in, Dhirubhai shook off his village mentality—which perhaps he never did have—and learnt to spend money, city-style. In his eyes, it wasn't extravagance, but a broadening of the mind, another lesson picked up from Burmah Shell. 'Suppose you and I go to the Taj to have drinks,' he explained once. 'One bloody drink costs sixty-five rupees. But all the same we have a few drinks and come out as if nothing has happened. If a person from my village comes to know that I have spent five hundred rupees on just a few drinks, he'll be shocked. He'll say this fellow has gone mad, *saala company ka diwala nikaal deyga*. What I am trying to say is that I have developed a broadness of mind which my friends in the village cannot think of having.'

One of those who often shared a drink or a round of bridge with the upcoming tycoon was Murli Deora, president of the Bombay Regional Congress Committee and like Ambani, then an impecunious yarn trader. With a wry smile, Deora recalls business trips to Delhi where since neither could afford a hotel room, they had a storage arrangement with Ashok Hotel for their briefcases and returned to Bombay by the last flight.

Sunday evenings were reserved for the family and they would roam Chowpatty beach or Dadar Circle for the best snacks and juice parlour in town. Remembering those days, Anil said, 'We had a great deal of attention from both my father and my mother. Somehow he used to find the time. My father believed that the childhood years are when character and motivation are developed. Sundays were very important in our lives. He used to take us out to football or hockey matches. At that time, the options were very clear. We had the choice of two snacks or one drink and one snack. We used to jump when Sunday arrived and we would be thrilled because we would be taken to an Udipi restaurant for idli sambhar. Sunday was an important day.'

Most excursions were by bus. As a school kid, Dhirubhai's biggest ambition had been to own a jeep. 'I was a member of the Civil Guards, something like today's NCC. We had to salute our officers who went around in jeeps. So I thought: one day I will also ride in a jeep and somebody else will salute me.' In the mid-'60s, the government introduced an export promotion scheme where earnings from the export of rayon fabrics could be used for the import of nylon fibre. Ambani's attention switched from spices to the textile trade. And he bought himself not a jeep but a Mercedes. A few years earlier, he had got a dull black Cadillac with dark tinted windows. Thirty years later, he's still using it. It's the most famous car in Bombay. And yes, there's no shortage of people waiting to salute him.

'GROWTH IS A WAY OF LIFE'

At first, there was little to differentiate Ambani from other yarn traders. Like them, he worked Bombay's hot and teeming yarn markets, living off tea shop snacks and endlessly chewing

paan. As his mind 'broadened', he started pulling away from
the crowd. In February 1966, at about the same time as the late
Aditya Birla, BK's son, was negotiating the purchase of Indian
Rayon, Ambani built a spanking new mill at Naroda, twenty
kilometres from Ahmedabad. Both were spinning mills and
produced roughly the same product. Birla paid Rs 3m to buy
Indian Rayon while the capital cost of Ambani's mill was one-
tenth that at Rs 280,000, which he borrowed. Ambani was then
thirty-four years old, Birla twenty-three. Both foresaw
synthetics as the fabric of the future though they arrived at this
common ground from opposite routes and different
backgrounds.

Ambani registered Reliance Textile Industries with a
paid-up capital of Rs 150,000 not as a composite mill but as a
powerloom unit. 'We got the licence for powerloom because
the regulation was that you could not make 100 per cent
filament synthetics except on licensed powerlooms.' Aditya
Birla latched on to the same idea. 'Not only Reliance, Gwalior
was a powerloom factory. I am telling you, Gwalior's Dornier
looms were also known as powerlooms! What a fallacy! People
think composite mills are first class, that powerlooms are
second class. I wanted to remove that feeling.'

As their name suggests, composite mills offer an
integrated approach, producing fabric at one location right
from spinning cotton into yarn, to weaving, printing and
processing. In contrast, the powerlooms of Bhiwandi and
elsewhere tend to be garage operations in size and structure,
small and unorganized. Typically they buy yarn from outside
and weave 'grey' or unfinished fabric which they sell to
process houses. After printing and other processing, the
fabric—generally unbranded—is sold to the wholesale trade,
which has financed the whole operation.

Ambani had been dreaming of integrating backwards for
some time. 'I was constantly thinking of going into

manufacturing,' he said at the time. 'My desire was motivated by the fact that we were not able to produce and supply a quality fabric to the export market. It was a question of integrating backwards. If I had a ready product then I would not be at the mercy of other units in the industry, and I could ensure the quality of the products myself.' Over time, backward integration would become a core Reliance strategy, the central theme for all strategic planning, and it remained paramount in family conclaves until recently.

But, at the time, it was hard to raise the piffling Rs 280,000 he needed to get into manufacturing, with sceptics outnumbering believers. Among the former was Viren Shah, a fiery businessman-politician and chairman of Mukand Iron and Steel. Like Ambani, Shah traces his roots to Chorwad where his family was the biggest landowner. Turning down Dhirubhai's request for a Rs 400,000 loan, Shah told a friend 'this project will not fly'. He couldn't have been more wrong. In the first year itself, seventy workers manning four warp-knitting machines and a small dyeing section notched up sales of Rs 90m and a profit of Rs 1.3m. By 1977, the year Dhirubhai went public, the mill was earning a tidy profit of Rs 43.3m from revenues of Rs 700m.

Each year he added to the mill, and every time a new piece of machinery was installed, Ambani, a God-fearing man, would call a pandit and hold a *puja*. Mukesh recalls, 'As kids, we used to go around and say: *Aaj kiska puja ho raha hai?* And we would be told that some new stenters have been bought, so we are praying to them.' The *pujas* were perhaps more a manifestation of Dhirubhai's social conditioning, a kind of insurance taken out from the pantheon of Hindu gods and particularly Ganesha, the god of good beginnings, rather than a matter of personal belief. 'Yes, I believe in God, but I don't perform a daily *puja*. I don't have any gurus. *Ek baat hai, destiny koi cheez hai,*' Dhirubhai said reflectively. 'I am not a believer in religious rituals. I was brought up in the Arya Samaj environment which taught us to shun rituals. *Puja*, of course, but simple, elegant and brief.'

The *prasad* flowed as the Naroda complex grew. Sales were brisk, and fixed assets rose from Rs 280,000 in 1966 to Rs 145m in 1977, more than doubling to Rs 370m in 1979. By 1983, on the eve of its entry into petrochemicals, Reliance would become India's largest composite textile mill, sprawling over 280,000 sq.m., producing three million square metres of fabric per month, and employing 10,000 workers.

To help him manage the exploding business, Dhirubhai turned to his family and close friends. Ramniklal shifted from Aden to Ahmedabad to look after administration and production at Naroda. Rasik Meswani, their brother-in-law, and Natwarlal stayed back in Bombay to look after the finance department. Also in finance was an old Aden hand, Indu Sheth, who had been a clerk like Dhirubhai in an export house. Indu's brother, M.F. Sheth, became the brains behind Reliance's export strategy.

This habit of plucking talent from wherever available would become a classic Reliance management strategy. The Ambanis don't rely on paper qualifications. On the contrary, whoever shows initiative, gets the job. So Reliance's first marketing manager was one Natwarlal Sanghvi who used to sell petroleum products. Its knitting manager used to be an auto spare parts salesman. On the technological side, however, Dhirubhai's approach was radically different. Over the next few years he systematically poached the best talent from his competitors. Reliance had to have the best: JK Synthetic's best yarn technologist, New Swadeshi Mills' chief engineer, Grasim's senior supervisor. No major synthetic textile unit was spared.

In building his industrial empire, Ambani shared Aditya Birla's view that when buying machinery, it must be the latest and the best. 'Play on the frontiers of technology. Be ahead of the tomorrows,' he kept telling his new team. According to Minhaz Merchant, founder-editor of *Gentleman* magazine and *Business Barons*, the matric-pass Dhirubhai has 'an uncompromising commitment to quality and what could almost be called technological avarice—an obsession to be the first in India with the finest technology the world can offer'. In 1975 a World Bank team visited twenty-four leading textile mills and reported that 'judged in relation to developed country standards, only one mill, Reliance, could be described as excellent'. The rest they described as slums.

'Our expansion was dictated by the exigencies of the export markets. When there was a very high demand in the international market for texturized and crimped fabrics, we decided to import texturizing machinery. The import entitlements that we were permitted against exports enabled us to import the most sophisticated and latest technology from abroad. Gradually we kept expanding the capacity of the mills, integrating vertically all the time. Now we have a fully integrated composite mill,' said Indu Sheth, now retired.

Much of Reliance's investment into state-of-the-art equipment was financed by huge trading profits. As a private company, Ambani didn't need to puff his performance. Until it went public, Ambani used to plough every paisa of profit into the company, rarely treating himself to a dividend.

The heftiest profits came from the High Unit Value Scheme which the government introduced in 1971, through which polyester filament yarn could be imported against the exports of nylon fabrics. This was a game which Ambani already knew how to play. He admits that Reliance Commercial Corporation accounted for over 60 per cent of exports under the scheme and was therefore its largest beneficiary. Rumours spread that the scheme had been devised solely for him. At the Mulji Jetha market, polyester was then called *chamak*. Ambani became the *chamatkar*.

Even at that time, Ambani strongly disputed this argument. 'You can hardly blame us for taking advantage of the schemes when others kept their eyes shut. You do not require an invitation when there is a profit. I do not consider myself cleverer than my colleagues in the industry. If there was a very large margin of profit, why did they not take advantage of it? If anybody says that Reliance benefited immensely from the High Unit Value Scheme, they are giving me credit at the expense of their ignorance.

'The scheme remained in force for eight years. Many companies participated in it. If others did not do well, perhaps they could not export their goods. We used to hold fashion shows in Russia and in Poland and exported our fabrics. We took planeloads [of fabrics] to Zambia, Uganda and even Saudi Arabia. At that time our strategy was to export because export gave a lot of prestige with the government.

'You have to look at the economy in its totality. Imports and exports have to be combined together to get a totality of profit. Against exports of rayon fabrics we were getting import entitlements for nylon fibre. In some areas, some cash incentives were also available. The premium on nylon filament yarn was 100 to 300 per cent. It only once touched 700 per cent. We were exporting rayon fabrics and importing nylon fibre and supplying it to mills. The profits were between 15 per cent and 25 per cent net. We were one of the largest exporters and our turnover must have ranged between Rs 15 and 25 lakhs. When the High Unit Value Scheme came, we were manufacturing and exporting. We used to be allowed to import polyester filament yarn against export of nylon fabrics.'

When the scheme ended in 1978, Ambani turned to the domestic market. 'About 10,000 metres was being produced when I entered the market. All that I needed was a small gap which I could penetrate, and I did so successfully. Our only difficulty was that we were not sufficiently known or established in the domestic market. Our first priority was to establish our Vimal brand name. We therefore launched a crash advertising programme,' recalled Ambani.

Dhirubhai supported Reliance's entry into the domestic markets with an advertising blitz that was unprecedented in India. Then and now, it outspent its competition with a budget which is on par with consumer giants such as Hindustan Lever. Billboards, radio, print, and television—once a distribution network had been established—blazoned the mill's message, ONLY VIMAL, and the baseline, 'A woman expresses herself in many languages—Vimal is one of them.' The brand was named after Vimal, Dhirubhai's eldest nephew, Ramniklal's son.

'People don't want the headache of comparing and shopping around. They would rather go straight for quality. Right from the start, I knew that brand image was the most important part in order to win the consumer's confidence,' says Ambani. To achieve this objective, 'We tried to emphasize that we were producing a superior fabric by laying stress on the technological sophistication of our unit in all our advertising. Simultaneously we took steps to evolve our own distribution system as we found that the existing marketing channels were inadequate and unsatisfactory. So much of our success in marketing was a function of three factors—choosing the right product mix, identifying our market and establishing a viable distribution structure.'

This strategy was enormously successful, so much so that an industry analyst once commented, 'In terms of market positioning, Vimal has always been a bit of a paradox. Although it has always been positioned as an upmarket product and has also been priced that way, its customers have stubbornly continued to be in the middle bracket.'

Before that happened, Ambani had to jump the first of many hurdles. 'When Reliance entered the domestic market it met with a lot of resistance from the traditional cloth market whose loyalties understandably were to the older mills,' said a Mulji Jetha market trader at the time.

Confronted with a problem, Ambani thinks laterally. In this case, he bypassed the traditional wholesale trade, opened his own showrooms, tapped new markets and appointed agents from non-textile backgrounds. According to Ghoshal, while Ambani did not pioneer the concept of company stores—Reliance's competitor Bombay Dyeing had innovated this practice—he 'pursued this strategy on a grand scale'.

Ambani untiringly toured the country, offering franchises to shareholders. To those who agreed and had the shop-space, he promised that Reliance would provide financial and advertising support. Many accepted. In his drive to achieve high volumes, Ambani spotted an entirely new market—the non-metro urban segment—and opened it up. Other mill-owners watched enviously as Ambani scooped rich profits from fabric marketing in smaller towns, as the first to both recognize and exploit their potential.

For three years, between 1977 and 1980, almost daily a new and exclusive Vimal retail outlet would open its doors to business. 'In fact, on a single day in 1980 we opened as many as one hundred Vimal showrooms,' said K. Narayan, president of the textile division, who prior to joining Reliance in the '70s had been a professor of commerce in a local college. By 1980, Reliance fabrics were available all over India through twenty company owned retail outlets, over 1,000 franchised outlets and over 20,000 regular retail stores. Ambani's success in franchising and his speed in opening retail outlets is perhaps comparable to that of Benetton, the Italian knitwear company, or McDonald's, the American hamburger chain.

In his relationship with his dealers, Dhirubhai established a paternalistic attitude. According to Narayan, who is one of his oldest managers, 'I used to tell my trade—doing business with us is risk free. If you lose, come back to us. If you make profits, they are yours. Textiles is a trade driven product. Consumer acceptance is necessary but then trade must help too. Most traders are small entrepreneurs. So when I specify targets to a trader he should do his damnedest to perform.'

Traditional stockists, however, still hesitated to buy Vimal's synthetics range because it was too upmarket, too expensive. Indian entrepreneurs had not yet begun manufacturing man-made yarns and fibres locally. The government believed that India was too poor to indulge in synthetics and so discouraged imports by levying stiff customs tariffs.

Ambani questioned this we-know-best attitude. 'For a poor country, for poor people, from the utility point of view, synthetics are the best. More and more people don't mind paying a little more provided they have the assurance of quality,' he insisted. 'Do you remember Bri-nylon? When it first came, anyone who came in wearing a Bri-nylon shirt would be walking two inches above the ground! That is how people felt and seeing that, I chose to go in for synthetics. And at that time the duties were not so costly. That came later.'

The government refused to listen, hiking duties and capping production. As local supply fell short of demand, smugglers got into the act. Dhirubhai's research showed that a staggering Rs 30bn worth of textiles were annually smuggled into India in the '80s. In arriving at this number, Dhirubhai painstakingly collected data on supplies reaching the United Arab Emirates from such sources as Japan, Korea, Taiwan, Hong Kong and Singapore—and became an authority on smuggling in India. His insight into consumer patterns may have been due to his personal background. He didn't look down on consumers or take them for granted. The polyester pasha had stumbled on a huge market which the older mills had missed completely.

By 1980, sales were Rs 2.1bn and growing, but Reliance's production couldn't meet demand. Ambani stretched the mill's production capacity to its outer limits, continuously upgrading the technology and replacing slower looms with faster ones, but he couldn't install more looms. The government's licensing policy favoured the powerloom sector and large mill-owners, even Ambani, found it difficult to get sanctions for capacity expansion. To overcome this constraint, Ambani started sourcing grey fabric from the powerlooms of Surat, processing it at Naroda and selling it under the Vimal brand name.

The Naroda mill was a watershed in the Ambani saga. It transformed Dhirubhai from a mere yarn trader into a mill-owner, the top of the Christmas tree in Bombay's high society and that of Ahmedabad, the two cities which mattered most to him. Often referred to as the Manchesters of India, Bombay and Ahmedabad have grown rich on cotton textiles. Most mills were set up during the British Raj, their brown owners acting as blue-blooded as the Prince of Wales. Generations of Mafatlals, Sarabhais, Wadias and Lalbhais dominated western India's banking circles and the Taj Mahal Hotel's ballroom off Bombay harbour. In this rarefied atmosphere, the earthy Ambani with his swarthy complexion and robust hail-fellow-well-met manner was a powerful presence.

As a yarn trader, Ambani used to kick his heels outside

the custom-designed offices of the big *seths*, waiting for the opportunity to make a sale. Some bought from him, others didn't. One of those who didn't was Nusli Wadia of Bombay Dyeing, a young Parsi mill-owner of impeccable pedigree who would later clash with the older, brash, go-getting trader (of which more later). Today, the boot is on the other foot, but 'I call them my *seths* still because I can't forget my old days,' says Dhirubhai. 'This is my nature, my culture.'

Under the *seths*, often third and fourth generation scions raised on a rich diet of culture and *bon ton,* the Indian textile industry was beginning to look as if it had gone into terminal decline. More often than not, it was referred to as a 'sunset' business, one where there was no fresh investment, no aggression. Whereas the old mills resembled cobwebbed museums, Reliance's Naroda unit could have been in any developed country. 'Once I had successfully put up a textile mill,' said Ambani, 'I decided I must have a world scale, fully integrated plant. All I wanted was to be competitive with countries like Japan, Taiwan, Korea.'

Like first generation trail-blazers in the mould of Mafatlal Gagalbhai (1873-1944) who started out hawking cotton cut-pieces on wayside roads and ended up founding one of India's largest business dynasties, Dhirubhai infused the textile industry with his dynamism and confidence in the future. It took Bombay Dyeing a hundred years to reach a sales turnover of Rs 1bn. It took Ambani under a dozen.

Ambani's success bred jealousy. Whispers started wafting through textile circles that Reliance's phenomenal success owed less to good management and more to manipulation. The allegations forced a protest. 'We have always worked within the laws of the country and the guidelines set by government. People are jealous,' Ambani grumbled. 'Many of these people were cotton mill-owners and they started to say this when we threatened their leadership in the industry. There is no difference between our methods and those of anybody else—the only difference is that our motivation and dedication is much greater.'

During his days as a Mulji Jetha yarn trader, a rival once floated the rumour that Ambani had gone bust. This was not the first time Ambani would have to fight for his reputation, and it would not be the last. Dhirubhai reacted by scrawling a public notice on the market board inviting everyone to whom he owed money to come and collect their loans. 'He didn't have a single rupee in his pocket at that moment,' says Uniyal, 'but he had a tremendous faith in himself. He knew that once he offered to pay back the loans, nobody would ask him for them. And none of them did. He truly understood the minds of men.'

Another time, Ambani was accused of black marketing. Defamation had gone too far, he felt. To counter this latest attack, he asked D.N. Shroff, the then president of the Silk and Art Silk Mills Association and a long-time friend, to call a meeting of its executive committee. Most were big names in the synthetics business. Looking them straight in the eye, Dhirubhai lashed out: 'You accuse me of black marketing, but which of you has not slept with me?' Since each of them had at one stage or another bought yarn from or sold it to Ambani at the going rate, that one question silenced them all.

Reliance outpaced the rumours. Sales doubled every two years from Rs 49m in 1970, to Rs 127m (1972), Rs 302m (1974), Rs 628m (1976), Rs 1,201m (1978) and Rs 2,097m (1980).

It was time to shift from Kabutarkhana to more salubrious environs. Ambani bought a flat in Usha Kiran, then the poshest block in town, paying half a million rupees. Later he would buy two more, one each for his brothers. In the lift, once in a while, Dhirubhai would bump into another mill-owner,

Jagdish Prasad Goenka, scion of one of Calcutta's oldest business families, an art collector of rare Indian miniatures and head of Swan Mills. As the days went by, Goenka's *namashkars* would become less enthusiastic, the smiles forced. Ambani's star was in the ascendant, but Goenka *seth's* star seemed to have forsaken him. Swan Mills' financial troubles multiplied so badly that he abandoned it in 1987. Reliance went from strength to strength.

EQUITY CULT

A few years before shifting to Usha Kiran, Ambani went public. In November 1977, as in 1967, Dhirubhai had a hard time convincing people to trust him with their money. D.N. Shroff tried to persuade friends in government to buy Reliance shares but with practically no luck. According to Anil, 'If we asked somebody to buy a hundred shares, he would back out and buy ten instead.'

Fifteen years later, Reliance toppled Tisco as the most traded company in India. In 1993, Reliance's daily turnover was 386,000 shares or Rs 97.6m; Tisco's 161,800 and Rs 35.7m.

No one understands the psychology of capital markets and of the Indian investor better than Dhirubhai. Riding the crest in 1985, he ebulliently declared: 'My holding is 16 per cent, but I can't keep control over the company by my shareholding. I keep control over the company by showing performance and winning the confidence of the shareholder. I have never been afraid to expand my capital base because I know that I have the confidence of the shareholders. I don't mind if my shareholding gets diluted—and it is getting diluted—because as you must be knowing, very few chief executives of a company are loved by their shareholders as I am loved.' The words would haunt him during the fight for Larsen & Toubro.

To keep his shareholders happy, he made sure that the price of Reliance shares performed better than the BSE index. For example, the High Unit Value Scheme ended shortly after Reliance went public. Ambani stumbled. To buy time, Reliance's annual accounts were extended by three months, ostensibly to bring Reliance's financial year ending into line with the calendar year (this at a time when most companies were shifting over to a March year ending). Despite the dip in profits, Ambani declared a 27 per cent dividend. He had given 15 per cent in 1977. The next year (1979), in addition to a 25 per cent dividend, Ambani issued bonus shares on a 3:5 ratio. The share appreciated by 450 per cent.

Dhirubhai has a knack of introducing innovative financial instruments and giving fresh twists to old ones. In 1979, Reliance needed money to finance a worsted (wool-blended) spinning mill and Dhirubhai picked up a forgotten financial instrument, the partly convertible debenture. It was not an innovation—Standard Alkali had issued them earlier—but Dhirubhai found it difficult to get permission from the controller of capital issues. Arguing that it gave investors a guaranteed return through interest as well as offering the prospect of capital appreciation through the conversion into shares, Dhirubhai relentlessly lobbied the government until it accepted the concept. Investors liked the idea so much that the 1979 issue was oversubscribed six times and convertible debentures (both partly convertible and fully convertible) became the instrument of choice for managements and investors.

Between 1979 and 1982, Reliance made four successful debenture issues. The 1979 issue (for the worsted mill) was quickly followed by one in 1980 (for modernizing its textile mill), 1981 (to finance PFY manufacture) and a record Rs 500m one in 1982 at the time of the attack by the infamous bear syndicate which had forced the closure of the BSE and made Ambani a national figure.

Later, Ambani would insist that he had had no choice but to defend the share price. Reliance's Rs 500m debenture issue was slated to close on May 20, 1982. It was until then the biggest issue. The next biggest offer was that of Telco, which had raised Rs 470m—and Telco was at that time India's second biggest non-government company, while Reliance wasn't even in the top twenty. To place the magnitude of Reliance's issue in context, it is worth remembering that in 1990, the BSE raised Rs 1.7bn in a good week but in 1980, Rs 1.7bn represented the whole year's resource mobilization. Ambani wanted to raise one third of that at one go. The stakes in this game were phenomenally high.

Secondly, virtually every company making a public issue pushes up its share price just before its issue opens. Aware of this, bears cash in by selling short just before the issue—when prices are high—and deliver after the issue—when prices slump. During the 1982 bear raid, Ambani's obdurate stand against the bears ruined several brokers, earning him some powerful enemies. Someone began to ask how and from where Ambani had got hold of Rs 120m to pay for those shares. While throwing out baits, his fishing expedition hooked an unexpected nugget, one which shook the credibility of the finance minister and questioned the sanctity of Parliament.

It was quite a fluke. In answer to a spate of questions on July 26, 1983 in the Rajya Sabha on the nature and extent of NRI investments in Indian companies, Pranab Mukherjee, the then finance minister, named eleven companies which had invested over Rs 225m in Reliance between April 1982 and March 1983. The question was probably aimed at Swraj Paul's takeover bid of Escorts and DCM. It found an unexpected target. But for Mukherjee's reply, nobody would have known that Reliance was the biggest beneficiary of the controversial NRI scheme.

The names hinted at shady deals. Could companies called Iota, Crocodile and Fiasco be for real? Who would give their companies such bizarre and funny names? The Calcutta-based *Telegraph* picked up the scent first and in September 1983 broke the news that eight of the eleven companies were not even in existence in the UK when the investments were made and that the registrations took place a day after Mukherjee's statement in Parliament.

When Parliament reopened after a recess on November 15, a number of MPs drew the finance minister's attention to the *Telegraph* report and demanded an explanation. Two privilege notices were submitted against Mukherjee, one in the Rajya Sabha by Satpal Malik (Lok Dal), and another in the Lok Sabha by Madhu Dandavate (Janata). A khadi-wearing idealist and dyed-in-wool socialist, Dandavate was then a lowly MP of a party which had little prospect of ever being in power. He would play a pivotal role in Ambani's career in the future.

The Fiasco-Crocodile-Iota riddle slowly unravelled. In the first breakthrough, investigative journalists discovered that the eleven companies had been registered in the Isle of Man, an international tax haven, between November 1979 and July 1982 and were owned by several Shahs, some related, others not.

The clue left more questions hovering in the air. The companies had acquired Reliance shares after Ambani's battle with the bears in May 1982. Was there a link between the two events? The companies appeared to act in unison—at least six bought Reliance shares on the same day—so there was probably one ultimate owner. Who was he and from where did the Rs 225m come? The companies' share capitals were small, no more than £200 apiece, and only three had borrowed money to pay for their purchases. Whoever controlled them also seemed to be remarkably well informed about Indian regulations. Three days after the finance ministry had relaxed constraints on NRI investments (on August 20, 1983), three companies applied to the Reserve Bank of India for more Reliance shares.

It was all highly embarrassing for the government but as the mystery man's identity remained unknown and it became clear that technically the letter of the law, if not the spirit, had not been broken, the media's interest fizzled out, especially after an RBI scrutiny committee appointed for the purpose could not find any chink in Reliance's exhaustive replies to its numerous queries on the issue.

PATALGANGA

But what happened to the Rs 225m? Some of it must have gone towards paying back loans taken out during the big bear fight. Ambani would have paid about Rs 120m to buy 850,000 shares and perhaps as much again to support the share price during its extraordinary swings. Meanwhile, at Patalganga, a sleepy village seventy-one kilometres from Bombay which takes its name from the river on whose banks it is located, the polyester yarn plant was almost ready to go on stream and bills were pouring in.

Work on the Rs 800m plant had started in 1981. Right from the beginning Ambani had an ambitious vision. It would be a world class plant, with the best machinery, all well laid out.

Ambani's keenness for the project was not merely due to his confirmed belief in backward integration. He saw in it a way to improve his competitive position. As he later explained: 'I was a buyer of this product all over the world and I was observing what was going on—not only with the producers in India but also abroad. I went to a major company in the West

and saw how inefficient they were . . . people were not working
. . . were having long lunch hours. The bosses too were not
committed . . . and the cost of all these inefficiencies was
loaded on to the product and was being passed on to me. I knew
that we could manage the business a lot better, make more
money than them, and yet supply better and cheaper products
to our mills.'

Ambani's opportunity to break into PFY manufacturing
came when the Indira Gandhi administration threw open the
doors of this business to the private sector in early 1980. This
was the moment Dhirubhai had been waiting for and Reliance
applied immediately for a licence. So did forty-three others.
Ambani knew he could build a great plant but pitched against
him were the heavyweights of Indian industry: the Tatas, the
Birlas, the Bangurs, the Garwares, the Mafatlals and the
Thapars. It was then believed that amongst those whose
opinion counted in the selection process were Veerendra Patil,
the then petroleum minister, and Pranab Mukherjee, who
headed finance. According to the grapevine, four business
houses had been shortlisted during the first round, but
Ambani's name was not on it.

However, when the selection process was finally over, the
winner was Reliance. The surprising decision left the Mehras
of Orkay, the Jindals, the Singhanias and the Mafatlals out in
the cold. On the cocktail circuit, gossip linked the
government's decision with Dhirubhai's formidable political
contacts, symbolized by a lavish party which he hosted in a
New Delhi five-star hotel for Mrs Gandhi immediately after
the January 1980 Lok Sabha elections. This was a crucial
election which saw the end of the Janata Party rule (1977-80)
and Mrs Gandhi's triumphant comeback despite the excesses
of the Emergency (1975-77). Dhirubhai's party was almost
Mrs Gandhi's first public engagement after becoming prime
minister.

Kapal Mehra's name apparently had been on the shortlist. According to Perez Chandra of *Business India,* 'The Mehras of Orkay had to make a representation to Mrs Gandhi to get a licence. They were eventually granted one in 1985 but even then the licence of 10,000 tpa that Reliance got was more than 40 per cent above that of Orkay. In addition, Pranab Mukherjee's parting gift to Dhirubhai included a licence to expand capacity to 15,000 tpa.'

Dhirubhai disputes the suggestion that his political links played a role in Reliance getting the licence. 'My proposal was financially better structured,' he claimed. 'I told the government that I was putting my company's own resources, and that the others would have to borrow from the financial institutions. My main edge was that we could mobilize our own resources.' But what about Pranab Mukherjee's role? Didn't he help to get this and four other projects cleared? 'People who wanted to criticize Pranab Mukherjee used me as gunpowder. Pranab was in the finance ministry, which does not issue licences. Also, how many people have got licences in India, and how many have implemented these licences? The country should salute people who implement projects quickly.'

Dhirubhai had already built up a reputation for quick project implementation. Earlier, he had set up a worsted spinning plant within eight months of getting a licence. At Patalganga, where Reliance acquired an area twenty times larger than necessary for the polyester filament yarn project, the villagers didn't know what hit them. The PFY plant came up in eighteen months. Perhaps the best accolade came from Richard Chinman, the then director of Du Pont International: 'In the US it would take us not less than twenty-six months to erect and commission such a project.' Later, when building its huge petrochemical plants at the Patalganga and Hazira (Gujarat) complexes, Reliance would be driven by a sense of urgency because it couldn't afford cost overruns. Ambani, like Aditya Birla, knew that delays in project implementation could tip profits into losses. And once plants were up and running, they had to work at full capacity, round the clock.

To help him build the PFY plant, Dhirubhai pulled his eldest son Mukesh out of Stanford where he was studying for his MBA and dropped the untried, untested twenty-four-year-old chemical engineer from Bombay University into the deep end.

'My father told me: "You will take this over and I will only give you one person from Reliance. Everybody else has to be new,"' recalls Mukesh. 'So a team had to be established, we had to select the right technology. The first thing that happened was that I came to the office and found there was only one person with whom I would work for ten or fifteen years. Gradually we got the other people. We are a very professional set-up.'

'When we started the plant, everybody was recruited on merit. We advertised and we were very proud. The credit for this decision should go to my father. I told him that it's a Rs 100 crore project and shouldn't he hire a guy who has worked twenty-five years in the polyester industry and maybe pay him Rs 20,000 per month. He said: "No, you do it. If you think you're going wrong you come back to me but go ahead and do it." That's the kind of encouragement that is required today. Initially everybody was pessimistic, everybody I talked to said it's difficult. But we went in with an open mind and tried our very best. We were on stream in forty-eight hours.' On November 1, 1982, bare months after the bear raid which made a legend out of his father, another Ambani won his spurs.

In selecting technology for the plant, father and son honed in on USA's Du Pont de Nemours. Explaining their choice, Mukesh said: 'We already had a good working relationship with them, so it's not that Du Pont did not know Reliance. We used to buy fibres from them. We made a presentation to them about what we wanted to do and also told them this could be an opportunity we were losing. If we didn't do it, somebody else would. They kind of stuck to the idea. After setting up our plant, their business with India has grown—they've sold technology to five joint sector projects. It was the right decision for them.'

To get Du Pont to sell him their technology, Dhirubhai promised everything but equity. 'Technology is available for the asking in the international bazaar,' pointed out Dhirubhai. 'So why do I need to make a foreign company my partner and give them 51 per cent?'

Some Indian businessmen seek tie-ups with global giants for technology, a few to share risk and others for funds. Ambani's need for the latter lessened as the government reduced restrictions on local companies. As he said, 'Now I get my rupee funds from my investors. For my foreign exchange requirements, I can access the international markets. But we are open to consider joint ventures where we have an active role to play.' By 1994, Dhirubhai had negotiated over fifteen collaborations with the world's best companies but he refused to take on any of them as a partner.

Like Rahul Bajaj, Ambani hasn't taken partners because he could never play second fiddle. And Dhirubhai likes to move fast. He could never accept the conditions under which B.K. Birla worked in Century Enka, a synthetic yarn maker and a joint venture between the Birlas and Holland's Enka International. 'At Century Enka, everything needs Enka's approval,' said S.P. Sapra. 'Enka is used to the slow growth European environment. So they are incrementalist and cautious. They slow down the Birlas . . . If Dhirubhai had created an alliance with Du Pont everyone in India would have said, "Great, he has got Du Pont in India." But it would have slowed everything down.' And passivity is anathema to Dhirubhai. D.N. Chaturvedi, a long-time financial consultant, understates the case when he says, 'Once a decision has been taken, Dhirubhai becomes an impatient man until the project is implemented.'

As a Burmah Shell clerk, Dhirubhai recognized that 'whatever information must come, must come'. As an exporter, he had had to overcome the reluctance of foreign buyers worried about Indian companies and their unpredictable delivery schedules. Perhaps that's why Dhirubhai named his company Reliance. He met every commitment on time, regardless of cost. Narayan, president of the textile division, provided an example. 'In 1973, the rotary machine at Naroda broke down on a Friday evening. The import of the component to be replaced would have normally taken two or three months. So I went abroad the same night, bought the component and got it back on Sunday night and the plant was in production from Monday afternoon.'

To meet Dhirubhai's deadlines, Mukesh's young project team discarded several established business practices in favour of unconventional methods which have now become part of Reliance's corporate culture. One of these was letter writing and paper shuffling, which Mukesh sought to abolish totally. 'Problems were discussed at face-to-face meetings with contractors and decisions were communicated directly. If each contractor were to write to the other and then to us, we would have wasted valuable time,' said Mukesh. Another tenet dispensed with was that of choosing the lowest bid in a tender. 'Sometimes we accepted tenders which were two and a half times higher than the lowest bid,' he recalled. Reliance's criterion was whether the contractor could deliver on time.

In his climb to the top of the corporate ladder, Dhirubhai

had already absorbed and adopted the two key strategies of self-reliance and speed. In implementing the PFY project, Ambani adopted two other co-related strategies: size and sales. He would use this set of four values over and over to drive Reliance's spectacular growth.

At a time when the size of the PFY market was 6,000 tpa, Ambani built a 10,000 tpa plant with a built in provision for a further 15,000 tpa expansion. According to H.T. Parekh, who as head of ICICI sanctioned Reliance's first institutional loan, 'Dhirubhai always spoke of international standards and sizes. Initially I admit that I had some doubts whether he would really be able to carry it through. But he has disproved me by his resourcefulness.'

Most businessmen, uncertain of demand, played safe by building small plants. Ambani turned the concept on its head. According to Sapra: 'Dhirubhai would systematically remove the barriers that were constraining demand.' In the case of PYF, Ambani felt that there was tremendous latent demand, but that it was curbed because at the time the government reserved PYF for small-scale weavers in the 'art-silk' industry. The big mills had to use cotton. This was the key barrier to consumption and a limited market.

To get round this problem and stimulate demand, Ambani launched a 'buy back' scheme where Reliance sold its 'Recron' brand of yarn to small powerlooms who then sold the grey cloth back to the company for finishing and eventual sale under the Vimal brand name. In a sense this was a repeat of the Naroda experience where Dhirubhai had used powerlooms to get round government limitations on production. He would also repeat the careful nurturing of suppliers just as fabric vendors had been nurtured during the hectic days of 1977-80 which saw a new Reliance outlet opening virtually every day.

Huge capacities in a relatively underdeveloped market put

intense pressure on Reliance's sales and marketing teams. 'We gave a fantastic amount of financial support to the little weavers,' said Sapra. 'We gave them ninety days credit to create demand.' Once the positive loop of supply-led demand creation became fully operational, the company would revert to its tight-fisted operating policies. 'Today, 90 per cent of our sales is on cash basis. Whatever we ship today, payment is received by 2 p.m. tomorrow.'

By 1983, PFY had replaced textiles as the major revenue earner in Reliance's portfolio. Ambani kept adding to capacity, upgrading technology and modernizing. 'This continuing growth allowed Reliance to emerge as the lowest cost polyester producer in the world,' says Ghoshal. 'In 1994, its conversion cost was 18 cents per pound as against the costs of 34, 29 and 23 cents per pound for West European, North American and Far Eastern producers.'

Before this happened, there was a major hiccup. On the night of July 24, 1989, a vigorous monsoon downpour filled to overflowing the nearby 'apology of a river' and Reliance's Patalganga complex was damaged by flash floods. Technical experts from Du Pont flown in at considerable cost estimated a minimum period of ninety to a hundred days before the complex could be operational again. Local newspaper reports, based on the opinion of India's best experts, were even less optimistic. Reliance had the entire complex fully functional in twenty-one days.

K. K. Malhotra, head of manufacturing operations, explained how they did it: 'Understand the havoc. After the water receded, we had to remove 50,000 tonnes of garbage—silt, dead animals, floating junk—before we could get to the actual recovery work. All our sophisticated electronic and electrical equipment had been under water for hours . . . We set up a control room to connect the site with the outside world. Then we took time to carefully look at the damage and quantify the work. Based on that quantification, we set up objectives for each plant, when it would be on track. Each day at 11 a.m., I would have a meeting for an hour to review the work. On the third day, I asked the Du Pont people, "What do you think?" We had planned to get our two huge compressors ready in fourteen days. They said, "Out of two, if you can get one ready in a month, you will be lucky." I phoned Mukesh that evening and said, "I want those guys out of here. If they say this, it will percolate . . . it will break the will." We had the compressors one day ahead of schedule, and the whole plant going a week ahead of plan.'

The real secret to speed, according to Malhotra, lay in two things: careful planning to quantify tasks and then saturating the tasks with resources. 'Most companies do not quantify the tasks, do not quantify the resources required . . . Anyone who says we will do this in twenty-four months has not done a proper estimation, for only by accident can the real requirement match such a nice round number . . . We assess the requirement precisely.'

He continues: 'And then, once the plans are done, we saturate resources. We put in the largest amount of resource that the task can absorb, without people tripping over each other . . . If I had all the time in the world, I would optimise. But given my opportunity cost of lost production, it almost does not matter how much it costs because, if I can get the production going earlier, I always come out ahead . . . Only when you put the value of time in the equation do you get sound economics and then saturation almost always makes sense.'

'And, finally, we follow the dictum: coordinate [operations] horizontally, when in trouble go vertical. That dictum—both parts of it—are also vital for speed.'

While Mukesh was proving his mettle at Patalganga, Anil

(a chemical engineer from Bombay's KC College) was studying for an MBA in marketing at Wharton. On his return to India in April 1983, Dhirubhai sent him to Naroda to cut his eye-teeth. 'I left America in four hours flat after writing my last examination paper,' recalled Anil. 'When I came home I said, "Dad, I've graduated." He said, "No big deal. Come on, let's go to office." I asked, "There's no rest, no holiday?" My dad said, "Nothing doing, no holiday."'

Events in Delhi, however, were spinning at mach I velocity. Hardly had Anil established a regular routine for shuttling between Bombay and Naroda than the government finished processing Dhirubhai's applications for the manufacture of four new products calling for fresh capital investment of almost Rs 8bn. Once again Patalganga was humming with activity as the brothers began implementing two of the approvals.

LOAN MELA

Ambani's philosophy of life is simple. Based on a loose interpretation of karma, he believes that every individual is born into an orbit in which he will probably remain for the rest of his life. The world is a series of orbits, hierarchically stacked up with peons and clerks at the bottom and leading industrialists and politicians at the top. To be successful, you must break out of your orbit and enter the one above. After a spin in that orbit, you must break into the next one, and so on until you reach the top. Even as a teenager, he knew he would graduate into new orbits.

Ambani crashed through the first orbit when he graduated from being a petrol pump attendant to a clerk. He shot through the second when he chucked up the security of a salaried job for a riskier life as a self-employed yarn trader. As a mill-owner, he invaded the fourth. He stormed the topmost orbit when he decided to invest in petrochemicals.

In keeping with his core philosophy of backward integration, he started with PTA (purified terephthalic acid), one of the petrochemicals from which PFY and PSF can be made. Over time, he integrated sideways into LAB (linear alkyl benzene, used by detergent manufacturers), into thermoplastics such as PVC (polyvinyl chloride), HDPE (high density polyethylene), LDPE (low density polyethylene, used by plastics processors), and then worked his way backwards through intermediates such as MEG (monoethylene glycol), paraxylene, and n-paraffin, to the basic raw material, ethylene and ultimately the source of petrochemicals, oil. Work is in full swing on an ethylene gas cracker and an oil refinery, and Reliance is a regular bidder for oil exploration contracts. The former petrol pump attendant is inching his way to realizing his dream of building a company like Burmah Shell.

Work on the PTA plant started immediately Dhirubhai got the licence in 1984. His hold on PTA production would become so strong that no one dared challenge it for over a decade. Several businessmen, including Aditya Birla, applied repeatedly to the government for licences but were consistently turned down. Only after the Narasimha Rao administration initiated its liberalization programme were other PTA plants sanctioned. The first off the mark was Mahesh Chaturvedi of ATV Projects who in 1993 announced plans for a 120,000 tpa plant at Mathura.

In tune with Dhirubhai's strategy of backward integration, the PTA plant supplied Reliance's PFY facility. It would also feed a new PSF plant, coming up fast in the same complex. Indian textile mills use both PSF and PFY, and the two are largely substitutable.

Ambani was always a panoramic thinker, and the PSF plant represented his incredible capacity to take risks. At the time Ambani applied for permission to make PSF(1984), it was in short supply. Mills preferred to use PSF because it was cheaper than PFY largely due to higher excise levies on PFY. Local PSF production was 37,000 tonnes and another 10,000 tonnes was being imported. Ambani applied for a 45,000 tonne capacity, or 4.5 times the current import, knowing full well that half a dozen PSF licences, albeit smaller ones, had been awarded to other industrialists.

To feed these capital-hungry ambitions, Ambani needed huge injections of cash. In 1983, despite the ever-larger public issues and substantial profits from the Patalganga PFY plant and the Naroda textile mill, Ambani was feeling hungry. The reason for his sudden appetite was a small but significant change in company tax laws.

A financial wizard, Dhirubhai's amazing tax planning meant that virtually from its inception, Reliance had paid zero taxes on corporate earnings. He could do this because Reliance's continuous capital investments enabled him to set off the profits from operations against the tax credits he was allowed on the investments. In a bid to make companies like Reliance actually pay taxes, Pranab Mukherjee, the then finance minister, announced in his 1983 budget that zero-tax companies would have to compulsorily pay tax on 30 per cent of their profits.

Reliance, however, managed to retain its zero-tax status. It changed its accounting practice. As against the earlier practice of capitalizing interest on long term debt obtained for the purchase of fixed assets till the date of commissioning of the assets, Reliance capitalized interest for the entire contracted period of the debt. This it did on the assumption that 'interest accrues at the time of availment of the loan till the date of repayment of the said loan, and all loans shall be repaid on due dates'.

'It's simple,' said Anil. 'We had accumulated depreciation. A lot of other companies cannot do this because accumulated depreciation can come only from massive capital expenditure. If you spend more money, you get more depreciation. We had projects on hand at that time which were capital intensive. The next year's budget removed the minimum tax.'

In early 1984 Ambani was once again suffering his usual cash-strapped itch. The Crocodile-Iota-Fiasco money had been a shot in the arm, but it had been all used up. Mulling over money-making schemes, a brainwave hit Ambani. Why not convert Reliance's non-convertible debentures into shares? As a rival said at the time: 'Ambani is adept at the intricate jugglery of high finance. The basic concepts underlying his schemes are simple, but with a kind of simplicity that borders on genius. And the man is an unabashed go-getter.'

The only problem was that the scheme didn't quite comply with the controller of capital issues' rule-book. How could an instrument which was initially sold as non-convertible, which was priced differently and offered different rates of interest, be put in the same category as convertible debentures? It would reward some investors at the expense of others. But they managed to convince the finance ministry and everything went through smoothly without a hitch.

Four times over the past five years Reliance had issued partly convertible debentures collectively worth Rs 930m. The convertible parts, worth around Rs 230m, had already been converted into equity shares. The non-convertible parts were quoting at a discount ranging from 15 to 18 per cent. Ambani in April 1984 offered to exchange every Rs 100 worth of debentures for 1.4 shares. The then market price for a debenture was Rs 84, that of a share, Rs 115. For debenture holders, it was an attractive offer. It was even more so for

Ambani. Cash outflows on servicing would go down. The debentures carried 13.5 per cent interest. Even the most generous dividend on a Rs 10 share would be less. In Reliance's balance sheet, a huge Rs 700m debt would disappear (as accountants regard debentures as borrowings), share capital would go up by about Rs 100m, and it would look healthy enough for the next round of fund-raising. Magic!

After the 1982 bear raid 'Dhirubhai became the small investor's stock market deity, but this image got further reinforced when Reliance offered to convert the non-convertible portion of the debentures issued between 1979 and 1982 into equity,' says Ghoshal. This was perhaps the last time that Ambani could act without rivals snapping at his heels, without questions being raised in Parliament and in the media, on stock exchanges and the bazaars. Indira Gandhi was assassinated on October 31, 1984. Her son, Rajiv, became prime minister.

For almost a year, Ambani did not fully appreciate the effect the changes in New Delhi would have on his business. And why should he have? The new administration was prompt in granting permission for Reliance's application for a PSF plant. In fact, according to Anil, 'the first letter of intent to be cleared by Rajiv Gandhi at the first cabinet meeting was for Reliance. It was the Rs 460 crore polyester fibre plant. Later it approved a number of our projects and schemes like the PVC and foreign exchange financing schemes. I don't need to say anything more.'

That year, Reliance made a record profit of Rs 710m. Dhirubhai was on a roll. It seemed as if his juggernaut was unstoppable. But it was. And it was a rude awakening.

The man applying the brakes was Vishwanath Pratap 'Mr Clean' Singh, Rajiv Gandhi's new finance minister. While cracking down on corporate corruption, Singh followed a carrot and stick policy. On the one hand, he drew up a June

1986 black list of twenty-one business houses who had large outstanding excise payments to the government, and unleashed a raid raj of unprecedented severity, but at the same time, he eased up the Licence Raj. As far as Reliance was concerned, they had reduced access to the finance ministry. Singh refused to meet any industrialists privately and Mukesh was photographed sitting at one of Singh's open house sessions like any other businessman.

The first hint of future trouble was the government's sudden decision to shift imports of PTA from the open general licence (OGL) to the 'limited permissible list' in the Exim Policy notification of May 28, 1985. Anyone can import an OGL item, but anything on the restricted list has first to get clearance from the director general of technical development.

Most laypersons at first believed that this decision was designed to help Dhirubhai. Reliance's new PTA plant was under construction and would go on stream soon. The new barriers on imported PTA would help the sale of his local PTA. The reality was quite the opposite. It would be a year more before Reliance's PTA plant would go on stream. Until then, Dhirubhai needed to import PTA to feed his PFY plant. He could use DMT (di-methyl terephthalate) as feedstock, but the local DMT was Rs 4,000 per tonne costlier than imported PTA. His raw material bill could shoot up by Rs 600m.

Dhirubhai still hadn't lost his old touch, however. Sniffing out news of the imminent change, he moved at lightning speed. Negotiating with international suppliers, he contracted the purchase of literally a whole year's supply of PTA—something in the region of 60,000 tonnes—and instructed several banks to open letters of credit for him. From May 27 to 29, 1985, the Bombay branches of Standard Chartered Bank, Société Générale, State Bank of India, Canara Bank and Banque IndoSuez worked furiously to issue almost a dozen letters of credit worth a stupendous Rs 1.1bn. The last one was opened barely a couple of hours before the government announced the changed policy.

Predictably, the finance ministry was none too happy that Ambani had managed to double-guess its plans, and struck back with a 50 per cent import duty which would nullify his gains. Ambani promptly challenged the tariff duty but he had lost the round.

Dhirubhai's failure to import PTA at concessional rates at first appeared to be an aberration, an accident. The next incident was a public slap in the face.

The Reliance board was to meet on Wednesday, June 11, 1986 in Bombay to consider the conversion, for the second time, of non-convertible debentures into convertible ones (the E and F series). For weeks stock markets across the country had been humming with excitement in anticipation of the announcement. Punters were convinced that Ambani would pull off the coup this time as he had in April 1984, though the government had refused countless similar requests from other companies.

This time V. P. Singh refused to play ball. On Tuesday evening, the finance ministry announced that it had decided not to permit such conversions. Within the hour, the news was on the agency wires to newspaper offices, and government officials called Doordarshan with instructions to carry the news item on the 9.30 p.m. news—an unusual step for a TV network that didn't carry hard-core financial reports until the mid-'90s. According to V. P. Singh, he took this step 'to curb unhealthy speculation'.

Anil Ambani was at Delhi airport, waiting for a delayed flight to take him back to Bombay in time for the crucial board meeting the next day, and didn't hear of V. P. Singh's decision until he reached Bombay. The next morning the headlines screamed the disastrous news. The board meeting fixed for that day was adjourned. On the BSE, one series of Reliance's debenture prices halved from Rs 220 to Rs 120, the other from Rs 210 to Rs 134 and 1.5 million Reliance investors lost anything up to Rs 3bn in a few short hours.

V. P. Singh's action was probably influenced by a series of articles published in a national daily. Three months earlier, on March 22, the *Indian Express* had front-paged an article on debenture conversions entitled 'Sub-rule or subversive rule', and called on the finance minister to 'prevent this prejudicial tendency from becoming part of the system'. The paper and its sister publication, the *Financial Express*, had been carrying on a campaign against Ambani for some time. It ran three articles from May 16 to 18, 1986 on a loans-for-shares scheme which Ambani had developed in June 1985 and which the paper dubbed the 'Reliance Loan Mela'.

According to the *Indian Express*, ten or more banks had lent over Rs 600m as overdrafts to a bewildering assortment of sixty investment companies without any track record against the security of Reliance shares and debentures. The newspaper claimed that these companies belonged to Reliance and that they borrowed money from the banks at 18 per cent interest to buy debentures which earned only 13.5 per cent interest in one case and 15 per cent in the other. The only way this transaction made sense was if the Ambanis planned to convert the debentures into Reliance's overpriced shares at some stage.

In a knee-jerk reaction, the Department of Banking Operations and Development in the finance ministry ordered an inquiry. A senior RBI team rushed from Bombay to Delhi to help out and Bimal Jalan, the banking secretary, cautioned that 'while there is nothing illegal in advancing loans against shares and debentures, the purpose for which the money is used has to be kept in mind'. Heads would roll, predicted banking circles.

The top official of a bank uninvolved in the scheme said: 'When I saw the first article on the Reliance Loan Mela in the May 14 *Financial Express,* I nearly dropped my cup of tea. I must say I was very relieved, after a close scrutiny of the report, not to find the name of my bank in the published list of sixteen banks.' Against this, a banker who was involved said that the scheme was irresistible. His bank would advance loans against blue-chip Reliance shares after providing a 50 per cent margin. In addition, his bank was assured of a deposit twice as large as the advance, so that besides risk, funding the loan would not pose a problem.

It was commercially sound banking. Reliance shares were appreciating, and the scheme promised profits for everyone. There appeared to be nothing illegal in Ambani's scheme, nor did it flout any RBI guidelines. In the West, such schemes were common. In India, it raised a brouhaha. Eventually the RBI called back the loans.

MURPHY'S LAW

All through the latter half of 1985 and for most of 1986, it seemed as if Dhirubhai had been overtaken by Murphy's Law which says that whatever can go wrong, will. Apart from Nina's glittering wedding to Shyam Kothari in December 1986, there didn't seem to be any good news.

Standing on the dais at the wedding reception next to Nina and Shyam, with Kokila by his side, jocularly greeting friends as they lined up to wish the happy couple, Dhirubhai's thoughts drifted to another family wedding two years back. At Dipti's wedding to Raj Salgaonkar in December 1983, as the father of the bride, he had hosted a lunch for the 12,000 workers at the Naroda mill. To see the workers participating in the Ambani family's happiness had multiplied Dhirubhai's own happiness. Having once been a blue-collar worker himself, his attitude towards his workers was genuinely paternalistic, not a management strategy.

It pinched Dhirubhai to know that there wouldn't be an opportunity to host a similar function when his second daughter was getting married. Somewhere along his headlong career, the affinity he used to share with his workers had disintegrated. The looms at the Naroda mill were silent, the workers on strike, and a celebratory lunch was out of the question.

Dhirubhai felt even more hurt by clashes between Anil and Ramniklal over the negotiations with the workers. Impetuous and outspoken, Anil had found it difficult to work with uncle Ramnikalal right from the beginning but now a family split seemed inevitable. Had sending Anil to win his spurs at Naroda been a mistake? At the time, keeping Mukesh at Patalganga and sending Anil to Naroda had seemed a logical decision. Natwarlal had already walked out a few years earlier. Now Ramniklal. Separating from his brothers was hard for Dhirubhai. Family means a lot to him and he and his brothers had been close to each other. There was a price to pay for riches and power, and the bill had been presented.

Smiling his trademark grin, pumping hands vigorously, slapping a friend's back and cracking the usual wedding jokes, Dhirubhai hid deep inside him the strain he was going through. Nothing should mar Nina's wedding. He pushed aside his mounting business problems.

Reliance, so often described as a bubble, seemed about to be pricked. Dhirubhai had not then heard of Bill Gates and *The Road Ahead* had not yet been written, but Gates's description of a company in trouble precisely described Reliance in the mid-'80s. 'A company in a positive spiral has an air of destiny while one in a negative cycle feels doomed. The press and analysts smell blood and begin telling inside stories about who's quarrelling and who's responsible for mismanagement. Customers begin to question whether, in the future, they should continue to buy the company's products. Everything is questioned, including things that are being done well,' Gates would write. He could have been talking about Reliance.

Rumours about technical hitches in the new PSF plant coming up at Patalganga were gathering momentum. It had been built in a record fourteen months and the Ambanis had hoped to get the plant started in April 1986, but teething troubles delayed commercial production to August, allowing press speculation to blow up the issue. Mukesh and Anil tried to point out that such teething troubles were normal, but the Ambanis' reputation for quick implementation nose-dived. More serious were the problems in implementing the PTA licence. The Ambanis had initially thought they would have the plant up and running by mid-1986. It would eventually be commissioned in November 1987, more than a year behind schedule.

What really hurt Reliance badly was a gaping hole in operating profits caused by a variety of factors. Sales were booming, moving up by 24 per cent to Rs 9.11bn in 1986 but nobody was cheering at 222 Nariman Point. Yarn prices crashed after PSF was put on the OGL. Project costs of the PTA and LAB plants ballooned by Rs 3bn partly because of a rise in capacity but also because of cost overruns. The government delayed clearing one of Dhirubhai's mega debenture issues. The triple-whammy resulted in operating profits plummeting from Rs 710m in 1985 to Rs 140m in 1986. To narrow the gap, the Ambanis sold off some of the family silver—Rs 370m worth of UTI units—but were forced to increase bank borrowings from Rs 380m to Rs 1.36bn and step up unsecured loans from Rs 700m to Rs 1.44bn.

The Naroda strike, the PSF plant's teething troubles,

Ramniklal and the family divorce, the glitches in the PTA plant, the crash in yarn prices, the delay in the G series, the hole in Reliance's profits, the cash crunch—the problems relentlessly stacked up on each other. On February 9, 1986 Dhirubhai succumbed to the pressure and suffered a paralytic stroke from which he would never totally recover.

Doctors moved him out of the Jaslok Hospital's intensive care unit within days, but recommended treatment by American specialists in San Diego. Typically, Dhirubhai called a board meeting the day before he left. And to scotch rumours or a run on Reliance's share price while he was away, he met with leading journalists in an informal press conference in his all-white office. 'I had come to attend a board meeting and thought why not meet some friends before going on a holiday for a few weeks,' he told them cheerfully. He returned to India for the abortive June 11 board meeting and the annual general meeting but left almost immediately for further treatment in Switzerland. August of that year saw him on his feet at the EGM, the crowds cheering as speaker after speaker praised Reliance and its dynamic chairman.

In the years to come, Dhirubhai's health would be the subject of intense speculation. But it was obvious that his legendary will to succeed would be applied to the matter of his poor health as well. In 1989, he gave a lively interview to S. N. Vasuki of *India Today*. To the poorly punned question, 'We would like to have your last word on the subject,' Dhirubhai quipped: 'Why do you need my word? I'm here before you. How do you find my health? I feel fit. I'm here at the office as I used to be, doing my hard day's labour.'

However, the mind can control the body only up to a point. After that 1989 interview, Dhirubhai turned reclusive. He made a rare public appearance at Hazira in an informal press conference in August 1991 to announce the merger of the group's two big companies, Reliance Industries and Reliance Petrochemicals, where he 'appeared confident, spoke in Gujarati, slurring over some of his words'. This was followed by the Reliance AGM in October, where 'ill as he obviously was, looking tired and wan, and with an almost totally disabled right hand, Mr Ambani nevertheless proved that he had lost none of his wonted powers of persuasion and people management. Awkward questions were either avoided altogether, or averted with a charming invitation to "come and have a cup of tea and clarify everything" with the chairman,' reported the *Times of India*.

As Reliance struggled through a negative cycle, Mukesh and Anil looked for scapegoats—and identified Nusli Wadia. Convinced that the elegant chairman of Bombay Dyeing and Britannia Industries was behind their troubles, they found it difficult to forgive or forget Jinnah's grandson.

Wadia is ten years junior to Dhirubhai. Gutsy, England-educated and with a sharp legal mind, the Christian-turned-Parsi is as tenacious as the man who created Pakistan. His business empire doesn't figure among the top twenty but Wadia could have been India's number one industrialist. A favourite of J.R.D. Tata, Wadia repeatedly turned down his godfather's offers to head the Tata group. Interestingly, he has impinged on the lives of half the business maharajas in this book—Ambani, Aditya Birla, Rama Prasad Goenka, Brij Mohan Khaitan and Ratan Tata—almost by accident, but every encounter would become a turning point.

Wadia told *Business India* that the Ambanis 'are making me out to be some kind of James Bond figure, running around the globe . . . and destabilizing the nation. It is almost like a Hindi film. It has sex, espionage, forged passports—everything for a blockbuster.' In a sense the war between the young aristocrat and the older self-made entrepreneur was inevitable. The clash stemmed from the unhealthy nexus between business and politics which had developed during the '80s. Both are politically well connected. Neither hesitated to involve their political patrons to suit their personal ends.

What sparked the Ambani-Wadia feud? There are so many stories, it's impossible to know which is true, especially as neither Wadia nor Ambani have ever come forward with their versions. One thing, however, is certain—it had something to do with Wadia's decision to build a DMT plant and Dhirubhai's entry into PTA.

Both are raw materials for the manufacture of polyester yarns and fibres (PSF and PFY). During the Janata Party rule (1977-79) Wadia obtained permission to build a 60,000 tpa DMT plant and purchased a second hand plant from USA's Hercofina, but before his letter of intent could be converted into a licence, the government changed. Under the new Congress administration, his licence was delayed on one pretext or another until 1981. His plant was finally commissioned five years later.

As a PFY manufacturer, Ambani could use either DMT or PTA but Dhirubhai was convinced his choice was the raw material of the future. Moreover, in the days when Ambani used to hawk his yarn from door to door, Wadia had refused to buy from him. Now it was Wadia's turn to be disappointed.

The conflict ignited once Dhirubhai obtained a licence to build a PTA plant; it would become a fireball after Reliance built its paraxylene facility (paraxylene is a vital input in DMT manufacture). Despite Wadia's bitter opposition the PTA plant came up anyway and the '80s and '90s saw both tycoons trying to gain an advantage in terms of customs and excise duties on DMT and PTA in their favour. There was one abortive attempt at reconciliation. In December 1985, Wadia attended Nina's wedding. Photographs of the two tycoons shaking hands made it to every celebrity magazine in town.

It wasn't long before the truce broke down and once again the two went hammer and tongs at each other. Reportedly one of the major reasons for the cease-fire's short life was a campaign launched by the *Indian Express*, owned by the late Ramnath Goenka. Ironically, he was drawn into the fray as a common friend of the two mill-owners. When Goenka's mediation attempts backfired, he backed Wadia and turned against Ambani.

THE OLD FOX

Described once as 'a paper cannon that fired in eight directions', Ramnath Goenka (1904-1991) was proprietor of the second biggest newspaper chain after the *Times of India*. During the anti-Reliance exposures, Goenka was criticized for using his paper to fight his friends' battles but he had always wielded it as a weapon, before Independence and after. He gave a job to Feroze Gandhi (Indira's husband) in the *Indian Express* at Jawaharlal Nehru's request, but would run fearless campaigns against Indira for splitting the Congress Party, for nationalizing banks, for abolishing privy purses, and for establishing the Emergency.

Completely hands-on, the 'Old Fox' hired and fired editors with little sympathy for their sensitivities, yet every newshound of repute worked in his stable at some point in their careers. Goenka loved the *Indian Express* and its reputation as crusader. His editors toppled A.R. Antulay, the chief minister of Maharashtra, in a cement scandal. They puffed up Devi Lal and then brought him down. For the Reliance campaign, Goenka hand-picked Swaminathan Gurumurthy, an unknown chartered accountant from Madras. To help him, Gurumurthy collected a small coterie around him, including Maneck Davar, then the unknown editor of a small legal newsletter.

But the half decade before Goenka died was not only about Wadia and Goenka's battles with the Ambanis. Arun Shourie and Chitra Subramaniam were unveiling the Bofors scandal. There were messy leaks about the government's purchases of the HDW submarines. The Fairfax case, the clashes between Rajiv Gandhi and V.P. Singh, Gandhi's locking of horns with cousin Arun Nehru and old friend Arun Singh, Amitabh Bachchan's tossing away of his membership of Parliament, the stories unfolded faster than reporters could type.

Apparently unsophisticated in his crisp white cotton dhoti-kurta and simple black chappals, and given to language peppered with colourful Hindi abuse, Goenka's looks were deceptive. As much a legend as Ambani, a bania like him, and as doughty as his antagonist, Goenka had a natural appetite for a fight. He allegedly flouted regulations and cut corners to build his empire, but his personal lifestyle was above reproach. The living room of the twenty-fifth floor penthouse of Express Towers where he spent most of his time was a stark room with large windows, a couple of rexine sofas and bare tiled floors. By the mid-'80s and at the height of the *Indian Express*-Reliance war, Goenka had become bald, his full lips pursed into a tight grin, but the dark eyes were still sharp behind the thick glasses although he was beginning to be shunted in and out of hospital.

Goenka first met Ambani in 1964. 'This is not something I like to brag about, but I am the man who introduced him to Dhirubhai Ambani,' says Murli Deora. 'They met at a small dinner that I had organized at the Taj in Delhi. Ramnathji spent the entire evening examining Ambani and I could sense that he was trying to dissect him. I asked him afterwards what he made of Dhirubhai. "What I like about him," he said "is that he is not a hypocrite." This was an ambiguous remark but I had the feeling he had taken to Ambani. And sure enough he saw a lot of Dhirubhai after that.'

The two sometimes played cards together on a Sunday afternoon. What turned the publisher against his friend? There are several conflicting stories on the provocations which caused Goenka to hound Dhirubhai and why the *Express* became Ambani's 'punching bag'.

By one account, at a coincidental meeting on a Bombay-Delhi flight, Ambani apparently told Goenka that everyone had a price, that *Express* reporters were on his payroll, and that even Goenka had a price. This, the story went, was later sought to be explained away as an off-the-cuff jest, but the elderly baron took great offence. A variation on this theme was the story that the Ambanis had influenced the Press Trust of India (PTI) to write an article contradicting an *Express* report that the CBI had been asked to investigate Reliance's affairs. Goenka, apart from owning the *Express*, was chairman of PTI.

Vir Sanghvi, editor of *Sunday,* a leading political weekly, has his own theories. 'Mine is simple,' he says. 'Goenka believed that Ambani had betrayed him. And Ramnathji never forgave what he regarded as treachery. Goenka regarded Nusli Wadia as a son. He thought that Wadia was being persecuted by Ambani (*"Woh bechara Englishman hai, mere jaisa bania thodi hai"*). Because Ambani was a friend, he believed he could get him to stop persecuting Nusli. A meeting was set up at Express Towers. Dhirubhai promised to lay off. And then—or so Ramnathji believed—he went back on his word. For Goenka, that was the ultimate betrayal. And he never forgave Ambani.'

'Betrayal! That's interesting,' says Uniyal. 'I was present at several meetings between Dhirubhai and RNG (Goenka) during those days. At every meeting, RNG would pledge to

Dhirubhai to call off the *Indian Express* attacks on Reliance, only to go back to his Sunder Nagar guest house to plan for a fresh assault in the next morning's edition. Then he would be the first to call Dhirubhai in the morning to express regrets for what happened, using the choicest abuses for his editors for defying instructions. It all became almost a daily affair. Daily war and daily truce.'

'Hypocrisy is the armour of a valiant warrior like Ramnathji,' Dhirubhai once told Uniyal with a smile. 'I respect him for trying, even if I am not totally fooled by such hypocrisy.' Dhirubhai felt Goenka's campaign was born of envy. 'Ramnathji was not my enemy. My success is my worst enemy. In conditions where too many try and very few succeed, the success of someone like me is bound to cause envy, and the envy becomes ever more intense the more its designs are frustrated. The sole motivating factor behind Ramnathji's campaign of character assassination is envy.'

With his father in hospital in 1986, Mukesh decided to take the bull by the horns and sought a meeting with Goenka, but his calls were not returned. Dhirubhai then asked Mukesh to barge into Goenka's flat in Sunder Nagar, even without an appointment if necessary. Mukesh did that—and was kept waiting on the doorstep, only to be told that Goenka could not see him. He was on his way down the stairs when he was called back up and thus began a series of meetings between the aging press baron and the young inheritor.

Goenka hurled charges and recriminations at Mukesh, who nervously stammered apologies. He also pleaded that the *Indian Express* should stop publishing reports about Reliance until his father was better. Realizing that Mukesh was not making much headway, Dhirubhai, who had returned by now from San Diego, himself asked for a meeting and offered to go across to Express Towers. But Goenka said the mountain would come to Mohammed and drove over—minus driver as usual—to Ambani's office, a stone's throw away. The meeting, which lasted all of forty-five minutes, was stormy but Goenka promised to refrain from publishing any fresh stories on Reliance until July, when a new editor was to take over.

Some feel that the truce might have lasted for longer than the three weeks it did had it not been for the missiles that the two sides had already fired at each other. The whole of June 1986 saw an unprecedented media blitz where newspapers, magazines and week-end tabloids unleashed blistering attacks on the Ambanis. Only the fortnightly *Onlooker* took pot-shots at Wadia. According to *India Today*, the Ambanis through Murli Deora made a last-ditch attempt to stop the *Onlooker* article from appearing. Unfortunately, its proprietor was away in Tirupati, the editor in Cork and the presses kept rolling on. The truce crumbled.

In time the Ambanis got inured to the attacks, shrugging off accusations and landing a few punches of their own whenever they could. 'I believe my best defence is my deeds,' said Dhirubhai. 'In a few years from now, what will stand tall above all these so-called controversies is the work I'll have done and left behind me to make Indian industry great and big and competitive at home and in the world market. I'm not sure how many will really bother to remember the daily venomous outpourings of the *Indian Express*. The campaign has become so hackneyed that I do not think it necessary or useful for me or for the paper's readers to defend myself against all the lies, half-truths and distortions which it keeps printing.'

Nonetheless, in the beginning the *Indian Express* campaign must have been a frightening experience for Mukesh and Anil—then in their late twenties—as they struggled to put up a stiff defence. While Dhirubhai was recovering, they shielded him from the worst onslaughts. In his first major interview, on the heels of the Reliance Loan Mela articles, a visibly flustered Mukesh deftly answered every hard question thrown at him by the seasoned T.N. Ninan, who was business editor of *India Today*. A few weeks later, Reliance issued a series of fifteen advertisements in ten major newspapers across the country, including the *Indian Express*. As a damage control exercise, paid advertisements are blunt tools with an inherent credibility problem. However, the Reliance ones tried to pull the rug from under Goenka's feet by containing key phrases like 'concern for truth', 'allegiance to ethics', and 'commitment to growth'.

Goenka hit right back with another hail of headlines. Among the reports was one alleging that Reliance had built capacities in excess of the licences by smuggling extra machines into the country. This eventually led to a show cause notice from the Customs authorities and a duty and penalty claim of Rs 1.19bn on Reliance. Even as Ambani's lawyers prepared to battle the case, in July 1986, the government abolished a customs levy on imported PFY around the same time as a new Reliance PFY unit was being commissioned. The finance ministry's action was triggered by the accusation that domestic producers—and Reliance foremost—were making windfall profits because of the duty.

This last attack struck the Ambanis right on the bottom line, but Wadia and Goenka also suffered their fair share of hits. In the mêlée, it was discovered that *Imprint*, a magazine edited by R.V. Pandit which had been particularly vitriolic in its attacks on Reliance, had until 1985 been partly owned by Nusli Wadia and his father, Neville. Even more damaging was the revelation that Goenka, his relatives and friends had all either acquired or been allotted Reliance debentures.

Perhaps the biggest setback to the Wadia-Goenka campaign was the success of Reliance's G Series. In December

1986, the Ambanis approached the capital market with a massive Rs 5bn offer of fully convertible debentures. The issue was labelled in one section of the press as a public referendum on Reliance. The Ambanis were fighting back the only way they knew—by a direct appeal to the investing public. The issue was oversubscribed seven times with an unprecedented number of 1.75 million applications for allotment before the offer's closing date. Despite the allegations and setbacks, they had retained the confidence of millions of shareholders. This time it was an exhausted Goenka who had to be admitted to hospital.

The tide began to turn. A series of events—the success of the G Series, a secret meeting (probably in October 1986) between Dhirubhai and Rajiv Gandhi brokered by Amitabh Bachchan, and the shifting of V.P. Singh from the finance ministry to defence—seemed to point towards a revival of sorts. A number of favourable government decisions followed. Some licences, pending for quite a while, were suddenly cleared. Imports of PSF were canalized through a state agency, thus preventing direct imports by end users. A customs levy of Rs 3 per kg on PTA (which Reliance was still importing) was abolished. The Patalganga complex was granted refinery status, entitling it to a lower level of excise duties for raw materials like naphtha. Early conversion of the G Series debentures into equity was permitted which resulted in an estimated saving of about Rs 330m in interest costs. Reliance declared a hefty profit of Rs 800m in the next accounting year, though this was extended to eighteen months to coincide with the commissioning of the new PTA and LAB plants.

Murphy's Law seemed to have abandoned Maker Chamber IV in favour of Express Towers. A key editor, Suman Dubey, resigned in April 1987. On September 1, there was a massive nationwide raid on the *Express* group, leading to over

250 cases filed being against it in various courts across India. The Delhi office went on strike (October 28) and Goenka's fifty-five-year-old daughter, Krishna Khaitan, died a few days later. Goenka's visits to the hospital became longer and more frequent. After the Old Fox died in 1991, Vivek Goenka, his successor, lobbed the occasional grenade but the punch was missing.

CORPORATE DEMOCRACY

In the winter of 1986, Larsen & Toubro, better known as L&T, was in turmoil. A power struggle among its top executives had erupted as a result of which embarrassing skeletons started tumbling out: irregularities in its shipping division, controversial resignations and financial fiddles such as a company flat being sold at a throwaway price. L&T was in dispute with the finance ministry over employee stock options and with the Company Law Board over its accounts. As an independent company whose owners were no longer handling its affairs, L&T was particularly vulnerable. Its two foreign promoters, S. Toubro and Henning Holk-Larsen, had left India years ago and the shareholding was widely dispersed. By the summer of 1988, L&T was ripe for plucking. Because its management was in a row with the government, whoever got the powers that be on their side could walk away with it.

The Ambanis were tempted. It was India's biggest construction company (sales 1988: Rs 5bn; 1995: Rs 33bn) with an excellent track record, and promised considerable synergy with Reliance. Mukesh and Anil got to work. They obtained a nod of approval from the finance ministry and the prime minister's office, elbowed out Manu Chhabria, and got N.M. 'Nikky' Desai, its chairman, on their side. Confident that they had covered their bases, they acquired a block of L&T shares.

In the middle of its Rs 800m convertible debenture issue, at a September 23 L&T board meeting, Desai moved a resolution inviting Mukesh and M.L. Bhakta, a chartered accountant and long-time Reliance director, to join L&T's board. Both bought the hundred shares a director needs and accepted Desai's invitation. A couple of weeks later, Mukesh and Bhakta were formally inducted as directors. Anil was coopted as a director on December 30, and after Desai's resignation on April 28, 1989, Dhirubhai became L&T's chairman.

A year later almost to the day, he penned a remarkable letter of resignation.

What happened in the interim? The first hint of trouble was Desai's changed attitude. When he had invited the Ambanis, he was fighting with his back to the wall. L&T's other managers were baying for his blood. The finance ministry, through the CLB, had issued show cause notices charging L&T and its directors with favouring Desai and his wife. The allegations included allowing them to buy a flat at a rate far below market value, of donating funds to organizations his wife and daughter were associated with, and of misconceived diversifications leading to huge losses. Both Chhabria and the Ambanis were keen to acquire L&T, but Desai favoured Dhirubhai as a white knight who could bail him out. Above all, Desai agreed to the Ambanis' offer because he thought he would continue to run L&T and that the Ambanis' contribution would be limited to 'strategic inputs' on long term direction. It was a naive view, surprising in a master strategist. It took Desai all of four months to realize that he'd miscalculated.

At Reliance, the Ambanis are hands-on managers but in L&T, they initially felt they had a good man in Desai. He had been in L&T since he was twenty-two years old. After he took over as chairman, L&T's sales, assets and profits had grown substantially. The Ambanis needed someone to run L&T for them and automatically assumed that Desai fitted the bill. But once in L&T House, Dhirubhai revised his opinion. If L&T had to deliver the kind of results the Ambanis were used to in Reliance, the existing management would have to be overhauled. It didn't take the Ambanis long to discover that between 1982 and 1989—during Desai's tenure—L&T's return on revenue had halved from 8 per cent to 4 per cent, as had return on net worth (from 22 per cent to 10 per cent) and that return on assets had crashed from 7 per cent to 3 per cent. So Desai was told—gently at first and then not so gently—that he no longer ran L&T and that a new Ambani team would take over.

For Desai, the realization that L&T was no longer his company was hard to accept. He had been so keen on the Ambanis that his family had even sold shares to Trishna Investments, an Ambani company (he later tried to deny this, but L&T claimed that the transfers were on record). His attempts to protest before a board meeting in April 1989 resulted in his exit.

In August 1989 the takeover ran into its second obstacle. S. Gurumurthy of the *Indian Express* started investigating the acquisition and was outraged by what he found. He argued that the takeover was effected by buying shares from financial institutions with a new company, BoB Fiscal, as the middleman. But, he said, the institutions were not allowed to sell to private parties, so a fraud had been committed.

In mid-1988, four Ambani satellite companies (Skylab Detergents, Oskar Chemicals, Maxwell Dyes & Chemicals and Pro-Lab Synthetics) had deposited Rs 300m in an investment company which in turn deposited this amount with BoB Fiscal. In July 1988, BoB Fiscal bought 330,000 L&T shares from

LIC, GIC and other FIs. A few weeks later, Trishna adjusted the difference and took delivery of the shares. Bazaar purchases were added to this nucleus and on January 6, 1989, 390,000 shares under BoB Fiscal's name in L&T's registers were transferred to Trishna Investments.

In a series of articles in the *Indian Express,* Gurumurthy wrote that Reliance needed L&T to stay afloat, that the L&T acquisition was no more than a means of funding Reliance Petrochemical's Hazira project. Reliance had promoted Reliance Petrochemicals, raising Rs 6bn in debentures from the public but, according to Gurumurthy, the Rs 6bn had already been squandered on unproductive activities such as a support operation for the Reliance share price and therefore it needed money. And sure enough, on August 21, 1989, L&T announced a Rs 8.2bn debenture issue. With this money, L&T would give Reliance Petrochemicals supplier's credit of Rs 6bn. The Ambanis had finally found the money they needed to build their petrochemical plant.

In September 1989, the matter moved to the courts. Two petitioners challenged L&T's issue and questioned the role of the FIs in handing over L&T to the Ambanis. Justice Kotwal of the Bombay High Court rejected the petition, ruling that the Ambanis didn't control L&T—despite large advertisements for the issue which referred to it as a Reliance Group company. The petitioners appealed and the case moved to the Supreme Court. They pointed out innumerable irregularities in the BoB Fiscal-Trishna transaction. They also demonstrated that the family of BoB Fiscal chairman Premjit Singh profited Rs 0.5m a year from the Ambanis.

Sensing that the case was not going well, the Ambanis offered to sell the shares back to BoB Fiscal. At first they wanted a no profit-no loss transaction, but after the finance secretary (S. Venkitramanan had been replaced by Gopi Arora) objected, they agreed to take a Rs 120m loss and by November the transaction had been reversed. The Ambanis hoped that the matter would end there but of course it did not. Several new allegations surfaced—such as the revelation that L&T had spent Rs 750m on buying Reliance shares. As these shares were depreciating in value, the petitioners said, this was hardly the best way to spend shareholders' money.

It was at this point that Ram Jethmalani, the petitioners' lawyer, called for an EGM to allow shareholders to decide whether the Ambanis should continue on the board of L&T or not. Despite Dhirubhai's charisma and reputation as the small shareholder's champion, the call posed a serious threat. Rajiv Gandhi had lost the December 1989 general elections and V.P. Singh was now prime minister. People expected heads to roll and they were not disappointed. Premjit Singh was asked to go on leave in December 1989, Manohar Pherwani, head of UTI, joined him in March 1990. The government decided not to wait for the Supreme Court judgement and in April asked the LIC to request an EGM and the removal of four directors from the board: Dhirubhai, Mukesh, Anil and Bhakta. Replacing them would be faceless bankers and bureaucrats from LIC, UTI, GI and IDBI.

The Ambanis immediately issued a press release in Bombay: 'We have been anticipating this illegal and anti-democratic move by the government . . . amply demonstrates that this government is spurred only by its petty pursuits of revenge and repression . . . the government has been misled on this issue by a vicious disinformation campaign conducted by the *Indian Express* . . . we will take our cause to the people.'

Twenty-four hours later, Mukesh faced the Delhi press corps. 'He seemed nervous, flustered even, but this was perhaps more a reflection of his introverted personality than a lack of confidence,' said Olga Tellis of *Sunday* who would later join the Ambani-owned *Sunday Observer*. Pointing out that 'the action to remove the Reliance directors is illegal', Mukesh said that the group would 'go to both the courts and the people'. LIC had not assigned any reason for wishing to replace the directors and this violated the law. Moreover LIC's action hurt Reliance and the Ambanis in their capacity as shareholders. Journalists protested that LIC had every right to call for an EGM whenever it liked and challenged Mukesh to substantiate his charge that illegalities had been committed. He began to enumerate some, was interrupted by the press and the meeting lost its focus.

Realizing he was at a disadvantage, Dhirubhai resigned and D.N. Ghosh stepped into his shoes in April 1990. These would prove to be a little too big even for an ex-chairman of the State Bank of India. Ten months later, on a pleasant winter morning, he too would resign.

With his silver hair and bespectacled scholarly face, Ghosh had been picked by Bimal Jalan, the then finance secretary, for the job. From the Ambanis' point of view, the choice was not particularly felicitous. A few years earlier, in June 1985, at the height of the Reliance Loan Mela affair, Ghosh had publicly criticized the Ambanis. 'I drafted the original RBI guidelines in 1970, when I was a junior officer. And this was not the purpose for which banks were supposed to give loans,' Ghosh had said in anguish at the time.

During Ghosh's ten-month tenure, he cut the size of L&T's mega issue to Rs 6.4bn, denied supplier's credit to Reliance for its petrochemical projects, and offloaded a chunk of Reliance shares held by L&T.

Three months after Chandra Shekhar took over as prime minister from V.P. Singh, Yashwant Sinha, the then finance minister, called Ghosh to Delhi for a meeting on February 15,

1991. Nothing personal, Sinha told Ghosh. Ghosh made no comment but simply handed over the resignation letter he had had typed in anticipation. In Bombay, Anil was getting married to the glamorous film star, Tina Munim. He couldn't have asked for a better wedding present.

Predictably, Ghosh's resignation sparked off a media skirmish. The *Indian Express* protested that L&T was once again being sought to be returned to the Ambani fold. The *BPO* took up cudgels in defence. What was unusual was the vituperative language used by Uniyal, the *BPO's* managing editor. Rarely had media debate fallen to such levels. Unfazed, Uniyal says cheerfully that he 'enjoys invective. I used to be in the UK where it's quite common.'

Colourful language aside, there were several legal hurdles to overcome before the Ambanis could be re-inducted into L&T. The Supreme Court cases were still on. Parliament was in session, Chandra Shekhar's problems were multiplying, and unwilling to allow this hot potato to overshadow House proceedings, it seems likely that the prime minister's office headed by Kamal Morarka, an idealistic Bombay businessman, advised the Ambanis to have patience. In the event, Chandra Shekhar's government fell after the Congress withdrew its support and general elections were called.

In June 1991, the Congress Party came to power, and soon after his appointment as Narasimha Rao's finance minister, Manmohan Singh promised that if the shareholders approved the Ambanis' return, the FIs would remain neutral. Since any shareholder with a 10 per cent stake can call an EGM, Trishna Investments now did so. The meeting was set for August 26.

Before that, there was a hectic proxy drive. Mukesh and Anil worked the phones, calling up large L&T shareholders, asking for proxies. They hired 800 people to collect proxy forms and had 83,000 by the time the anti-Ambani camp realized what was up. At the tumultuous EGM, LIC asked for an adjournment and the meeting was postponed to September 17. Meanwhile, perhaps under pressure from the finance ministry, Trishna withdrew its EGM request. A rumour—unsubstantiated—was floated that Dhirubhai had been arrested, leading to a sharp crash in Reliance shares.

The chairmanship issue remained unresolved. The board had met occasionally through the year but in the uncertain political climate, the issue wasn't even placed on the official agenda until Holk-Larsen suggested to the finance ministry in late September that U.V. Rao be appointed.

No friend of Nikky Desai, Rao had resigned as vice-president of the profitable switchgear and electronics division in 1988 because Desai had promoted S.R.R. Subramanium as president instead of Rao. And Rao also stayed away from the October board meeting and EGM when Desai helped induct the Ambanis into L&T. After Desai's exit, the Ambanis mended fences with Rao and in April 1989 offered him the managing directorship which he accepted. After Rao became chairman in 1991, however, he joined with Subramanium in distancing himself from the Ambanis. 'We don't want the Ambanis or the Chhabrias or the Hindujas or Swraj Paul. We L&T-ites are capable of managing the company and taking it to greater heights,' said Rao. 'We don't require any outsiders to manage us,' echoed Subramanium.

With Manmohan Singh taking a neutral stand and uncertain of victory in any move to oust Rao and Subramanium, the Ambanis decided that patience was the better part of valour.

For a moment, in 1994, it looked as if the winds of change were blowing their way. The two staunch Ambani opponents retired in April and the nineteen-member L&T board began to tilt in their favour. D.V. Kapur, an independent professional, was considered an Ambani suppórter, four FI nominees were expected to vote for them and two others might follow their lead. With Mukesh, Anil and Bhakta already on the board, that made the Ambanis ten-strong in a numbers game. All that remained was the finance ministry's blessing—which Manmohan Singh withheld. Once again the Ambanis decided to wait for a more favourable time.

'THERE'S NO INVITATION TO MAKE PROFIT'

It is often said that Ambani is an acronym for ambition and money. If Dhirubhai was driven by these, what about the sons? What do Dhirubhai and his sons have in common? And crucially, what are the differences? The Reliance of today no longer resembles its earlier incarnations. Not only is it ten times bigger, but its profit centres have changed. Over the years, exports have given way to textiles, textiles to polyester, polyester to petrochemicals and by the year 2000, the refinery will become the biggest earner. His textile background shaped Dhirubhai, his children are petro kings. Ambani senior flourished under the shade of the Licence Raj, the two juniors operate under the beam of the 1991 New Economic Policy.

Earlier, the last lights to be switched off at the Reliance group headquarters, after he had typically put in a twelve-hour day, were those in the Chairman's suite. Today, Mukesh and Anil are the last out. Designated Co-CEOs by their father, they've been the main decision makers since the early '90s. Asked how they see themselves, Mukesh answered: 'As two bright young Indians, without the historical baggage—of saying we are a great big multinational company, or with a hundred-year family history. We have a fire in our belly, *ki kuch kar ke dikhana hai*. That is what keeps driving us.'

As in all Indian business houses, the family is clearly and firmly the ultimate decision maker, but equally the Ambanis believe that Reliance is a professionally-run company. Anil, usually the first person in to work, insists that 'one must not mistake entrepreneurs who actively manage the business as unprofessional. We are equipped with qualifications from leading educational institutions and are building professional motivated teams to seize opportunities.'

How do they operate? 'As a team. We revolve areas among ourselves, so that we are both well rounded. Control of finance and people are the most important things. What kind of training, what kind of people, our future, we discuss everything,' said Mukesh. Adds Anil: 'My role, along with my father and Mukesh, is one of providing leadership, vision, strategy and, whenever needed, to be the fire brigade. Day-to-day we don't run any of our businesses. Our business leaders do that.'

'They're very close to each other,' says one of their associates. 'They spend three hours a day together. A list of Mukesh's appointments for the day is regularly sent over to Anil's office and vice versa. They're closer than most husbands and wives though there are many forces trying to split them apart. They realize it and are taking precautions.' Was the 'associate' protesting too hard? To scotch rumours of sibling rivalry, the Ambanis permitted *Business Today* to publish a September 1995 cover story on a reshuffle of its top management structure. The move boomeranged. 'Team Reliance' ruffled sensitive egos down the line. Nor did it end speculation about company men aligning themselves to one brother or the other.

Dhirubhai set high targets for himself and those around him. 'Motivated manpower is the most important thing, I tell you,' he once said. 'At Reliance we work like anything, leave no stone unturned, work round the clock, to achieve something which is the best. I have a rapport with all my people, they can reach me any time they want. I myself do not give attention to anything except Reliance.'

The Ambanis expect the same devotion from their executives. Qualifications aren't as important at Reliance as they are at other corporations of its size, and designations are less important than responsibilities, but standards of performance are high and burnout common. For those who fail to achieve targets, the consequence is simple and inevitable. Next time, he's not given an important job. The best reward in Reliance is to be called by Dhirubhai for special jobs. Non-performers are rarely sacked, just sidelined. They quickly get the message. Being seen to be close to the Ambanis is important.

'We do not have formal delegation of authority in our company,' says Prafulla Gupta, a Harvard MBA who joined the Ambanis after working for almost twenty years around the world with Booz, Allen and Hamilton, the international strategy consultants. 'There's nothing like in position X you may have a Y level of signing authority, etc. If there are two people at the same level, one may have the authority to sign a cheque for an eight-digit figure and the other for trivial amounts. It varies with the role and the confidence the person can evoke.'

According to Ghoshal, 'The result of such a structure is a high degree of ambiguity but also a high degree of flexibility. People can be brought into the organization from the outside quite easily; responsibilities can be adjusted without openly declaring winners and losers; and positions can be created and abolished overnight.' In his well-researched study, Ghoshal discovered a senior management team consisting of people with three very different kinds of background, all reporting directly to the family.

In the first set are Dhirubhai's early associates, some of

them old Aden hands. They used to be his intermediaries in his financial operations, in his relationship with government officials and in debottlenecking his implementation plans. By 1994, their role within the group had diminished though some of them are still involved in a consulting capacity.

In the second set are top managers brought in from India's largest companies, mostly the public sector. 'Most private sector CEOs had the view that the public sector managers were useless bureaucrats rather than managers, incapable of taking decisions and only good at creating files that protected their own hides. Dhirubhai, on the other hand, recognized that in India only the public sector companies had any experience of executing projects of the size he was contemplating,' said one. It was this group which built the Hazira petrochemical complex. Today, these older men are losing their value. 'The PSU culture cannot drive the organization on the global path,' says Akhil Gupta, chief executive, operations.

The place of the first and second set is being taken over by a younger group of managers, including a handful of foreigners, carefully chosen by Mukesh and Anil. Typically educated in the best management and technical schools in India and the United States, they often have considerable experience of working with international suppliers and customers.

According to Ghoshal, Reliance needs to consolidate these three sets, but the question is, how? Earlier, the spectacular growth had been fed by outside talent. There had never been time to create a team spirit or for systematic development of people from within, but the lack of teamwork is becoming a constraint. There's too little cooperation within the senior management group heading the different businesses and functions. Given the diversity of their backgrounds, each of them has a different style and is the product of a different culture. The existing organization provides little incentive for them to collaborate horizontally or to build a shared culture across the units they manage. 'There's a need to create a more organized process for nurturing and developing the company's human resources and this may require a far more radical change in management style than a change in its formal structure,' says Ghoshal. The development of a fast track for potentially high calibre executives and greater transparency in Reliance's promotion policy are two avenues which Mukesh and Anil are currently trying to establish to deal with this issue. 'Once there's greater transparency, we hope executives will be more motivated,' says Mukesh.

Dhirubhai's attitude towards his employees was paternalistic. 'I know that if something goes wrong and my family is in trouble, the Ambanis would put the entire Reliance corporate muscle behind them to support me,' said K. Narayan. 'And this is not restricted to the top. What they do at the top, I do to the people down below. Often the issues are not big. For example, if a clerk's child is seriously sick, I send a car for him to use at that time.' Will the new generation continue the tradition? It's anybody's guess.

Like Ratan Tata, the Ambanis are finding it difficult to get the right managers. According to Prafulla Gupta: 'Now we are getting into oilfield development and production. For these businesses, there is lots of technical capability in India but not enough management capability. At the same time, these are $100m to $1bn plays, and we must run these with absolutely world class competence. So we have three choices. We can identify suitable people abroad and hire them and help them get used to working in India as quickly as possible. Alternatively, we can license or purchase the technology as we did for polyester, and grow our competence as we go along. Or we need to review our strategy with regard to alliances and be willing to get into more and more partnerships to quickly enter the new businesses.'

To cope with tomorrow's environment, Mukesh and Anil will need to hone their management team. Under Dhirubhai, Reliance became India's number one company. Today, others are catching up. Anil admits it's a formidable challenge: 'In every business that we have, our second largest competitor is a multinational.'

According to S.P. Sapra: 'The visibility and success of Reliance has made others develop the courage to think big. The Reliance formula is no longer a secret. Also, they will not have the impediments we had. They will be on tested grounds. More importantly, they will be able to benchmark themselves against us. At the same time, there is also a big change in the global companies. Earlier, they were not very interested in India—the country did not have credibility. Now they see India as a major growth opportunity. So they will provide a driving force. They will push their technology . . . they will educate our domestic competitors.'

Overall, the easing of entry barriers does not appear to worry the Ambanis. As Anil argued: 'It would cost Shell $8bn to replicate our position in India. Given their worldwide resource needs, they cannot commit that amount of money to one market.' Nonetheless Dhirubhai, Mukesh and Anil are huddling with executives to identify the kind of company Reliance should be in the years to come and to reassess the group's fundamental strategies.

The first tried-and-tested formula under review relates to diversification. The group's historical growth was built on the strategy of backward integration at a time when other business houses hedged their bets by investing in a basket of industries. The company took great pride in being the only large company in India to be totally focused in a single vertical chain. But deregulation has offered a number of one-time opportunities in potentially giant sectors such as telecom, power and insurance. Should Reliance use its proven competencies in resource mobilization, in creating large new markets and in managing mega projects to jump into these unrelated businesses? In order to do so, would they have to take partners?

It's not as if Dhirubhai never considered diversification. Like Aditya Birla, he flirted with glass shells and picture tubes used in colour televisions before abandoning the project in the mid-'80s. In the '90s, he debated over and rejected a car project. In 1995, under Mukesh and Anil, Reliance is mulling over options such as power, telecommunications and insurance. It will be interesting to see the view they adopt. As Dhirubhai used to say, 'There's no invitation to make profit. Assess the situation and make the best of it.'

These are the problems of success. The fires of 1986 and 1989 have been put out long ago. Most of their enemies have either died or are reconciled, at least superficially. Dhirubhai has cheated those who predicted Reliance was a bubble which would burst at any moment. It didn't then and it's too big to happen now. As Anil says, 'One side of the coin is criticism, the other side is our results which speak for themselves. Perhaps my father's only fault has been that he thought too big and clearly ahead of his time.'

Though he now attends office for only a few hours each day, Dhirubhai's appetite for growth is undiminished: 'Growth has no limit in Reliance. I keep revising my vision. A vision has to be within reach, not in the air. It has to be achievable. I believe we can be a Rs 300bn company by the end of the century.' New ideas come tumbling out in a cascade of wildly enthusiastic variations on the theme of 'Why not let's try and make something new and exciting?' There's so much to do.

Sitting comfortably on a favourite marble swing in his terrace garden overlooking the bright sparkle of the Queen's

Necklace, his grandchildren playing by a pond nearby, there's an aura of immortality about Ambani. Of a tough businessman who hasn't aged or lost zest for life, money and power. Others may think that he has finally arrived, he himself thinks that he has only just begun.

Chapter 2

Rahul Kumar Bajaj

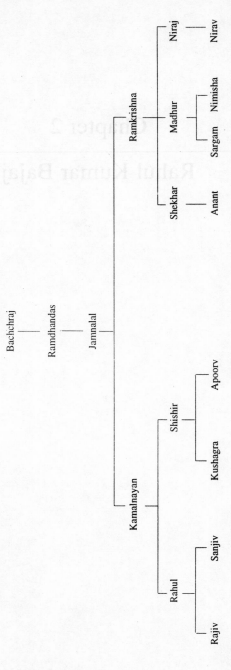

THE BAJAJ FAMILY TREE

Akurdi
June 17, 1979

The thirteen-year-old boy standing on the veranda edged closer to his mother, his fingers reaching out for hers. A thick clump of trees on one side prevented them from seeing fully what was going on below and a little way away, but it didn't cut off the sounds of anger and violence. The sun had barely risen. It was a monsoon morning, the air heavy with moisture.

'My mother and I were standing on the balcony of the old house. There had been tension in the air all through the night. At the time I did not know what was wrong. . . . Suddenly we saw flames. Later I found out that the workers had overturned a police jeep and had torched it. A few moments later, there were gunshots,' recalls Rajiv Bajaj, now thirty.

The police firing on that damp morning was the backlash of a labour dispute which had been simmering through the summer of 1979 at Bajaj Auto, a scooter company located at Akurdi near Pune. The union had recently acquired a new leader, Rupamaya Chatterjee, a fiery young Bengali socialist keen to establish himself as Pune's Datta Samant. The management was headed by Rahul Bajaj, Rajiv's father. Barely forty at the time, Rahul's determination to improve the company's performance matched Chatterjee's zeal.

Events at Bajaj Auto started getting out of control on the evening of June 16. Two workers called for a tool-down strike, but when the management sought an explanation from Chatterjee, he disowned the action. The management then warned the two workers in writing against indulging in 'unauthorized' actions. Interpreting this as a charge-sheet, they and their supporters walked out and squatted on the lawns in front of the factory building. According to the police commissioner, the security officer's provocative language to the workers triggered off the trouble. The workers went berserk and began breaking the window panes. When the police were summoned later, they showered metal equipment spares on them, injuring about twenty-five policemen.

Before that, they stormed the head office. Rahul Bajaj was working on the first floor of the old office building. 'Our chief security officer's head was gashed from the stone throwing but four watchmen reached my office before the workers came charging up. Somehow they contained them. There was some slogan mongering and speechofying (*sic*). After the police came, they dispersed.'

But not to bed. Tension built up during the night, and the management called in the police to stand in front of the gate to prevent further damage when the factory re-opened the next morning. The workers began trickling in from 6.00 a.m., but within the hour, were in the grip of a mob mentality. About 900 workers turned violent and upturned a police wireless van and burnt it. The police fired tear gas shells which the mob hurled back, along with stones and metal parts. The workers threw acid and rolled barrels across the road to prevent the police from following them. Then they made bonfires out of wooden cartons and scrap. Unable to control the situation, the police fired twenty-nine rounds. Two workers and one bystander were killed. Forty policemen were injured.

Maharashtra's home minister, Bhai Vaidya—a former trade union leader, incidentally—immediately instituted a judicial inquiry. While it dragged on, Chatterjee and Bajaj arrived at a settlement, and the factory reopened after five months. But to date no worker reports for work on June 17. On that day, the conveyor belts don't move, there's no clash of steel on steel, no sparks fly from the welding machines.

Fourteen years after the incident, the Bombay High Court fined thirty-one workers Rs 100,000 each. These were the highest ever fines imposed on workers. A lower court had earlier sentenced them to three years of hard labour. Significantly, there has been no strike at the Akurdi plant since then (though there was an eight-month lock-out at the Waluj plant in 1987).

Bajaj attributes this remarkable peace to the fact that 'somehow, we managed to create a situation of win-win and relations became better and better, and that is how my relationship with Chatterjee became excellent. After that we signed another agreement. And after Chatterjee died, we signed another agreement with his main deputy Ambedkar when everything was beautiful.'

Bajaj, the only industrialist at Chatterjee's funeral, is all praise for his antagonist: 'He was a gentleman. I don't know the inside story of the man, but he lived simply. He used to ride a bicycle. Even in the '70s, union leaders used to ride in cars, or on scooters at the very least. But not Chatterjee. He used to eat *chanas* and dressed absolutely like a worker.' Bajaj has less kind words for the workers. 'After so many years, what is the point of staying away from work, losing production and wages?' he asks acerbically. 'Why don't they work and donate part of their earnings to the families of the three men who died?'

Such pragmatism is Bajaj's hallmark. It has earned him a

rare reputation as one of India's most successful industrialists. Successful people tend to be highly entrepreneurial but oddly enough Bajaj doesn't quite fit the bill. Compared to his peers in this book, Bajaj appears colourless rather than dynamic. Squeaky clean, he has never been involved in shady takeovers. He doesn't engage in street fights with other industrial magnates, nor has he ever hijacked someone else's project. He hasn't burnt tyres during a hard drive for meteoric growth. On the contrary, he is something of a plodder, routinely burning the midnight oil, and devoted to the virtues of hard work. Yet he is India's most admired industrialist along with Dhirubhai Ambani and the late Aditya Birla.

Uday Kotak, India's top merchant banker, makes a pertinent comparison between Bajaj and Ambani. 'Apart from the fact that they are two very different personalities, Dhirubhai is a much greater risk taker. Rahul is much more analytical. He moves very cautiously.' Over the past ten years, the lanky (6'1") and handsome (but balding) Marwari has been on the cover sixteen times in magazines as varied as *Asiaweek* and the *Poona Digest*. The Indian business press adores him because he has built Bajaj Auto (sales 1995: Rs 22bn) into the world's fourth largest two-wheeler manufacturer. Non-business journalists keep tuning in to Pune's BBC (Bajaj Broadcasting Corporation) for his unflinching frankness and varied opinion on every topic under the sun.

For Bajaj has a view on everything. Consistency matches conviction. In his personal life, this means a ten-a-day Dunhill Red addiction. In business, it translates into an abiding determination to stick to the knitting. Bajaj has been cranking out scooters since 1964 and is perfectly happy to continue doing so in the next century. 'If Bajaj Auto cannot be a world player in its field, I do not deserve the right to diversify. You should diversify from a position of strength, not from a position of weakness,' he thunders. Pune's scooter manufacturer controls 6 per cent of global production in its area, but to date its market is almost wholly limited to India and its product would need substantial technological upgrading to make it internationally acceptable.

Curiously, for a man with his formidable track record, Bajaj's appetite for media coverage is insatiable. He loves reading about his company and himself. His two secretaries, V. Hariharan and Mohan Keyyath, meticulously file every clipping. They are also responsible for keeping his hectic travelling and appointment schedule on track, an often impossible task. Bajaj's meetings have a habit of overshooting allotted timespans. The charitable ascribe this to Bajaj's habit of getting to the root of a matter. The uncharitable, to his loquacity. 'He uses a hundred words when ten would do,' says T.N. Ninan, editor of *Business Standard*. Most meetings are held in Bajaj's vast office suite dominated by brown leather chesterfields, rich wood panelling, and a huge picture window overlooking lush gulmohar trees and colourful lantana bushes. Facing Bajaj's desk, across a massive expanse of cream carpeting, hangs a painting of a cumberously turbaned Rajasthani by the Jaipur artist, Jaya Wheaton.

For such a vibrant man, it is a strangely impersonal office. There are no knick-knacks to bare its owner's personality. Rahul approved the layout and furniture but his wife Rupa chose the painting. Three clocks, part of a motley collection of gifts and trophies, dot his dark table and the surrounding wall unit. The outside world intrudes in this oasis of cultivated calm through a 14-inch television perched behind his desk. Normally it is tuned to CNN. Its news bites have much in common with this restless and somewhat imperious man. Bajaj can be amazingly cruel to those not in his mental league. Nor does he suffer fools. His attention span is short but his judgement is incisive. This 'A' type hyperactive is always fidgeting, his long, thin arms wheeling around him when he talks.

His innate restlessness is particularly evident when Bajaj sets off for work every morning at 10.30 a.m. The Bajajs live inside the factory complex. The journey is under 150 metres. After a heart attack in August of 1984, the walk would undoubtedly do him good. Yet the left-handed Bajaj prefers to drive his creamy yellow 1990 Mercedes 300D to work at top speed for all of one minute flat. Once he hops out, the chairman-cum-managing director's vehicle is the only car parked alongside the spotless kerb.

The Mercedes is the sole status symbol Bajaj allows himself. As one of India's most powerful executives, he could have built a mansion as priceless as the opulent Juhu palace of Viren Shah, his partner in Mukand Ltd, a special steel rolling mill outside Bombay. The most luxurious objects in Bajaj's Akurdi residence are the exotic orchids which Rupa grows.

A FAMILY OF PATRIOTS

Rahul was born on June 10, 1938, in Calcutta to Savitri and Kamalnayan (1915-1972) Bajaj, a Marwari businessman. The family was comfortably well off and in the process of moving from trade into industry. He schooled at Bombay's elite Cathedral and John Connon School, and graduated from Delhi's St. Stephen College with a BA (Hons) in Economics in 1958. Back in Bombay, Bajaj did a two-year stint at Bajaj Electricals, clocking in after morning lectures at the Government Law College. He spent most of 1961-62 as a junior purchase officer at Mukand and with some work experience under his belt, he left for Harvard. He passed out of the class of '64 with an MBA degree. In between (December 1961), he married Rupa Golap, a Maharashtrian beauty queen and an up-and-coming model. They have three children, Rajiv (b.1966), Sanjiv (b.1969) and Sunaina Kejriwal (b.1971).

Like his contemporary the late Aditya Birla, Rahul was raised in an intensely political family. Mahatma Gandhi treated his grandfather, Jamnalal Bajaj (1889-1942), as his fifth son. His grandfather was also a close friend of Jawaharlal Nehru. He contributed to the nationalist movement and the Congress Party, and was its treasurer for some years. The political tradition continued into the next generation. Between 1939 and 1947, most of the adult members of [the Bajaj] family found themselves behind prison bars in the cause of Indian freedom. Kamalnayan later became a Congress member of Parliament. When the Congress Party split in 1969, he left Indira Gandhi to join the Congress (O).

Though Bajaj has no personal political ambitions, he likes the company of movers and shakers. The Bajajs and the Nehrus have been family friends for over three generations. Kamalnayan and Indira Gandhi studied at the same school for a short time. Jawaharlal Nehru himself picked the name Rahul for Kamalnayan's first-born, a gesture which made 'Indira Gandhi hopping mad as she had wanted it for her own son', recalls Rupa. (Coincidentally, Rahul and Rupa named their first-born Rajiv, and Rajiv and Sonia Gandhi named their son Rahul). As prime minister, Rajiv Gandhi reportedly turned to Bajaj for advice. Closer home, Bajaj has been in the kitchen cabinet of Sharad Pawar, four times chief minister of Maharashtra.

Unlike Birla, however, Bajaj was brought up in a spartan atmosphere, unusual for a business family. Kamalnayan grew up in Gandhi's ascetic ashram at Wardha. His children (Rahul, Suman and Shishir) grew up in relatively more luxurious surroundings, in the leafy bylanes of Bombay's posh Carmichael Road. Rahul's upbringing and values owed more to Mahatma Gandhi than Jawaharlal Nehru, being more middle class than aristocratic. Holidays were often spent playing with the workers' children in the family's factories. Given this background, the idea of living inside an industrial complex did not appear as ludicrous to Bajaj as it would to his peers in the Marwari aristocracy. 'Actions speak louder than words. I did not and do not believe in absentee landlordism,' Bajaj is fond of declaring.

Bajaj's first office was simple: a Godrej table, a Godrej chair, and not much else. 'Though I was an MBA from Harvard, I didn't have any fancy ideas that I must have staff, or a secretary,' he remarks virtuously. His no-nonsense, hard-nosed, direct approach soon created an aura around India's king of the road. It is an image which affords Bajaj immense satisfaction.

His efforts at projecting a 'middle-class' image are, at times, a touch ridiculous. Such as the superfluous identikit badge dangling from the pocket of his half-sleeved safari suit. Why does a gold stripe embellish Bajaj's laminated mugshot when those of his executives are mere silver? Would any of the security personnel have the temerity to question, let alone check, the boss's walkabouts?

Rupa chuckles at the thought. They have been living in the factory complex for almost three decades. On shifting from Bombay to Pune, they were allotted a 10' by 12' room in a Bajaj guest house. The rest of it was reserved for the general manager of Bajaj Electricals, a group company now run by Shekhar Bajaj. Dussehra 1965 saw them finally in a house of their own. Rupa has no complaints. Like her husband, she enjoys colony life despite tense moments such as those following the police firing in 1979.

'That night we hardly slept. We received a couple of crank calls saying it would be better if the children and I go away, maybe to Bombay. Rahul and I thought about it. I said no. I wanted to be with Rahul and I didn't want people in the colony to think that Rahul's wife and children could just take off for Bombay when things became difficult. I also thought that if I went away, it would be a long long time before I could come back. Once you go away in such a situation, it is very difficult to feel secure enough to come back. Since there was firing, an inquiry would take place which would be a long drawn out thing. The workers were in a mood to fight the management for a long time. I wanted to stay here with him,' Rupa recalls.

But times change. The next generation has its own views. 'I don't think one should be rigid. There are business families who live in big cities, away from their factories. I believe it is important to know how the company works and the kind of management systems it follows,' says Sanjiv. Sanjiv might have thought differently had he been in his father's black Bally sandals on November 26, 1964, the day a twenty-six-year-old Rahul joined Bajaj Tempo Ltd.

TEMPO TANTRUMS
His first job was as a deputy general manager. 'I had to see the commercial side which included purchasing, marketing, sales, accounts, finance, audit, everything but the production.' His boss was Naval K. Firodia (b.1910), then chief executive of Bajaj Auto and managing director of Bajaj Tempo.

Thin and ascetic-looking, his starched white khadi Nehru topi proclaiming his Gandhian convictions, Firodia was a lawyer from Ahmednagar who had spent time in Yerawada prison during the 1942 Quit India movement, and got to know the Bajaj family in the '20s through the Congress Party. Following Independence, Firodia joined the Bajaj Group, and helped them tie up joint ventures to manufacture auto-rickshaws and scooters in India. In August 1957, Bajaj

Tempo was promoted to make three-wheelers using German technology. The first Indian Vespa from Bajaj Auto operated out of a garage shed at Goregaon, on Bombay's outskirts, and Bajaj Auto had its manufacturing facility at Kurla. Later both plants were shifted to Akurdi, with a grass strip separating them. Today there's a wall on this strip.

The wall is a constant reminder of the rift between the Firodias and the Bajajs. Earlier, members of either family would simply stroll across the strip whenever they felt in the need of company or advice. Today, even if the wall hadn't been there, neither would dream of casually walking over to the other side as in the past. The earlier friendship between the two families deteriorated into a cold war and by September 1968, a twenty-year-old partnership lay in tatters. Rahul Bajaj resigned from Bajaj Tempo and N.K. Firodia from Bajaj Auto. The Firodias walked off with Bajaj Tempo and the Bajajs held on to Bajaj Auto. The sales of the two companies were roughly Rs 70m apiece. Small beer even in those days.

Neither side wants to talk about why the fight broke out but each feels it got the short end of the stick. 'I felt they had taken away our company. Of course, they have their side of the story,' is all that a reticent Bajaj is willing to say. The Firodias were equally unhappy. Though they had Bajaj Tempo, they felt they should have got Bajaj Auto, a company which they felt they had built up, which was in a monopolistic market, and which had great potential, while they considered that Bajaj Tempo's 'immediate prospects were not very bright'.

According to a friend of both families, the relationship between the Firodias and the Bajajs began to sour shortly after Rahul Bajaj joined Bajaj Tempo. 'You have to view the fight in the correct perspective,' he said. 'Even the Bajajs accept that N.K. Firodia played a crucial role in establishing both Bajaj Auto and Bajaj Tempo and that he and his brother, HK, are very good managers and have done a lot for the two companies. But you have to remember that for many years, Firodia had been working for Bachraj Trading at Rs 500 a month. Later when Bajaj Tempo and Bajaj Auto were promoted, the Bajaj Group provided the financing though the Firodias held a quarter share in the managing agency firm. But after Rahul joined the business, the Firodias began buying shares in the market, possibly from mid-1967 onwards, trying to quietly strengthen their position in Bajaj Auto. When they found out, naturally the Bajajs took umbrage, especially young Rahul. Ironically, he was looking after the commercial side of the business, and so the shares which the Firodias had bought came to him for transfer, which of course he refused to do. I believe this was the genesis for the fight.'

Before the parting of the ways, the battle for Bajaj Auto—fought first in the boardroom, then on the stock market with both the Bajajs and the Firodias trying to acquire its shares—was fierce. Initially, the Firodias had 13 per cent of Bajaj Auto's issued share capital of 104,250 shares but by the end of February 1968, they had managed to hike it to 23 per cent. The Bajajs started out with 28 per cent and gradually built this up to 51 per cent. One of the better-known skirmishes in this battle was a bid to acquire a critical 4 per cent block held by financial institutions such as the LIC and the UTI. Basing their calculation on the share's market price of Rs 260, the Firodias offered Rs 262.50 per share for the block. Rahul Bajaj, on the other hand, was much more agressive and boldly submitted an offer of Rs 411. Outflanked, the Firodas walked out of the auction disdainfully, saying 'they didn't have money to throw'.

From the boardroom and stock markets, the war progressed to the courts. In round one, the Firodias moved the Supreme Court in an attempt to arm-twist Rahul into transferring the shares they had bought from the stock market. The Supreme Court refused to oblige. In 1988, antagonism flared publicly. The *Sunday Observer* carried an interview where an angry Bajaj declared his 'firm conviction that Bajaj Tempo will one day be a part of the undivided Bajaj Group'. 'A bullock does not die as a result of a crow's curse,' Firodia countered, quoting a Maharashtrian proverb.

The mud-slinging and the legal actions didn't subside for two decades after the war's outbreak and even today the tension between the two families threatens to blow up any time. The conflict is partly due to the fact that both families continue to hold significant chunks of stock in each other's companies even after the divorce.

The problem was, the Firodias held 23 per cent in Bajaj Auto, which ensured that Rahul couldn't get a special resolution passed without their permission. However, in the early '90s, in order to fund an ambitious expansion programme, the Firodias gradually sold off some of their Bajaj Auto shares, bringing down their holding to 13 per cent. While this move considerably eased the pressure on the Bajaj camp, the Firodias found their position worsening in Bajaj Tempo.

After the split, the Firodias had carefully built up their stake in Bajaj Tempo from 13 per cent to 26 per cent, but their expansion plans forced them to make a number of rights issues which diluted their holdings. As their stake plummeted, for a brief moment in 1991-92, the possibility of a hostile bid arose and cash-rich Bajaj gleefully seized the tempting opportunity. Initially, the Bajaj group held 23 per cent in Bajaj Tempo. Now Rahul acquired a dangerous extra 3 per cent so that the Germans, the Firodias and the Bajajs each held 26 per cent with the balance 22 per cent scattered among the public. The opportunity vanished, however, when Bajaj Tempo made yet another issue (in 1993) and persuaded Daimler Benz to renounce their rights in favour of the Firodias.

Currently the Firodias probably have 36 per cent, Bajaj 26 per cent, and Daimler Benz 16 per cent and Rahul admits there's no possibility whatsoever of acquiring Bajaj Tempo (sales 1995: Rs 5.65bn). So why does he hold on to these shares? What are his intentions? Bajaj offers a tongue-in-cheek reply: 'It is a good investment. The Firodias run Bajaj Tempo very well. Their track record shows that. Whenever I want to sell my shares, I will make a good profit on them.' This attitude combined with Rahul's ability to block special resolutions is an Achilles heel which has left the Firodias feeling vulnerable. So long as that sentiment endures, and Bajaj doesn't appear to feel any desire to allay or dispel it, there is unlikely to be a thaw in the cold war between two of Pune's giants.

Bajaj has an equally tempestuous relationship with another scooter maker, Piaggio, owned by the Agnellis of Italy. The powerful Turin-based family runs an industrial empire which, according to David Lomax, author of *The Money Makers,* is 'so big and influential that no Italian government would dare either to ignore it or to adopt policies which would damage its overall interests'.

Piaggio and the Bajaj group tied up in early 1960 to assemble scooters in India. Vespa in India was as loved as Vespa in Europe, the first wheels alike of the rich and the poor. A young Sir Terence Conran, the British designer, scooted round London on his. In New Delhi, the college-going Bajaj found that his Vespa boosted his popularity. The technical collaboration ended in 1971 when the Indira Gandhi government refused permission to extend its term. Some analysts felt this was a blessing in disguise. 'With Rahul's tough and disciplined approach, the company soon found its footing in the market and Bajaj Chetak and Super became legends,' commented one.

On the day the collaboration officially ended, Piaggio wrote to Bajaj, thanking him for years of 'really friendly cooperation' and wishing Bajaj Auto 'the most successful future'. It was dated April 1—All Fool's Day—an unintended irony. A decade later, Piaggio would accuse Bajaj of pilfering Piaggio designs in a California district court.

Piaggio's move appears to have been a knee-jerk reaction to Bajaj's export thrust. Pune's scooter king had started dreaming of becoming a global player. Between 1978 and 1981, Bajaj Auto's export sales jumped from Rs 63.5m to Rs 133.2m. A euphoric Bajaj even ran a campaign in *Time* magazine, perhaps the first Indian advertiser to do so. But he was still just a country cousin. Piaggio's production in 1981 was 905,000 vehicles, that of Bajaj Auto, 173,000. Piaggio's sales were L626bn (about Rs 4.7bn at the then current rates). Bajaj Auto's were Rs 1.16bn.

Bajaj's euphoria evaporated as Piaggio initiated legal action against him in the USA and West Germany. The Italians claimed that Bajaj had violated the terms of their collaboration, had not returned Piaggio's original drawings and so had no right to manufacture scooters.

Bajaj claims he had Piaggio's tacit permission. 'How else could it have been? We couldn't be expected to invest crores of rupees in plant and equipment and then one fine day cease to manufacture and let our investment go to seed. And, if Piaggio had not acquiesced in our action, it should have taken legal action *then*, not ten years later.' Piaggio's lawyers—Indian—took a rather dim view of this attitude. 'It's a matter of national importance that Indian companies abide by the agreements that they enter into with foreign companies. We want a greater inflow of foreign technology. How can we inspire confidence if we violate agreements?'

Bajaj brushes aside the argument. 'I remember a whole

week in Genoa with four of my colleagues in 1975. A deal was about to be finalized. Everything was done. Without charging any royalty and fees, without any equity in our company, Piaggio would give the plans of their scooters and three-wheelers. In return we would give them the worldwide right for exporting our vehicles. We fixed the minimum value they would export each year for the next ten years. It got stuck on one small point. We wanted R&D cooperation. They wouldn't agree to that. But we broke amicably as we had done in 1971. Later our exports increased a little bit. They were still chicken feed. But Piaggio thought it was a threat.'

Hiring Baker-Mckenzie, one of the largest international law firms in the world, Bajaj poured $1m into his defence. It was a huge figure for an Indian company at the time.

The great scooter war ended on a whimper. In the USA, Piaggio offered an out-of-court settlement. The millions of dollars compensation demand was scaled down to $50,000. Bajaj 'refused to budge and in the final settlement only gave a promise that he would not sell Bajaj scooters of Piaggio design in the US. By then there was no demand for the scooters in the US anyway.' In Germany, Bajaj Auto lost in the lower courts but won in the supreme court.

If Bajaj didn't lose, neither did he win. 'The case took four to five years during which our exports suffered. Piaggio succeeded in their aim to that extent. Our Indonesian and Taiwanese exports, our two major markets at that time, did not stop. They stopped later on for other reasons, local economic and political reasons.' Bajaj is philosophical.

'Journalists like to dramatize but quite frankly there was no hate. It was a serious business fight. In their position I might have done the same bloody thing.' What really hit Bajaj between the eyes, however, was the sight of Piaggio nonchalantly scooting into his lane. And he couldn't do a thing about it.

In the mid-'80s, following the relaxation of constraints in the light commercial vehicles (LCV) industry, the government reluctantly permitted fresh investments in the two-wheeler industry. The move led to a wave of foreign collaborations. Piaggio was quick to put its foot into the crack in the door by signing a technical collaboration with Deepak Singhania of Lohia Machines (better known as LML) and with Andhra Pradesh Scooters.

Bajaj was and is still sore. Piaggio came here claiming they had better technology, a better vehicle and a better deal for the Indian customer. 'If they were so much better than us, they could have easily beaten us in America and Germany. Why did they take recourse to the courts? But then, they are in business. We are in business. My anger was directed against the government of India for allowing them to enter again. It made my blood boil. This was a wrong policy. I was not afraid of competing with them, and time has shown [this]. They should have been told to withdraw their cases against an Indian exporter and *then* come to India.'

October 1989 brought signs of an accord. Piaggio's home turf was under attack from the Japanese. In India, LML was doing badly. The Italians began to wonder whether the LML investment had been such a good idea after all. Giovanni Alberto Agnelli, nephew of the legendary Gianni Agnelli, the heir to the Fiat empire and Piaggio's vice-president, brokered a secret visit by Bajaj and his team to Piaggio headquarters in Pisa to work out a strategic alliance. A key element was a 10 per cent cross-holding in each others' companies. Also on the negotiating table was a collaboration for spare parts and the ending of a few remaining bits of the long-running German court battle.

As before, this attempt too fizzled out. Meanwhile LML slipped deeper in the red. To rev up its image, Piaggio picked up 25.5 per cent of its equity for Rs 80m in 1990. The fresh fuel injection soon got used up. In 1993, LML's losses hit Rs 360m. From the sidelines, *Business India* smirked: 'Piaggio tried to dent Bajaj's growing market share but only got its nose bloodied.' September 1993 saw a third futile attempt at reconciliation. Agnelli junior flew from Turin to Pune. Piaggio wanted to replace the Singhanias with a new Indian partner. Would Bajaj consider this? Bajaj instead revived the idea of a 10 per cent cross-holding between their companies. The talks came close to success, but broke down when Piaggio apparently started talking of raising the cross-holdings. Suddenly LML's asking price began to look too high. If Bajaj gave in to Piaggio's demand for more equity, he would expose his soft underbelly. In 1993, of Bajaj Auto's Rs 370m share capital, about 51 per cent was controlled by the Bajaj family, roughly 10 per cent by company dealers, and around 20 per cent by the Firodias. If Bajaj gave away more than 10 per cent, his biggest foe could use it as a dangerous lever if things didn't work out with Piaggio later.

Scenting an opportunity, other Indian industrialists immediately made a beeline to Italy. Among them were the Nandas of Escorts and the Munjals of Hero Motors. At one point it looked as if Rajan Nanda, Escort's vice-chairman, had clinched the deal. Eventually, Piaggio decided not to separate from the Singhanias. Since the Agnellis and Bajaj continue to keep careful watch over each other, this chapter is still open.

YOU CAN'T BEAT A BAJAJ

Driving through the cavernous manufacturing facilities at Akurdi and Waluj (near Aurangabad), it is difficult to imagine that this company has frequently been the victim of government paranoia. The '70s and '80s were particularly difficult. The Bajaj family has had close connections with the

Congress Party since the '20s, but the goodwill evaporated abruptly when Kamalnayan spurned Indira Gandhi during the party's 1969 split. Subsequently, her administration stubbornly refused to allow Bajaj Auto to expand its manufacturing facilities on socialistic grounds as Bajaj Auto was a monopoly.

'My blood used to boil. The country needed two-wheelers. There was a ten-year delivery period for Bajaj scooters. And I was not allowed to expand. What kind of socialism is that?' asks Rahul Bajaj.

His vociferous criticism of economic policy cost Bajaj—who has always voted Congress—more brownie points. Outwardly, the relationship between the Nehru-Gandhi dynasty and the Bajajs was cordial, but 'my family never had the kind of contacts you are talking about. We were very much in the freedom struggle but we never used those contacts for our business purposes. Maybe some others have. In any case I don't think such contacts would have meant anything to the then government in power, either the Congress government under Madam Gandhi, or when the [1979 Akurdi] strike took place, the Janata government under Mr Morarji Desai.'

What about money power? 'Even if giving money could have bought any licences, I can categorically say we did not give any ministers or any senior bureaucrat a single penny to get us a licence.'

Despite its straitjacket, Bajaj Auto prospered. In its start-up year (1962), it manufactured 3,995 scooters. It immediately initiated a successful indigenization process which sheltered it when the Gandhi administration refused permission to extend the Piaggio collaboration. By 1971, the Bajaj scooter was a completely local product without any imported Italian parts. Since 1994, it has been producing over a million two-wheelers annually.

It's generally accepted that Bajaj Auto's success is largely due to Rahul Bajaj. In 1970, after the managing agency system was abolished, he became managing director, moving up to chairman on his father's death in 1972. He made the Bajaj scooter so popular that a flourishing black market developed. A customer fortunate enough to be allotted a Chetak or Super could sell it the next moment at double the price. Dealers charged customers huge premiums—unofficially—to jump the queue. A Bajaj scooter is still a regular dowry demand among middle-class families. In Indian movies, scooter chases were as popular twenty years ago as computer-generated images are today.

Bajaj refused to exploit the situation. Holding the price line became an ethical issue, a modern twist to Gandhian trusteeship concepts imbibed during childhood. 'Ensuring that the consumer obtains the best possible product at the lowest possible price and the employee gets a fair wage for a day's work is the criterion of ethics in business,' he insisted. The government admitted that Bajaj had not taken 'any undue advantage of its dominant position', but it still refused to relax production restrictions. Lobbying by competitors like UP Scooters Ltd and Automobile Products of India fanned official anxiety about the power of big business.

For Bajaj, the Licence Raj was a 'nightmare' and a time of 'great difficulties'. 'I know how difficult it can get to chase someone in New Delhi for a licence. Then some fool delays the whole project by procrastinating, because he wants something for himself.' India is probably the only country in the world which threatens to penalize management for overproduction. Bajaj thumbed his nose at such rules, 'but thank goodness I was never actually penalized though I was quoted often for saying that I was ready to go to jail for excess production just as both my parents had for the freedom struggle.'

Interestingly, the long-desired permission for major capacity expansion came during the Janata Party administration (1977-79). George Fernandes, as industries minister, allowed Bajaj Auto to double its licensed capacity to 160,000 two-wheelers.

There was to be a question mark about this permission. Rahul Bajaj's *Congresswala* image and his personal friendship with Sharad Pawar is well known. Why did the Janata Party grant something which the Congress had withheld for years? Was there a quid pro quo? Rumours centred round Fernandes, a close friend of Viren Shah. Shortly before the end of the Emergency (1975-77), an arrest warrant was issued for Fernandes for his alleged role in the Baroda Dynamite Case (1977). Shah claims he 'did not shelter Fernandes', but admits that he knew where Fernandes was hiding and that he organized interviews with the international media for Fernandes while he was underground. Sensitive to international disapproval about the excesses of the Emergency, Indira Gandhi called for elections in 1977. After she lost and the Janata Party came into power, did a grateful Fernandes repay the debt?

'Rubbish,' says Viren Shah. 'Petty Indians will think and say such things, but George is just not that kind of man. He is a man of principles. He genuinely believes that we have to have more industry, more factories. Just look at his record. During that time, he permitted so many companies to expand.' Unfortunately for Shah's protestations, Fernandes is better remembered as the minister who forced Coca-Cola and IBM to leave India, thereby alienating the international business community and choking off foreign direct investment for years, and for comparing the Indian business community with rats.

Bajaj Auto received its second major permission to

expand capacity on October 7, 1982. By this time Indira Gandhi had begun to heed her son Rajiv's views on the need to open up the economy. 'It's true that Rajiv could not dismantle the industrial licensing system, but he gave us as many licences as we desired,' said Bajaj. Narain Dutt Tiwari, who was industry minister, allowed Bajaj Auto to build a 300,000 unit at Waluj. The Rs 2bn plant was built in a record fourteen months. President Zail Singh inaugurated it on November 5, 1985. Three years later, during Rajiv Gandhi's prime ministership, capacity was upped to a massive one million scooters.

The last permission came just in time. In the last decade, local and international competition has been hotting up, and the fact that Bajaj Auto has a world-size plant gives it a vital edge. Economies of scale help make it an extremely profitable operation. 'Our scooters are 20 per cent cheaper than that of the nearest competitor *and* we enjoy a 20 per cent profit margin,' says Rajiv Bajaj smugly.

'POLITICAL VENDETTA'

Government sleuths keep a watchful eye on these hefty profit margins. Twice they suspected that government coffers weren't getting their fair share of them and instituted 'search and seizure' proceedings. The first, conducted on May 18, 1976, during the Emergency, was carried out on the entire group. The second, on December 17, 1985, when Vishwanath Pratap Singh was finance minister, was limited to Bajaj Auto. Each time the raiders went away empty-handed. On both occasions, instead of the Bajaj family being feathered and tarred, it was the government which came under flak for using its muscle to harass businessmen for their political convictions.

Ironically, both times, a Congress administration authorized the raids though ever since the party was formed, the Bajajs have always voted for it. So why did they fall out of Indira Gandhi's favour? Why did she order the mammoth three-day raid in 1976 where 1,100 income tax sleuths simultaneously swooped on 114 Bajaj establishments across the country? They questioned even Jankidevi, Rahul's eighty-four-year-old grandmother, who had renounced all worldly possessions after Jamnalal's death in 1942 and who lived in an ashram at Wardha.

Eighteen months later, Rahul and his uncle Ramkrishna (1923-1994) aired their suspicions to the Shah Commission, a committee set up by the Janata Party to examine the misuse of political power during the Emergency. In a written note read out by Ramkrishna to the Commission, the Bajajs claimed that the raid was 'an act of political vendetta'. Outlining the background of the raid, Ramkrishna deposed that the family's relationship with the Gandhi dynasty started deteriorating with his brother Kamalnayan's opposition to Indira Gandhi's first bid for prime ministership in 1966. 'Ever since then the previous regime had assumed that our family was against them, especially as it was their stand that those who were not with them were against them.'

Ramkrishna had lost favour because he refused to allow the government to take over the Vishva Yuvak Kendra in Delhi of which he was the managing trustee. The fact that Viren Shah, an accused in the Baroda Dynamite Case, was their partner didn't help the situation. The relationship nose-dived after Jayprakash Narayan (1902-1979), a respected socialist freedom fighter, condemned the Emergency and urged the public to protest against it from his death-bed in Bombay's Jaslok Hospital. The links between Narayan and the Bajajs were strong and several Bajaj members had visited Narayan during the Emergency, buttressing Mrs Gandhi's belief that the family was against her.

If further kindling was needed, it was provided by the family's relationship with Acharya Vinoba Bhave (1895-1982), a staunch Gandhian and a leader of the Sarvodaya movement for social reform. In January 1976, Ramkrishna's brother-in-law, Shriman Narayan, organized a *sammelan* for the high priest which was partly funded by the Bajaj Group. Bhave, who initially had indirectly supported the Emergency, now turned against Mrs Gandhi and used the *sammelan* as a forum to protest against the Emergency, calling for its revocation and the release of all political detenus. As preparations began for a second *sammelan*, the Gandhi regime tried to get it postponed or cancelled. Describing the incident to the Shah Commission, Ramkrishna told an enthralled audience of how a common friend contacted him to 'use' his influence over Shriman Narayan and Bhave himself. Ramkrishna excused himself. It would be neither right nor proper. He could not help the government. Delhi was not amused.

Ramkrishna Bajaj's deposition provoked a spat in the income tax department over who had ordered the raid. Under persistent grilling by Justice Shah, part of the truth emerged with the needle of suspicion pointing to S.R. Mehta, the chairman of the Central Board of Direct Taxes. In March 1976, an assistant director of inspection had been dispatched to Bombay to collect dirt on the Bajaj group. The mission was unsuccessful, but his advice was ignored and a raid was ordered by Harihar Lal, the director of inspection (investigation). Gradually, more sordid details tumbled out about procedural 'lapses' and a messy 'smirch' Bajaj campaign but very little extra came to light about who and what exactly triggered off the raid.

Rupa has her own suspicions. 'Rahul had gone to Ahmedabad where he made a speech at some meeting where he criticized Sanjay Gandhi or made a negative comment about him. Afterwards we were told—but it has never been confirmed—that perhaps that sparked the raid.' Rahul is noncommittal: 'This is all conjecture. We don't know anything for sure. At the Shah Commission hearings the income tax officers concerned gave evidence that there was no justification for the raid, and everyone knew we were against the Emergency.'

If political vendetta lay behind the 1976 raid, the reasons for the 1985 raid are even murkier. Authorized by V.P. 'Mr Clean' Singh, then Rajiv Gandhi's finance minister and prime minister-in-waiting, the income tax investigation on Bajaj Auto was part of Singh's campaign to clean up corporate India. During this campaign, 6,000 raids were conducted, about 100,000 residences searched and almost half a million people subjected to interrogation.

Apparently keen to demonstrate total impartiality, Singh's victims were selected from a broad spectrum: from noted industrialists like S.L. Kirloskar, a visionary Pune-based entrepreneur, to doctors, lawyers, film stars, drug barons and smugglers. The scale of attacks and the humiliating media coverage engineered by Singh's team culled from the Directorate of Revenue Intelligence, the Directorate of Enforcement and the Directorate of Anti-evasion, initially froze businessmen into numbness. Once this wore off, mass hysteria set in, to be replaced by roars of resentment, ultimately leading to Singh's transfer from the finance ministry to defence (on January 24, 1987).

As word spread of the nationwide income tax raid on Bajaj Auto, the initial reaction was one of disbelief. After all, this was the company of which the government itself had declared that 'despite its dominant position, the company has not tried to take undue advantage of its dominant position'. Barely a few years after the endorsement, the government was claiming that it was committing income tax fraud. With their backs to the wall, the government officials tried to justify themselves, the thrust of their argument being the high premiums commanded by Bajaj vehicles. For example, Bajaj Auto produced nearly 33,000 three-wheelers. On an official price tag of Rs 27,000, the premium ranged between Rs 10,000 and Rs 20,000. In this situation, tax officials felt there was considerable scope for under-reporting income.

According to government sources, their suspicions were aroused when a raid on a Bajaj Auto dealer in Patna led to the recovery of duplicate books showing that Rs 1.2m had been paid to a top company executive. The raid report was sent to the finance ministry which authorized further research and a more detailed report. The investigation was entrusted to D.N. Pathak, Bombay's newly appointed director of investigation who had just arrived from Uttar Pradesh (Singh's home state). For five months, Pathak and his team studied the market, gathering information piecemeal, collecting lists of Bajaj dealers.

One day before the raid, a deputy director of intelligence visited the Bajaj plant disguised as a schoolteacher to check out the various entry points and sensitive locations. The Pune commissioner of income tax was requested in a letter sent in a sealed cover to collect a hundred people at his office and also to arrange buses and taxis. On December 17 at 7.45 a.m., 285 income tax officials in Pune and Bombay fanned out to sixty-five locations. Pathak had signed a hundred and one search warrants.

But when the party reached Bajaj's residence, its owner wasn't there. He had left the previous night for Bombay. Caught off-guard by this elementary gap in their information, the party recovered enough to call Bombay and request a local team to be despatched immediately to Mount Unique, a skyscraper off busy Peddar Road. The Bombay-Pune lines hummed with anxious inquiries until the tax sleuths finally caught sight of the tycoon engaged in his favourite activity—chatting on the telephone. Once Bajaj had satisfied himself about the correctness of their identity, he agreed to their 'request' to accompany them to his office at Bajaj Bhawan at Nariman Point. There he was interrogated for six hours.

After three days of exhaustively searching Rahul Bajaj's house, office and bank lockers as well as those of his executives and dealers, the raiders called a press conference where they triumphantly announced the 'seizure of unexplained cash of nearly Rs 20 lakhs, jewellery and other valuables of Rs 80 lakhs, 1,500 US dollars and a few other currencies'. The press note added that 'a substantial part of the seized assets have been admitted by the concerned persons to be their concealed incomes and wealth'. Significantly, the note did not mention any names.

Up in arms against the income tax department's press note, Bajaj issued his own. Denying any wrongdoing by Bajaj Auto, he claimed that the premiums were collected by dealers and not by the company. If he were allowed to increase capacity and meet consumer needs, the premiums would automatically disappear. Asked to counter Bajaj's allegations, the income tax department sheepishly admitted that the company's book-keeping was indeed clean as a whistle and that whatever seizures had been made, were from the dealers.

Ironically, barely five months after his finance minister raided Bajaj, Rajiv Gandhi invited him to be chairman of Indian Airlines (IA). It was the first time someone from the private sector had been selected. Was the appointment a gesture of atonement? Bajaj scoffs at the idea: 'No, no it had nothing to do with the raid. It might have been a bit of an embarrassment for Mr V.P. Singh, but I don't think my appointment had anything to do with the raid at all.'

The IA chairmanship brought with it free seats on international flights, greater access to the prime minister, lots of publicity, an official rendezvous opportunity with co-director Sharmila Tagore, the glamorous film star—and a boxful of headaches. The airline's flights rarely took off on time, morale was low, customer satisfaction even lower, and aircraft maintenance dangerously poor because of a perennial shortage of planes. Incidents were taking place which ranged from the bizarre and tragic to the ridiculous. On October 19, 1988, 133 people were killed on a Bombay-Ahmedabad flight. Earlier, as 279 passengers waited to disembark, an IA airplane fell flat on its nose because the two pilots were not on talking terms with each other. On two occasions, pilots apparently forgot to open the undercarriage before landing. As a non-executive chairman, Bajaj ruefully realized he couldn't do a thing.

His helplessness rankled. At a meeting of the CII (Confederation of Indian Industries) in Calcutta, he trenchantly criticized boards of directors for being mere legal entities with no responsibility for achieving corporate excellence. For months before this, the media had speculated about wranglings between bureaucrats at the Ministry of Civil Aviation, politicians, the airline's management and its board. How many aircraft should be purchased; should there be more general sales agents; at what price should IA sell redundant aircraft to Vayudoot (a smaller, sister domestic airline); what about non-smoking flights . . . there was too much political interference and the decision making process too long drawn out for the scooter king's patience. It was no consolation knowing that squabbles at Air India, headed by Ratan Tata, were even more acrimonious.

The disarray immensely pleased the legion of bureaucrats and politicians who had been against appointing business tycoons to such positions in the first place. For example, in March 1987, the powerful Parliamentary Committee on Public Undertakings had grilled IA officials over Bajaj's chairmanship. Even after several hours of questioning, the committee reproved the officials for being 'unable to furnish a satisfactory explanation' as to why Rajiv Gandhi wanted Bajaj and Tata to be on the boards of the two airlines.

By roping in Bajaj and Tata, Gandhi had hoped to introduce greater efficiency and professionalism into the management of the national carriers, but as an experiment, its success was clearly mixed. At IA, on the positive side were a slew of decisions taken by the board to improve the airline's operations. 'We had set three objectives at the beginning,' recalls Bajaj. 'To increase aircraft availability, to streamline marketing practices, and to intensify training inputs.' By the end of his twenty-one-month chairmanship, IA was reporting better profitability, had inducted over a dozen new aircraft into its fleet, and was planning to increase the number of sales agents, which had remained frozen at 400 for five years. On the downside was the Ahmedabad crash, the realization that pilot training was way below par and increasing customer dissatisfaction. As the howls became louder, especially around January 1989, a pugnacious Bajaj dug in his heels. 'To leave now would be cowardice. I'm not going to be a rat who leaves a sinking ship,' he barked. His detractors promptly sniped back, 'Who made the ship sink in the first place?'

The frustrating episode finally ended in December 1989. Rajiv Gandhi lost the general elections. Along with Ratan Tata at Air India, Bajaj resigned. The public praised the gracious gesture. Looking back at his turbulent chairmanship between

September 1986 and December 1989, Rupa says simply: 'The chairmanship meant a lot to Rahul.'

'MONEY ON THE TABLE'

In 1986, the two people who most worried Bajaj—the Firodias and Japan's Honda Motor Company—tied up with each other to produce scooters in Bajaj's own backyard. Eighty-three production facilities in forty countries makes Honda a fearsomely difficult company to compete against. The world's biggest two-wheeler manufacturer boasts an expertise and innovation in engineering which ensure that rivals choke on its exhaust fumes.

For years, Honda had been eyeing India and its huge domestic market. It was quick to rush through the threshold when the Indian government cracked open the investment door in the two-wheeler business, and immediately announced its intention of coming to India with one or more joint venture partners. Over 150 applications poured in, and with typical Japanese conscientiousness, Honda painstakingly narrowed the list to twelve hopefuls. In order to further prune the list to the best three, during 1983-84 Honda executives visited the manufacturing facilities of all twelve. It quickly became apparent that Rahul Bajaj, the Firodias, and Brijmohan Lall Munjal of Hero Motors, a Delhi-based cycle manufacturer, led the pack by a wide margin. Back in Tokyo, Honda directors decided to tie up with the two weakest. The Firodias and Munjal were preferable to Bajaj. A partnership with the latter would not work because Bajaj 'wanted too much'. In 1984, Honda entered into a technical collaboration with the Munjals to make motorcycles through Hero Honda Motors, and a joint equity venture with the Firodias to make scooters through Kinetic Honda.

As Honda flexed its muscles in India, Bajaj faced a few

añxious moments. Sophisticated consumers in the Pune area loved Kinetic Honda's new scooter, its sleek design, low fuel consumption, and hi-tech features. The rest of the country looked at its stiffer price tag. Bit by bit, Bajaj relaxed. In 1993 Kinetic Honda sold 85,000 scooters (11 per cent market share) compared to Bajaj Auto's 538,000 (76 per cent).

Honda, firmly committed to a leadership position in India, viewed these statistics through a different pair of glasses. According to Koji Nakazone, their man in India, Kinetic Honda had done very well in reaching sales of 85,000 scooters at a time when the market itself had shrunk by 12 per cent. In 1993, the Japanese hiked their stake in Kinetic Honda to 51 per cent, beefed up their representation on the board, and enlarged its scooter capacity.

Bajaj may be miles ahead today, but he is preparing for the mother of all scooter wars. To the merchant banker at Bajaj Auto's road show on October 20, 1994 in Kleinwort Benson's London office who asked 'How can you expect to win this war with a twenty-five-year-old Vespa model?' Bajaj gave a snappy reply. 'What do people want from a scooter? Shape, fuel economy, cost, and emissions. Honda brought into India the latest and best technology, but customers want change, not necessarily technology. My engine is as good if not better. Shape, yes, customers want a new shape and in 1997 it will get more contemporary.'

The hard-as-nails money men walked out of the luncheon meeting eating out of Bajaj's hand. Bajaj wanted $150m. He pulled in $800m worth of demand. Bajaj Auto's October 1994 GDR issue was an overwhelming success with fund managers begging for allocations, but Bajaj was cooler. He knows that reputations are at stake here, and that he takes four years to execute changes which Honda does in two.

Bajaj is readying himself to take on the Honda challenge.

For decades Bajaj Auto had had no marketing department—only . dispatch. As the golden days of ten-year-long waiting lists slipped away, he remedied this. The new whiz kids he hired drew up a multi-pronged strategy. Over a hundred new dealers joined the Bajaj network. Forty of these had been wooed away from competitors. Bajaj Auto introduced four new models and more are on the way, with something for everyone. Overnight it has become one of India's biggest advertisers with some of the slickest ads on television. Lastly a new hire-purchase and leasing company, Bajaj Auto Finance, was promoted to help cash-strapped customers. As his domination of the Indian market surged, the *Financial Times* applauded from the sidelines: 'Bajaj is one of the few large Indian companies which competes successfully with the world's best . . . most recently its market share has been rising.'

Meanwhile, Honda was having a rough time on the motorcycle front. In 1985, Hero Honda ran an outstandingly popular advertisement which snapped the punchline, 'Fill it, shut it, forget it', based on its motorcycle's fuel efficiency; but by the '90s, Bajaj's new KB 4S (made in collaboration with Japan's Kawasaki) was racing alongside, pressuring Honda into pumping on all cylinders in order to maintain its lead. A 1995 independent analysis of leadership positions in the motorcycle industry by Crosby, an international financial services group, reported that Hero Honda was steadily losing out to Bajaj Auto in the war of market shares. Bajaj Auto had roared ahead to 30.54 per cent, Hero Honda was 28.18 per cent and TVS Suzuki, 13.35 per cent. Hero Honda started offering free petrol with its model.

What about the future? In India, the two-wheeler world's biggest giants—Honda, Yamaha, Suzuki and Piaggio—are jostling with each other and with the local number one. On

Bajaj's northern flank is Yamaha, the world's second largest two-wheeler company, which has a collaboration with Escorts, and is planning to pour in money and technology into its Indian operations. To the south is Suzuki and the TVS group. Piaggio is perhaps the weakest of the four, but Bajaj cannot afford to underestimate it as its products are the most similar to his. Towering above them all is Honda.

'In the case of Yamaha, Suzuki and Vespa, everything depends on the strength of the companies back home. If they remain very strong there, they will be strong competitors here,' says Bajaj, who is planning to turn the tables on them by invading their home territories. For Bajaj Auto, though the Indian market is growing, the next frontier is very clearly global leadership. 'Rajiv is very keen to take Bajaj Auto to be the leader of the world. I only talk of being number two, after Honda. Piaggio and Kawasaki we have already beaten. The rest don't matter,' says Bajaj modestly.

It will be interesting to see how Bajaj plans to conquer the world for he doesn't have an internationally acceptable product. Only Indians and Italians like scooters. The rest of the world either uses cars or motorcycles. Bajaj Auto doesn't make cars. Motorcycles—mostly Kawasaki knock-offs—are currently a small percentage of total production.

One strategy could be through the acquisition of an existing global player. The cash-rich Bajaj could buy Piaggio, suggests Pradip Shah, former chairman of Crisil and now an associate of George Soros, the American financier. 'They've lost their leadership, don't forget. It is entirely possible that the [Agnelli] family one day could say that we will concentrate on Fiat and the other businesses.'

Does Bajaj want to be an international takeover shark? He shrugs his shoulders enigmatically.

Bajaj could attempt to develop a popular range of

powerful motorcycles. The problem is, Bajaj Auto's R&D
department is nothing to write home about, not surprising in a
company which sells its production like hot *chappatis*. He
needs to acquire technology but will anyone give it to the
potential giant-killer?

Kotak dismisses the argument. 'India is a very large
market and knowing his strengths here, the best thing for
anybody would be to get into Bajaj Auto. It is Rahul Bajaj who
is not willing to tie up with anybody. There would be plenty
of people who would be prepared to tie up with him in a manner
in which he would get 50 per cent or 51 per cent.' Bajaj
disagrees vehemently: 'I do not want in my own country to
share power, authority making and ownership with a foreigner.
I have nothing against foreigners. That is not the point. But
General Motors does not have foreign equity. Honda does not
have foreign equity. Nor does Sony or IBM. The weak do.'

'I HAVE NOTHING AGAINST FOREIGNERS'

His truculent attitude left Bajaj eating dust at the starting line
of the 1993 car race. Once the government flagged off the entry
of the private sector into passenger car manufacture, a dozen
businessmen went into top gear to tie up with the world's
biggest and best. One by one they reached the marriage
registry. General Motors tied the knot with Chandra Kant Birla
of Hindustan Motors, Ford with the Mahindras, the jeep
makers. Peugeot liked Vinod Doshi of Premier Auto,
Mercedes preferred Ratan Tata of Telco. Honda decided to
make the Civic and Accord in India with the Shrirams. Bajaj
began to look like the rejected belle at the ball.

Predictably, Bajaj came in for some heavy ribbing from
his friends. At a September 1995 seminar organized by the CII,
R.C. Bhargava, Maruti's chairman and managing director,
teased Bajaj: 'If we'd only known how keen he was to make a

car, Maruti would have tied up with him.' Bajaj responded badly to the joke, issuing Bhargava 'a standing invitation to head my company'. An alert *Financial Express* reporter promptly buttonholed Bajaj after the session and the next day published a report quoting the scooter maker as being in talks with Chrysler, Renault, and Fuji. The Bajaj Broadcasting Corporation was working overtime. 'Why open one's mouth that one's talking with all three?' asked one of the seminar's attendees rhetorically.

With the best bridegrooms having been snapped up, Bajaj had to make do with the leftovers. As Chrysler didn't have a small car suitable for the Indian market, the Mahindras had already rejected them. Getting Bajaj would be a step up for Chrysler, but compared to Ford (with whom talks had broken down and who subsequently joined hands with the Mahindras), getting Chrysler was certainly a step down for Bajaj. Similarly, the Hindujas had rescinded their MoU with Renault and were close to sewing up a deal with Daihatsu, a Toyota subsidiary. With his insistence on a majority stake, was Bajaj setting too stiff a price?

'Not at all,' says Bajaj. 'Contrary to media reports, this was not an issue. Both Fuji and Renault were willing to give me 51 per cent. With Chrysler, we were talking of 50:50 partnership, but until and unless the project is right and we have the right product, we won't get into cars. What's the point in several manufacturers making 20,000 cars each? You've got to make at least 100,000 cars, preferably 200,000, in order to overtake Maruti. If I can't do that, I don't want to be in cars.'

By mid-'96, Bajaj Auto was the only automobile-related company without a foreign partner. Others in the car business are heaving sighs of relief. 'Can you imagine how formidable a Bajaj-Toyota combine would have been? Together, they would have cleaned out the market. Toyota with the Hindujas,

I can deal with,' said one. In the event, towards April 1996, the Toyota-Hinduja MoU went the Renault way leaving Toyota free to come alone or reopen talks with Bajaj.

A family of four brothers, the Hindujas, according to the *Sunday Times,* are the UK's eighth richest family, richer than the Queen of England. Vegetarian, non-smoking, non-drinking Sindhis, they reportedly made their fortune in Iran in the days before the Khomeini revolution toppled the Shah. Today the two eldest (Shrichand and Gopichand) are settled in London, Prakash is in Geneva where he heads a bank, and the youngest, Ashok, lives in Bombay. From the mid-'80s, the family has been linked, rightly or wrongly, to several major controversies, in particular the Bofors gun deal which eventually led to Rajiv Gandhi's electoral defeat in 1989.

After signing the MoU with Daihatsu in London, the Hindujas weren't thinking about the controversies. The engagement would prove to be short-lived but while it was on, it was celebration time, and the brothers were busy toasting each other in grape juice spritzed up to resemble non-alcoholic champagne. At a chance encounter with Bajaj on a London-Bombay flight, Gopichand flung out his arms in a fair attempt at commiseration: 'I know, I know. First Ashok Leyland, and now Toyota. But what can I do? These things happen, you know!' Seven years ago, the Hindujas had outgunned Bajaj for the Madras-based Ashok Leyland, India's second biggest truck manufacturer (after Telco).

The Bajaj-Hinduja tussle began in June 1987, when the UK's Rover Group put its 39 per cent shareholding in Ashok Leyland on the auctioneer's block. Hill Samuel, the merchant bankers who held the mandate, received almost twenty offers from several countries including India, Japan and Holland. According to press reports, three contestants led the pack in the first round of bidding in London in September: Bajaj, the

Hindujas, and M.R. Chhabria, a Dubai-based electronics trader who had acquired Dunlop India, a tyre company, in partnership with R.P. Goenka.

Initially analysts reckoned that Bajaj would clinch the deal. He was keen (he had been stalking the company for the past three years); he had experience in the automotive business; he already held 2 per cent of Ashok Leyland's equity; and the Rover Group knew him. Bajaj shared the optimism: 'I'm told—but there is no evidence of this—that the chairman and the finance director of the Rover Group favoured our bid because of our track record. The Hindujas, for no fault of theirs, are a very wealthy trading family who were not in any industry at that time, leave alone the automotive industry.'

By late September, Bajaj and the Hindujas were running neck and neck with Manu Chhabria falling behind —his bid was roughly £5m lower than the others.

Make-or-break point came when all three bidders were invited to London in the autumn of 1987. On October 12, the Rover group board met the Hindujas, and followed it up with talks with Chhabria and Bajaj over the next two days. At the meetings, the Rover management stressed three concerns: the size of the bid, technological support for Ashok Leyland, and the 'comfort' of the local management. Shortly before the Rover board met finally on the 16th, Bajaj upped his bid by 10 per cent to $27.45m.

Having done all he could to sweeten his offer, Bajaj left London for Pune without being officially informed about Rover's final decision. Though his last offer was significantly higher than that of the Hindujas and with the payment spread over a shorter period, he was sure they would breast the tape ahead of him. Months back he had sensed what Hill Samuel would tell him later—that the non-executive Rover directors preferred the Hindujas. Why hang around for bad news? The formal announcement came after a short delay, on October 26. Clearly, non-financial considerations were involved.

One of the terms had been the 'comfort' of the local management. Was Ashok Leyland's managing director, R.J. Shahaney, rooting for the Hindujas? It would be understandable. Were Bajaj to take over, he would be a hands-on manager but the Hindujas, with their strengths in trading and financial services, could be counted on to leave the management in the hands of a capable professional manager. No comments, said Shahaney.

Was it because Bajaj didn't have truck technology? It could have been a factor. This was a big hole, and to plug it, Bajaj tried to finalize a tie-up with Italy's Iveco but the talks fell through. According to an Ashok Leyland director, 'If Bajaj had gone ahead with Fiat Iveco, he would have got the company. He certainly tried hard enough to get it. The talks failed, according to Merrill Lynch and ANZ Bank, because Iveco wanted to bring its own technology into Ashok Leyland whereas Bajaj wanted to keep his options open. Apparently Iveco was also unhappy with the composition of the consortium and disapproved of Bajaj's plans to hold a rights issue in Ashok Leyland if his bid succeeded.' Nonetheless both parties continued the dialogue until the end of September, when Iveco pulled out in favour of the more amenable Hindujas.

According to a merchant banker who had a ringside seat, 'the Hindujas have a lot of influence, from the prime minister downwards'. Their contacts in the UK are equally impressive. Margaret Thatcher, as prime minister, for example, attended the Hindujas' annual Diwali party. This may have had a role in their success. Bajaj disagrees. 'It could have been a minor consideration but I don't think British companies work that way.' Bajaj bid £27.45m, the Hindujas £26m. 'Ours was the higher bid, but we lost primarily because they had the foreign exchange and I didn't,' he says.

Bajaj Auto had a massive Rs 1.2bn war chest (at a time when $1 was equal to Rs 20) but no dollars. Unlike many business houses, the Bajaj Group has no offshore funds. For the acquisition, Bajaj needed government support to access foreign exchange. The Rajiv Gandhi administration refused to free the necessary foreign exchange and Bajaj turned to the big international merchant banks. Merrill Lynch came to his rescue, putting together a consortium of international investors who would underwrite his bid. The Rover Group would be paid by Merrill, and the consortium repaid through a rights issue once Bajaj got control of Ashok Leyland.

Today, Bajaj is resigned: 'The Rover Group's non-executive directors were not very happy about the kind of deal I had made. They made all sorts of conditions but basically [my] money was not on the table, whereas with the Hindujas the money was.' At the time, he could barely contain his exasperation. 'When an Indian company on Indian soil controlled by a foreign company.is put up for sale voluntarily by the foreigners, the government should consider ways in which a resident Indian wanting to buy it should not be at a disadvantage as compared to a foreign company or an NRI. The Hindujas did nothing wrong. They had no foreign exchange constraints. I can't blame them. I can't blame the seller. I can only question our government.'

Not for the first time and not for the last. In 1993, he was at it again, this time accusing the government of not giving Indian business a level playing field in its mad rush for economic reform. The protest splattered Bajaj's whiter-than-white image with the hues of a protectionist. He argued in vain that he was not against reforms but the stain refused to wash out. 'The whole idea got completely *ultofied.*

We want Indian companies to become multinational corporations and for that Indian firms need to grow . . . All we were saying was that the government should enable us to face competition.' Bajaj was not alone. He had the backing of a group of industrialists, dubbed the Bombay Club because of the venue of their first meeting at the Belvedere.

In a city of exclusive clubs, the Belvedere probably gets top marks. Gleaming granite, rich wood panelling, and deep leather chesterfields in chocolate and maroon carefully orchestrate an aura of tranquil luxury. Members enter through a discreet entrance in The Oberoi's lobby where white-gloved waiters, selected from the hotel group's elite training college, hover unobtrusively to serve the demanding clientele.

In the dining area, one entire wall is taken up by huge picture windows. It is a favourite of the city's prominent businessmen for their power lunches—a place to see and be seen. The cool air-conditioning and sparkling white napery and exotic foods are an added bonus. Just off the lobby leading to the dining room are a couple of private conference rooms. Outside, below swaying palm trees, beggars ply their trade. Inside, billion rupee deals are made and unmade—quietly.

On a warm September morning in 1993, as usual, there were a few members idly sipping pre-lunch aperitifs at the well-stocked bar. Nobody looked up when Rahul Bajaj walked in. The rich and famous walk into the Belvedere all the time. A few glanced up curiously when Hari Shankar Singhania entered. But everybody's attention switched on when a dozen other big daddies from Delhi, Calcutta and Madras trooped into the club, heading straight for a private room just off the Belvedere's lobby. There were a few gasps of surprise, hastily disguised. Men like Lalit Mohan Thapar, M.V. Arunachalam and Dr Bharat Ram control some of India's most valuable companies. Something was obviously brewing, but what? And where did Bajaj fit in?

As details of the meeting leaked out, businessmen, politicians, bureaucrats and economists polarized into pro- or anti-Bombay Club factions, with the antis winning the shouting stakes.

The bloodthirsty outcry made several wince. 'It was just chance that I didn't go for that meeting. I simply got held up by something else. Given the agenda—about which I didn't know anything when I got the invitation—I had a lucky escape,' said one industrialist with profound relief. In private he doesn't mind admitting he shares the Bombay Club's views, 'but why announce them from the roof top and get slaughtered?' Others hestitated to give away even this much.

When asked to join the new forum, some like R.P. Goenka and the Essar Group's Shashi and Ravi Ruia flatly refused. Others, like Dhirubhai Ambani, diplomatically softened their rejection. 'I'm 100 per cent pro-liberalization. I don't think any industrialist is against it,' said Ambani. 'But we should protect our industries from unfair competition. The world is in recession and the fear is that we may be exposing ourselves to recessionary competition and large-scale dumping. At our stage of development, we cannot afford to do that.'

The majority, like Aditya Birla, sympathized but only in the privacy of their private conference rooms. Birla was as prompt in declining the Bombay Club's invitation as a Goenka or a Ruia but according to Dr Fredie A. Mehta, an economist-executive with the Tata Group, the viscose and cement tycoon's image as its vehement critic was a media-fiction. 'He told me that if the Bombay Club stood for a fair level playing ground between Indian and foreign industry, he was totally with the Club. The public at large had drawn many wrong inferences from the way the Bombay Club put forth its theses, and it was necessary for the Club to declare that it was not trying to hide under protective walls.'

Evidently the Club stood for the interests of Indian industrialists against foreign competition, but what exactly was its agenda? And why did someone like Rahul Bajaj whose company was rock-solid feel threatened enough to join hands with a rag-tag band of men with completely different corporate cultures and ethics?

For Bajaj, the issues were simple. The government had not allowed Indian industry to function freely for decades. When opening up the economy and laying out the red carpet to foreigners, it owed Indian industry the chance to put its house in order before forcing it to compete against global giants.

For the Club's other members, the reasons varied. Some felt threatened by a spate of high-profile acquisitions which had taken place a few months earlier. Ramesh Chauhan sold his soft drink business and Thums Up brand to Coca-Cola, Adi Godrej took Procter & Gamble as a senior partner (an alliance which would subsequently come apart), and the Tatas shrugged off Tata Oil Mills to a Unilever affiliate. Multinationals were buying up India, went up the cry. In the year 2000, would any Indian brands still exist?

Many Indian managements felt sore that multinationals such as Colgate-Palmolive had been allowed to hike their equity stakes in their Indian affiliates at dirt cheap prices but they were forbidden to do so as it would be a move against the interests of minority shareholders. But in order to improve their outdated factories, Indian management needed money. Companies would have to raise funds, but few businessmen had the resources to officially subscribe to new issues in order to retain their holdings. It was a catch-22 situation brought on by the draconian income tax laws of the past. The Bombay Club therefore demanded non-voting shares or other devices. The Indian government would plug the loophole in 1994 but much damage had been done by then.

Two months after its first meeting, on November 9, 1993, the Bombay Club presented a thirteen-point charter to Manmohan Singh, the then finance minister, and Montek Singh Ahluwalia, his special adviser. These demands were simple and most centred on new ways to raise money as well as to lower interest costs. If that was all that the Bombay Club wanted, no rationalist could object.

'If we want to make our companies world-class, we also need rules and regulations that are in line with global corporate and financial norms,' commented Swaminathan S. Anklesaria Aiyar, the editor of the *Economic Times*. 'We should not need the Bombay Club to tell us this.' Manmohan Singh promised to be sympathetic and Pranab Mukherjee, then commerce minister and a former finance minister, added that the government would not allow Indian companies to be 'wiped out'.

Unfortunately, the line between giving Indian industry a fair chance and protectionism was a dangerous tightrope. How much time should Indian industry be given? In India, the cost of money is higher than in the West and the gaps in infrastructure so wide that the playing field can never be truly level. There were no easy answers and the Club was criticized as 'a group of inefficient producers fearing competition'. Frightened by the backlash, over the next few weeks, several founders backed out discreetly. By the end of the year, the Bombay Club's membership had been whittled down to Thapar, Singhania, Arunachalam, B.K. Modi, Bharat Ram and Bajaj. By the close of 1994, 'it was a club of one', says Bajaj ruefully.

HAMARA BAJAJ

In 1987, the Ashok Leyland takeover had earned the Hindujas

a cover story in *Business India*; in October 1993, the magazine published one on Rahul Bajaj. Called *'Hamara* Bajaj'—a takeoff from Bajaj Auto's famous advertising slogan—the cover photograph showed Rajiv kneeling at his father's feet. Both the title and the photograph suggested that Rajiv was Bajaj Auto's heir apparent. Was it coincidence or did the reporter hit the right button? As of 1995, the Rs 40.25bn Bajaj Group is parcelled between five active members: Rahul and Shishir (Kamalnayan's sons); and Shekhar, Madhur, and Niraj (Ramkrishna's). Excluding Mukand Ltd, which is a partnership with the Shahs, the group consists of over twenty companies in a range of engineering businesses and employs 29,000 people. Bajaj Auto is by far the biggest and most profitable company in the group. After Uncle Ramkrishna's death on September 21, 1994, Rahul became head of the group.

Broadly speaking, Shekhar looks after Bajaj Electricals (sales 1995: Rs 1.9bn), a consumer electricals company. Madhur was recently promoted from being chief executive in charge of Bajaj Auto's Waluj unit to president of Bajaj Auto. Niraj is managing director of Mukand (sales 1995: Rs 9.13bn), while Shishir runs Bajaj Hindustan (sales 1995: Rs 1.52bn), a sugar manufacturer. Rajiv joined Bajaj Auto three years ago and today is in charge of marketing, production and research and development. Waiting in the wings is Sanjiv. Sunaina doesn't expect or want a management role in any Bajaj company. Their eight cousins (Shishir's two children, Shekhar's two, Madhur's two and Neeraj's two) are still in school.

In the *Business India* cover story, Madhur is conspicuous by his absence. Sanjiv—who wasn't photographed in the story either—claims this was a mere coincidence, that 'the photographer came to Akurdi when we were at Waluj'. Quite possible, but the excuse doesn't quite deflect the uncomfortable fact that the succession issue is one of the trickiest problems facing the family. Every time there is a divorce in another big business family, speculation about the Bajajs breaks out. Will Rahul Bajaj break away from the group? Can Rahul Bajaj keep the family together? Will Madhur accept Rajiv and Sanjiv or will he feel threatened enough to ask for a split? Will Rajiv give Madhur the respect he should? Neeraj has as much right to Bajaj Auto as anyone else, so how long will he accept being shunted off to Mukand? Does he want a position in Bajaj Auto? Most of the time the Bajajs manage to ignore the whispering around them.

Apparently the way to achieve this difficult task is to accept realities and work on them. One member explains: 'The family always maintains that if x brother is not capable of running something, but he is a Bajaj and a part owner of the whole thing, he will remain there. Maybe the family has to find the right managers for him.' As for Rajiv and Sanjiv, 'their careers may have started in Bajaj Auto but at no point of time can they say that it is their birthright'. Unwilling at first to give his views, Bajaj gradually admits that over the past twelve months several family conclaves have been held on the issue. 'If there is a split, it can be 1:4 or 2:3, there is no other possibility. If one guy wants to go, there is no problem. He just goes, and if the four don't want to give him anything, he doesn't get anything. He'll get his money and his wealth according to his share. But he cannot get Bajaj Auto, whoever it is, including myself.'

'If two want to get out, it depends on which two. If it is me and my brother, it is one situation. If it is me and one of the other three, it is a slightly different situation. Then the group would split into two entities. So the guys who are three should probably get Bajaj Auto and the guys who are two would, according to calculations and divisions or whatever of profit or sales—that's a matter of detail—get the rest. I don't think Bajaj Auto can be split and it shouldn't be split. People worry about a split in the Bajaj group, but according to me they have nothing to worry about. If two and three separate, so they separate. Where there's 1:4, the picture is not seriously disturbed. And the way we know people, it won't happen till I am there. After me, I can't say what will happen'.

'We have to see what happens. I think people get unduly worried ten years in advance and spoil ten years of a good life, whether it is business life or married life, in anticipation of questions like this. At the worst what will happen? There will be brothers fighting. And the group will break. I am putting it as if I am underestimating the implications of that, that's not the point, but if that happens, that will happen. The only problem happens when two exit—which I don't think will occur in the next ten years—so I say bullshit. If it happens, we will face it.'

A day before this conversation, on the evening of August 12, 1994, the 57-year-old Bajaj stretched himself lazily in his favourite armchair. Outside, a light drizzle fell, and a gentle breeze wafted in the smell of grass. Inside, Rupa was checking dinner. All three children were at home, the boys' fiancées were expected. Picking up the latest copy of *Business World*, Bajaj started leafing through it. Its cover story on India's investment boom made him pause. All around him, businessmen were aggressively rooting for new avenues of growth. New names, people he had never heard of, were putting up vast infrastructural plants. The size of projects had ballooned. Who spoke of anything less than a Rs 1,000 crore venture any more? But what was he doing? He didn't have a Rs 500 crore project on the anvil, much less a Rs 1,000 crore one. Was he going to be left behind in the corporate sweepstakes? But did the rat race really matter?

Since childhood, Bajaj has been used to being in the driver's seat. In school he normally stood first in class. 'I was a prefect, house captain, captain of the boxing team and what not.' For three decades, he had run Bajaj Auto as his personal fiefdom, insisting on overseeing every detail, signing the smallest of cheques. Before the current corporate office was built, Bajaj's office was right inside the factory, with windows overlooking every activity. By the time he was fifty, he had accomplished all he had set out to achieve. Was it time to slow down and let the new generation take over? Was he *actually* getting saddle weary?

In the '80s, Bajaj Auto was the fastest growing company in India. During the decade, sales grew from Rs 519m to Rs 18.5bn, making for a 1,852 per cent growth rate. In contrast, Dhirubhai Ambani's Reliance Industries grew 1,100 per cent, with sales moving up from Rs 2bn to Rs 18.4bn.

But if he didn't work, what would Bajaj do? As a student, the boxing champ used to play table tennis, but his busy life hadn't left time for hobbies, even if he had wanted them. 'People say having some diversion is a good thing. Maybe it's good for some people. I've never needed it,' Bajaj used to say proudly. Like all workaholics, he doesn't know how to spend his leisure hours. He reads magazines, 'but not a lot'. Nor does he take holidays. 'This concept that people should take holidays to enjoy themselves is a cliché. I believe in enjoying my work. Between 1965 and 1984, I took only four vacations.' According to Sanjiv, Rahul likes to watch English movies: 'Westerns, thrillers, action, not just mindless violence but with a story. Also Eddie Murphy type movies, with some slapstick. We all enjoy watching them, so when he is at home, we sit together.'

'Maybe there's no fire in the belly any longer,' he muses. After his heart attack, he loosened the reins a bit at Bajaj Auto, allowing senior executives some say in policy and execution, insisting simultaneously that he 'has delegated, not abdicated. I am totally with Lee Iacocca in one thing—I don't believe in consensus decision-making. I ask for other people's opinions in key matters and I give them a fair hearing. But I don't take a vote. I make the decisions.' These days he doesn't walk around the factory as he used to earlier. When he does stroll over to check scooters ready for delivery, there is a mild panic. As a peon rushes off to get petrol, engineers give a silent sigh of relief as the Chetak Classic kicks to life under Bajaj's foot.

To some extent, Bajaj is coping with the extra free time at his disposal by reinventing his job. He has always taken a keen interest in trade associations. Now he is presenting himself not just as the head of one India's biggest business houses, but as India Inc's senior statesman in the mould of Sir Harvey-Jones of UK's ICI or the late Akio Morita of Japan's Sony Corporation. Bajaj played a major role in forging the CII into a more powerful voice than Assocham and Ficci. For over a decade, he has been leading the Indian delegation to the annual Davos symposium organized by the World Economic Forum, and he is a key patron-member in the Indo-British Partnership Initiative.

Today, the old warhorse appears surprisingly content. Sometimes articles like the *Business World* one get under his skin but on the whole he is not much bothered about being left behind. Or perhaps it is not so surprising. In the '80s, analysts criticized him for sticking to his knitting rather than diversifying, and for preferring to pay hefty taxes rather than taking advantage of dubious tax loopholes. Public opinion never bothered him then. Why should it bother him now?

Chapter 3

Aditya Vikram Birla

This chapter was completed shortly before Aditya Birla died on October 1, 1995.

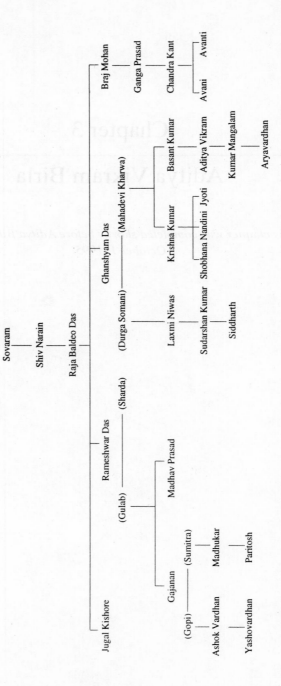

THE BIRLA FAMILY TREE

Sovaram
Shiv Narain
Raja Baldeo Das

Jugal Kishore — Rameshwar Das — (Sharda) — Ghanshyam Das — Braj Mohan

Braj Mohan
Ganga Prasad
Chandra Kant
Avani   Avanti

Ghanshyam Das — (Mahadevi Kharwa)

(Durga Somani) — Laxmi Niwas
Sudarshan Kumar
Siddharth

Krishna Kumar
Shobhana Nandini Jyoti

Basant Kumar
Aditya Vikram
Kumar Mangalam
Aryavardhan

Rameshwar Das — (Gulab)

Madhav Prasad

Gajanan — (Sumitra)
Madhukar
Partiosh

(Gopi)
Ashok Vardhan
Yashovardhan

Il Palazzo
May 27, 1995

They say birds of a feather flock together. The rich do. In Hong Kong, it's the Peak; in London, Mayfair; in Bombay, Malabar Hill. Clinging precariously to the hill's southern slope is Il Palazzo, a social climber's dream. It's a busy block with over a hundred flats. Towards evening, the tempo starts winding down, and by eleven o'clock most lights are out.

The evening of Saturday, May 27, 1995 was no exception. It had been a hot day, with the mercury climbing to over 35°C, and long after the sun had set, the heat continued to lie over the city like a thick duvet. The building's security personnel loitered listlessly under it, sweat beading their foreheads even in repose.

The screech of an ambulance pulling up in front of the tall wrought iron gates snapped them out of their lethargy. A quick whisper and the gates were flung open. A few bored drivers hanging around the open parking lot strolled over to see what was the matter. They were shocked to see nurses and paramedics whisking Aditya Vikram Birla, lying on a stretcher, into it. The world-famous industrialist had lost weight and looked tense, haggard and in pain. Doors banged as doctors, family and key executives climbed into a small cavalcade of cars to accompany Birla to Sahar airport.

The entire exercise was over in a few minutes. The block was quickly back to normal. Few of its inmates saw or even heard the movements outside. It would be some weeks before word of mouth spread details about the panicky night flight on a British Airways aircraft to John Hopkins Hospital in Baltimore, USA. Nobody dreamt that Birla would not come back to India alive.

The ambulance and its cavalcade cut straight across the tarmac to the waiting plane, bypassing the airport's grey administrative building housing customs and immigration. The short notice given to British Airways personnel had been insufficient for them to be able to convert any part of the plane into a stretcher bay. Even fully reclined, the first class seat was a poor option. Birla's pain intensified. For the anxious party accompanying him, the long hours before he could be wheeled into the famous American cancer hospital were a prolonged purgatory.

Two weeks later, the *Economic Times* front-paged an article on Birla's prostate cancer. Speaking from Baltimore, his father, Basant Kumar (BK) Birla airily dismissed the report: 'Aditya is suffering from a slipped disc. He is speedily recovering and should be all right soon. We will be returning to India in about two weeks.' As the weeks merged into months and he remained hospitalized, few were taken in by the sciatica subterfuge, but went along with it anyway. There was too much goodwill for the man who had single-handedly built a billion-dollar corporate empire and yet had remained a good guy, though not everyone thought so. One of the hallmarks of the Birlas is the family feud which has been consuming them for over a decade.

Unlike American and European proprietors, Indian newspaper barons are notoriously tight-fisted, so the Birlas were spared the ordeal of having newshounds sniffing them outside the hospital or buttonholing doctors and nurses to check out BK's story. Instead, reporters took to asking local members of the family about the condition of the most famous member of the clan. They immediately ducked out of sight. 'He has to keep information of his illness quiet. Imagine what would happen to share prices!' said a cousin before firmly closing the door.

The extended family found the questions highly embarrassing, but not for the reasons the media believed. Aditya Birla didn't want to talk about his illness, especially not to cousins and uncles he didn't trust. His friends remained mum. It was only after the cremation, as rumours circulated furiously and had to be scotched before they became outrageously fanciful, that BK authorized the announcement that Birla had indeed suffered from prostate cancer. Was this secrecy imperative, I asked Rajashree, Aditya's wife of thirty years. Wasn't it counter-productive?

'He didn't want people to talk about it to him or be sympathetic about it, that was the only reason,' she explained. 'Because when one is sick, people keep talking about it. That's a sort of reminder to your mind that you are sick. Hardly two or three close friends were told about it. For instance, like even my mother—he didn't want to hurt her. He just wanted to lead a normal life. And the cancer spread so fast, before we realized that something had gone wrong. He didn't complain of pain, he kept working . . . . We knew in August 1993—there is a test called PSA, at the end of May he had a PSA done, and everything was fine, normal.'

His need for privacy was in keeping with the man. Reclusive to a fault, the only Indian businessman to routinely make it to Forbes' list of the world's billionaires would decline to meet the press unless a specific aspect of his business demanded it. Birla was always more comfortable running his companies than talking about himself. In the late '80s he briefly emerged out of his shell. When he did, it was with style. A string of dinners in the four major metros to celebrate his father's seventieth birthday, another set of celebrations for Kumar Mangalam's wedding, a painting exhibition (of which more later)—Birla shared these family celebrations with everyone he had come in contact with, and they flocked to congratulate him. It's doubtful whether anyone—from the Ambanis of Reliance Industries down to the smallest yarn dealer—ignored the royal invitations. The party over, Birla withdrew into his ivory tower.

Unfortunately, the family feud had a habit of intruding during such happy moments. Rajashree recalls a particularly galling moment.

August 8, 1988 started out as one of the happiest days in Birla's short—barely fifty-three years—life. For the past couple of years, Rajashree and he had been searching for the perfect match for their only son, Kumar Mangalam. In Neerja ('lotus flower') Kasliwal, they thought they had found her, but like all fond parents trying to put together an arranged marriage, were uncertain about their judgement until the two youngsters agreed. The previous night, it looked as if they might. By the late afternoon, most of the finer points of the match had been discussed with his future in-laws.

A call from Calcutta shattered Birla's tranquillity. 'He didn't want to go,' recalls Rajashree. 'He could have been in Bombay calling people, close friends, those whom he wanted to inform personally, about the engagement. He couldn't do that. I had to do it for him.'

On his way to Santa Cruz, Bombay's domestic airport, through the heavy evening office traffic Birla's thoughts must have been mixed. Instead of a delightful celebratory dinner, he was on the last flight out eating off a plastic tray, and heading towards an unpleasant showdown with his cousins and uncles. He was used to frequent travel, catching perhaps a hundred flights annually. Making a rough calculation, Birla reckoned the flight from Bombay to Calcutta would take two hours and twenty minutes. With luck the drive from the airport to Basant Kumar Vihar, his childhood home, a rambling bungalow quite unlike the modern block of flats in Bombay where he now lived, would take well under forty minutes. Hopefully he could tumble into bed before 11 p.m. He needed to be alert the next day.

Resigning himself to the inevitable, the born fidget's fingertips beat an impatient tattoo on the armrest of the uncomfortable Indian Airlines club class seat. In 1994 Birla would treat himself to a neat little Cessna Citation S-2 ('a business necessity, not a luxury'), but for now, he had no choice but to travel on commercial flights. He tried stretching his cramped muscles but gave up. Stuffing some more cotton-wool into his ears, he attempted to dull the ache from a chronic childhood ear ailment which made flying a torture.

Once the plane had docked, Birla strode quickly through the terminal to the car waiting for him. Few of his co-travellers realized that Birla had been on the flight: he had an ability to fade into the wallpaper at will. His face was squarish, like his thick dark-rimmed glasses. His passport description would fit that of most Indian males of his age: features, regular; skin colour, wheatish; height, 5' 6"; eyes, dark brown. The first impression was disappointingly *ordinary*. Except for his deep, strong voice. He used words sparingly, but emphatically, calling a spade, a spade, an unIndian habit.

Be it at a Euromoney Conference in New Delhi or in London's Dorchester or at the Bombay Gymkhana, only the cognoscenti could recognize India's most dynamic billionaire in his dark suits, starched white Swiss cotton shirts and expensive and muted silk ties. He made no concession to fashion: he wore the same cut for three decades but he stopped short of the neo-colonial safari suits favoured by Marwari businessmen like Rahul Bajaj and Rama Prasad Goenka.

The next morning, Birla got up at his usual 7 o'clock, well in time for the crucial meeting. He was a man of habit, not one who liked change for change's sake, with a fetish for punctuality and a brisk businesslike manner, sharp and to the point. In the event, the family conclave proved to be a major triumph. Aditya had been on the verge of losing Grasim and Hindalco, two of his biggest companies, to a rival faction, but he succeeded in twisting near defeat into a major victory. Coming to Calcutta had been worth it.

Khushwant Singh in his column, *With Malice Towards One and All,* once wrote, 'To most people, the name Birla means just one thing: money.' For thirteen years, six branches of the Birla clan were engaged in fighting over it. The row's trigger had been the death of the clan's founder, the legendary Ghanshyamdas Birla (1894-1983), known to all simply as GD. On June 11, GD had collapsed outside the Singapore Airlines' London office on Regent Street. He died within hours, leaving behind a tangled legacy.

At stake were assets then conservatively estimated to be worth Rs 30bn, and probably hugely more; over a hundred companies, half of them blue-chips; large tracts of prime real estate; and a rich portfolio of investments. Not even the income tax department knew exactly how much the Birlas were worth.

The Birlas tried at first to maintain a dignified and united front. After the cremation at Golders Green in London, they flew together for the condolence meetings in Calcutta at the Alipore residence of Laxmi Niwas, GD's eldest son. In a noble show of 'rock-like' solidarity, ten adult male members representing three generations posed together for an *India*

Today cover in a classic photograph clicked by Raghu Rai. In the accompanying text, the Birlas individually and collectively assured T.N. Ninan, then an upcoming reporter, later to become editor of *Business World* and *Business Standard*, that the group would never split up.

It was a classy cover-up. The family was at war with itself. While GD was alive, individuals couldn't, or didn't dare, express their real feelings. His word was law. He gave and he took away. The best, he left to BK and Aditya. The other Birlas felt they had been given the short end of the stick.

TEMPLE BELLS AND LADDOOS

Back in 1943, however, there were no fumes of acrimony to spoil the sweet scent of incense burning in the family home. India was still a part of the British Empire, and as Mahatma Gandhi's footloose ambassador, GD was either lunching with His Majesty the King or 'having to defend Englishmen before Bapu and Bapu before Englishmen', as he put it in his autobiography, *In the Shadow of the Mahatma.* His three sons and various nephews were busily working in his burgeoning industrial empire of jute mills, cotton textile units, sugar companies, airline and trading ventures. It was a time to build, not snipe at each other.

So temple bells pealed and laddoos were distributed when a son was born to Sarala and BK in Room No.3 of Birla House, New Delhi, at 11.07 p.m. on Sunday, Marg Shirsha Krishna 3, Samvat 2000 (November 14, 1943 in the English calendar). Two daughters followed Aditya: Jayashree Mohta in 1951 and Manjushree Khaitan in 1957.

By all accounts, Aditya and his sisters had a very happy childhood, enlivened by regular annual vacations where the day would be spent trekking, sailing, and riding. In the evenings, the family would play *antakshari* and charades. The fact that she always had to wear a sari and keep her head demurely covered didn't stop Sarala, a lively woman with a passion for life, and a perfect foil for her more restrained husband, from pursuing her interests. In the family album an old black and white photo shows a radiant Sarala skiing in the Alps, her silk sari billowing around her slim figure.

Aditya spent most of his childhood in Calcutta, living in Birla Park until 1955, and then in Basant Kumar Vihar which BK built. (Birla Park was later converted into the Birla Industrial and Technological Museum). His first school was the Mahadevi Birla Shishu Vihar at 4 Ironside Road, founded specially for him. After two and a half years, he went on to the Hindi High School. Classes didn't end at 4 p.m., there were tutors waiting at home. After his matriculation, he joined St. Xavier's College, graduating in science.

Aditya's school and college track record was commendable, unlike his father's who admits candidly that he 'was no great shakes in college'. Just before a major examination, GD asked BK to go abroad. BK heaved a sigh of relief. 'Had I failed in my exams, the humiliation and shame would have haunted me all my life. Perhaps God sent me on the foreign trip to save me from that lasting stigma.'

After his B.Sc., Aditya was keen to study abroad. He would be the first Birla to do so. BK was racked by doubt. The Beatles, flower power, and the sexual revolution were shaking up Western society. What if his only son succumbed to such influence? Talking it over with Aditya, BK warned: 'The Birla family has its name, status and values—uphold the tradition fully. You must have only one goal—to study. Do well in your academic work and successfully return to your home, your motherland. In that lies your dignity—and ours.'

With Sarala, BK debated whether they were 'doing the right thing in packing off an eighteen-and-a-half-year-old to a foreign land for such a long period of time. He had every possible comfort in India: his own personal servant Harshu, a car at his disposal, tutors to guide him, the care and love of Dadoji, his father, mother, sisters, other members of the family, and friends. When needed, a doctor was at hand, who would pay house calls as often as required. Never once in Calcutta did he find any occasion to ride a tram, bus or taxi. There would be no such help available in America. He would have to do it all by himself—cooking, washing dishes and clothes, cleaning his flat, polishing his shoes, using public transport.'

Resolutely, BK put aside his fears. In September 1962, Aditya flew to Boston, coach-class. For the next three years, he was—almost—an ordinary citizen. Until he got the measles and had to be hospitalized. In India, Sarala and BK were frantic with worry. 'Travel abroad in those days involved a long-drawn out process of obtaining governmental permission. Chachoji quickly arranged to get the P-Forms,' recalls BK.

Rushing straight to the hospital from Boston's Logan Airport, they found Aditya sick and demoralized. He had quarrelled with his landlord and had had to change flats. He couldn't understand the American accent, and liked neither cooking nor Boston's icy winds. He was the youngest boy in the class, the course was tougher than expected and he was worried that he would be unable to complete it. Chuckling over the period, BK remembers buying groceries which Sarala would cook. 'Our presence helped him to recuperate fast and gave him a new lease of life. No more household chores—and delicious meals into the bargain!' Not surprisingly, a maid was dispatched to Boston soon after Sarala returned to Calcutta.

As expected, Birla had no problems after that in obtaining his MIT (Massachusetts Institute of Technology) degree. Like the other freshly-minted graduates, he lost no time in getting new visiting cards printed. The typeface he selected reflected his character: bold and solid, with a complete absence of frilly curlicues or flamboyant flourishes. There was a strong pragmatic streak in his make-up. Asked once whether his chemical engineering background influenced the group's choice of projects, Birla retorted impatiently: 'If I'd used too much of my expertise, the group would perhaps have gone bust by now.' He saw his role as providing leadership, imparting entrepreneurship, giving direction, enthusing people and encouraging them to work as a team, 'but one great advantage of my technical background is that no one can bluff me. I certainly know what's happening'.

Like his grandfather, early on in his career, Aditya displayed an incredible hunger for business. On a bone-chilling November day in 1963, while still a homesick Indian student at MIT, he had written to his parents in Calcutta:

Respected Ma, Kakoji

Today, is the 5th of November. My birthday is on the 14th.

Ma, I don't know why, my outlook has changed a lot. So far, I thought of only studies—studies and studies. Now I feel that studies will be completed in 7 months—thereafter, I have to work. I now feel that I should enter business at the earliest—and create something really big—something really big—really BIG. I now realize that studies would be over soon. Until recently, the aim was to join MIT—then it shifted to getting the degree from MIT. Now the aim is to become very big and important in business. Big and important not only in business—but also in other aspects of life.

Nowadays, I keep my room very tidy. Even when we did not have a maid, I kept my room very tidy. Everything is neat and clean. I now realize that your advice was correct: the aim to study only—is not very important. A person must be perfect also in other finer points of life. I don't know how this change in my outlook has come about. Nowadays I dress well. Recently I did some shopping, which included some good clothes.

Sometimes, I really remember you all very much. When I think of my birthday—then I remember you even more. On such occasions, I really miss you very much.

I am happy. Please do not worry about me.
Yours lovingly
Aditya

Six months after he returned to India, Aditya was married to Rajashree (nee Rajkumari) Forma on January 19, 1965. He had been engaged for seven and a half years—GD had betrothed the two children in 1957, when Aditya was fourteen and Rajkumari ten. By the age of twenty-two, Aditya was a father. Kumar Mangalam was born on June 14, 1967, and Vasavadatta on June 10, 1976. Recalling her wedding day, Rajashree comments: 'It was like two young children getting married. He was not nervous, but quite serious on that day. Recently I saw our marriage film and I thought why was he so serious? Maybe he was taking even the marriage thing as seriously as he used to take his business, but basically by nature he was fun-loving, wanting to have adventures.'

But Birlas aren't supposed to have adventures. Family

protocol, an army of devoted retainers, and an abundance of doting affection work against such a proclivity. However, once in a while Aditya succeeded in kicking off the confining traces. After completing his MIT course, tired but on a roll, Aditya mapped out a three-week driving holiday to criss-cross the US with flatmates Ashwin Kothari and Om Bhalotia before flying back to India. An impatient GD refused permission, demanding imperiously that Aditya return immediately to India. When BK and Sarala backed Aditya, GD camped out in New York, pugnaciously insisting that Aditya phone him three times a day.

Dutifully, Aditya agreed. Even BK, a nervous father, found such solicitude absurd. One day, when Aditya and his friends checked in an hour ahead of schedule, GD worried that they were driving much too fast. BK remonstrated. 'If the boys come ahead of schedule, he worries. Reach late, he worries. After three or four hours of driving, you had better be on the dot—or else worry will pile on worry!'

'SOMETHING REALLY BIG'

Back in India and shortly before Aditya's wedding, GD wanted to induct him into Hindalco, an aluminium manufacturer and one of the group's bigger companies. BK had other ideas. While Aditya's American classmates were still filling out application forms, his doting father had lined up not one but two projects for his only son.

The first was a small spinning mill for which BK had acquired an industrial licence. The Birlas were not the government's favourite business house at the time and it had taken BK time and patience to obtain the licence. Mahatma Gandhi had been dead for a while now, the Birlas were never really close to the Nehru dynasty and the winds of socialism were blowing through Indian polity. Under the British, the profit motive was a perfectly legitimate and admirable human trait. Under Nehruvian socialism, it became a dirty word. Big business families were now referred to as monopoly houses.

Handing the valuable licence over to Aditya in July 1964, BK told him, 'This permission is just a piece of paper. If you are interested, take it up. If not, tear it up.' The second job was to overhaul Hindustan Gas, a Rs 30m company which BK had founded in 1944.

The Eastern Spinning Mill wasn't the 'something big' of the MIT-returned youth's dreams, but the Rs 8m project offered tremendous opportunity. Though his father kept a watchful eye, the callow graduate had complete freedom to employ whomsoever he liked, order machinery as he thought fit, and construct buildings to his own design. 'I wasn't worried,' recalls BK. If, in this process, Aditya lost Rs 1m-1.5m, it wouldn't matter. If he profited from the failures and learnt the right lessons, it would be a small price to pay for thorough training.

Within a year of setting up the mill, Birla was impatient to expand. Coincidentally, Shantilal Thar, a family friend, showed him the way. There was a small spinning mill for sale. Were the Birlas interested? GD was inclined to brush it off. The seller wanted his money within a couple of days. 'How, in such a short time, can one arrange Rs 30 lakhs? You should have given at least a week's advance notice,' he protested. Aditya's interest was caught, however, and he wheedled the money from his grandfather. It would always be so. Whatever Aditya wanted or needed, arrived on a platter. 'In 1945, our son Aditya was just two years old. We were discussing plans for his education. It occurred to us—why not open a new school?' remembers BK.

Close by and around the same time that Aditya bought Indian Rayon for Rs 3m in October 1966, a small unknown yarn trader was building a spinning mill at Naroda in Gujarat for Rs 0.3m. Six months later, Dhirubhai Ambani's Reliance Textile Industries couldn't produce fast enough while Birla's investment looked as if it would go up in smoke.

Unaware of the trouble brewing hundreds of miles away, Aditya and BK were finishing dinner on the evening of April 21, 1967. They were spending a few days in Birla House, an exquisite palace just off Napean Sea Road in Bombay which now belongs to Aditya's nephew, Yashovardan. It had been a busy day, but father and son were looking forward to relaxing in the lush gardens at the back or in one of the several elegant sitting rooms on the ground floor when they received an urgent call from their manager at Veraval. A fire had broken out at the Indian Rayon factory.

It raged fiercely from around eight at night until five the next morning. 'It was a nightmare,' recalls BK. 'The whole night we were sitting in one room waiting anxiously for news that the blaze was under control—the machinery safe, the factory still standing.' Unable to control his fears, Aditya paced the room, calling Veraval every ten minutes or so. He was just twenty-four years old. Indian Rayon was his first major independent business decision, and neither GD nor BK had thought much of the idea in the first place.

'Aditya was thrilled by Indian Rayon,' says BK, but there were problems from the beginning. It was too small to be viable and had accumulated arrears of Rs 37.5m in the books even before the buy-out. After the takeover, the workers went on strike, the fire broke out, and losses spiralled. GD kept reproaching Thar. 'You mounted Aditya on a decrepit steed,' he grumbled incessantly. BK demurred. 'But it wasn't really Shantilal's fault. We went into this business with eyes open.' His mettle stung and his business acumen under doubt, Aditya went into overdrive in his bid to turn Indian Rayon into a commercial success.

Aditya's immediate priority was to run the plant to its full capacity, the second to raise it to more economic levels. Yarn production moved slowly from 5 tpd to 12.5 tpd, rising to 22 tpd by 1971. After that, progress was faster. In the weaving division also, Birla kept adding spinning machines. To get better prices and chunkier profits, he pushed up yarn quality, and pioneered coloured yarn. Losses became profits. During the '80s, Birla diversified the company's product mix, adding cement and carbon black. In the '90s, divisions for the manufacture of argon gas and sea water magnesia were commissioned.

In 1974, when Thar sold Indian Rayon to Birla, neither could have foreseen that Indian Rayon would become one of India's most valuable companies in the private sector (23rd in 1995). After GD inducted Aditya into Grasim, analysts and the media would refer to the bigger company as Aditya's flagship, but in a sense Indian Rayon was the kernel which nurtured Aditya and the phenomenal growth of his group.

Shortly after buying Indian Rayon, Aditya shifted base from Calcutta to Bombay. The family gave him a suite of offices in Industry House, an inconspicuous building in the Backbay Reclamation area, close to Nariman Point and the Bombay Stock Exchange.

Today, the office is as it was when its occupant was alive. In a room bright with fluorescent lighting, one entire wall is a plate-glass window overlooking a small balcony green with plants. Birla used to sit at a large wooden desk topped by a shiny sheet of smoked glass. On the right is a red leather diary. Patterned on the UK's *Economist* desk diary, Birla had designed it himself, adding reams of extra information on India. Every year he would gift an updated edition to friends and relatives. On the same side is a computer monitor, and directly across it, a luxurious leather suite for visitors. Behind the plain black leather executive chair hangs an early M. F. Husain from the artist's horse series.

The fourth floor suite has a comfortable, somewhat dated but not shabby feeling, like the rest of the building, with its wood-panelling and art deco motifs, and quite unlike the clinical severity of Ratan Tata's office in Bombay House. Photographs are scattered all over the room. Frames in silver, wood, and gilt jostle with the usual motley collection of silver-plated trophies. Each photograph records a particular watershed in Birla's life: with Indira Gandhi, with Rajiv Gandhi, with various world leaders, and at ribbon-cutting ceremonies of factories, large and small. Some capture particularly emotional moments such as the family portrait of Aditya with Rajashree, daughter Vasavadatta, son Kumar Mangalam, and daughter-in-law Neerja, resplendent in wedding finery. There is a particularly tender one of BK smiling at Sarala at the opening of a temple BK had had built. In another, a young Aditya sits cozily next to GD.

The office used to be a beehive of activity. Today, Rajashree quietly got up from behind the desk to greet me. The last time I had been in this room, Aditya had been pacing up and down, telephone glued to ear, shouting down it, 'I want a project. We've got to have a new project, otherwise we will be paying out too much in taxes.' His body tense, he had placed one foot against the table's edge, flexing his hamstrings, in an attempt to release impatience and restlessness. He had been talking to one of his executives, perhaps in Gwalior. A meeting was scheduled for the following week, and Birla wanted him to come prepared with a slew of new ideas for the group's huge investible surpluses. Birla spent a lot of time in this office, spinning his strategies, drawing up blueprints, keeping busy his four secretaries (two in Bombay, one in Delhi and one in Calcutta).

No other Indian businessman can claim to even remotely match Birla's ability to build factories from scratch. The only comparable entrepreneur is perhaps Walchand Hirachand (1882-1953), a visionary who pioneered India's entry into businesses of national importance such as shipbuilding and aircraft manufacture as well as building huge waterworks and key trunk roads. Like Walchand, Birla inspired others. One of his many fans was Sanjiv Goenka, head of CESC and the man responsible for short-circuiting Calcutta's power cuts. 'I've never really been in direct touch with him but Aditya Birla is a kind of idol,' said Goenka. 'See what he has achieved in such a short span of time! I think if I could achieve one-tenth of it, I would be great.' Within the Birla clan, there was a mixed reaction to its most famous member. They respected Aditya for his achievements and the person he was but found such adulation, constantly voiced, difficult to bear.

Over a span of twenty-five working years, Birla built some seventy plants manufacturing acrylic fibre, aluminium, aluminium fluoride, anydrous sodium sulphate, argon gas, bleaching powder, carbon black, carbon di-sulphide, caustic soda, chlorosulphonic acid, coconut oil, fertilizer, flax, hosepipes, hydrogen peroxide, industrial machinery, insulators, lightning arrestors and condensors, palm oil, poly aluminium chloride, paper, polyester filament yarn, polynosic and other speciality fibres, portland cement, rayon grade pulp, sea water magnesia, sponge iron, sodium tripolyphosphate, STPP (a detergent intermediate), sulphuric acid, textiles, viscose filament rayon yarn, viscose staple fibre, and white cement, besides a string of small power plants. A human factory-making factory, other industrialists said, and acknowledged his achievements by calling him 'Aditya babu'.

Age and cancer couldn't diminish his zest. On the contrary, if anything, they made him more entrepreneurial. For a brief moment in 1990, he had paused, saying, 'After a point, one has to consider the load on oneself. Today, it is not a question of obtaining a licence. That era has gone and licences are freely available. Now the things to consider are the availability of good people, the tying up of the finance and time. Perhaps I am becoming more content in the last five years. I start thinking of the load on myself and whether a new project is worth it.' Three years later, in his fiftieth year, with the bad news from the doctors ringing in his ears, he declared, 'We will get more aggressive now.'

According to Rajashree, during his illness, work became his only hobby. 'He was a fun-loving, very very adventurous person but in the last three-four years, he was working harder. Previously we used to go to plays, watch videos—he used to like Amitabh Bachchan movies—but for the last few years, it was just work.' Blueprints for vast factories used to shower like confetti from his desk; after 1993, from his sickbed.

Coincidentally, around the same time, the Narasimha Rao administration was opening the doors of several businesses previously reserved for the government to the private sector. The liberalization programme enabled Birla to think and plan big, bigger than anything he had done earlier, and he prepared a rich smorgasbord of ideas. Seizing the opportunity, he outlined humongous plans: a petrochemical complex as large as Dhirubhai Ambani's at Hazira in Gujarat; a 1,000 MW power station similar to the one the Hinduja brothers are erecting at Vishakhapatnam in Andhra Pradesh. While his backroom boys worked out the details, Birla pushed to complete an oil refinery, a copper smelter, a hot rolled coil steel mill, and an entry into the sunrise telecom sector. Meanwhile there was a takeover deal fermenting in Tanzania, and the Romanian government wanted to sell him a carbon black plant belonging to Aperchim, a state-owned enterprise.

Among the trophies, however, there is one brass farthing. It was fortunate for Birla's reputation and bottom lines that in the one instance where he erred, the group was large enough to absorb its negative impact. Few beyond industry insiders and a handful of savvy analysts supected that his flagship was bleeding badly because of his gamble in Vikram Ispat, Grasim's sponge iron division.

Within the group, it was another story. There was no attempt to sweep the problem under the carpet. According to Rajashree, Aditya 'was worried about the sponge iron plant because every day a new problem was coming up. They used to solve one problem and just after a week a new problem would start. He wasn't upset about it, he just took it as a challenge. Once when he was giving a speech, the boys asked him, which is your favourite factory? So he replied that the one which is in trouble, because a father always has a soft corner for the weakest child. I think he was talking about Vikram Ispat.'

Sponge iron is a raw material in steel-making and a substitute for imported steel scrap used by Indian rolling mills. In 1984, the Indira Gandhi administration liberalized sponge iron manufacture in an effort to boost steel production and reduce expensive scrap imports. Like half a dozen others, Aditya Birla jumped onto the bandwagon. After his mother's assassination, Rajiv Gandhi took over and speeded up the process. Practically everyone who applied for a licence got it: the Ambanis of Reliance, Shashi and Ravi Ruia of the Essar Group, Umesh Modi of the Delhi-based Modi group, M.L. Mittal of the Ispat group, Neelkant Kalyani of the Bharat Forge group, P.B. Bhardwaj (a London-based businessman), and, of course, Aditya Birla.

The government's unusual efficiency and generosity were greeted by shocked dismay. Indian businessmen were in the habit of looking upon a government approval as an automatic licence to print money but if the government gave everyone a chance and every letter of intent was implemented, the current shortage would slip into a case of serious oversupply. The government lobbed a second bombshell: Birla and the Ruias were permitted to build huge 800,000 tpa gas-based plants, the rest had to be content with 100,000-150,000 tpa coal-based plants. One by one promoters backed out, leaving just four in the field: Birla, the Ruias, Modi and Bhardwaj.

Two years down the road, Modi, Bhardwaj and Birla were still struggling to implement their licences when the Ruias commissioned their sponge iron plant on August 1, 1990. 'It was a stroke of luck,' says Ravi. In a hotel room in Emden (Germany), Shashi was leafing through a bunch of trade magazines when he noticed an advertisement for a five-year-old mothballed gas-based plant with two modules having a capacity of 440,000 tonnes each. Its owners, Nordferrowerk GmbH, had operated it for barely six months in 1981 before shutting it down because of high gas prices. 'Buying a second hand plant is like buying a second hand car. It could turn out to be a fantastic deal or a dud,' continued Ravi.

On checking it out, the Ruia brothers realized that the Emden plant was definitely no dud. In fact, buying it would be the smartest move of their lives as it bankrolled their push into steel and oil exploration and oil refining. From being a small shipping company on ONGC's fringes, the Essar Group would become one of the fastest growing business houses of the decade.

What had come down in the West, came up in India. The Ruias clinched the deal for the proverbial song in January 1987. It took them twenty-four months to dismantle, ship and re-assemble the 17,000 tonne plant, piece by piece, at Hazira. In all the Ruias had to spend Rs 4.16bn on the plant but it was dirt cheap at the price—and not just because Birla's spanking new one would cost double. The Emden plant had already weathered teething troubles under its previous owners. 'This plant was built by Germans for West Germany and they designed it to be the Cadillac of sponge iron plants,' says Ravi. 'From day one, it worked like a dream.' The time factor—a two-year lead over the pack—gave the Ruias a crucial advantage. Despite a 15 per cent cost overrun, Essar had saved on interest charges and could capture a sizable chunk of the market.

Birla also took a hit on technology. The Ruias chose proven technology while Birla flirted with the unknown. For his sponge iron plant, Birla turned to Mexico's Hylsa S.A. de C.V. who promised him the latest and the best in manufacturing and processing technology. The only drawback was, it was also untested. For the first time in his life, Birla could not contain costs or remain on schedule. Two new kids on the block had breasted the finish tape ahead of 'Babu'. Outwardly Birla appeared unperturbed, but Vikram Ispat's slow progress must have been galling for the man who had won his corporate spurs on the back of speedy project implementation.

Even today, Vikram Ispat isn't out of the woods though it has been commissioned. Setting the plant on its feet is going to be a major challenge for Kumar Mangalam, says an industry insider. 'Why didn't Mukand and Musco get into the sponge iron business?' he asks pertinently. 'They were offered the same project but putting up a merchant plant doesn't make sense. Why make a product that competes with a commodity? One can never hope to make a profit. Kumar Mangalam will need to integrate forwards, put up an HRC (hot rolled coil) plant. At one point, Vikram Ispat was bleeding Rs 800m. The Ruias' project was different. They thought like traders and had the devil's own luck in timing. They bought the plant and put it up when there was a tremendous shortage of scrap. Within three years, they've made such good money that they've recouped all that they had spent on the plant.'

INDIA INC.

An astute and cautious businessman, Birla must have deliberated over these angles before plunging into sponge iron manufacture, but perhaps he didn't consider them overwhelming enough. The project offered the opportunity of getting a toehold into a business for which the Birlas have hungered for half a century. One of GD's greatest—and unfulfilled—desires had been to own a steel mill like J.R.D. Tata's Tisco. In the mid-'70s, Aditya too had tried to get into this core sector but had ended up burning his fingers.

Knowing how much steel-making meant to his grandfather, Aditya had once sketched out a project report for a pig iron plant. He had tested his skills in Eastern Spinning, Hindustan Gas and Indian Rayon, and had felt ready to take on a new challenge. Having built one plant and turned around another, and brimming with the confidence of youth, he felt confident enough to embark on a mega project. And promptly fell flat on his face.

A more experienced businessman would have known from the start that it was an overly ambitious plan. Where a veteran like GD had failed, could Aditya succeed? For a moment it seemed he could. Travelling to the USA, the twenty-something managed to convince Kaiser Corporation, one of the world's biggest metal companies, to join hands with him in building a $100m plant in Bihar. Flying back to India, Aditya hugged himself.

The bubble burst when the Indian government withheld its approval. Integrated steel plants were, as per government policy, reserved for the public sector. The episode was not a total fiasco, however. Jawaharlal Nehru, who was prime minister, and T.T. Krishnamachari, his finance minister, awarded the young lad a consolation prize in the form of Hindalco.

Returning to the USA, Aditya renegotiated his deal with Kaiser, switching from steel to aluminium, and Hindalco became one of GD's 'dearest' companies. But, tenacious as always, Aditya never gave up on steel. When regulations permitted it, he would launch Vikram Ispat. Despite his disdain for acquisitions, he initiated negotiations for Vizag Steel (which broke down). In December 1991, Century Textiles would announce its intention to build a Rs 6bn pig iron plant near Midnapore in West Bengal, and in 1995, the Jayalalitha administration in Tamil Nadu would sign an MoU with Grasim for a Rs 33bn integrated steel plant.

The earlier pig iron foray made a deep impact on Aditya's mind. Fed up of red tape and pen-pushing bureaucrats, he looked outside India for growth opportunities. 'There were so many restrictions. So many clearances were required. So much time was being taken up that I decided to move out. Of course, recognition was probably the motive force. Everyone wants to make his own contribution and whatever I might do in India would be only a drop in the ocean. Going overseas was the only course if I had to make it on my own,' he said at the time.

And make it he did, by a wide margin. In computing the size of his operations, Birla refused to benchmark himself against Indian yardsticks, preferring to pit himself against the world. Till 1994, Birla was the world's number one viscose producer, the largest producer of palm oil, the third largest producer of insulators and the sixth largest producer of carbon black.

Strait-jacketed by Indian foreign exchange regulations, Birla's pockets weren't exactly bulging when he started scouting for projects. Anything in America or Europe was way above his means, but a fistful of dollars could buy quite a lot in South East Asia. Moreover, GD and President Ferdinand Marcos of the Philippines knew each other well. Aditya dropped by to visit his grandfather's old friend who promptly appointed him honorary consul for the Philippines in India. For the youngster, granting visas and scribbling his autograph on passports was a heady feeling.

From a material point of view, however, Thailand offered better opportunities. In the late '60s and early '70s, it was opening up its economy to foreign investment. Incentives included exemption from corporate tax and dividend tax for eight years and no duties on the import of capital equipment. Birla's first international venture was a Rs 10m textile mill; his first major order, uniforms for its air-hostesses' uniforms from Thai Airways. The tiny mill became a springboard for three more mills, one each in Thailand, Indonesia, and the Philippines.

These plants spawned other ventures. By the mid-'90s, Birla was operating the world's biggest palm oil refinery in Malaysia, but his biggest investments were in Thailand. According to the *Nikkei Weekly,* Birla was not merely the largest Indian investor in Thailand, but also its second-largest holder of assets in the country. Between 1970 and 1980, Birla promoted ten companies in South East Asia with aggregate sales of $100m.

In 1986, he lost one. A coconut oil refinery was nationalized after Ferdinand and Imelda Marcos fled to the USA in the coup which brought Corazon Aquino to power. The textile mill remained untouched, however. Swallowing his disappointment, Birla went back to the drawing board. As

Aquino gave way to Fidel 'steady Eddie' Ramos, the Philippine economy revived and Birla was back in business. In 1987 he announced a $55m project to make 23,000 tonnes annually of rayon fibre. In 1991, he established his fourth company in the country, Indo-Phil Corn Chemicals.

In 1990, Birla headed a Rs 12bn overseas empire of twelve companies in Thailand, Malaysia, Indonesia and the Philippines, making his group perhaps the only true Indian multinational. By 1995, there were seventeen companies in fourteen countries with aggregate sales of Rs 52bn. An overjoyed BK exulted: 'Other Indians started ventures in these countries but, till 1984-85, most of the endeavours had failed.' Within the Birla clan, they wondered, was this merely a father's pride talking, or was it a snide dig at CK's African enterprises and SK's Singapore operations?

Until early 1990, few back home knew the extent of Birla's operations in South East Asia and the speed with which he was growing there. From Birla's point of view, the less said the better. The MRTP, FERA and other regulations didn't encourage transparency. In any case, very few bothered to bypass the fuzzy smokescreens to make out the real picture. Most of his international companies are closely held. Only two—Thai Rayon and Thai Carbon—from a stable of thirteen, are quoted on the local stock exchanges.

After 1990, Birla allowed the smokescreens to melt away. It was a good time to showcase his achievements. He had already reversed his decision to keep away from the limelight, and most companies were reporting spectacular profits. 'Inspite of ruthless competition from the Americans, the Japanese, the Europeans and the South East Asians themselves, we are making super profits,' declared Birla smugly. 'Last year, we gave 50 to 100 per cent as dividends. I wish we had kept more shares for ourselves.'

According to an international banker, Birla had an ulterior motive in handing out the generous payouts. 'Birla's own holdings in his companies abroad tend to be small, but he controls them through management contracts except in Malaysia. In most of his companies, there are several large NRI investors, mostly Palanpuri Jain diamond merchants such as Rashmi Mehta of Gembel. As these companies are private, investors cannot count their gains through capital appreciation of shares, so Birla keeps them happy by giving generous dividends and frequent bonuses,' he explains. On a more worried note, he continues: 'The question is, will Kumar Mangalam be able to maintain the grip his father had on these companies?'

The foreign banker's theory undervalued the importance of a core Birla tenet: Aditya's preoccupation with the bottom line. Birla's local companies are amongst the most cash-rich in all of India. In 1993, for example, a *Business World* survey found that Grasim was India's second richest company, and Hindalco ranked sixth (ICICI, Grasim, Telco, Tata Chem, HDFC, Hindalco, ITC, Tata Tea, Nocil, Spic). Birla rarely entered a business which did not generate a minimum 22 per cent return on equity. Dubbed the 'Fail-Safe' man by *Business Today*, Birla was as risk-averse internationally as in India.

For one, Birla didn't dabble in businesses he wasn't familiar with. Mostly, his overseas ventures mirrored his Indian experience. Most products Birla made abroad, he also made at home. The lessons in industrial management learnt in India were applied internationally. For example, in 1966, he acquired Indian Rayon, then a small spinning mill. Three years later, in 1969, he built Indo-Thai Synthetics, a Rs 10m, 12,768 spindle mill. Similarly, at the same time (1974) that Grasim was beefing up its rayon programme, Birla established Thai Rayon, a joint venture between Grasim and Thai entrepreneurs. In mid-1988, Birla introduced carbon black into Indian Rayon's portfolio of products. From a small 20,000 tpa unit (beefed up to a more respectable 50,000 tpa in 1989) in India, he gradually built a global presence with plants in Thailand and Egypt, becoming the sixth largest manufacturer in the world of this tyre intermediate. More recently, he had received offers for carbon black plants in Poland and Romania.

As a further precaution, many products are linked to the country about whose economy Birla was best informed. Most of Birla's Malaysian palm oil is exported to India as are many of his Thai products.

Thirdly, globally and locally, he kept away from consumer products that needed savvy marketing, and concentrated instead on a spectrum of industrial intermediates: viscose and acrylic fibre, carbon black, synthetic yarns, palm oil, fatty acids, detergent intermediates, epoxy resins, hydrogen peroxide. Many saw Birla's unwillingness to enter the high-risk high-profit areas of consumer brands as a major weakness in his managerial make-up.

Allegations that he couldn't face competition used to touch Birla on the raw. 'We are not afraid of competition. Let competition be afraid of us,' he challenged. 'I thrive on competition,' he told me. 'How many Indian businessmen know how to face international competition? In South East Asia, there is no protection. The Americans, the Japanese, the Europeans and the South East Asians themselves—all are there in the market. We are one of many. And in the industries we are in, we are open to ruthless competition. But we are making super profits.'

As news of Birla's success spread, heads of state came knocking on Aditya's door with flowers, trying to seduce him to their countries. In February 1993, the King of Bhutàn paid a state visit to India. He wanted an Indian entrepreneur to exploit Bhutan's limestone deposits, build a cement plant there and export some of it to Assam and West Bengal. The royal homework shortlisted two names: Aditya Birla and Suresh Neotia of Gujarat Ambuja Cement. In November 1994, Chaun Leekpai, the Thai prime minister, came to personally congratulate Birla on the silver anniversary of the group's presence in Thailand. The king left empty-handed, Leekpai left with promises of $400m in fresh capital investment.

The Russians followed. Birla was always short of rayon grade pulp, would he be interested in a pulp plant in Russia? If so, they had for sale a 120,000 tonnes plant employing 700 workers in north-east Russia, a three-hour flight from Tokyo. It was going cheap: it had been closed for the past four months. In December 1994, a virtually invisible press release announced the group's entry into yet another country. Significantly, that year Birla's aggregate Indian production with a 90 per cent market share was 120,000 tonnes, or equal to Indian Rayon's new purchase. In one stroke he had doubled his production.

If in India Birla's illness spurred him on to be more dynamic, the pattern would be repeated in South East Asia. Thailand is to become the group's second manufacturing base after India. But there are plans for a textile mill in Vietnam, a major expansion of existing carbon black facilities in Egypt, besides a gaggle of smaller projects in Malaysia, the Philippines and Indonesia. An editorial in the *Economic Times* patted him on the back: 'Well might Mr Birla declare that foreign competition should be scared of him.'

GREAT EXPECTATIONS

Inevitably envy trailed Birla's success at home and abroad, and family members suffered the debilitating emotion more than outsiders. GD's death unleashed emotions which had been reined in for too many years. They resented GD's partiality for BK and affection for Aditya. They were jealous of the fact that GD stayed with BK when he was in Calcutta and with Aditya when in Bombay. Respect for GD had forced vocal restraint, but in private their rancour ballooned under repression. Under their sober suits and conservative ties, they seethed with envy every time the media hyped Aditya's Midas touch, or referred to him as GD's logical heir. It's hard to be a Birla. The surname demands success.

Tensions were exacerbated by the Hindu joint family system. Some among the younger generation felt that their inheritance had not been equitably distributed after GD's death. They were unprepared to accept the terms proposed by the older generation and were willing to fight for what they perceived to be their just rights. The issue still hadn't been completely resolved by the time Aditya died.

In reality, the seeds of the Birla *mahabharat* were probably sown much before GD's death. Some trace it to the late '70s when GD inducted Aditya into Hindalco and Grasim. They sprouted into green shoots of jealousy when GD 'made it very clear that he wished Aditya to take over their reins after his demise'.

In 1983, Birla patriarchs, represented by GD's three sons (Lakshmi Niwas, Krishna Kumar and BK), and their cousins, the brothers Ganga Prasad and Madho Prasad, tried to bank down the fires. At first it looked as if they would succeed. During the official mourning after GD's death, Laxmi Niwas (1910-1994), a talented speculator, prolific writer and now titular head of India's second largest business house, spoke to *India Today*. 'We are not a group in the sense that the public normally sees us,' he was quoted as saying. 'Each member of the family has his own companies in whose functioning the others do not interfere. There is no one central authority and at the end, my father had direct responsibility of only a few companies that were especially dear to him.' It was a clear message that GD's wishes were sacrosanct.

The most important of the 'especially dear' companies were Hindalco and Mysore Cement, so it was only 'natural' that one grandson, Aditya, should assume charge of Hindalco, in which he was already involved; while the other grandson, Sudarshan (SK), would get charge of Mysore Cement. GD had six granddaughters from his three sons and several grandsons from his three daughters (Chandrakala Daga, Ansuyiadevi Tapuriah, and Shantidevi Maheshwari) but in a traditional Marwari family, the baton passes from father to son. Females don't count except in dowry exchanges. Like the Tatas, the Birlas are not a particularly fecund family, and old habits die hard.

In executing GD's expressed desires, his sons carefully left unsaid the fact that Hindalco was ten times the size of Mysore Cement. (Hindalco's sales in 1983 were Rs 1.87bn, Mysore Cement's, Rs 178m). Also left unsaid was the fact that between them, BK and Aditya controlled the largest and most profitable of the Birla companies. 'And why not?' argued Aditya's friends. After all, wasn't he responsible for substantially building up many of these companies in the first place?

In a rare moment of candour, Aditya once admitted that the Birla most unhappy with the settlement was Sudarshan. In the autumn of his life, even GD appears to have suffered a few guilty twinges. Shortly before he died, he allocated Jiyajeerao Cotton Mills and Saurashtra Chemicals to Sudarshan but the scales were still tipped in Aditya's favour when he was made chairman of Grasim. In 1985, the family belatedly made amends by handing over Cimmco to Sudarshan's son, Siddharth.

By 1986 a revolt against the 1983 settlement was gathering momentum led by SK and KK. In 1983, KK, a Rajya Sabha Congress member of Parliament, had observed that carving up the empire would 'not be easy, even if someone wants to, and I don't think it is going to happen'. Post-1986, his unhappiness matched that of his nephew and he was ready and willing to wield the scalpel.

'I know that KK is bitter about the fact that he has not got any of GD's major companies. Grasim, Century, Hindalco and Kesoram have all gone to BK and Aditya, while KK has got nothing,' said one of KK's friends. Virtually all KK's companies (Zuari Agro, Texmaco, Indian Steamship, the sugar units) were founded, acquired or managed from the start by KK himself. 'The absence of an inheritance may be partly because KK has three daughters and no sons, partly because KK had turned down offers from GD to move into one of his companies, and partly because father and son did not always see eye to eye,' said Ninan. Bad luck also played a role. Some of his major units—in coal, insurance and copper—were nationalized, while a starch unit in Burma, the family's first overseas venture dating back to the '40s, had to be sold because of troubled political conditions in Burma.

With so many forces at work, even the genial BK admitted that the formula was under strain. 'After 1983, it was clear that unless some kind of division was agreed upon, there would not only be problems in course of time but also misunderstandings and even unpleasantness.' At the same time, 'there was, I think, some hesitation in all four of us about how to start discussing the division.' And where to start.

Unravelling the group would be a difficult task. An intricate structure of cross-shareholdings bound the group companies together. This was not a planned strategy such as Ratan Tata was trying to introduce at Bombay House but a historical legacy from an era when companies floating new ventures·had to turn to sister concerns for raising funds. The original four Birla brothers had promoted enterprises jointly, using manufacturing companies, family trusts and a clutch of investment companies which eventually became 'mother' units. So Century (controlled by BK) held a substantial stake in Zuari Agro (KK), while Grasim (Aditya) had a large holding in Mysore Cement (Sudarshan), and so on.

Management control was often divorced from ownership. A clean break would involve selling shares to each other at market prices where the real beneficiary would be the tax collector. Apart from the heavy capital gains tax which everyone would have to pay, the legal bill for untangling Gordian knots would be hefty. In 1983, the family had agreed that for the time being, they would try out GD's principle of 'line of actual control', i.e., group companies would be partitioned but the cross-shareholdings would remain intact. By 1986, everyone accepted that the knots would have to be snipped even if they had to shell out Rs 250m to Rs 500m to the taxman.

The skirmishes were initially limited to GD's side of the clan with the Braj Mohan and Rameshwar Das branches maintaining a neutral distance. They would later be drawn willy-nilly into the scuffle because of their immensely valuable shareholdings. No longer were Aditya and SK portrayed as GD's only grandsons. 'We were four and now again we are four,' reminded the new generation, referring in the first instance to GD and his three brothers, and in the second to CK and Ashok. The advent of proxy battles raised the price of forgotten share certificates in dusty *tijoris*. And as the battleground became bloodier, family members would join hands with each other to create power blocks which would shake the principle of de facto control of companies and bring about massive upheavals.

During the bitter backroom wrestling, one Birla retained his dignity. Paying him a tribute, BK wrote: 'Ashok's attitude during the discussions was the best. He attended only one meeting; he explained his point of view and told the other members of the family: "This is my opinion; please give me whatever you feel you want to give me; I don't want to enter into any wrangling over this matter. Whatever basic settlement and valuation is agreeable to Aditya, is acceptable to me." Up to the end he totally stuck to his decision.'

BK's eulogy, published in *A Rare Legacy*, came too late. On February 14, 1990, flight IC 605 crashed at Bangalore airport claiming ninety victims. On board had been Ashok, his wife Sunanda, their daughter Sujata, and many of Ashok's key executives. They had been flying to Bangalore for the opening of a new factory, a joint venture with USA's 3M. The only member of the family to survive was Yashovardan, who was then studying in the US.

KK triggered the 1986 round of skirmishes by apportioning his companies among his three daughters. Shobhana Bhartia provided the immediate provocation by promptly moving onto the *Hindustan Times* board, attending office in Delhi and interviewing prospective candidates for the paper's editorship. Some Birlas felt 'this was a bit too hasty, rushing before formalities had been really been sorted out. Besides these members liked to believe that the paper, and the authority that went with it, belonged to the family as a whole and not to any particular segment.'

In April 1986, at a conclave in Calcutta, Ganga Prasad was asked to oversee a fresh effort to resolve the deadlock. The family met on August 15, Independence Day, for an hour. The next day, the ten Birlas resumed their talks. It was all very civilized: the youngsters deferred to their elders; those who spoke, did so in calm, even tones. It was also inconclusive, and the tensions were never far below the surface. But 'after four months of discussions, intense consultations among ourselves, much concerted efforts to arrive at an equitable and fair division and allocation, a settlement came in sight', said BK. The basis for valuation for quoted companies would be the market price on August 14; for unquoted companies, it would be their net worth; and for investment companies, their intrinsic value.

Within weeks, it was clear that this grand composite plan wasn't going to work. 'We had hoped that all the major issues would be resolved but for various reasons, the proposed settlement fell through. Four months of serious effort went down the drain. Naturally, an element of bitterness crept in,' said BK. From Rs 150m to Rs 200m, the 'liability' for BK and Aditya had apparently swelled to Rs 2bn and they started examining the valuation very closely. All through 1987, 'the atmosphere was polluted by arguments, wranglings and antagonisms. Hope and despair alternated like day and night,' BK sighed.

As in 1986, so in 1987, the year's first skirmish involved KK. This time it was a straight fight between KK and Ganga Prasad over Upper Ganges Sugar. Originally promoted by Braj Mohan, Ganga Prasad held over 30 per cent of its stock but KK had been looking after it for several years. In accordance with the 1983 settlement, KK continued doing so. In 1986, however, the tiny company doubled its sales, from Rs 388m to Rs 619m, showing good profits. In the vitiated atmosphere of 1986-87, Ganga Prasad demanded it back. A hurt KK claimed that 'a gift is not meant to be returned', and offered to buy Ganga Prasad's shares, but the issue became deadlocked over price. In the ensuing scrimmage, the Calcutta Stock Exchange had to step in to regulate trading.

The most embarrassing skirmishes were those when the clan bid against each other for blocks of shares held by relatives. In Bombay, Sudarshan approached his aunt's family, the Maheshwaris, who owned between 10 and 15 per cent of shares in some key Birla firms, including Pilani Investments. The Maheshwaris thought Sudarshan was buying them for a 'pool' account. By the time Aditya knocked on their door, he was too late and failed to get the prize despite a higher bid. In defence, Sudarshan explained that he was merely carrying out a family commitment that had been given earlier because the Maheshwaris had said they wanted to sell.

Sutlej Cotton perhaps witnessed the biggest exercise of the Birlas' incredible money power. An ostensibly insignificant company, in 1986, Sutlej Cotton's net worth was around Rs 95m; sales, Rs 350m. But it was a 'mother' unit, holding a valuable portfolio of Birla stocks including 1.85m Grasim shares (8.5 per cent of its total equity); 1.24m Hindalco (9 per cent); 1m Zuari Agro; 0.5m Universal Cables; 650,000 Ratnakar Shipping; 64,000 Pilani·Investments; and 6,750 Century. In the books, these shares were valued at a historical figure of Rs 29.8m. At 1986 market prices, the Grasim shares were worth Rs 170m, and those of Hindalco, Rs 120m. Sutlej's shareholding was divided between the financial institutions (11 per cent), the general public (25 per cent), and the Birlas (64 per cent). Of this latter portion, KK owned about one-third, i.e., 20 per cent.

Keen to establish unchallengeable supremacy, KK tried to strengthen his grip on it. First he quietly acquired a part of General Insurance Corporation (GIC) shareholding in Sutlej. Shortly thereafter he tried to make a rights issue. In early 1986, the *Hindustan Times* carried an item that Sutlej Cotton proposed to make a rights issue of 240,000 shares of Rs 10 face value at a premium of Rs 15 per share. The market price was

Rs 23. In effect, the issue would double the company's equity base.

Apparently KK did not discuss the Sutlej rights issue with the rest of the family before announcing it. The other Birlas objected, saying that Sutlej was owned by the family as a whole and no single branch had a majority. The hefty premium also became a hot topic. However, KK refused to back down and the action moved to the stock market. Its price rocketed from Rs 25 to Rs 35 in August 1986 to an astronomical Rs 118 a year later. Again the Calcutta Stock Exchange had to intervene. KK was forced to abort the issue.

The jostling propelled the clan into unexpected alignments. Ganga Prasad, Pryamvada (Madho Prasad's widow) and Sudarshan (all net sellers in the latest settlement) found themselves on common ground and ganged up against BK and KK (who were net buyers).

Almost imperceptibly, around the same time, KK began to realize he had more in common with his younger brother BK than he had thought. In 1987, KK published *Indira Gandhi: Reminiscences.* While writing it, vivid childhood memories poignantly returned. And Aditya was not such a bad lad after all, recalled KK. During the 1971 Lok Sabha elections, 'my young nephew Aditya, my brother Basant Kumar and his wife Sarla *(sic)* helped me a lot. They had worked tirelessly and were very disheartened over my defeat', remembered KK emotionally. 'Aditya was particularly sad. He almost broke down; that was the saddest day of his life, he declared with all sincerity.'

For Aditya, Uncle KK's tacit support could not have come at a more opportune moment. The GP-PMP-S combine controlled more than half the shareholding in two crucial 'mother' units, Pilani Investments and Jiyajeerao Cotton Mills, which held large investments in key BK-KK companies. For a moment, the Birlas rocked on a precipice. There was a real fear that Aditya could lose Grasim and Hindalco.

Smelling money, outside punters swung into action. Between July and August 1987, share prices of Birla companies swung madly. Jiyajeerao Cotton shot up from Rs 18 to Rs 34 in one week; Grasim rose from Rs 76 to Rs 100; Hindalco, from Rs 74 to Rs 117.

This was perhaps the most dangerous moment in Aditya's entire business career, but he played his cards shrewdly, always a step ahead of the rival combine. For the past couple of years, he had been judiciously shoring up his stakes through 'some clever and timely' purchases on the market. Most of his purchases were made in small lots through small brokers. In addition he had an ace in his hand which the others couldn't beat. In a crunch, the financial institutions who held large stakes in his companies would surely back him. Now he played the trump card. The others agreed to sell out to him. By August 1988 a truce had been hammered out. Tempers cooled and Aditya was firmly in the saddle.

Kumar Mangalam's wedding to Neerja was a welcome respite from the family fireworks, but the truce didn't last long. As soon as the wedding was over, the clan returned to its favourite pastime. The unpicking process occupied the better part of the next three years, but by and large, the cross-shareholdings had been delinked by 1990. By May 1996, a power-sharing formula for Century Textiles, the last festering sore, had been worked out. Nobody was completely satisfied but at least workable compromises of sorts had been achieved and the clan would stop breathing down each others' necks. The sums involved in this exercise were enormous. BK and Aditya probably made a payout of between Rs 1bn-Rs 2bn to the others and the taxman.

For such an astute man, one with his formidable

intelligence and business savvy, how and why did Birla permit himself to be cornered over Grasim and Hindalco? 'Perhaps he was too trusting,' says Rajashree. 'He was very large hearted and too trusting. He always considered the family as a whole and shareholdings didn't worry him. That such problems could arise didn't even occur to him.'

'He really did not bother to consider that his part of the family didn't have a majority and that another part did because he thought the whole family was his whereas some other parts of the family, they made sure that they had a majority,' agrees Kumar Mangalam. 'I am not blaming anyone—I am just saying that times change and I think as far as my father was concerned, he, I mean, everyone thought, that it was impossible for him to lose his companies. I think the important thing was that at the end of the day, no one from the family could say that he was unfair to them, or even that he was rude to them. It was all done in a manner that he did not have to have any regrets. It was all very dignified. There was nothing surreptitious or underhand about it. And he did all of this by himself, without any support from the family.'

KALLUVETTUKUZHIYIL MOOSA

On the morning of February 7, 1988, Kalluvettukuzhiyil Moosa walked out of his house to the nearby tea shop to read the newspaper over a cup of tea. It was thirty-one months to the day that he had been following this routine, ever since the factory he worked in had closed down. Skimming over the previous day's events, he read an article saying that once again talks between the Kerala state government and the management of Grasim's pulp and viscose fibre plant at Mavoor had broken down. Folding up the paper, Moosa returned to his house and hanged himself.

Some would later say that Moosa's death was not in vain.

Twelve other workers had committed suicide before him but no one had taken any notice. This time, the Marxist government made a serious effort to break its deadlock with the Birla run company so that the plant could reopen.

The crux of the conflict was wood. To feed the pulp plant, the Grasim management had purchased 30,000 acres of forest land in 1965. At the time, the state government had promised that these forests would not be nationalized for sixty years. The government changed and the new administration reversed the decision. In 1974, a new agreement was hammered out where the government agreed to supply 200,000 tonnes of raw material, or two-thirds of its needs, to the plant. From 1981, even this dwindled and the plant was running to less than one-fifth its capacity. Starved of inputs and with mounting losses, Birla shut down the plant in July 1985, declaring his willingness to reopen whenever the government supplied it with raw materials at competitive rates.

The plant's closure threw 4,000 workers out of work, an enticing vote bank for every politician in Kerala. The on-off negotiations with various Marxist ministries didn't help. There were threats of nationalization, but each time the government backed off. The brinkmanship finally ended in January 1989. The government blinked, not Birla.

Broken promises and other incidents made Birla cynical about politicians and the way they ran the country, both at the Centre and at state levels. Like his contemporary, Rahul Bajaj, Aditya was conscious of his political heritage, but unlike the scooter king, Birla shunned the company of politicians, saying simply, 'It is better to keep out of the limelight and let the balance sheet speak for itself.' In the '90s, when industrialists started coming out in support of the BJP, Birla refused to be drawn into the debate, merely commenting curtly, 'We must remember that we are Indians first.'

In the '60s and '70s, under Indira Gandhi, despite K.K. Birla's personal rapport with the Congress leader, the clan was in a corporate doghouse and several of Aditya Birla's proposals were either rejected or blocked. Resentful of bureaucratic restraints, Birla had turned his attention to South East Asia. As he used to say, 'Look, one must enjoy doing one's job. If not, it's better to just leave it. Confrontation doesn't get you anywhere. I have the whole world in which I can put up industries. I have no compulsions that I must limit my activities to a particular country. So I do not need to beg to influence anyone. All over the world, if we are doing business, it is on the strength of our management and people. Not on the basis of talking to the governments.'

But India was and would always be his home base, and he built wherever he could. 'In the past one was not guided only by choice or gut feeling. A lot of decisions were taken because licences were available in certain areas. And this was wrong. For instance, high growth took place in the cement industry because it was delicensed. If the industry had been deregulated, maybe we'd have gone into sponge iron much earlier,' he said.

Characteristically, Birla seized every opportunity for growth that presented itself. If that happened to be cement, so be it. In the '70s, ACC, a Tata group company, was India's largest cement producer. By the turn of the '90s, Birla was in a race for the leadership position. Did he want to be the biggest player in the Indian cement industry? 'I have no such ambitions. I'm told we are quite large, but how we compare in size with others doesn't matter to me. Whatever we run should be run efficiently. I'd like to feel that the units with which I'm involved are run at excellent capacities and produce quality'.

As the Narasimha Rao administration's liberalization programme gained momentum, Birla welcomed it but commented warily, 'There are too many rules and regulations and just too much of government in every sphere of activity. Now we're taking conscious steps to break away from the system and I think the government is doing an outstanding and truly remarkable job. In a very short time, phenomenal steps are being taken, but it has to percolate down the line. To change the culture of an industrial organization takes several months. So to change the culture of a whole country and its government apparatus isn't going to be easy—it'll take time.'

He started drawing up new investment plans, but his wariness towards politicians and bureaucrats didn't wane. 'We will not put up a manufacturing unit in India unless there is an inherent advantage in doing so. Gone are the days when business plans were finalized keeping just the Indian market in mind,' he warned. It was no more than expected from a man whom the government had kicked around so much.

Bureaucrats took eleven long years to clear the Mangalore Refinery project, nine for the sponge iron one, six for the polyester filament yarn plant, three for the one making argon gas and hydrogen peroxide, and two for the fertilizer unit. Birla abandoned the glass shell project because the government dragged its feet for so long that business conditions changed and it became unviable. There were many projects which he could not get cleared at all. These included Indian Rayon's proposal for a huge 1,000 MW power station in Andhra Pradesh which the Narasimha Rao administration eventually awarded to the Hindujas, a caprolactum plant, a float glass project, and a petrochemical complex. The Mangalore Refinery case, in fact, is a classic example of the frustrations Birla had to put up with.

In September 1985, the cash-strapped Rajiv Gandhi administration, desperate to increase the country's oil refining capacity, decided to invite private entrepreneurs to build refineries as joint ventures with the public sector. Several projects were offered, among them Karnal (in Haryana), Auriya (Uttar Pradesh), and Mangalore (Karnataka).

Coincidentally, Birla was then in the middle of building Indo-Gulf Fertilizers and mulling over sponge iron. The Mangalore project caught his eye as it had a large naphtha cracker attached to its refinery. Birla had been keenly watching Dhirubhai Ambani's progress in petrochemicals, and Aditya was keen to have his own cracker. The Mangalore project seemed the ideal vehicle. Moreover, the entire hydrocarbon sector was opening up. To get into petrochemicals and oil simultaneously was a seductive combination.

Others had the same idea. Sixteen business houses jumped into the fray but Birla gradually inched ahead. In November 1986, he topped the petroleum ministry's shortlist. His nearest competitors were Shashi and Ravi Ruia of the Essar Group. Uncle K.K. Birla was in third place. By early 1987, Birla limped past the finish tape. Or so he believed. On February 2, the Centre issued a press release saying it was 'exploring the possibility of entering into a memorandum of understanding with Indian Rayon Corporation as co-promoter for the Mangalore petrochemical complex and for preparing a detailed project report'. The note raised more questions than it answered. Why was it so tentative? If no decision had been taken, why issue a press release? And the note mentioned only a petrochemical project. What about the refinery?

Clearly someone was working against the project, but was he gunning for the state government, Birla or merely trying to stall the project? The question remained unanswered when Birla signed an MoU with Hindustan Petroleum Corporation (HPCL) to jointly build a 3m tpa refinery and a 250,000 tpa naphtha cracker in June. Provision was built in for the future addition of six downstream petrochemical units. Birla rolled up his sleeves and got to work though all the requisite permissions hadn't yet come through, confident that he had the backing of the state government.

Barely had the ink dried on the approval when it came under low-intensity fire once again. Birla's most vulnerable moment was to come in April 1989. In a highly unusual decision, an inter-ministerial committee meeting directed the Project Investment Board (PIB) to review the Mangalore project. The committee justified its order on a report by Abid Hussain, a member of the Planning Commission. Hussain suggested that India should have crackers based on gas rather than naphtha. If the suggestion were accepted, the government's decision would favour Ambani's cracker and indirectly pencil out Birla's cracker though not the refinery.

The committee's sudden decision to refer the Mangalore project back to the PIB despite its earlier clearance and the Rs 200m spent by the promoters sparked parochial resentment in Karnataka. The Centre had not discussed the matter with local officials before issuing its directive. Karnataka was worried that Uttar Pradesh—which had been sanctioned a gas cracker at Auriya—would hijack the project. The Janata Party and Janata Dal started gearing up to protest. The project was by now well and truly enmeshed in political and bureaucratic intrigue without a brick having been laid.

Birla survived the attack but objections to the project continued under V.P. Singh's administration. In December 1989, Veerandra Patil, Karnataka's chief minister, flew to Delhi to raise the issue with Singh who had taken over as prime minister from Rajiv Gandhi on December 2. Singh, known to be wary of Ambani, promised an answer by February 1990. Birla allowed his hopes to rise: 'I think only three crackers will go through—ours, Haldia and Dhirubhai's,' he told friends. He was in for a shock. In March 1990, the government let it be known that because of the resource crunch, 'expansion of existing facilities was preferred to new ones'. In Delhi, politicians like Ramakrishna Hegde, a former chief minister of Karnataka who had become vice-chairman of the Planning Commission, and M.S. Gurupadaswamy, then petroleum minister and also from Karnataka, lobbied hard on Birla's behalf, but like the Red Queen in *Alice Through The Looking Glass*, they seemed to be running to stay in the same place.

A visionary who had had pragmatism hammered into him during the Kaiser episode, Birla now seriously reassessed the situation. He had spent over five years trying to get permission for the Mangalore complex. His attempts at getting a licence to manufacture purified terephthalic acid (or PTA, a petrochemical input in synthetic textiles and a business dominated by Reliance) had gotten nowhere and the proposal was blocked, gathering dust somewhere. The government had repeatedly turned down Grasim's requests to put up an HDPE (a petrochemical used by the plastic industry) unit as well as one for LAB (a detergent intermediate). Birla felt almost certain that the cracker was slowing down the progress of approvals for the refinery. Five years had gone down the drain. Perhaps it was time to cut his losses, quit pushing for an entry into petrochemicals, drop the cracker and get on with the refinery.

At the next meeting of the PIB in November, 1990, however, the powerful committee didn't take any decisions because of the uncertain political climate. Two days later, Chandra Shekhar was sworn in as prime minister.

This was just the opening Birla needed to make up for lost ground. One of Chandra Shekhar's first acts was to grant PIB approval to the Mangalore refinery, but he didn't stop there. Throwing the door wide open, on April 11, 1991, his government showered letters of intent on all serious applicants. Much of the earlier rivalry was made redundant. Yet somehow

Birla's project was still lost in the woods.

Normally a reticent man, as businessmen have to be, in April 1992 Birla was pushed into venting his frustration: 'We have created systems that have gone out of control. There are not many players in this country who will put up such a mega project. The refinery project has been subject to a lot of bureaucratic delays. The memorandum of understanding was signed four years back and it has been hanging fire for God knows what reason—some permission, some clearance here or there.'

Towards the close of 1992, he managed to gather all the necessary clearances but petrochemicals remained an elusive dream. Undaunted he threw down a gauntlet, promising that 'after the refinery, we'll go in for a petrochemical unit'. Birla re-applied for a cracker in October 1994, and a PTA licence in 1995, even as the Ambanis were gearing up for their refinery. The clash of the titans in direct market competition for the first time should be interesting.

Were roadblocks being deliberately erected to stall the Mangalore project, I asked Kumar Mangalam, who in December 1995 was facing opposition from a group of fisherfolk at the refinery's proposed site. 'No, no. The troubles we've had are the normal ones faced by any large project. I don't think there is or was anyone's hand behind them,' he denied firmly.

If there were no roadblocks in this case, it's no secret that there were unseen forces at work slowing down Aditya's entry into hydrogen peroxide.

The gas is used extensively by the textile and paper industries in India, and its production had been the monopoly of the politically well-connected Nusli Wadia for decades. Until Birla decided to challenge it. Nonetheless, it took him over four years to get a licence. Once he had all the licences in hand, Birla moved swiftly to tie up with the USA's FNC, the world's largest producer of the profitable gas, to help him erect facilities in Madhya Pradesh and Bangkok. The Nagda plant never came up but once the Thai plant had gone into full commercial production, it was time to administer some sharp taps on a few wrists.

In May 1994, Thailand announced that it was considering slapping a 30 per cent 'punitive tax' on certain Indian companies on the ground that they were 'dumping' hydrogen peroxide. The foreign trade ministry's announcement was prompted by a local company, Thai Peroxide, which was worried that Indian companies were offering the gas at prices lower than the cost of production. India's ex-factory price was Rs 26.60 per kilo while the export price was Rs 15.36. If Indian companies kept dumping their production, local manufacturers would be saddled with a mounting pile of unsold stock, warned Thai Peroxide. Indian companies exporting hydrogen peroxide to Thailand should be asked to give detailed information on their cost of production, demanded the Birla-run Thai company with mock virtuosity, knowing full well that only extreme duress would make any company part with its trade secrets. Wadia's National Peroxide retreated from the Thai market.

Though the government shot down so many of his proposals, there was one area where Birla ruled supreme: viscose. The steady profits yielded by its manufacture were the source of his greatest strength, his financial muscle. Until 1994, Birla was the world's number one viscose staple fibre producer. In India, between BK's companies and his own, the duo control 90 per cent of viscose fibre manufacture and 60 per cent of viscose filament yarn. As fiercely as Ambani protects his PTA hegemony, the Birlas jealously guard their turf. As Aditya once said, he wasn't in business just for fun: 'I'm a hard-headed businessman.'

Most businessmen know when not to meddle but not Satish Kumar Modi, an aggressive Delhi-based businessman. The youngest of five energetic brothers, he was used to being bossed and had learnt early on to fight for what he wanted. During the '70s, the Modi Group grew from next to nothing and by the '80s it was among the top twenty business houses of India. When Modi announced his intention of setting up a viscose unit, the Birla engine went into overdrive.

Right through the '80s, newspaper headlines screamed details about the Modi-Birla tussle. Birla, then and later, insisted that there was no stop-Modi campaign. 'We are not fighting Mr S.K. Modi. If we did not want to encourage competition, why would we agree to sell a plant to the Thapars. Earlier we set up a plant for South India Viscose. But we are machinery manufacturers and suppliers. If the Modis want to buy a plant, naturally I would like to sell my machinery to them. And if, according to DGTD regulations, they advertise in a gazette for machinery, how can we not come forward. We have the capacity to build world-class plants having supplied to South Korea, Cuba, Thailand and Indonesia in the face of global competition. We are trying to sell machinery—not to stop competition.' Considering that Birla's monopoly remains intact, it doesn't need to be said that Modi is still waiting for the requisite permissions.

SMALL THINGS COUNT

Inevitably, Birla's amazing career poses the question: How did he do it? How did he keep so many balls in the air without dropping one? What special managerial skills did he draw upon?

In an age when B-schools didn't exist, MBA tutors were your father's trusted managers, and textbooks were ledgers of thick cream paper bound in red quilting filled with crabby accounts, Indian Rayon provided Birla's initial management education. Either it was a very good school or Birla was a very good student.

In the spinning mills' early days, perhaps the first management tenet Aditya learnt was the value of continuous growth. Every year he kept adding to Indian Rayon's spinning and weaving capacity. This lesson became a crucial concept, one which he applied to every company under his charge. On taking over Hindalco after GD's death, he immediately introduced an expansion programme. In 1983, the company's production of primary metal was 93,883 tonnes. Ten years later, production stood at 157,826 tonnes. Continuous growth is today a primary goal in the group's corporate philosophy.

'To keep on modernizing, updating, debottlenecking, cost cutting, increasing production (including capacities) by technological improvements, this is what we enjoy. Running a plant day in and day out in the same manner gives one no joy. The basic aim of technological advance should be to reduce the cost of production—not technology for technology's sake,' he once explained.

Birla's companies are profitable powerhouses not through spectacular growth but through hundreds of seemingly trifling improvements. In this he differed diametrically from Dhirubhai Ambani's philosophy. Ambani's visions were always 70mm. He wanted to build the biggest PTA plant in India and it had to be of global size from day one. When planning an oil refinery, he started out by demanding a licence for a 9m tpa capacity plant. Birla, in contrast, proposed a 3m one.

Ambani forced the government to change its myopic views on the minimum economic size of plants and to allow Indian businessmen to build large plants. Birla, on the other hand, worked within the government's parameters, without getting into confrontation. He would start small and build up capacity ·slowly but constantly, applying annually for innocuous permissions to expand production. The end result for both businessmen was probably the same. Birla eventually hiked the Mangalore Refinery's capacity to 9 million tonnes, equalling Reliance, for example, but only after obtaining clarifications and wringing some concessions on the way. If Ambani was India's polyester pasha, Birla was its viscose king. Both were monopolists. But in Ambani's case, perhaps the going was harder. Both were frustrated by bureaucratic red tape shackling their entrepreneurial drive.

If he picked up the concept of continuous growth in Indian Rayon, Birla realized the value of quick project implementation during the early days of empire-building in South East Asia. A simple business mantra, it's not unique to Birla. Others have stumbled upon it and used it well. Dhirubhai Ambani learnt it in Aden. Rahul Bajaj applied it when he was erecting Bajaj Auto's Aurangabad plant. Aditya Birla picked it up in the Philippines.

In 1975, the Indo-Phil Textile Mills Inc was commissioned in a record time of five months and eleven days. With production in full swing and cash rolling in, it became clear to Birla that the project's quick implementation had not only brought its cost down substantially but also had a tremendous bearing on profitability. Having mastered this lesson, he applied it faithfully. His next major project was Pan Century Edible Oils, a partnership with a group of Malaysian investors. At the time, it was Birla's most ambitious project and his largest overseas venture. The plant was constructed within twelve months and started commercial production almost immediately.

Back in India, reporters watched in awe as Birla rigorously applied his mantra and vaporized the *chalta hai* attitude for which India is so famous. Indo-Gulf Fertilizers, a Rs 7.2bn gas-based ammonia and urea fertilizer complex located at Jagdishpur (Uttar Pradesh) won kudos from bankers and bureaucrats for its under-budget and before schedule commissioning. Within thirty-eight months of zero date, it began trial runs and went into commercial production at its rated capacity almost immediately (November 1, 1988). A few months earlier, Indian Rayon's carbon black plant achieved 80 per cent capacity utilization within the first year of commercial production. Every time and for every proposal, the strategy paid dividends and Birla's managers down the line recognized that on this issue the boss would accept no compromise, no excuses.

According to Mahesh C. Bagrodia, the most powerful of Birla's executives, 'Babu was willing to do even things he wouldn't otherwise do to ensure that projects came up on time.' While putting up Indo-Gulf, problems regarding the gas supply cropped up. To sort things out, Birla personally made a trip to Delhi to meet the chairman of the Gas Authority of India. 'It makes a difference when the chairman of such a large group takes care to smoothen out even minor problems. Suppliers are then aware of the urgency of deliveries and they do deliver,' he said.

Business World once dubbed him the 'Big Birla' and the label stuck. Talking about size, he said: 'Even though I believe in diversification, at the same time, I feel that plants should follow economies of production and be big. And this policy has been followed in our plants. In viscose staple fibre we are the biggest; in palm oil we are the biggest in the world; in India, in caustic soda, we are the second biggest; Vikram Cement is one of the biggest cement companies at one site in the world.'

While Ambani's Reliance Industries is tightly focused, many of Birla's companies—the older ones particularly—are highly diversified. Asked about his interest in unrelated businesses at a time when several groups are restructuring and honing their core competencies, Birla replied: 'These are all basic requirements. For instance, VSF is basic to clothing requirements. Sponge iron, steel and cement, you need them to build a house. We cannot go wrong as far as the demand for these is concerned provided we give good quality. And I think our quality is excellent because of our tight management control. My philosophy is that a company should be well-diversified so that the cyclical ups and downs of each industry will not hit it very sharply.'

His entry into hyrdogen peroxide exemplified his attitude to size. Per se, it's not a big business, but it is profitable and it was an area tightly controlled by one businessman. For four years, Birla doggedly pursued government approvals. I once asked Birla why he wanted the project so badly and whether breaking the monopoly had become the issue. 'No, no. I wouldn't like to put it this way,' he had disclaimed. 'We are not trying to break Nusli Wadia's monopoly. We go into a product if it is profitable, if there is a demand for it and whether at that demand level, a plant of the minimum economic size can be built, and finally if there is an adequate return on a plant of that size and that cost.'

After continuous growth and size, another area in which Birla placed great importance was quality. When he lobbied for its introduction within the group in the '70s, he was flying against a Birla tradition. GD a shrewd bania who grew up in an era of shortages, didn't believe in quality. Profits were the cornerstone of GD's management philosophy and in a seller's market, consumers had no choice but to tolerate the shoddiness of Birla products. In the bazaar, a cliché was born: Birlas look after shareholders; the Tatas, consumers. Aditya took a longer view on quality than GD and tried to turn the cliché on its head.

'Earlier we used to compromise on quality machinery. I realized that it is better to spend a little extra for better machinery because it pays in the long run. If the machinery is good, the product is good, sales are good and profitability is good,' he said. 'Now we produce the best aluminium, the best insulators. In our category of suitings, we are the best. In carbon black we are the best both in India and abroad and you can check this with our competitors in Indonesia. In acrylic fibre and in sodium phosphate we are the best. In filament yarn, we are not the best but one of the best.'

Hammering this concept down the management cadres, Aditya's factories began picking up awards. In 1974, for example, Grasim's Harihar rayon grade pulp plant received the Sir P.C. Roy award for the development of indigenous technology. Some years later, Grasim built a $7m viscose staple fibre plant in Korea, whose production the Japanese Synthetic Textile Inspection Institution declared was 'equal to Japanese export products'. In 1979 a team of World Bank experts highlighted the efficiency of Indo-Phil Textile Mills' textile machinery. More recently, in October 1994, Indo-Gulf became the first Indian fertilizer manufacturer to receive the ISO 9002 certification. Such recognition meant a lot to Aditya.

GD probably wouldn't have understood what the fuss was all about. Concerned more with profits, he had no compunction about cutting corners. Paying foreigners for technology was one such corner. Why pay when one can copy? The strategy might have worked in the '50s and '60s, but the quality-conscious engineer inside Aditya baulked. Instead he signed one technical collaboration after another with the best companies in the world. Aditya's carbon black plant near Bangkok was set up with know-how bought and paid for from America's Phillips Petredeum. Grasim's engineering and development division at Nagda tied up with Germany's

Neumag for its capital equipment.

Which is not to say that Aditya didn't respect GD. On the contrary, Aditya proudly acknowledged GD's influence in his 'ideals, ethics and zeal for developing business'. At the same time, Aditya paid tribute to BK for teaching him the nuts and bolts of business, and the 'especially important training in how to control companies through the finance function'.

Under BK's supervision, Aditya acquired a meticulous knowledge of accounts, particularly the *partha*, the centuries old traditional Marwari system of monitoring and financial control. Though its use was widespread among Marwari firms in the nineteenth century, most gave it up gradually. Today, it is almost unique to the Birlas who use it extensively. In the late '80s, Aditya convened a conference of his top executives from all over the world to discuss the *partha,* and compare it with other systems. By the end of the conference, 'he realized that through it the group was saving Rs 100 crores. He was very pleased about that,' recalls Rajashree.

In essence, *partha* simply asks 'What does it cost to make?' In a pre-Lotus spread-sheet era, the Marwaris developed a manual system to determine input costs and the daily cash profits as compared to budgeted profits. GD further refined the system by adding more detail and insisting on rigid compliance. Each company had to draw up a series of informed estimates of how much it should cost to manufacture a particular volume of production, sell it and generate a specified profit. Both BK and Aditya imprinted the system with their own stamps. In Aditya's case, he considered *partha* to be the ideal vehicle for combining the conflicting needs of central management control and executive delegation. 'It really gives executives full power to do what they want and to monitor what is the effect of what they are doing,' he said.

According to Siddharth Birla, one of Aditya's nephews,

'This system has many advantages. Essentially it emphasizes the speed of reporting, even sacrificing some accuracy in the process. There is mental pressure on the manager to perform daily. It has a very short reaction time. Then costs are carefully monitored, there can be no fiddling of the accounts, and the law is laid down that if there is trouble, contact the boss straightaway.' Uncle Ganga Prasad Birla says the family widely adopted the system during the depression years. 'Money was tight, credit was not easily available, and you had to worry about money more than anything else.'

Anxious to increase operating efficiency, Aditya honed the *partha* to added sharpness. The system involves analysis on a daily basis of input costs, and the extent and reason for variance from pre-determined operating targets. These targets are set for each employee and unit of group companies up to divisional level, after consultation with the employees and units concerned. Deviations from the *partha* are reported daily to Birla's Bombay office. 'If you have employed more labour or used more raw materials on that day, it will show. If you have produced less, that will show too,' he said.

'During our monthly meetings, I look at three reports. One is the *partha,* the second is the monthly progress review, and then we have the position paper statement. The *partha,* or the costing, is drawn up once every six months, and executive performance is drawn up according to how well he does compared to the norm. At the monthly progress review, a target is set at the beginning of every month according to market changes. In the review, we look at deviations from the target. If we haven't achieved it, we discuss the reasons, what steps we will take to make sure that next month we do achieve the target. The position paper statement is like an agenda.' Once targets were set, he left executives to get on with the job. This strategy had the effect of ensuring consistent performance.

While a Tata success depended on the performance of individual executives, the Aditya Birla group depended on its systems.

In keeping costs under control, along with the *partha,* Birla used a second key tool: benchmarking. According to Rahul Bajaj, 'I can quite categorically state that he was the one person who thought about and practiced benchmarking on costs on a competitive basis almost ten years ago. His rivals and contemporaries started doing so only five years ago. Aditya would personally see to it that his products and costs were benchmarked against the best in the country and even abroad. He would even benchmark his raw materials.'

'I remember one incident. At one of our meetings, Aditya asked me what Bajaj Auto's overtime policy and expenditure were, and what its ratio was to our total employee costs. Then he did some quick calculations, and found that we had a more favourable ratio than he did. Suddenly he turned serious and then, half-jokingly, said: "Rahul, your ratio can't be better than mine. I am more efficient than you are."

'I was amazed that the chairman of such a vast industrial empire would immerse himself in such details. That's not all. A few days later, I found that some of his senior managers had got in touch with us, wanting to know how we were managing overtime costs and what our policies were. All this also shows that Aditya was very sharp and fiercely competitive.'

After 1993 and his illness, Birla introduced two major changes in his corporate philosophy. Earlier, he had avoided buy-outs, but in 1995, he began talks with the Romanian and Tanzanian governments to acquire companies in those countries. And right from the beginning he had preferred to work on his own but in 1994 he took a partner: AT&T.

In his reluctance to buy companies, Birla stood out from the crowd. Several of India's most aggressive businessmen, such as Rama Prasad Goenka of RPG Enterprises, Manu Chhabria of Jumbo Electronics, B.M. Khaitan, the tea baron, and Vijay Mallya, the brewer, have built their empires through this route, but not Birla. Takeovers were not his style, though he knew how to fend them off and had demonstrated his skill when members of his own family launched hostile bids on his group companies. The buy-out talks after his illness were a major departure from Birla's normal business philosophy, but by then he had become a man in a hurry.

'I have nothing against takeovers but the right proposal must come,' he used to maintain. Hopeful brokers would offer him the best, which was rarely good enough. In the past he rejected ITC 'because of its excise problems. I would not take Jokai because I am not interested in the eastern tea gardens'. He admitted that takeovers per se did not excite him. 'Every person has his own objectives. My objective is that you must try to put up new greenfield projects. That gives me most satisfaction because you are actually creating wealth. If you take over an existing company, you are not creating wealth, you are only acquiring something somebody has already put up. That does not give me as much satisfaction.'

ALL THE KING'S MEN

According to Shashi Ruia, the key to Birla's success lay in his ability to organize himself and everyone around him. 'He was very systematic. And he drove his people hard. He drove himself hard also, but he knew how to get the most out of his people,' says Ruia admiringly—and enviously.

Birla knew that in order to translate his paper blueprints into concrete monoliths, he needed people, good capable people upon whom he could rely. His trustful nature allowed Birla to delegate easily and build up an inner circle of talented professionals on whom he depended. Explaining how he did this, he once said: 'What do you do to attract people? You give them tremendous powers and independence while monitoring their performance. We give our executives tremendous powers of decision-making, policy-making. This along with monitoring is the reason for our success.'

Most had joined the Birla organization in the '60s, more or less around the same time as their boss. Today, these men are Kumar Mangalam's five-star generals. They know more about the organization and Aditya's dreams than does the son and they are the grass-root lieutenants who helped Aditya build seventy factories in twenty-five years.

Key decision makers are the Bangkok-based Shyam Sunder Mahansaria (chief of Birla's South East Asian operations), S.B. Agarwal (Indian Rayon), A.K. Agarwala (Hindalco), Indu Hemchand Parekh (Grasim), and Bishwanath Puranmalka (Indo-Gulf). The first among these equals is Mahesh C. Bagrodia, 'the only person besides myself who knows the big picture', Aditya had once said.

One Birla, rather less successful than his cousin, uncharitably insinuated that the credit for Aditya's success should go to GD's carefully selected team which he inherited, but BK denies this, claiming that when Aditya launched his enterprises in the mid-'60s, he was encouraged to pick his own men. 'I did not want to give him my men, as they would have been constantly looking over their shoulders towards me. And I must say he picked an excellent team.'

Almost to a man, they are Marwaris like their chief. Most trace their roots to within a fifty-kilometre radius of Pilani. Birla denies having a bias in favour of his own community. 'I have four secretaries, two of whom are south Indians and one is Maharashtrian. If I had a bias, I would have kept only Marwaris for such a confidential position.' Birla nonetheless agrees that his top management is Marwari, just as that of the

Tatas is Parsi. 'It is natural. There is an affinity and I will never feel embarrassed or compromised if there are more Marwaris. Is there any group which does not have more people of its own community percentage-wise?' he asks.

Mirror images of their chief, Birla's generals tend to be teetotalers, vegetarian, non-smokers, workaholic globe-trotters. It is said that senior Birla executives are sacked for only two reasons: misappropriation or a 'loose' lifestyle. Otherwise they can be as entrepreneurial as they like. 'The biggest part of the pay packet is freedom,' Birla had said. Along with this was lifelong job security. But there is also intense pressure to deliver and to keeping thinking up new projects for the boss. Birla protested: 'We are not a company without a soul. Each individual president is literally the chairman of that unit. It [a new project] is his baby.'

Today, it's a greying power structure which has its plus and minus points. Mahansaria is nudging sixty, Bagrodia fifty-six but Kumar Mangalam is twenty-eight so the average drops to respectable levels. However there is a question mark over the future of the old guard. Will Kumar Mangalam induct a new team or will he retain his father's? Birla generals stay in their harness just like their bosses. Lifetime security means just that. At the same time, there are many new faces today. Unlike J.R.D. Tata who weakly refused to tackle a similar problem in the Tata Group, Aditya's succession planning at the senior executive level has been admirable.

He did a lot of the interviewing and hiring himself. Before he left for his last trip to the USA, he tried to ensure that the organization was a fit fighting machine where 'we have not just a very strong second line, but a strong third line too. As many as 80 per cent of our top executives have grown along with their companies and there is still a host of talent within the group waiting to take charge. Not contented, we are concentrating now on building a strong fourth line.' It was typical of Birla to leave every detail tidy and ship-shape behind him.

Cast in the sons-of-the-soil mould, none of Birla's generals are high-fliers *a la* Darbari Seth or Russi Mody. Nor do they have fancy degrees or abbreviations after their name. It's not as bad as the Shahs' organization where three MBAs rattle around in a crowd of thousands, but there is a distinct preference towards chartered accountants similar to Mukesh Ambani's partiality towards engineers.

If there are few MBAs, ·there are even fewer women. Denying any prejudice against them, Birla points out that in his operations abroad, almost 80 per cent, both staff and officers, are female. In India, he argues that there are few women because of the traditional nature of the companies' culture. One or two women here and there would only feel awkward.

As to his preference for CAs, Birla insisted: 'I have nothing against MBAs. They are brilliant boys, extremely bright and enterprising. There is nothing wrong with the man, but the training that is given is better suited to multinationals. CAs have a very good background. Their whole educational upbringing is such that they have a very good grasp of the basics, of all that is happening in India, in company law, in accounting. They are also not anglicized nor do they become brown sahibs. On the other hand, management graduates are generalists. A CA can fit into a specific slot when he joins business. He can start by being an accountant and then go up the ladder. Business institutes unfortunately have a bias for sales and also their whole culture is Westernized so they do not really fit in with Indian culture.'

Part of the reason for the disdain for MBAs lay in the fact that for years, Birla didn't need marketing whiz-kids. He has a monopoly in viscose, and most of his products are industrial materials, intermediate building blocks used by many industries and there are few consumer products which need advertising or brand equity building skills. Secondly, the organization is strongly finance-driven. But as the group moves into new areas big changes are taking place. More non-Marwaris are coming in, a new HRD programme is in place and Birla head-hunters can be spotted at the campuses of the Indian Institutes of Management recruiting MBAs for the organization.

A chemical engineer himself, Aditya practised what he preached where Kumar Mangalam was concerned. 'He's highly qualified. He's done his CA (which gives him specific job-related expertise) and MBA (which gives him wide vision). I think this is the best combination of degrees that a person in his position could ask for. Even in our organization, there's not a single person who has this educational combination. In addition he has been thoroughly trained for two to three years in every aspect of the business by me. I hope he is the most successful amongst all four of us.'

His attitude to daughter Vasavadatta, on the other hand, was far more conservative. Like most Marwari families, the Birlas saw no point in teaching girls skills beyond those needed in a well-behaved corporate wife: a basic graduate degree, cooking and flower arranging. Around the time Kumar Mangalam was drawing up lists of possible universities for a Master's in business administration, I asked Rajashree whether Vasavadatta would be allowed to go abroad for higher education. 'No, I don't think we want to go so far. We are training up Kumar, but for Vasavadatta, I think a good convent school and then marriage,' she answered firmly. Five years later, on a flight from London to Zurich, BK remarked that 'Vasavadatta wants to go abroad to study. We are thinking about it. The educational standards of colleges in Bombay have deteriorated, and she is very keen to go.'

If Vasavadatta wants to work, would she be allowed to? 'I would not object to my daughter joining the business, but I would advise her that there are better things she could do. Many women run their businesses very successfully, but I think they have a far more important role to play in society. Bringing up the family, they can contribute to cultural, social and so many other aspects of life. Why not do that?' Aditya had countered then.

'Maybe we were wrong, the thinking has changed now,' Rajashree said sadly. 'Girls should be able to stand on their feet. Vasavadatta is learning accounts now. Let's see how she does.' Recently Rajashree joined the boards of four major companies. The winds of change are blowing, but softly.

'HOW PRIVATE IS THE PRIVATE SECTOR?'

'Aditya Birla doesn't like bankers,' a banker confided in me over a couple of drinks. I looked up in surprise. This particular banker was supposed to be close to the Big B, and had helped him put together some great deals. 'Because he's so important, he wants the best. He gets it, and then he asks what more we can do for him. And we have to find ways of satisfying him.' Maybe bankers don't like him? 'No, no. We do. He's straightforward. He delivers. You know exactly where you are with him. I don't know why he doesn't like bankers.'

Maybe Birla had this attitude because bankers weren't always straight with him. Once bitten twice shy goes the hoary cliché and Birla knew the feeling. Unfortunately, he needed them. They provided him the money to grease the wheels of production. After his executive managers, they were perhaps the next most important group of people Birla dealt with directly but the way bankers played around with Hindalco's

1994 GDR (global depository receipt) issue merely confirmed Birla's distrust of money merchants. It would be his worst experience, but not the first negative one.

For an Indian company, tapping the international capital market is a big deal. Getting greenbacks from tough Western fund managers brings in hard cash and wins the acclaim of peers and the finance ministry. According to Rajashree, her husband 'felt it was a big achievement. Putting up plants in India had become routine for him. He knew how to go about it, but the Euro-issues were completely new and challenging.'

He wasn't the first Indian to issue a GDR offering to tap this market. That honour belonged to Dhirubhai Ambani, a man powered by an instinct to pioneer innovations. Birla was perfectly content to follow in Ambani's footsteps. Aditya wasn't a trailblazer, he was more interested in the premium he could get for his equity.

The Ambanis are accused of many sins, but carelessness is not one of them. Mukesh and Anil, Dhirubhai's sons, began preparing for the $150m issue in November 1991. Conscious of the path-breaking role the issue would play, every angle was examined, every question anticipated, the offering circular meticulously worded. Travel details—the roadshow would wind its through most of the financial capitals of the world—were coordinated, appointments with potential investors checked and re-checked. As the months slipped by, the tension at Maker Chamber IV in Bombay, and at Lehman Brothers' ultra-modern headquarters in Broadgate, London, was palpable.

Finally, in May 1992, the Reliance team decided to go ahead—and was promptly plastered by the eruption of the Harshad Mehta affair. The stock exchange and banking crisis, popularly known as the Scam, was triggered by the financial irregularities in the operations of Bombay's biggest bull,

Harshad Mehta. A judicial investigation into his affairs exposed grave lacunae in India's banking and stock market regulations. Nervous fund managers disappeared into their burrows.

In Industry House, Birla huddled with his executives and merchant bankers, Citicorp (the bookrunner) and Merrill Lynch (joint lead) and discussed threadbare every aspect of Reliance's experiences. The Tatas were also due to tap the Euro-market, but Grasim was scheduled to be the second Indian GDR offering. Hindalco would follow if Grasim went well. Birla and his team were ready, in fact had been so for several·months, but the conditions didn't look promising. Ideally, more time should have been allowed to elapse before the market was approached, but fund managers were expecting the issue and a postponement wouldn't necessarily ensure better conditions with the Scam still unfolding. Birla resolved to take his chance.

It was a brave decision, but then Birla was never knock-kneed. The roadshow began in November 1992 and flopped badly. At least Reliance had been fully subscribed; Grasim barely managed to raise $90 out of $100m, even after pricing at a deep discount.

According to Dilip Maitra, a reporter with *Business Today*, even this $90m was suspect. He calculated that it was only 60 per cent subscribed. 'In a desperate bid to beef up the issue, Grasim's management was forced to turn to Birla's companies abroad for succour. Some of these chipped in with around $30m. As it was difficult to arrange for such a large amount of cash at a short notice, Citibank came to their rescue with short-term bridge loans,' wrote Maitra bluntly.

Grasim's difficulties punctured the bubble of Birla's enthusiasm. Normally as close-mouthed as an oyster, his success in Asia had drawn him into an out-of-style boast. 'I have no problem selling shares abroad,' he had proudly declared barely a few months earlier. 'It's very easy for me. Today, if I put up a new venture in any South East Asian country, I would have requests for ten times the capital that I have to float. It is a difficult job for me to allot capital. We don't sell, we allot.' Worse was to follow. Mangalore Refineries's non-convertible debentures to raise Rs 5.6bn also bombed. These were unlucky days for Birla.

Why did the Grasim issue do so badly, especially as it had several advantages which Reliance lacked? Apart from the whiplash effects of the Scam, the Ambanis had had to leapfrog a number of invisible barriers. Fund managers felt the Ambanis had a questionable reputation. They felt Morgan Stanley, the issue's joint lead managers, had an even more questionable one. At the Reliance roadshow in London, at the Savoy Hotel on the Strand, a fund manager from Touche Remnant asked Morgan Stanley how they could 'realistically bring a deal like Reliance into the market after getting their research view so wrong on an Indonesian company'. Despite the misgivings, the Reliance issue was subscribed and sold reasonably close to market price.

Grasim in contrast had to be sold at a deep discount though there were no questions about Birla's integrity. One possible answer could lie in the choice of the bookrunner. According to one jealous syndicate manager who admits he had lobbied hard—and failed—to get the mandate, 'Citicorp won the mandate because of the relationship they had with Birla but they are basically a commercial bank. When the book was being built, who could they call? They didn't have an investor base. Merrill did, but they were joint lead.'

The only upside to the Grasim deal was that fund managers made money. At the time, Birla didn't realize the full implications of this statement. He had had to sell his equity cheap and it was a bitter pill to swallow, but the next time he approached the market he was surprised to see how happy fund managers were to see him again. Birla had made a poor start but he more than made up lost ground in the following years. If Dhirubhai was the acknowledged wizard of Indian stock markets, Birla would become the star of the GDR market.

By January 1994, Birla was riding the crest. He had set a record of sorts for emerging markets when Indo-Gulf and Indian Rayon between them elicited a demand of $3bn. He had asked for $250m. In November 1992, Birla had sold at discount. Now he wanted a top dollar rate and got it. The $30m hit proved to be cheap at the price. Surprisingly enough, Kumar Mangalam, who made his debut during the roadshows, was the cooler of the two. 'There was a herd mentality at the time,' says Kumar. 'One investment manager bought a scrip. Others thought he had done his research and just copied him. And every Indian issue, including ours, did well.'

Birla's success made him the target of some unsavoury manipulation. His next deal, which happened to be Hindalco's second GDR offer, became a sitting duck in a shooting match played by skilled marksmen. They moved so quietly that neither Birla nor his advisers heard them coming. By the time they did, it was too late. Hindalco was hit, badly.

On the evening of Thursday, July 7, 1994, in London, Birla was cloistered with syndicate managers to price Hindalco's $100m issue and to institute damage control. The next morning, each GDR was offered at $24.

This price meant a discount of 8.5 per cent over its Bombay Stock Exchange price. However, right through the road show, Lehman Brothers, the book runners of the issue with J.P. Morgan as joint lead, had indicated a price range of $26-$27. This would peg the new GDRs slightly cheaper than the old GDRs, then trading at a mid-price of $29.25. So why did Birla allow the new Hindalco shares to be sold at $24? Especially since in India, Hindalco was quoting at Rs 920 and there was reasonable demand for the new GDRs in the Euro-market. A Lehman spokesman admitted that Hindalco had 'met with good demand, with balanced distribution between Asia and the USA, and the book was oversubscribed'.

The answer lay in the wild movements of Hindalco stock on the Bombay Stock Exchange on Wednesday, the day prior to pricing in London. In a matter of hours Hindalco's local price plummeted from Rs 920 to Rs 825 before moving up to Rs 860 just before the close of the day. Reportedly, an FII had offloaded a huge chunk. The possible motive? To force down the local price in order to push down the international GDR price. The fund manager could then sell high in India and buy low in Europe. On the first day of trading, Hindalco's new GDRs opened at $26.50. All those who had bought the issue made a cool profit of $2.50 per share within hours.

There wasn't much Birla could do about the situation. He might have been soft-spoken, but he was no pushover, and he fired back straight from the hip in the only way open to him. On Friday, July 9, Jonathan Boyer, head of Jardine Fleming India Investment Trust, phoned Birla. He was irritated that his fund had not been allocated any Hindalco stock. 'Do you know who I am?' he asked Birla. 'I'm the most important FII there is.' Birla's voice was cool. 'You live in Hong Kong. I hear there is a harbour there. Why don't you jump into it?'

It wasn't just European bankers that Birla distrusted. He wasn't too fond of Indian ones either. Although they had obligingly bailed him out during his battle with the GP-PMP-S combine to retain control over Grasim, Hindalco and Century, he was sufficiently irritated by the breed in 1990 to launch a campaign on the need to preserve the private sector from the FIs. Convinced that they were 'destroying the privateness of the private sector', for over a year he lobbied the finance ministry; wrote articles in newspapers, and distributed detailed technical notes on the subject.

The crux of his argument was that 'there are a large number of companies in which FIs own 40 per cent of the equity capital, even 50 per cent and 60 per cent. This is ridiculous. We are supposed to be a mixed economy, but if so-called private sector companies are controlled by the FIs, then where is the private sector? In most companies, the promoter entrepreneurs control 25 per cent of the equity or thereabouts. If the institutions control twice that percentage, the entrepreneurs' feeling of ownership of the companies they control in theory is eroded. The result is that the entrepreneurial spirit is destroyed and that is the dangerous thing because India's greatest asset is its entrepreneurs. The government is destroying this wealth by allowing FIs to take control of companies.'

Angrily, Birla asked: 'The funny thing is that the FIs keep complaining that they are short of funds. Then why do they grab all the shares of companies that they can get? Why do they compete to get control of companies? Why can't they liquidate their holdings in existing companies to generate funds for new investments?'

Birla's outburst surprised many, though had they linked it to its timing, they might not have found it so odd. Ambani was in the middle of his fight to gain control of Larsen & Toubro, whose chairmanship swung like a pendulum with every change in government. Birla had barely begun to breathe freely after several long-drawn battles to retain control of Grasim and Hindalco from family marauders. Over at Bombay House, Ratan Tata was enmeshed in a bloody double-fronted war against Russi Mody and Darbari Seth. The events hammered home, even if GD's advice had faded, which it had not, the truism that businessmen should hold majority stakes in the companies they manage.

There was a widespread perception that Aditya Birla held large shareholdings in his companies, but the campaign hinted that this might not be the case. In order to fund his expansion drives, he had been forced to reduce his stakes, sometimes to dangerous levels. Way back in the '80s, GD had warned Aditya of the risks he was taking. Aditya, however, was determined on growth and he was the only member of the Birla clan who could afford to ignore GD's advice.

In 1981, for example, Aditya wanted Indian Rayon to issue convertible debentures, a financial instrument energized by Ambani. According to BK, 'My father was opposed to the idea because this would reduce the family holding in the company from 18 per cent to something lower than that, and we would be risking our control of the company. But Aditya said that he wanted to expand his operations and could not get money any other way. So despite my father's opposition, and in fact his anger at the proposal, Aditya went ahead.' It wasn't that Aditya disagreed with GD's view, but he had no choice. In 1993, he managed to push up his stake from 13.2 per cent to 20.4 per cent through a Rs 3.4bn rights issue.

Eighties onwards Birla was forced to reduce his shareholdings every time he took a loan from an FI because he had to mandatorily sign a convertibility clause which enabled FIs to acquire substantial blocks of equity in his major companies. In his campaign, Birla suggested a more equitable option: 'I think there should be a limit on how much of a private sector company's equity the FIs can hold. Perhaps 25 per cent at most. If they hold more, let the government pass a law making the excess holding of a non-voting type. That way, the private entrepreneur has a fair chance in the event of a contest. Right now, with the FIs holding 50 per cent and the private entrepreneur holding 25 per cent, the latter has no chance.'

There were few takers for Birla's advice until Manmohan Singh became finance minister. The economist-turned-politician may not have done anything much about it but at least he listened. And in the process came to appreciate the blunt tycoon who dittoed the sentiment. Their rapport was such that Manmohan Singh would be the first to hear and share good news. On Sunday, January 14, 1994, the finance minister was staying at the Tata-run St James' hotel in London when he got an excited call from Birla, who was then staying minutes away at BK's ground floor flat at Arlington House near the Ritz. Indo-Gulf had set a new record by getting a $1.5bn response for its $100m issue.

Their friendship proved to be a mutually beneficial association of the kind singularly lacking in post-Independence India between businessmen and politicians. More usual is an attitude of confrontation between businessmen and politicians, businessmen and bureaucrats, or, for that matter, bureaucrats and politicians. A small example proves the point.

In 1994, the Euro-market for Indian paper was in a tizzy and there was a desperate need for a strong, big issue to lift the GDR market back to buoyancy. VSNL's jinxed issue was waiting to come back along with forty or so private sector companies. Tube Investments, DCW and BILT were small issues and cautiously priced to make sure that they would not bomb. In a market as volatile as this, the finance ministry needed a star performer and after the January 1994 blockbusters, Birla fitted the bill perfectly. None of the twenty-odd companies—not even savvy groups such as Reliance or RPG Enterprises—which tapped the market around the same time, matched Birla's impeccable sense of timing. The market was either going up or down.

In early May, the FIIs handling the offering informed Birla that he should tap the Euro-market immediately. The appetite for India paper, lukewarm for so long, was beginning to firm up. Three issues (Tube Investments, DCW and Ballarpur Paper) had gone through smoothly and there was a definite rally in the secondary market. Birla agreed. He had been preparing for this for months and Grasim was ready to tap the market for a second time. Its roadshow began on May 31 in Singapore and ended on June 7 at Edinburgh.

The odd thing was, nobody—not even Barclays de Zoete Wedd and Citicorp, the lead and joint lead managers—knew until May 21 that Birla was ready. They had ten short days to get a roadshow up and running, inform potential investors, build up media hype, book hotels and flights for a whole team of specialists, compile an audio-visual presentation and print cartons of literature. And there was one minor hitch. The finance ministry hadn't cleared the issue. Birla picked up the phone and called Manmohan Singh. The show was on the road. Priced at $20.50 per GDR at a small premium, the issue was fully subscribed. Singh's trust in Birla's perspicacity had not been misplaced.

THE ARTISTIC SIDE

In between factory blueprints and account ledgers, Birla reserved time and energy for some serious hobbies. One of these was the Sangit Kala Kendra, a non-profit cultural organization which started operations out of his office. For its structure, he borrowed heavily from Calcutta's Sangit Kala Mandir started by BK in 1945. Members pay a nominal yearly fee and the money is used to organize programmes exclusively for them. In any given year, members enjoy plays in English, Hindi and Gujarati, vocal and instrumental recitals, concerts and quiz shows, a talent contest and a fun-fair. The Kendra offers incredible value: the cost of attending these events is half the normal rate. Cards reach members on time, every performance starts on the dot. Like everything he did, Birla ran the club smoothly and efficiently.

A weekend artist, he revealed a closet passion for copying the masters at a one-man show in September 1990. The thirteen canvases on display in B. Vittal's trendy gallery at Bombay's Nariman Point took Birla sixteen years to paint. Unwilling at first to allow the public a glimpse of his hobby, he was pleasantly surprised by the critics' reaction. 'My exhibition attracted more attention than any of my multi-crore projects,' he said at the time with a wry smile.

Birla discovered his talent when he was laid up in bed for three weeks in 1974. Bored, he asked for paint, brushes and an instructor. His canvases show a marked taste for portraits and Himalayan scenery: Leonardo da Vinci's *Mona Lisa* rubs shoulders with a Svetoslav Roreich mountainscape. There are no tempestuous paintings in the mould of Pablo Picasso or Satish Gujral. 'I paint for relaxation. When you are painting, you think of painting, you don't think of business. These are moments which give you some peace of mind, some happiness in creating something . . . I have yet to paint an original. Maybe the next one.' There wasn't to be a next one.

Birla's short life is paradoxical in a family where respect for health is a big tradition. Generally, Birlas eat well, sleep early, live long, and prosper. GD died handling the reins at eighty-nine. GD's brothers, Jugal Kishore, Rameshwar Das, and Braj Mohan died aged 84, 81 and 77 respectively. According to BK (a cool septuagenarian who enjoys zipping around Europe), this is a result of a proper lifestyle. 'Smoking, drinking and dancing are bad. These are taboo in our family's culture,' says the strict vegetarian. Which explains why the family is not in the catering, hoteliering or leather industries.

GD in fact had laid down a comprehensive set of rigorous tenets to which every Birla was expected to adhere: eat only vegetarian food, never drink alcoholic beverages or smoke, keep early hours, marry young, switch off lights when leaving the room, cultivate regular habits, go for a walk every day, keep in touch with the family, and, above all, don't be extravagant.

Only the black sheep—of which there are few—broke the taboos. Never Aditya. GD's favourite grandson completely absorbed and adopted this credo in his personal lifestyle. According to the picture painted by Rajashree, it was austere. 'He would get up at about seven. He would read the newspapers and while reading the newspapers he used to have his massage. Then he would have his bath, pray for a few minutes and get ready for breakfast, and would leave for office between 9 and 9.30. He would be in the office till about seven normally, but sometimes he would be late, say 9.30 or 10. Dinner we used to have at nine whenever he would come at seven. Three times a week he would play badminton. He didn't generally bring work home, but sometimes he did.' There was little time for socializing, less for partying.

When in Bombay, Aditya lunched in a private room on the top floor of Industry House, screened off from the larger dining area used by his executives. But wherever he happened to be, the meal was always a working affair. In between mouthfuls of uninteresting but nutritious menus washed down with glasses of freshly squeezed orange juice or salted lassi, Birla would catch up with the grapevine. Most days there would be a guest whom he either wanted to get to know better or with whom he was planning a deal. At the table there would generally also be a couple of regulars such as Gangaprasad Loyalka, Ashwin Kothari, Om Bhalotia, Sunil Daga, Suresh Taparia or Pradip Jajodia whose role it was to keep the conversation from flagging. In his will, Birla left sizable endowments for his friends, making them each a *crorepati.*

A fitness enthusiast, Birla used to play regularly at the Bombay Gymkhana, an elite city sports club. Invited once to flag off a tournament, Birla sportingly stripped off his suit jacket to lob a shuttlecock at badminton ace Prakash Padukone—and won a round of applause along with two points for some fluid stroking. Shrugging his jacket back on again, Birla had walked off the court on air, grinning broadly. He was also a competent horse rider, and had once won a school prize in fencing.

The benefits of regular exercise and a strict eye on calories showed. Birla's favourite holiday was a summer in London when he lost eight kilos in fourteen days and at fifty, his waist was nearly as trim as when he was twenty. Nonetheless, his hairline had begun to recede, and his thinning black hair had turned salt-and-pepper, but his face remained youthful and unlined until late 1993 when he suddenly aged ten years.

Aditya's extraordinary entrepreneurship bequeathed a mammoth legacy on Kumar Mangalam's young shoulders. He will not only have to defend his turf but also keep his team from being poached. Despite BK's wealth of experience backing him, just to keep the Rs 150bn empire intact and growing on its own momentum, the inheritor will need to be a real tiger. Pitched against him in the oil refining business are seasoned warriors such as Mukesh and Anil Ambani. In sponge iron and hot rolled steel, he needs to benchmark himself against Shashi and Ravi Ruia. Can he build a copper smelter quicker and better than the London-based dynamo Raj Bagri of Metdist? And these are just a few of his many rivals. Meanwhile, the handing over of the baton was marred by a series of disputes: family squabbles in Century, unrest among the fisherfolk of Mangalore, industrial action at Jayshree Textile Mill in Calcutta. In one of his early interviews, Kumar Mangalam had said: 'I've got very sharp ears and very sharp eyes. So I keep them open and use them to my advantage.' He'll need them.

Chapter 4

Rama Prasad Goenka

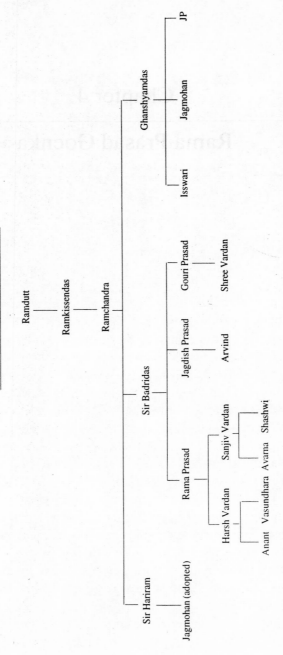

THE GOENKA FAMILY TREE

Ramdutt
Ramkissendas
Ramchandra

Sir Hariram
Jagmohan (adopted)

Sir Badridas

Rama Prasad
Jagdish Prasad
Gouri Prasad

Harsh Vardan
Sanjiv Vardan
Anant Vasundhara Avarna Shashwi

Arvind
Shree Vardan

Ghanshyamdas
Isswari
Jagmohan
JP

Naini Tal Jail
October 3, 1977

L eft alone finally, Rama Prasad Goenka sat on the cold stone floor of Naini Tal jail and looked about him. There wasn't much to see beyond rough walls and iron bars. Luckily his cell was empty and he didn't have to share it with a common felon. He'd been picked up and brought to the police station early in the morning. After hours of altercations and telephone calls, Goenka had resigned himself to the fact that no judge would give him bail that day at least. Peering in at the huddled billionaire, a kindly policeman tossed a blanket to him. Goenka fingered the coarse, torn, smelly material. Should he cover himself with it, or should he sleep on it? As night approached, it was getting chilly. In the end he covered himself.

Naini Tal is an elegant hill resort in the Shivalik Range near India's border with Nepal, 300 km northeast of Delhi. Twenty years ago it used to be a playground of the rich during the summer months. Its lovely lake and mountain scenery form a perfect backdrop for romantic movies. Star-spotting gave it an added attraction.

It's a leisurely place during the off-peak Diwali holidays. So how did one of India's most famous industrialists land up in its jail? The answer lay in New Delhi. Around the same time that Goenka was being escorted to his cell, the Delhi police moved in to arrest Indira Gandhi at her 12 Willingdon Crescent residence. Goenka was one of her closest corporate disciples. He was now being asked to pay the price of fealty.

Goenka's tryst with the Indian penal system was mercifully brief. Released the next day, he quipped: 'One day in jail was quite enough.' More seriously he adds: 'Before I was arrested I was scared. I worried about what the family would say. Afterwards, I did not have any fear.' Just as well, for his sang-froid was to be severely tested. During the Janata Party administration (1977-79), Goenka's homes and offices were raided forty-three times. It was the same administration which lifted Mrs Gandhi's tacit ban on Bajaj Auto's expansion and permitted Rahul Bajaj to build new capacity.

'Actually I became quite friendly with the officer in charge of the operation,' Goenka remembers. 'You cannot find incriminating documents every week. So he would ask me if he could watch cricket on my television set.'

More than the actual arrest, what really pained Goenka was the attitude of his fellow businessmen. 'Just before my arrest, they treated me like an untouchable, especially Bombay businessmen. People who earlier were running after me to get some introduction or some work done, they even stopped talking to me.' Also in 1977, Goenka faced one of his biggest business disappointments. 'We had negotiated to buy Assam Frontier. It was a very good deal for about £2.1m, 100 per cent share and a net valuation of 75 pence per kg. Jokai Tea was sold the previous year for Rs 22 per kg. On March 16, all the approvals were in hand, but we decided to remit the money a week later, after the Lok Sabha elections. The government changed and the deal fell through.'

Shortly before these elections, Mrs Gandhi had warned Goenka not to put all his eggs in one basket, i.e., the Congress Party. On the evening of March 1, 1977, he visited her at the

prime minister's office at 1 Safdarjung Road in New Delhi.
The outer sitting room was a mêlée. R. K. Dhawan, her
secretary and confidante, was trying to keep in order the sundry
ministers and future candidates clamouring to meet her.
Goenka, however, was not kept waiting. As soon as he saw
Goenka, Dhawan ushered him into Mrs Gandhi's office. She
came straight to the point. Losing the elections was a strong
likelihood. As a businessman, he should hedge against this and
meet the opposition. 'I told her, I would rather stand by you.'
To the press, he defiantly declared, 'I have only one vote and
that vote will go to Mrs Gandhi.'

Many businessmen believed RP's full-throated support
for Mrs Gandhi smacked of political opportunism. Amongst
RP's critics was J.R.D. Tata (1904-1993), head of India's
biggest business house. In a well publicized interview given to
Pritish Nandy of the *Illustrated Weekly of India,* the normally
diplomatic Tata, then eighty-two years old, said the Tata
Group's growth had been hampered by Indira Gandhi's
administration because of its refusal to compromise on
principles. He was particularly upset by the government's
rejection of Tata Chemicals' application to build a fertilizer
plant. 'Later, we heard that it was turned down because the
Tatas are too big. Though if we had been a Birla or a Goenka,
we would have got it,' said JRD.

Goenka's easy access to the prime minister galled JRD. It
contrasted sharply with his own relationship, which he
described as 'inanely social'. 'She would doodle or pointedly
ignore me while I spoke, cutting open envelopes and pulling
out letters. In all these years, I have never once been asked by
Mrs Gandhi: Jeh, what do you think? Never, never, never even
once.' Goenka, on the other hand, was invited to join the
Planning Commission and with the mantle of Mrs Gandhi's
approval draped over his shoulders, RP swung deal after deal,

vaulting smoothly over hurdles.

RP himself has always summarily dismissed suggestions that his friendship with Mrs Gandhi, and her advisers such as Dhawan and Pranab Mukherjee, helped him in his business deals. 'Nonsense. You may expect marginal latitude from a favourable government, but no government will go beyond that. Dhawan is not going to ring up an officer and say, "Do this, it is Goenka's work."'

Oddly enough, India's most famous takeover artist has no real office of his own. The corporate headquarters of RPG Enterprises (sales 1995: Rs 45bn) is Ceat Mahal in Bombay, under Harsh Vardan, Goenka's eldest son. Sanjiv, Harsh's younger brother, works from Victoria House in Calcutta. Goenka (RPG to subordinates, Rama Babu to friends) mainly operates out of a series of five-star hotels, any one of his half a dozen residences or even the first class cabin of an aircraft. Once on board, instead of quietly buckling himself into his seat, the gregarious Goenka immediately checks out who else is on the flight and settles down to serious networking. In the '90s, when the Indian government liberalized the import of private aircraft, several businessmen acquired executive jets but not Goenka. 'RP would be miserable sitting alone in his private jet,' teased Neelkant Kalyani, a Pune-based industrialist.

For the globe-trotter, home will always be a stately Alipore mansion where the resplendent atmosphere of Calcutta's nawabs mingles with the traditions of the Raj. On one side of the vast mansion's ground floor is a huge *gadda* room where you can throw off your chappals and bury your toes in sparkling white bolsters while playing 'sweep' (Goenka's favourite card game). Across the passage is a formal sitting room in mock-Louis Quatorze style, complete with European *objets d'art* and gilt sofas.

And books. Over the years, Goenka has accumulated a vast library which lies uncatalogued and scattered in a dozen cities. He won't disclose the titles of the books he enjoys, unwilling to let people glimpse his personality through them, and keeps them in his private sitting rooms, not in the large public entertainment areas. A complex man, the short, portly and balding Goenka relishes the idea of being an enigma and works hard to keep the mystery alive. 'In literature, my heroes are Nehru and Winston Churchill in English, and Jaishankar Prasad in Hindi. Amongst contemporary Bengali writers I try not to miss anything written by Shankar and by journalist Barun Sengupta,' he says.

Travelling, meeting people, reading, collecting modern art and antiques, watching Amitabh Bachchan and Meena Kumari movies on video during his daily half-hour evening massage, Goenka likes to pack something new into each day. Which is probably why he hates the nitty-gritty of day-to-day operations. He is in his element when on the scent of a possible acquisition. An experienced hunter, he masks his excitement. If anything, his hooded, bulbous eyes become more inscrutable, the dimple in his chin more pronounced. Once the kill is over, he leaves his sons, Harsh and Sanjiv, to complete the transaction. Later, expensive managers from public sector and top private sector companies are brought in to manage the acquisitions.

Officially, Goenka retired at sixty. Preparations for the big day started five years in advance, at Udaipur's sumptuous Lake Palace Hotel. Top executives from all group companies met there in January 1985 and received a blunt warning. 'I told them that in 1990 I would retire and that those who wanted to retire before me, fine, but those who were going to continue in the group should consider whether they would like to work under the chairmanship of Harsh. If they didn't want to work under him, they should say so now,' RP recalls. Among those who took RP at his word was P.K. Gupta, one of his most senior executives, who had been at RP's side for twenty-five years. RP shrugged ruefully and moved on.

At one stroke, Harsh (then thirty) became the youngest head of a major business house. Sanjiv was quick to back his father's choice, clearly and unambiguously: 'Of course, Harsh is the supremo. And I have accepted the second slot.' Cheerfully placing himself on the third rung of the new hierarchy, RP nonetheless covered his flanks. Retiring from the chairmanship did not mean he would 'leave the business'. 'I do not want to lean on my sons, or go to them for money, or be in a position where they can say, "Father, take this Rs 50,000."'

As Harsh lived in Bombay, the group's headquarters shifted from Calcutta to Ceat Mahal. With his love of politics, why didn't the group move to Delhi? 'To do what? Run after politicians? That is what I have been doing all my life. Let them [Harsh and Sanjiv] establish themselves as businessmen and then they can make their choice,' said RP at the time.

In this triumvirate, where exactly does RP's role end and that of his two sons begin? As chairman emeritus, legally he is a figurehead. He rarely attends board meetings, and doesn't receive monthly progress reports of group companies. Because of this, Tarun Khanna, a professor at the Harvard Business School, was lulled into describing RP's role as being limited to 'keeping active in a couple of deals'. In reality, nothing happens without his nod. Sanjiv is the only hands-on operations man in the troika. Harsh is mainly responsible for executive recruitment and lately of strategic planning.

RP also plays the essential role of opportunity spotter and keeps track of who is in and who is out in the political and bureaucratic scene. One of the reasons why he handed over the baton was to free himself for the mammoth task of promoting

Haldia Petrochemicals, a deal which eventually fizzled out. Today much of RP's energy is directed towards the power sector and the backroom manoeuvring necessary in a sector where the regulatory policy is still being written.

Goenka's clutch of twenty-two companies in twenty-six business areas is broadly divided into two groups. Sanjiv looks after companies in the east and south including CESC, while Harsh's playing field is western India and Ceat. This arrangement could lead to sibling rivalry. By the turn of the century, the Goenkas' investments in power (under Sanjiv) are expected to overtake their growth in tyres (under Harsh). A skewered balance between the brothers could develop into a flashpoint. RP disagrees: 'No, I don't think there is cause for worry because we are going into power in three to four different companies, and not just one. So if there is balance to be done with a brother, both have to sit down and do the balance.'

Today the trio are very close. They speak every day to each other from whichever part of the globe they happen to be. All three know who is meeting whom on a virtually hour-by-hour basis. The sons' staunch respect for RP is reciprocated. 'Emotionally, I do not get disturbed if there is a lock-out or a strike in any of my group companies. But the health of my children, and the attitude of Delhi towards me—these two things bother me and yes, they do worry me,' remarks Goenka.

In the autumn of his life, Goenka's fondest hope is that his two sons will work in tandem forever. The fact that Harsh and Sanjiv to date have just one son each may help. Though RP is optimistic, experience has taught him that keeping a fractious family together makes no sense at all. In 1963, the messy divorce between his father and his uncles made a deep impression on the young RP. Sixteen years later, the story repeated itself in RP's acrimonious separation from his brothers, Jagdish Prasad, fifty-nine and Gouri Prasad, fifty-six. It was perhaps the biggest crossroads of his life.

'TOO MANY LAPSES'

Rama Prasad was born on March 1, 1930, in Calcutta, the eldest of five children, to Rukmani Devi and Keshav Prasad (1912-1983) Goenka. He schooled in Benaras and graduated from Calcutta's Presidency College with an honours degree in history. At the age of twenty, he married Sushila Kanoria. Harsh was born in 1957, Sanjiv in 1961.

The Goenkas are blue-blooded members of Calcutta's Marwari aristocracy. 'In our community, we regard them as royalty,' gushes B. M. Khaitan, India's tea maharaja and one of RP's closest friends. By Indian standards, RP grew up in a rather Westernized household. The Goenka family fortune was founded on links with the British. Both RP's grandfather, Badridas and uncle, Hariram were knights of the British Empire; and Sir Badridas was the first Indian chairman of the Imperial Bank in 1933.

Marwaris are better known for their commercial enterprise than for producing scientists, but Sir Badridas was a physics and chemistry student, possibly the first of his community to graduate from Presidency College. His grandson, RP, an M.A. in economics, hungered for a doctorate from Harvard. 'I spent fifteen days in 1968 in Athens and three months at Harvard, researching. I wanted to do a comparison between Pericles and Chandragupta Maurya but they found too many lapses in my thesis,' he says.

Despite his liberal background, Goenka is an orthodox Marwari at heart. He expects those younger than him to greet him by touching his feet. The Goenka women stay at home, looking after the children, and RP brought up his sons to think in the same way. Lately, change seems to be in the air. In early 1996, Mala (Harsh's wife) started looking into the affairs of HMV, a music company.

In speech, Hindi phrases slip into RP's uneasy English. At home, and where appropriate, he wears a traditional cream silk kurta above a finely pleated Bengali-style dhoti. In the office, he prefers half-sleeved white safari suits, typical of Marwari businessmen of his age. For many years, however, Goenka wore a *jodhpuri* jacket over Western-style trousers. It was a silent protest against the subtle racism he experienced in his first job. After Independence, racism between the British and the Indians would be substituted by that between Bengalis and Marwaris. In 1991, Sanjiv would be refused membership of the swanky Calcutta Club amidst snide cracks about the need to stop the 'Bengali tiger [from] being cornered by the pot-bellied Marwari in the safari suit', but those incidents lay in the future.

At the close of the nineteenth century, the Goenkas practised the traditional Marwari occupation of moneylending. During the Raj, they acted as banians (commission agents) for European managing agency firms such as Rallis India (Armenian), Kettelwell Bullen and Bird Heilgers (English), and Duncan Brothers (Scottish). It was in the latter firm that Keshav Prasad obtained a job for RP as a covenanted assistant on the princely salary of Rs 350 per month.

Describing his first day at work, RP recalls: 'It was May 1, 1951. I went to the dining room. There were many tables. There were eight Englishmen and one Indian. One Englishman called out to another, "I say, old chap, do we allow people to have tiffin without a tie?" He answered, "No." "Then should we not ask him to leave?" I tendered my resignation and went home.'

Keshav Prasad was furious 'Why did you go against the

traditions of Duncan Brothers? They did not say anything to you They were talking among themselves,' he railed. RP was forced to retract his resignation but all through the fierce Calcutta summer he wore a *jodhpuri*.

Behind Keshav's recriminations lay dreams of heading Duncan Brothers, which, besides its flourishing trading activities, owned Anglo-India Jute and Birpara Tea. 'My only business ambition was to chair the board, own the company and totally Indianize it,' he told reporters many years later. Through a series of judicious loans and quiet tactics—Keshav Prasad liked to describe his management approach as '*ahista, ahista*'—he fulfilled the first part of his dream in 1957. Six years later, he achieved it in full. The event was described by the contemporary press as 'one of the biggest corporate coups' of the time.

As tea profits increased, Duncan Brothers became a rich war chest. With his sons by his side, Keshav Prasad hit the acquisition trail: Coorla Mills (1966), Asian Cables (1966), Jubilee Mills (1969), Swan Mills (1971), B. N. Elias Group (1973, including Agarpara Jute and National Tobacco), and Murphy India (1974). Among the trophies were a few failures: Rallis India, Balmer Lawrie, Remington Rand (which the elder Goenka bagged in a second attempt, from Keshub Mahindra, in 1991, but which was subsequently sold off for Re 1) and Bombay Dyeing.

The Bombay Dyeing deal was totally RP's idea, and in making a play for the venerable Parsi institution, RP displayed an odd mixture of audacity and naivete.

Bombay Dyeing has been owned by the Wadia family for decades. Currently the Rs 10bn textile and petrochemical producer is headed by Nusli Wadia, a corporate samurai who has crossed swords with Vishwanath Pratap Singh, Rajiv Gandhi, and Dhirubhai Ambani, among others. At age twenty-six, Wadia proved to be a feistier strategist then Goenka, then forty-two.

Goenka's play for Bombay Dyeing wasn't a hostile move. Bombay Dyeing's then chairman, Neville Wadia (Nusli's father) in 1971 put it on the auctioneer's block. Reportedly the company was in a financial mess, and the Wadias did not have enough resources to set things right. Unaware of his father's intentions, Nusli arrived in Bombay after completing his graduation abroad, expecting to find a job in the mill.

'We had signed the deal with Neville Wadia,' recalls Goenka. 'The contract is still lying in Jaswant Thacker's office. But after Neville Wadia had signed, Nusli baulked. Neville Wadia offered me Rs 5 lakhs to return the contract. Pallonji Mistry assured me that if the matter came to court, he would vouch for the legality of the sale and the presence of the contract. Like an idiot I told Neville: "If you offer me a drink, I'm prepared to cancel the deal." He rushed off to get the finest bottle of Royal Salute. But I was an idiot. There is no room for emotions in business.'

Pressure on Goenka to pull out of the deal came from other sources also. Among them J.R.D. Tata, who rushed to Nusli's rescue. The childless Tata's affection for Nusli was well known, as was his estrangement from Pallonji Mistry, a construction magnate whose shareholding in Tata Sons, a core holding company, was larger than that of the Tatas themselves. Mistry owned 40 per cent of Nowrosjee Wadia & Co, which in turn controlled 7 per cent of Bombay Dyeing.

Fortified by Tata's backing, Nusli drummed up support from within the company. He mustered 11 per cent of Bombay Dyeing's equity, some of it from his sister and their mother Dina, who were equally aghast at the prospect of Wadia losing his inheritance. The management cadre rallied round him and about 700 officers signed a joint statement saying they had saved money for a rainy day and were willing to offer this for buying the company's shares. The company union declared its intention to back the young master. With these four aces in his hand, Nusli flew to London for a showdown with his father. Goenka and the two Wadias met at the Ritz, a landmark on Piccadilly and Indira Gandhi's favourite hotel, where Neville was staying. Meanwhile, in India, JRD warned senior government and Reserve Bank officials that he would lead a public campaign if the government did not stop the sale from going through.

Did the controversial deal split businessmen along community lines? According to the *Business Standard,* a 'number of Parsi businessmen [came together] in Bombay to prevent a Marwari takeover of a Parsi concern'. Goenka shrugs off the comment. If there had been any anti-Marwari feeling, respected Parsis such as Pallonji Mistry and Pettigara of Mulla & Mulla would not have supported us.'

Later successes such as the acquisition of Ceat Tyres and Calcutta Electric Supply Company (CESC) have made Goenka philosophical about the petering out of the Bombay Dyeing bid. At the time, his failure rankled. In a sense, the abortive offer symbolized the stagnant phase the group was passing through in the '70s. In the '60s, Keshav Prasad and his three sons had acquired several mills and established a beachhead in Bombay through Asian Cables. This decade saw few accomplishments apart from the takeover of the B. N. Elias group of companies. RP felt stifled and wanted to set up his own office, independent of his brothers. In the process, he engineered the splintering of the entire Duncan Group.

'The separation was requested by me. My brothers did not want it. Both argued against it,' says RP. The friction among his three sons about the direction and pace of growth threw Keshav Prasad into a deep depression. The constant bickering wore Keshav Prasad down until he finally yielded. Some time in early 1979, at his opulent flat on Bombay's Carmichael Road, the disheartened father drew up three lists. He called in his youngest son, Gouri, showed him the three columns, and asked him to take his pick. Jagdish, the middle son, chose next. The last list was given to RP. In twenty minutes, fifteen companies with an estimated combined asset base of Rs 1.45bn changed hands. Each felt he had been given the short end of the stick.

Particularly RP. Mingled with regret, however, was relief. He could now put his past aside and start afresh. From now on, he wouldn't have to consider anybody else's sensibilities but his own, trust no one else's judgement but his own. He was free to make his own deals.

All through his childhood, RP had lived with the fact that Jagdish was their father's favourite. After joining the family firm, arguments with Keshav Prasad had become a daily affair. It seemed to RP that Keshav Prasad would scrutinize his proposals far more rigorously than those of his brothers. The tense relationship between father and son spilled over, souring RP's relationship with his brothers. The year 1963 was an especially difficult period for RP. He had spent considerable energy on a shipping proposal which his father scuttled.

'The government had given us permission to put together a fleet of twelve ships. Not that I was thinking in terms of all twelve, but Cochin Refineries had agreed to use three tankers. The scheme would have paid itself back in three years. My father was conservative. He wanted the money back in two and a half years, and the scheme fell through. I was having differences with my father at the time,' says RP with classic understatement.

RP's love for politics and politicians was another bone of contention both with his father and with his brothers. In 1966,

Indira Gandhi offered RP a place on the Planning Commission. Excited, RP nonetheless asked, 'Do I get twenty-four hours to respond?' Back home Keshav Prasad and his brothers shot down the idea. 'They said it was *bakwas* [nonsense].' As a member of a joint family, RP had no choice but to turn down the prime minister. Recounting the incident clearly brought back unpleasant memories. RP's voice hardened and for a few moments the thread of our conversation was lost as he stared ahead of him.

RP's loyalty to Mrs Gandhi during the Emergency and after the Congress debacle in 1977 exacerbated family tensions. 'While she was in power, sometimes we were out of favour and things would not go well, but equally something good would also happen. But when she was out of power in 1977-79, only the bad was noticed,' recalls RP bitterly.

Continuous sniping convinced RP that he was better off striking out on his own. He suspected that his two sons would have no future were he to remain in a joint family. 'By 1979, I was absolutely clear in my mind that nothing would induce me to stay.' Jagdish and Gouri were unprepared for RP's obduracy. They offered him a bigger slice of the family pie. 'They even said we are prepared to give you more work, more authority,' says RP with a cynical smile. The offer amounted to rubbing salt into an open wound. A few years earlier, without any explanation or warning, Keshav Prasad had summarily removed RP from the management of Anglo-India Jute Mills and handed it over to Jagdish. It was the biggest jute mill in the world under one roof, and RP would suffer considerable loss of face from the demotion.

After 1979, RP was a driven man. Though all three brothers tried to maintain a façade of cordiality, the battle lines had been drawn. Each was determined to establish a bigger corporate empire than the other. Franker than his brothers,

Gouri openly threw down the gauntlet. 'The question to be asked is: Ten years hence, which horse will win?'

According to the terms of the settlement drawn up by Keshav Prasad, all three brothers started out with a clutch of companies totalling roughly the same sales turnover: Rs 750 m. Each group contained a carbon black company, an input in tyre manufacturing and an industry in which the Goenkas held over 60 per cent of market share. Otherwise the companies in each group varied hugely in terms of profitability and potential.

RP's leftovers consisted of Phillips Carbon Black, Asian Cables and two duds (Agarpara Jute and Murphy India). Jagdish picked the textile interests and Anglo-India Jute. The prize, Duncan Agro Industries, went to Gouri. Both RP and Jagdish felt this keenly. The tea and cigarette manufacturer, with assets of Rs 540m, was 'an industrial status symbol like Birla's Century [and] the only Goenka company to figure in the list of one hundred top private sector companies,' according to *Business Standard*.

The split freed RP and he became more entrepreneurial. 'When we were together, the desire for business was not greater. But I was more careful. I think there is more adventurism in me now,' Goenka says. 'Also, when you are on your own, you can make faster decisions.'

And fleet-footed he was. Selling off Agarpara Jute to generate some cash, RP went shopping. His first purchase was Ceat Tyres of India in 1981, acquired just in time for RP to head its silver anniversary celebrations. It was then India's third biggest tyre company after Modi Tyres and Dunlop India. Profitable, rich with cash reserves and real estate, well-run and possessing strong brand equity, it was a dream company. A subsidiary of Italy's Ceat, it came on the market because the parent company was in a financial bind. Yet there were no takers.

Ceat Tyres of India was first offered to the Tatas, the company's original promoters. Moreover there was some synergy between the tyre manufacturer and Telco, the Tata Group's truck company. Telco's chairman, Sumant Moolgaokar, however, was uninterested and so it appears was J.R.D. Tata. When the Tatas turned it down, it was then offered to the Modis, an aggressive Delhi-based group who had entered the tyre business in 1971, but the Modis were in no position to purchase it. Modi Rubber was still overcoming teething problems.

Other possible buyers were put off by the uncertainty in the tyre business. During the '60s, tyres had commanded huge premiums, encouraging large investments in this sector. By the next decade, installed capacity had shot up. At the same time, the prices of raw materials had ballooned in the wake of the oil crisis of the mid-'70s. Overnight the premiums vanished. Ceat Tyres of India's future was bright but its prospects were decidedly chancy. Unperturbed, Goenka snapped it up. The deal, signed and sealed in Turin, Ceat's headquarters, was so discreet that not a ripple was felt in India.

Even after documents were exchanged, the only information which either party would release in India was that various investment companies belonging to Goenka had bought 11 per cent of Ceat Tyres of India's equity for Rs 205 per share (or Rs 12m); and that its 39 per cent foreign holding was still held by its Italian parent. The Goenkas would, however, manage the company, and on October 15, 1981, Harsh joined the board as a director. The share's market price was hovering around Rs 195. The announcement immediately aroused considerable speculation about why the Italians had virtually gifted the management of the company to the Goenkas. That question remains unanswered till today, though the Goenkas are known to have strengthened their holding.

Goenka's gutsy decision more than paid off. The parting from the parent company galvanized its Indian managers into performing better. RP was also lucky. The sector turned the corner. Once Ceat Tyres of India (later renamed as simply Ceat Ltd) started performing exceptionally well, Goenka had no hesitation in dipping into its impressive reserves. He bought KEC (in1982), Searle India (1983), Dunlop (1984, in partnership with Manu Chhabria), Bayer (1985, a minority stake which was subsequently sold off), and HMV (1988). The year 1989 was particularly spectacular for India's hungriest takeover specialist. Analysts watched breathlessly as he swallowed up a power company, two plantations and a computer hardware concern (CESC, Harrisons Malayalam, Spencer & Co. and ICIM).

These acquisitions added almost Rs 10bn to group sales of Rs 7.7bn in 1988, and propelled RPG Enterprises up from thirteenth to fourth rank in terms of size.

The 1979 split had left Goenka with a Rs 700m group. In 1992, RPG Enterprises joined the $1bn club (Rs 33bn). By 1995, group sales were Rs 45bn with profits of Rs 7bn.

GOOD PALS

Each victory whetted RP's appetite for more. In June 1982, Goenka started stalking Premier Automobiles Ltd (PAL).

At the time, PAL did not make very modern cars. In fact, its mainstay was the Padmini, an outmoded version of Italy's Fiat 1100, of 1966 vintage. It was also an unprofitable company, saddled with large debts. But until Maruti started churning out Suzukis, the Walchand group company was one of India's two car producers (the other being Hindustan Motors). And Goenka wanted to join the exclusive club.

Initially, having a go at PAL wasn't even a remote option in RP's mind. On the contrary he was mulling over setting up a new car factory. The idea and the ambition developed out of a chance meeting between Harsh and Giovanni Agnelli, chairman of Italy's Fiat. 'I was in London at that time. Harsh had gone to Turin, to Ceat's headquarters. There he met the chairman of Fiat, which also has its head office in Turin. The Fiat chairman offered Harsh know-how for a small car which they didn't want to give Premier. So Harsh got a letter to that effect from Fiat. With that we went to the IDBI office in Bombay. IDBI suggested that we join the board of Premier itself. With that letter from Fiat and the assurance of a seat on the board from IDBI, we thought why not take over Premier?' says Goenka.

Father and sons sat down to do their homework. The Life Insurance Corporation (LIC) held the biggest block of PAL's equity: 14.5 per cent or 115,000 shares. Within days of a meeting between Goenka and the LIC chairman, 28,000 shares were sent to PAL's share department for transfer from LIC to Ceat Finance and Ceat Investments. More were picked up from the market, bringing Goenka's holding to 8 per cent.

It was only then that alarm bells started ringing in Construction House, PAL's magnificent head office at Ballard Estate in Bombay. 'We were completely taken by surprise. We did not know what hit us,' says Vinod Doshi, the pipe-smoking, actor-industrialist who was elevated to PAL's chairmanship by his father. Doshi panicked. Collectively the Walchand group held 56,000 shares or a perilously low 7 per cent of PAL's equity. Collectively, financial institutions such as LIC, IDBI and the Unit Trust of India held 30 per cent. How much had LIC agreed to sell to Goenka? Who else would follow LIC's lead?

Sustained buying pressure by the Goenkas pushed PAL's stock up by almost 28 per cent in September 1982 and by early October, speculators in Bombay's towering new stock exchange building got wind of the takeover attempt. On October 5, the PAL scrip zoomed from Rs 395 to Rs 429. As its AGM approached on December 20, the air of panic and gloom in Construction House was almost palpable. Advertisements appeared nationally, listing the achievements of the management. Individual shareholders were approached for their support in case a proxy war broke out.

The Walchand family closed ranks. Vinod Doshi's job was to stall the transfer of Goenka's share purchases. Ajit Gulabchand, Doshi's cousin and chairman of the Hindustan Construction Company, flew to Pune to get Rahul Bajaj, the wel-connected and influential head of India's biggest scooter company, on their side. If Bajaj refused, Gulabchand would check whether Bajaj would act as mediator. His second task was to raise Rs 25m to cover share purchases from the market. But the role of Sharayu Daftary, Doshi's sister, was the most sensitive.

Shortly before the AGM, Daftary had paid Indira Gandhi a visit. After she left, an annoyed prime minister summoned Goenka to Delhi and ordered him to call off the takeover. He was not to disturb the company as it belonged to a freedom fighter.

Promising Mrs Gandhi that 'Lalchandji will not be disturbed in any way', Goenka left her private sitting room, went straight to R.K. Dhawan's room and phoned Harsh to double his holding. 'She did not ask me not to buy. The only assurance was that Lalchandji should not be disturbed,' he says without a blink.

What had really put Goenka's back up was the realization that the Doshis doubted his word. Two days previously, Goenka had met Vinod at Neela House, the Doshi family's mansion on Carmichael Road. Over a couple of drinks—'something special which comes in a cut glass bottle'—RP promised Vinod that he would call off his bid. So when Mrs Gandhi summoned him, Goenka was taken aback. 'Vinod and I spoke just two day ago! I have never gone back on my word. Now I wanted them to feel the presence of RP in Bombay, their very own city.'

As PAL's share price climbed, Doshi frantically kept up a hectic campaign to strengthen his position in the company. Goenka received phone calls from the Birlas, the Tatas and even Sharad Pawar, Maharashtra's chief minister, asking him to call off his bid. Only after Bajaj pacified them did emotions finally cool down. At Bajaj's insistence, Goenka agreed to sell his PAL shares at cost. 'We had to bear all the charges, so actually we sold them at a slight loss, but we had accepted Bajaj as a mediator and if that is what he ruled, we had to obey it,' said Goenka. A grateful Doshi heaved a sigh of relief.

Why did Goenka pull out at the crucial moment? The meeting with Doshi was almost a replay of Goenka's meeting with Neville Wadia in the 1969 bid for Bombay Dyeing. What made him change his mind and call off the attack? 'Peer pressure, maybe. I don't think India is ready for hostile takeovers. Which raids have succeeded? Strictly speaking, all the companies we acquired have been buy-outs,' Goenka explains. There was a willing seller in every company he seriously wanted. The only obstacles to his success were other bidders. In the Indian context, takeover skills mean getting a whiff of an upcoming sale before others, fending off rivals, astute pricing, and political muscle to obtain government clearances.

'MY THIRD SON'
Another businessman who has had occasion to cross swords with Goenka is Manohar Rajaram Chhabria. A trim Sindhi electronics trader from Dubai, Chhabria is proud of his

rags-to-riches story as the boy from Bombay's Lamington Road who made good in West Asia. For a brief moment during the 1982 Asian Games in New Delhi, the promoter of Jumbo Electronics held the title of the biggest Sony dealer in the world. In the mid-'80s, Chhabria stormed India's corporate citadel with a string of audacious takeovers. Each buy-out helped fund the next. By 1990, he had carved out a Rs 15bn empire. As his juggernaut moved on, M&A specialists shuttled between Goenka and Chhabria.

Nobody knows which of the two tycoons was first offered the Dunlop India deal. The only person who knew the answer died shortly after the sale was completed. He was Brijesh Mathur, a London-based banker with ANZ Grindlay, who had been given the mandate to get a buyer for the tyre manufacturer—India's eleventh largest company in the private sector—by its UK parent. Mathur engineered a curious partnership. The earliest indication of the secret conclaves in London was a bland announcement in mid-December 1984 that UK's Dunlop Holdings plc had sold 9.8 per cent of its share in Dunlop India to Chhabria and Sanjiv Goenka. Chhabria moved in as Dunlop India's new chairman; Sanjiv, then barely twenty-five, as deputy managing director.

In the small, incestuous circle of India's business elite, the news was greeted with startled disbelief for there could not be two more dissimilar men than R.P. Goenka and Manu Chhabria. If at all they share anything in common, it is a love of takeover roulette. Goenka is the quintessential Marwari aristocrat with a dash of Bengali culture while Chhabria is marked and moulded by his past. The contrast was specially evident at Goenka's sophisticated soirées, where Chhabria would often have to curb his pungent vocabulary and short temper while socializing or talking to Sushila, RP's soignée wife.

So why did Goenka tie up with Chhabria? Simply put, Goenka needed him. Apart from chipping in with hard cash, Chhabria's involvement would help overcome foreign exchange (FERA) and anti-trust legislation (MRTP) restrictions. As an NRI with considerable financial assets overseas, Chhabria could easily work out an offshore deal with Dunlop Holdings without any questions being asked. The MRTP was another landmine. Ceat's market share was 17 per cent. With Dunlop India, the Goenkas' share would top 35 per cent. RP was worried that rivals would work through the MRTP Commission to scuttle his bid for the Calcutta-based company as Jyoti Basu (West Bengal's communist chief minister), was already threatening to do so.

Some years later, while working on the Haldia Petrochemicals project, Goenka would establish a close rapport with Basu. At the time of the Dunlop deal, however, Basu regarded Goenka as just another Marwari industrialist who had abandoned West Bengal for Maharashtra. In August of 1984, Basu wrote to Indira Gandhi: 'In case the R.P.Goenka group succeeds in acquiring Dunlop (India), they will enjoy virtual monopoly in an industry which is a part of the vital transport sector.' He suggested instead that it be acquired by the state-owned Tyre Corporation of India.

During their short-lived partnership, Goenka affectionately referred to Chhabria—then thirty-eight—as his third son. The only problem was, few believed him. Shortly after acquiring Ceat, Goenka had told everybody that he was scouting around for a big company for Sanjiv to manage. Each of his sons should have a 'metropolitan base' from which they could spread their wings. After bagging Dunlop India, RP made no secret of his satisfaction. Harsh would have Ceat Tyres in Bombay, Sanjiv would run Dunlop India in Calcutta. But where would that leave Chhabria? Goenka's intimate title 'son' for his Sindhi partner began to sound stretched.

Trouble between the two billionaires would ignite a couple of years later. During the early days of the partnership, Chhabria would be too busy waging a protracted legal battle for Shaw Wallace to spare time for Dunlop India. After pocketing the liquor giant, he began looking at his investment in the tyre industry, and found much to dismay him. He took particular exception to Sanjiv sanctioning advances from cash-rich Dunlop India to RPG group companies but refusing loans for Orson Electronics, a Chhabria group company. At one stage Chhabria demanded the head of Dunlop India's chief financial officer, a demand that Sanjiv ignored.

The relationship between the two powerful men dipped further as Chhabria stopped looking up to the (physically shorter) Goenka. A subtle shift in the balance of personal equations also took place. Earlier, the association was mutually beneficial. Goenka had needed Chhabria to clear the legal hurdles in the Dunlop India takeover. As a newcomer to the Indian business and political environment, Chhabria had required Goenka to guide him through the pitfalls of North and South Block.

Initially Chhabria had found the going tough in a country where business deals are greased by political intrigue. His attempts to obtain clearance for his half of Dunlop India's equity are a perfect example of his difficulties. According to one observer, he couldn't get official clearance 'because of a red signal from the finance ministry'. In contrast, the Reserve Bank of India swiftly cleared Goenka's half of the purchase.

Chhabria was impressed by Goenka's political contacts. RP had published a book on Indira Gandhi, *Indira Priyadarshini*, and was friendly with her kitchen cabinet. He knew all the right politicians, bureaucrats and businessmen. By 1986, however, Chhabria had more or less found his way round

New Delhi's minefields and no longer needed Goenka's introductions.

'From being my son, he became my *chacha* [uncle] ,' quipped RP. Did he feel used? 'No. No one asked me to do it. I volunteered. So I should not feel bad about it. The only person to blame is myself.' At the heart of their falling-out was the question of who should change gears in the new turbo-charged Dunlop India.

The mud-slinging worsened as 'people close to the Chhabrias' and 'Goenka group insiders' began leaking stories of boardroom battles and behind-the-scenes tussles. The most public power tussle was over the appointment of Dunlop's managing director. The British incumbent retired on May 20, 1987. At Dunlop India's AGM in June, a shareholder suggested that under Sanjiv's stewardship, it had 'moved ahead and he should be elevated to the post of managing director'. Chhabria prevaricated. 'A decision would be taken soon,' he promised. Since he was obviously not going to be appointed MD, Sanjiv tried to abolish the post. He dropped this bombshell at a press conference—about which Chhabria claimed he was not informed—ostensibly called to announce Dunlop India's half-year results.

In hindsight, perhaps neither RP nor Sanjiv should have been surprised by Chhabria's urge to get his hands on the wheel. The ink had barely dried on contracts drawn up in 1984 when Chhabria had warned, 'It is not my intention to be an ornamental chairman.' Yet that was exactly how the Goenkas treated him. Gradually he 'began to demand [his] pound of flesh'.

Goenka claims it was never agreed that Chhabria would manage the company on a day-to-day basis. He points out that Chhabria had not objected when Dunlop India's British ex-chairman and managing director had welcomed Sanjiv as the man 'who will look after current operations'. 'But now, having tasted blood after acquiring Shaw Wallace and some other companies, he had got too ambitious.' As the rift widened, there was a patch-up attempt. The ensuing management reshuffle did little more than postpone the eventual partition by a few months.

Operationally, Dunlop India's performance was on the mend. In 1984, the Indian tyre industry was in the doldrums and so was Dunlop India. Its sales then were an impressive Rs 2.95bn but profits had dwindled to twenty million or so. When other Indian tyre companies started doing well, Dunlop did better. By 1988, sales were Rs 5.23bn; the bottom line, a healthy Rs 942.4m. International recognition followed. The *European Rubber Journal's* 1987 league ranked Dunlop India as the world's 28th largest rubber company. USA's Dunlop Tire was in 20th place.

Despite the kudos Dunlop India and Sanjiv were earning, by late June 1988 RP felt the time had come to cut free. 'Life for Sanjiv was getting very difficult,' he says. The Goenka trio unanimously felt that a slanging match with Chhabria was not worth it. Despite the loss of face, they would give up the prize. But on their terms.

In early July, Goenka went to London, ostensibly for a tooth operation. Harsh and Sanjiv joined him. Root canal treatment is always painful, but the dentist's drilling would be nothing compared to the drastic surgery about to take place at Dunlop. When Chhabria flew into London to meet them, he had no inkling of their intentions. An informal auction was set up: the highest bidder would get full control of Dunlop India. A select panel of bankers, lawyers and tax consultants declared Chhabria the winner. The Lamington Road boy had scored over Alipore's blue blood.

Or had he? A victorious Chhabria should have felt elated.

Instead, he was smarting. There was too wide a margin between the two bids. Chhabria realized too late that he had been adroitly led into stuffing a few extra millions into the Goenka coffers. The master strategist had struck again. In 1984, the financial media had speculated that the Dunlop buy-out must have cost the duo £7.5m each. Four years later, *Business India* pegged Chhabria's bid at between £30-37m.

Apart from Sanjiv's day-to-day hassles with Chhabria, there was a second, hidden, reason behind the Goenkas' desire to cut free from Dunlop. RP strongly suspected that one of the consequences of their rivalry was the income tax raid on his companies on March 17, 1988.

This raid, unlike the 1977-79 series, was embarrassing because it occurred when the Congress Party was in power. The corporate grapevine sizzled with questions. Why had the prime minister authorized it? What had Goenka done to upset him? It was true that Rajiv Gandhi distrusted Goenka, as he distrusted anyone friendly with R.K. Dhawan and Pranab Mukherjee, Indira Gandhi's confidantes. On the other hand, there was no apparent animosity. Secondly, the then finance minister, Narain Dutt Tiwari, was supposed to be close to Goenka. The business community was stunned by the headlines.

The raid was carried out with military precision. At exactly 8.30 on the morning of Thursday, March 17, a team of 311 income tax officials armed with search warrants and accompanied by colleagues from the anti-evasion wing of the customs, the central excise and the foreign exchange regulation departments simultaneously rapped on the doors of nineteen offices and residences of RP and his brothers in New Delhi, Bombay, Ahmedabad, Baroda, Hyderabad and Ranchi.

At his Prithviraj Road residence in Delhi, RP, not an early riser, was still in his pyjamas. Though surprised by the intrusion, he simply asked for the identity cards of the officials and let them get on with their job. Gouri was in Baroda, getting ready to address the annual general meeting of Gujarat Carbon. Jagdish was in Varanasi. Though RP's brothers received a fair amount of consideration, Sanjiv didn't get off so lightly and was interrogated for ten gruelling hours.

The government raiders spent four days sifting through mountains of paper before calling off the attack on March 21. Every evening they called a press conference to show off their haul of seized share certificates, jewellery and antiques. If the income tax officials had hoped to use the media to destroy Goenka's reputation, the plan misfired. Intimidated, industrialists kept silent, too cowed down to publicly condemn the raid, but the financial press jumped to Goenka's defence.

Business India fired a broadside at the government for turning 'into a bully boy against whom there is no protection', while *Business World* warned that such action 'will be disastrous for the country'. Gandhi was going overboard in his pursuit of populism, suggested Sujoy Gupta, a commentator with the Ananda Bazar Patrika Group of papers. If he wanted the Robin Hood title held by his ex-finance minister V.P. Singh, this was perhaps not the best way to go about it. The Bengali press was even more virulent, describing the attack on Goenka as one more example of the Centre's stepmotherly treatment of the communist state.

A defensive Ajit Kumar Panja, the then revenue minister and a Congressman from Bengal, tried to defuse the situation. Describing the raid as a 'routine action, taken in the 'ordinary course of administration', he insisted that 'searches have to be made to unearth unaccounted money'. In Delhi, the finance ministry defended the investigation, claiming that 'our officers do a lot of homework before we go in for a full raid. It is not a question of taking a sudden decision'. The words had to be gulped back when word spread that in their misplaced enthusiasm, officials had raided Shanti Prasad Goenka, a plywood manufacturer, who had no link whatsoever with RP or his brothers.

Before raids are conducted on any of the big business houses, permission is usually taken from the prime minister and the operation is overseen by the finance ministry. However, S. Venkitramanan, a former head of the Reserve Bank of India and the then finance secretary, claims that Rajiv Gandhi 'did not know that a raid was being planned on RP. He thought they were going to raid Ramnath Goenka'. [Ramnath Goenka (1902-1881) was the head of the Indian Express Group of newspapers, and the *bête noire* of the Gandhi-Nehru dynasty].

According to RP, three men knew and planned the raid. 'These were the revenue secretary, a minister of state, and the income tax investigation secretary. They kept the file away from the finance ministry,' he says. Venkitramanan nods, 'Yes, it's true. Even I didn't know about the raid.'

According to T.N. Ninan, then a reporter with *India Today*, Panja ordered the raid. 'The file reached the income tax headquarters in New Delhi on March 10 and officials placed it before the minister of state for revenue, Ajit Panja. Panja ordered the raid. Finance minister N.D. Tiwari initialled it and the file was sent back to Serla Grewal in the Prime Minister's Secretariat. Within twenty-four hours it came back with instructions that the raid be carried out. Next morning the action began . . . Tiwari was believed to be piqued at having been referred to by someone close to Goenka as being "manageable",' ran Ninan's version.

But why did RP suspect that the raids were a direct consequence of his differences with Chhabria? The clue lay in the choice of companies under investigation. The raid was specific and limited to three carbon black firms. Carbon black is an input in tyre manufacture and collectively, in 1988, the Goenkas controlled 60 per cent of the Rs 1.75bn market. The three companies under fire were Phillips Carbon (run by RP), Oriental Carbon (under Jagdish), and Gujarat Carbon (under Gouri). When the raiders came, they were well armed with detailed information of financial irregularities that would only have been furnished by industry insiders.

At the time, RP and his sons were discreet. Asked about the Chhabria angle, Harsh had said: 'We have an excellent relationship with Chhabria. In fact he was the first to call and offer help.' Nonetheless, RP couldn't resist one pot-shot. In an interview he gave to me for the *Economic Times* a few months after the raid, he declared: 'I am surviving and shall continue to survive—not on others' weaknesses but on my own strength. I will not indulge in actions which are aimed at attacking other businessmen in order to further my own case. I have not done so to date—and God help me not to do so in future.' It would take RP five years to feel comfortable enough to let down his guard: 'Manu is a fighter. If he had lost Dunlop, he would not have missed an opportunity to hurt me anytime, anywhere. So I simply went out. Today the situation in the country is different. I would not be cowed down by him.'

Though Goenka came out of the Dunlop India deal considerably richer, its loss left him bleeding. He needed to buy a big company quickly to repair his prestige and for Sanjiv to manage in order to maintain the balance with Harsh. As he brooded over this predicament, Chander Dhanuka came up with a solution.

A softspoken businessman, Dhanuka is virtually indistinguishable from hundreds of Marwaris like him who work in and around Calcutta's Burra Bazaar. Yet this well-connected, unassuming forty-something deal-maker has pulled off some astonishing deals.

One of these was the takeover of Calcutta Electric Supply Corporation (CESC), a professionally run, independent power generator and distributor. Most of India's power companies are government-owned and run except for a handful, such as the three Tata power companies, Bombay Suburban Electric Supply and CESC.

Dhanuka spent most of 1988 watching the movements of the CESC's scrip. Whenever it dipped, he would place a buy order. His purchases were so discreet that few realized that by early 1989, Dhanuka had collected 12 per cent of its equity. On a bright winter's day in February 1989, Dhanuka went to visit Goenka. Within days of this meeting, Dhanuka's carefully built block of CESC shares silently changed hands.

From RP's point of view, the deal couldn't have been better. On the surface, there was no reason for anyone to fancy the favourite whipping boy of Calcutta's citizens. Not only was it poorly managed, but its returns and dividends were heavily regulated by the government, and its licence would come up for renewal by the year 2000.

Goenka, whose gut instinct so far had never let him down, took a radically different view on the company. It had size, with revenues of over Rs 3bn. It also owned prime real estate whose value was grossly underestimated in its book of accounts. With one stone, he could kill two birds. CESC would fill the void left by Chhabria's driving off with Dunlop; and he could get a toehold into a business with great potential. Plans to open up the power sector to private entrepreneurs were being drawn up by bureaucrats such as S. Rajgopal, the power secretary. It was simply a matter of time before the new policies were announced. By acquiring CESC, Goenka would get in on the ground floor. The price was the real clincher. But the operation would have to be carried out quietly.

Dhanuka was equally pleased. To pull it off, the deal

would require exquisite skill and an impeccable sense of timing. Dhanuka was convinced RP had both. Taking the deal to Goenka rather than the Ruias or the Birlas had been the right choice. Not only did Goenka offer a good price, he was also able to pull off the deal. 'I knew that RP would be able to pull it off. To acquire a company with only a 12 per cent stake requires good contacts, both at the state level and in Delhi. I knew he had them. Seven or eight ministries were involved and he managed everything brilliantly,' says Dhanuka. Thrice before (Ceat, Dunlop, Bayer), RP had managed to establish management control of a company with a mere 10 per cent shareholding. He was confident he could do it again.

At the state level, Goenka's relationship with the Marxist government had undergone a sea change since the day in 1984 when Basu had written to Indira Gandhi advising against Goenka's takeover of Dunlop. In 1991, the Left Front government went out of its way to help comrade Goenka acquire CESC. During the intervening five years, Basu had come to appreciate the portly businessman as they worked together on the Haldia Petrochemicals deal. Gone also were the Naxalite days when journalists commented acidly that 'the Bengali world is that of the Red Star, the Marwaris of the five-star.' From being pariahs, Marwaris and other capitalists had become desirable bridegrooms, assiduously wooed by Basu's Marxist government. Mingled with esteem was some remorse for having eased RP out of the project in favour of Darbari Seth of the Tata group. For a deal of this importance, however, state approval wasn't enough. Goenka needed clearances from the PMO (Prime Minister's Office) and the finance ministry.

And here, Goenka was plain lucky. He was not particularly close to V.P. Singh, who had become prime minister after Rajiv Gandhi lost the 1989 elections, but at the time Goenka embarked on the CESC deal (February 1989), Rajiv Gandhi was still prime minister. And at the sensitive moment when CESC's chairman Bhaskar Mitter was to retire and RP·replace him, once again a Goenka well-wisher was in a pivotal position.

At the time Goenka was sewing up the CESC deal by hiking his shareholding and increasing his fragile·hold on the company, momentous events were taking place in New Delhi. In a craftily engineered coup in the Lok Sabha in November 1990, V.P. Singh was forced to resign and Chandra Shekhar took over the country's reins. It was a short reign (November 10, 1990 to June 21, 1991) but just long enough for Goenka to push through the CESC deal. On his first visit to Calcutta as prime minister, Chandra Shekhar had dropped in for lunch at Goenka's Alipore residence. Bureaucrats picked up the hint without any prompting. Why ask for trouble by stalling the ambitions of the prime minister's old buddy? On February 2, 1991, Goenka took over as CESC's chairman, Bhaskar Mitter became vice-chairman. A smiling Goenka 'gifted' CESC to Sanjiv, and made a quick visit to the temple to thank 'God Almighty'.

When discussing his business, Goenka frequently makes references to 'God Almighty', either thanking him or asking his blessing. He is a devout Hindu who takes his dharma seriously and attributes at least part of his corporate success to it. This is in stark contrast to other industrialists. Most of India's top tycoons pay token homage to religion, but few spend the kind of time, energy and money on their beliefs as does Goenka.

The late Aditya Birla, who used to pray ten minutes a day, believed that 'people who are successful, [find] it easier to see the hand of God'. For Goenka, religion provides strength—and humility. 'Belief in religion gives you self-confidence and, two, it makes you humble. When you believe in God Almighty's power, you realize yourself and your smallness. Humbleness helps in every aspect of life: business, politics and education,' explains Goenka. His religiosity, however, falls short of inducing a desire in him to emulate Birla munificence in terms of endowing charities or building temples, schools, and hospitals for the poor.

A vegetarian like Bajaj and Birla and most Marwaris, Goenka's dharma prevented him from joining hands with Sheraton International and Holiday Inn in the '70s. 'You cannot run five-star deluxe hotels without serving meat. We cannot be in the hotel business,' he had told them politely while turning them down. Of late, Goenka appears to have shed some inhibitions and become more pragmatic. *Hindutva* scruples didn't prevent him from acquiring Spencer in 1989. A Madras-based 130-year-old concern, Spencer not only owns and runs a hotel but is planning to set up an export-oriented shrimp farm. It also recently tied up with Wimpy to establish a chain of fast food franchises in south and east India.

Goenka is supposed to be a competent astropalmist and student of astrology, and does *puja* every day. Every *Falgun* (around February), he organizes a lavish *yagna* in the garden of his Prithviraj Road home in Delhi. There are seventy-one priests on his payroll (sixty-five of them in Benaras), praying for him daily, and for the success of his business. 'There is no substitute for doing prayers oneself. But sometimes, it is not possible. So you get others to do it for you,' he says smiling.

His greatest joy is to usher in the new year with a *darshan* of the god Balaji, in the Tirupati temple, of which he used to be a trustee, a position he felt honoured in holding. 'I had done eleven years of trusteeship. When Vijay Bhaskar Reddy became chief minister, he threw me out,' he says emotionlessly. For years, RP has been making an annual pilgrimage to Tirupati, turning it into a picnic for the whole family and a few chosen friends.

The dawn of 1990 was no exception. Well before the sun touched the horizon, thousands of devotees lined the streets leading to the temple. As they waited patiently for hours for their few seconds of *darshan*, Goenka's cavalcade of cars drove up to the temple and gained instant entrance. Once inside, Goenka bowed his head reverentially in front of the god. His prayers were a little more fervent than usual. A 'cherished dream' was turning into a nightmare. He needed divine help to get him out of it.

THE HALDIA HIJACK

Goenka's nightmare began in mid-May 1985 when he became a co-promoter, with the West Bengal Industrial Development Corporation (WBIDC), of a massive naphtha-based petrochemical complex at Haldia, about 200 km south of Calcutta. Goenka knew he was walking into a potential minefield, yet he went ahead anyway.

'It started with a courtesy call I made on Jyoti Basu. In order to sound impressive, I told him I was the chairman of Gujarat Petrochemicals. Jyoti Basu retorted: "What the hell are you doing for West Bengal?" He took the wind out of me. I asked for two days' time, went back to him and told him I was willing to shoulder the responsibility for setting up a petrochemicals complex at Haldia.' The charmingly disingenuous anecdote leaves out a few minor details. West Bengal was desperately looking for a new partner after its old one, the Union government, backed out in July 1984. And casual remarks are not Goenka's style.

Much preparation had gone into RPG Enterprises' proposed entry into petrochemicals. It had become a fashionable field and virtually every big business house was working round the clock to corner one of the half dozen or so projects which the government was likely to offer to the private sector. In the great petrochem race of the '80s were names like Dhirubhaï Ambani, Arvind Mafatlal, Vijay Mallya, Aditya Birla, and Shyam Bhartia.

For Goenka, then almost fifty-five, the Haldia project would become a personal Grail. During the long span of his working life, he had built up an extensive corporate empire but not once had he managed to build a successful factory from grass roots. One of the very few plants which the group built—a Rs 3bn tyre cord factory at Nasik—had to be sold in 1995. Another plant, a Rs 750m polyester staple fibre plant, India Polyfibres, promoted in 1987, wiped out its equity within three years of commercial production. More humiliating was the experience in the shaving blade sector where the Malhotra group nicked RP's Wiltech so badly that it had to be put on the auctioneer's block. Meanwhile several smaller ventures fared little better. Profits in a Rs 190m chemical plant, Cetex Petrochemicals, dipped so low that it had to be merged into the healthier KEC to keep afloat. Two tiny companies to manufacture printed circuit boards, Maple Circuits and Oak India, located in Kashmir, had to stop production because of the poor law and order situation.

The biggest and best companies in his group had all been built by others. Deep inside him RP had a need to be recognized as a greenfield man, in the manner of Aditya Birla or Dhirubhai Ambani with their world-class plants. They had translated their visions into concrete reality. Like them, Goenka wanted to leave a mark of his own. In 1988, he had drawn up a master plan, but none of the projects outlined succeeded.

When the Haldia proposal came up, he seized the opportunity with both hands. It would be the biggest project of his life, and a fitting climax to his career. To free himself for it, he eased away from RPG Enterprises, handing over the reins to Harsh. To the *Economic Times,* he announced: 'Haldia will get my immediate personal attention. . . If it makes my friends in the corporate sector feel reassured, I would like to make it very clear that I am no longer in the takeover game.'

When Goenka offered to shoulder Haldia Petrochemicals, Basu accepted the gesture gratefully. It was a project close to his heart but nobody else seemed much interested in it. The original letter of intent had been signed on November 11, 1977, but so far the West Bengal government had been unable to get vital clearances from the finance ministry and the IDBI. Goenka, with his connections at the Centre, might be able to push the right buttons and get the project off the drawing boards. Unfortunately, this didn't happen. Every time the two partners crossed one hurdle, another took its place. The frustrating delays sparked political bluster.

For example, on February 20, 1986, Nirmal Bose, the then state commerce and industry minister, charged the Centre with 'stalling' the project by delaying the approval of its product mix. He asked Left Front members of Parliament to take up the issue in the Lok Sabha. Seven months later (September 1986), the Centre cleared six foreign technical tie-ups. Nothing more happened for months. As tempers rose in Calcutta, Basu went to meet V.P. Singh, then finance minister, who promised to look into the matter. Still nothing happened. Basu griped that the 'government that works' [Rajiv Gandhi's famous slogan] should 'work a little more' on speeding up Haldia. The only palliative V.P. Singh offered was that the finance ministry's attack on Goenka's unpaid excise dues would have no negative effect on the project.

After Narayan Dutt Tiwari took over from Singh, Basu trekked to Delhi once again. Tiwari, an old friend of Goenka's, promised Basu on January 19, 1988 that the finance ministry would clear the project within ten days. Three months later, Basu grumbled that Delhi was still 'sitting on the file'. In April 1988, the Haldia question came up in the Lok Sabha. Had the Rajiv Gandhi administration given or not given all the permissions? Forty-four MPs belonging to various political parties urged Gandhi to clear it. Under pressure, the finance ministry approved its first phase on September 29, 1988.

Haldia's real hurdle was money. None of the three players had cash on the table: not Goenka, not WBIDC, nor the Left Front. Also, the project kept expanding like hot air in a balloon. The cracker's size more than doubled and additional downstream units were added to the blueprint. This, along with delays, hiked its cost from Rs 4.28bn in 1977, to Rs 10bn in 1985, and Rs 30bn in 1990. Banks didn't want to lend because they were unsure of its viability, and the Centre didn't want to commit its funds.

It was understandable, then, that Basu was astounded to learn that Rajiv Gandhi wanted to lay the project's foundation stone on October 15, 1989.

Smelling a rat but not quite sure where it was, Basu laid down conditions at a dinner hosted by Rajiv in Delhi on September 14. Among them was a commitment in writing that the Centre would take positive steps to clear Haldia Petrochemicals' funding. Gandhi agreed and on October 9, Gopi Arora (the finance secretary), met the financial institutions to hurriedly sort out the issue. On October 14, Buta Singh (the Union home minister) handed over the formal letter to Basu. Later that evening, Basu and Gandhi flew to Calcutta together. At the stone-laying ceremony on the 15th, the Congress tricolour and the CPM's red flag fluttered together in the wind. Next morning, newspapers were full of photographs of the two leaders standing chummily next to each other.

Two days later, Gandhi announced fresh Lok Sabha elections. A disgusted Basu realized that the stone-laying ceremony had been nothing more than an election gimmick to woo the Bengali voter.

In the photographs, Gandhi looked relaxed, Basu sombre and Goenka, glum. The cause of Goenka's unhappiness was Dhirubhai Ambani. Goenka's sensitive political antenna had picked up rumours that Ambani was about to pounce on Haldia. This would put Goenka squarely between a rock and a hard place. Taking on Ambani wasn't a prospect Goenka relished in the slightest but he had worked too long and too hard on the project to give it up without a murmur.

According to a friend, Basu's willingness to tie up with Ambani hurt Goenka to the quick. He couldn't believe that Basu could jettison him, not after all they had gone through over the past four years. Basu's point of view was that *even* after four years, Goenka had not been able to deliver. The Ambanis might do better. Basu had dropped hints of his disillusionment on earlier occasions but Goenka had failed to notice them. For example, after the 1988 raid on Goenka, Basu had told the state assembly that he was ready to sacrifice Goenka if keeping him meant jeopardizing Haldia.

Describing Goenka, a Calcutta industrialist once told *India Today*: 'You never know where exactly you stand with RP. He could be cutting your throat, but you won't know it till the knife is halfway across your neck.' This time, Goenka was at the receiving end. Ambani moved so discreetly that at first Goenka was not entirely sure that his suspicions were correct.

Ambani's name began to crop up sporadically in a seemingly casual manner. Soon after the stone-laying ceremony, Ambani hosted a private dinner for Basu in Delhi. It was the beginning of several rounds of talks in Bombay and Delhi where the Ambanis declared their interest in Haldia.

Arora's official letter of recommendation to the Left Front
came shortly before Rajiv Gandhi lost the 1989 general
elections.

From being a king on the chessboard, Goenka was reduced
to a pawn in the infinitely bigger game between Gandhi and
Basu. In 1988 a West Bengal minister at the Centre had
allegedly suggested to the prime minister that he should 'catch
Goenka to teach Jyoti Basu a lesson'. About a year later, in
October 1989, according to Indranil Ghosh of the *Indian
Express*, when Gandhi asked Arora to hammer out a new
financial package through the IDBI, 'he also asked Mr Arora
to ensure there was no change of the private sector partner for
the complex. Clearly he did not want to provide the Opposition
with a stick to beat him with before the election. So Mr Goenka
remained untouched.' Ambani had to wait.

The unsettling moves wore down Goenka's enthusiasm,
and he admitted as much to a friend. 'I do not want to stand in
the crossfire between the Centre and the state government. I
stood there for three years but since last year, I have been
feeling that my bravado is not worthwhile,' he said.

Late in the evening of Wednesday, December 13, Mukesh
Ambani arrived in Calcutta with the late Suresh Shankar
Nadkarni, IDBI's chairman and the first banker to be awarded
the Padma Bushan, in tow. The next morning they met Dr Asim
Dasgupta, the MIT-educated teacher of economics-turned-
politician and the then state finance minister, who welcomed
them with open arms. Ambani laid down his terms: Reliance
wanted four downstream units. Goenka would be left with the
remaining four as well as the mother cracker. A *Business
Standard* headline described the offer thus: 'Ambanis take the
cake, RPG gets the crumbs'. Crackers don't make money,
downstream units do, and the four units which the Ambanis
wanted were more profitable than the rest.

Meanwhile, Basu made one last-ditch attempt to persuade Goenka to accept Reliance as co-promoters. Dasgupta kept badgering both RP and Sanjiv but the Goenkas would not budge. To Basu, they cited their 'bitter experience with a partner' [i.e., Chhabria] as an excuse against the tie-up.

In anticipation of some fireworks, newsmen waiting on the steps of Writer's Building hounded Goenka for a reaction after Mukesh Ambani had driven off. Unusually laconic, Goenka briefly commented that 'if the state government wants us to work together, we have no alternative' and that 'as long as Jyoti Basu is there, no one can edge us out'. Not a man to be shafted without a tussle, Goenka had already formulated a rearguard action plan.

On the eve of Mukesh Ambani's visit, on December 10, BJP leaders called a press conference to allege that the Ambanis had roped in Chandan Basu, the chief minister's son, to put pressure on his father to oust Goenka from the Haldia Petrochemicals project. According to the *Independent* report, the BJP demanded that the Left Front government spell out Chandan Basu's role. Priya Ranjan Dasmunshi, who had been Rajiv Gandhi's commerce minister, added his voice to the outcry. He promptly wrote to V.P. Singh, who had just taken over as prime minister, asking him to investigate the BJP's allegation of 'favouritism and nepotism'. The accusation stung Jyoti Basu, as Goenka had known it would. Basu immediately threw open the downstream units to the highest bidder.

The day Mukesh Ambani met Basu, Viren Shah, chairman of Mukand, was seen having dinner with the chief minister. The next morning Shah and his sons, Rajesh and Sukumar, 'dazzled' Dasgupta and Tarun C. Dutt, the state's chief secretary, with their audio-visual presentation and willingness to invest Rs 10bn in West Bengal.

The next day saw the arrival of Mohan Lal Mittal, head of

the Rs 12bn Mittal Group, and his son, P.K. Mittal. Dasgupta spread out the welcome mat for them also. Mittal wanted Ambani's four downstream ventures, and said he was willing to invest between Rs 20m to 20bn in the project. The third day saw more hopefuls trooping in. Apart from Goenka, Ambani, Shah, and Mittal, there was B.M. Khaitan of Williamson Magor, Gouri Prasad Goenka of Duncans Agro, Bharat Hari Singhania of JK Industries, and Raunaq Singh of Apollo Tyres.

There was a new circus in town. Reporters covering the state government's secretariat had a hard time keeping track of prospective investors. Unfamiliar with the names and faces of businessmen who for years had avoided West Bengal like the plague, journalists buttonholed anybody who wore an expensive looking business suit. Visiting bureaucrats were mistaken for industrialists and grilled. There were as many gaffes inside the building as outside. A local businessmen remarked cynically: 'I will be damned if all those interested in Haldia Petrochemicals are really in love with the state as they claim to be. Some of them probably wouldn't be able to say which side of Calcutta Haldia lies on.'

It wasn't long before the press sniffed out Goenka's role as ringmaster. Gouri Goenka was RP's youngest brother, and Khaitan was RP's closest friend. Shah admitted 'having written to the Goenkas nearly two months back exploring the possibilities of a downstream unit at Haldia'. Mittal expressed his solidarity with Goenka: 'We are not going to compete with the RPG group which has initiated this prestigious project. But we will be happy to supplement RP-ji's efforts at implementing it.' Describing himself as RP's 'dear friend', Raunaq Singh said he was 'waiting for Rama to make an offer and discuss the feasibility of the projects'. Goenka's strategy was beautiful in its simplicity: if he had to have a partner, it was better to have two rather than one powerful one like Ambani, and better yet to have three, if not four. As the head of a consortium, he would be able to keep the project under his thumb.

Dasgupta and the other bureaucrats were overjoyed at the interest. For twelve years nobody had wanted Haldia and now there was a queue of at least eight suitors. Taking advantage of the situation, the Left Front government demanded a dowry. No one would get four downstream units. RP might get three, but the others would have to be content with one apiece. And the lucky fiancés would have to help revive selected sick units such as Scooters India or Titagarh Paper, for instance. Or make fresh investments in the state. Still no one baulked or withdrew.

More experienced than his administrators, the wily chief minister tried to maintain a distance from the noisy circus. He refused to talk about Haldia and when he did, he was cryptic, peremptory and dismissive. Basu took a shortlist to Delhi and offered the selection to the Centre. V.P. Singh threw the ball right back into Basu's court in their meeting in early January 1990. Basu then passed the matter to Dasgupta and Subrata Ganguli, the head of Indian Petrochemicals, the government-run Baroda-based petrochemical giant.

Officially, the policy was that co-promoters would be selected on their ability to attract foreign resources both as equity and loan; and on their financial strength and track record in implementing capital intensive projects and absorbing technology. There was no doubt that the Ambanis met these criteria. However, they were keen to commission the downstream units before the mother plant. Reliance's naphtha cracker coming up at Hazira could easily supply Haldia's ethylene feedstock requirements.

Basu preferred a more integrated approach. In fact, both Goenka and the Centre had suggested that the complex be set up in stages, but Basu had always resisted the idea in case the mother cracker never got off the ground.

As the days ticked by, the pressures on Basu and his team to pick a winner from among the contestants multiplied. In the contest between Ambani muscle and RPG stamina, who would win? The answer was Darbari Seth of Tata Tea.

One of J.R.D. Tata's most talented executives, Seth is a man of broad vision and large ambitions. From the mid-'70s the head of Tata Tea and Tata Chemicals had been trying to enter the fertilizer and petrochemical sectors, but none of his plans had worked out. From his office in Bombay House, Seth now kept a watchful eye on events in Calcutta. Finally, the opening he was looking for was at hand. Seth timed his centre-stage entry into the Haldia circus with impeccable finesse.

Basu grasped Seth's hand with the fervour of a drowning man. The Tatas, with their vast resources, seemed eminently capable of implementing Haldia. Basu would be able to easily blunt criticism from his detractors. On January 28, 1990, the WBIDC officially rescinded its May 1985 agreement with Goenka, and signed a fresh pact with Tata Tea. 'That day the tears came out of my eyes. I was the most humiliated person in all of West Bengal,' says Goenka. 'Hah!' says Seth. 'He wants to be a hero. Ask him, didn't I phone him to say that I would take up Haldia only if he turned it down? I call him *Bade Bhaiya*. Could I do that to him?'

Be that as it may, Goenka had the last laugh after all. 'The chief minister took the project away from me and gave it to Darbari Seth. And what happened after three years? I am told Darbari Seth is now *persona non grata* in Writers' Building!' he says with evident satisfaction. After Seth retired, Ratan Tata was left holding the baby. In hindsight, maybe Goenka had received divine help after all. He just didn't realize it at the time.

'MY GUT FEELING'

Like the sultans of old, Goenka's empire touches the lives of ordinary people in countless ways. Switch on a light, sip a cup of tea, have a shave, listen to music, drive to work—and you could be using products and services provided by CESC, Harrisons Malayalam, Wiltech, HMV and Ceat. But today, when it appears to be at a pinnacle, Goenka's empire is perhaps at its weakest moment. Too many of yesterday's strengths are looking like tomorrow's weaknesses.

In the '90s, focusing on core businesses has become the buzzword. Diversity, the staple strategy of the '60s, is no longer considered a strength. RPG Enterprises is an amalgam of haphazard growth and includes tyre companies, pharmaceutical firms, textiles, plantations, hotels, computer hardware businesses, cable manufacturers, a transmission tower outfit: Goenka has bought them all plus a few more. They were acquired by chance, not design, and without even lip-service to concepts of synergy. If a deal was offered at a good price, if the company seemed to be adequately managed, and if he had the money to buy it, Goenka bought it.

He picked some great companies—and some duds. How did he pick them? 'I hear that my sons are more comfortable when they have figures before them, but I have always preferred to listen to people,' says Goenka. He claims he didn't bother to look at Ceat's balance sheet before acquiring it. When the group was about to clinch CESC, he 'tried to study the CESC balance sheet but it was too complicated for me. My gut feeling is my only pathfinder.'

For the first time, Goenka's gut feelings are being questioned. In 1993, Harsh hired McKinsey, the international management consultants, to assess the group's performance and its ability to cope with changes ushered in by the government's liberalization programme. The results of the top secret study were unexpected, uncomfortable and unpalatable.

McKinsey repeated the trite truism that market leaders earn the highest returns. In the case of RPG Enterprises, the group has many companies with impressive sales turnover but none is a leader in its business. The notable exception is a small company called KEC International, manufacturing transmission towers. RP might not have noticed a slowdown in the group's profitability, but stock market punters certainly had. The McKinsey team calculated that the market capitalization of the entire twenty-two-company group was less than that of one Bajaj Auto. As of November 1993, Bajaj Auto's market cap was Rs 24bn, while RPG Enterprises netted Rs 16bn.

Worse was to follow. Because the group had largely grown through the acquisition route, it had not developed any technology of its own. Also, it had a habit of grabbing top-bracket names from other companies rather than building up managers internally. According to the McKinsey team, this was a lethal combination. Technology absorption was low; the companies were only as good as their worst managers; and the group had no intrinsic strengths to fend off competition when the market turned from a sellers' one to a buyers' one, as it was poised to do. In such a scenario, there was little point in leaning on the group's fabulous tie-ups with sixteen Fortune 500 companies. Access to the best technology in the world would not save the group if it did not consolidate.

The group's restructuring process is proving to be more painful than any of the three Goenkas had anticipated. McKinsey suggested that the group concentrate on three core businesses (tyres, power, and agri-business) and three potential core sectors (telecommunications, financial services, and retail services). Keep what fits, and sell off what doesn't. RP accepted the advice reluctantly. He allowed the sale of Ceat's nylon tyre cord division to Arun Bharat Ram of SRF—the unit had been an albatross round Harsh's neck for years and Bharat Ram was willing to pay Rs 3bn for it—but RP had major reservations about trimming the empire. If a company is doing well, why sell it off? It could become another 'potential core', couldn't it?

'I told Harsh and Sanjiv, that just because McKinsey had said something, it does not become a Vedic scripture. Yes, they are wise people, experienced people. Listen to them, but it does not mean that if you differ with them, you can't go your own way. Five years hence, I don't know whether this report will remain relevant or not,' says RP exasperatedly.

Dhirubhai Ambani had once said: 'At Reliance we believe two brains are better than one. We use consultants where necessary, but finally we use our own brains.' Why should RPG Enterprises be any different?

Clearly RP resents being tied down at a point when the government is encouraging private enterprise to blossom in fields which have been off-limits for decades. As a result of this he oscillates between the need to consolidate and the desire to grow. Harsh, like Ratan Tata, is conscious and worried about the need for structured strategic planning and appears to be concerned about his father's enthusiastic response to every opportunity that comes his way. 'Papa finds it very hard to say no. When chief ministers come to him and suggest a project, Papa doesn't say yes, but he doesn't say no also. The next day, we read in the papers that RPG is going to set up such and such thing.'

For the year 2000, RP, Harsh and Sanjiv have set an ambitious target for themselves and RPG Enterprises. The key objective is to ensure that RPG Enterprises retains its position as one of the top five business houses in India. Its corollary is to push the group's market capitalization to Rs 150bn (vis-a-vis Rs 16bn in November 1993). In its push for a leadership role in power, tyres and agri-business, the Goenkas will have to invest Rs 60bn to Rs 100bn over the next six years. From where will the money for all these projects come? Does the group have the resources? RP has been accused of building more castles in the air than on the ground. Are these plans as airy as his petrochemicals projects turned out to be?

Unperturbed by his critics, Goenka smiles. 'To succeed, you need to dream a little,' he says gently. 'Whenever funds have been required, I've always found them. I hope to survive another three to five years. During this time, I will outperform myself. Of this I am sure.'

Chapter 5

Brij Mohan Khaitan

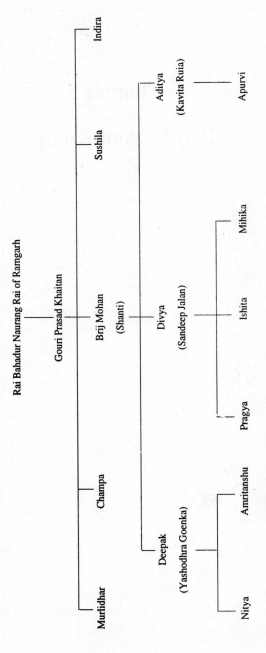

Harrods
Christmas, 1983

On the Saturday before the Christmas of 1983, most of London was out shopping. In the chic Knightsbridge area, Harrods was bursting at the seams. Close to 70,000 people were picking out last-minute gifts and presents from the gorgeous displays. Busily examining pieces of bone china or sampling the latest fragrances from Paris, few noticed the arrival of a police posse at one of its seven entrances. Scotland Yard had been tipped-off that the IRA, an Irish terrorist organization, had planted a bomb either inside or outside the famous building. Firmly and quietly so as to avoid a stampede, the police fanned out, asking shoppers to vacate the four-storied brick structure with its distinctive olive green trim.

Pushing their way through the lunch-time crowd were Brij Mohan Khaitan and Pradip Kumar (Pintu) Khaitan, a cousin and close business associate. They had flown into London that morning for an important meeting with Richard Magor, BM's English partner. Unwilling to arrive empty-handed at Christmas, the Khaitans had dropped into Harrods to pick up a food hamper before driving to the Magors' country house in Sussex.

'At that end of Harrods, where we were, there was no flurry. The police were pushing people towards gate number three. Our car was waiting for us at gate five We didn't know anything about the bomb. The chauffeur took the hamper from us and started putting it in the back. I reached over to the front of the car for my overcoat—it was cold—and Pintu was standing next to me. The time was 1.04 p.m. At exactly 1.05, the bomb went off,' says Khaitan.

A Scotland Yard investigation revealed later that dynamite had been concealed in the car next to the Khaitans' Volvo. Nine people in the immediate vicinity died, but BM and Pradip survived.

'Pintu was very badly hurt, and the driver was half burnt and became blind. Pintu and I were both thrown about twenty yards away, and we were lucky that we didn't fall on the corner of Harrods' show window. We just flew. There were people lying all over the place and the street was white with glass from the windows of all the buildings around. We were unconscious, I don't know for how long. Maybe four or five minutes. I became conscious first. And I saw Pintu lying on the road. Then we could hear some people shouting at the back. I was trying to get up, and they shouted, "Lie down, lie down." I was bleeding, and Pintu was bleeding badly. I patted him on the cheek and said, "Don't worry, we're still living, we aren't dead yet."' BM was no stranger to violence though this incident was the closest the tea baron had come to death's doorstep.

Within ten minutes the two cousins were lifted gently into ambulances. BM, conscious but delirious, was rushed to Westminster Hospital, next to the Houses of Parliament, and Pradip to St. Thomas's. Emergency surgery followed. 'They stitched me up—lots of my pieces were cut—and polished up my nerves. The treatment and service was extraordinary. I was flabbergasted.' He is less happy about the time the British authorities took to contact his wife, Shanti.

'For almost twenty hours, nobody in India knew what had

happened to us,' groused Khaitan. On the radio, Magor heard about the Harrods bomb blast, but naturally didn't link the incident with his guests' non-appearance. It would take him five hours to make the connection. Given the time difference, it was now well past midnight in Calcutta and Magor had to wait until the next morning to call Khaitan's Calcutta office. Shanti was at the Royal Calcutta Turf Club watching a polo match when a messenger finally reached her in the middle of the afternoon. Frantic with worry, she managed to board the evening British Airways flight, arriving at her husband's bedside a little before Margaret.Thatcher, the Archbishop of Canterbury and Princess Diana. A photograph of one of the world's most beautiful women sitting on his bed became a treasured addition to the rich family album.

Richard Magor, for whom Khaitan had purchased the unlucky Harrods food hamper, was a tea planter, and had been one all his life. In 1869, his grandfather, Richard B. Magor, had joined hands with one George Williamson to promote Williamson Magor to manage tea gardens in Assam, and Richard Jr duly took his place when the time came. Commuting between England and India with side trips to Kenya, Richard Jr was the archetypal merchant of the Raj with two pet elephants in his Sussex estate and a wardrobe full of rich shawls. Narrow-chested and long-limbed as are so many of the British aristocracy, with an aquiline intelligent face below a thinning mop of dark hair, under Richard's *zamindari*, the fortunes of the group's Indian tea business fluctuated as wildly as the politics of the age.

Today, the Magor family interests are looked after by Richard's only son, Philip, a geography graduate from Durham University and a chartered accountant, who drinks on average a dozen cups of tea a day, 'mostly of the Assam variety'. Pride in their heritage rings in Philip's voice when he brags :'My son, Edward Charles, who, I hope, will one day look after this business, knows the family business is tea; he's been taught that. The fifth generation of Magors will be here in India.'

Philip's prophecy may well come true, but the Magors have lost the lion's share of the business and now Khaitan is the major shareholder of the world's largest private tea group.

The end of Magor and Williamson rule over thousands of rolling acres of tea gardens more or less coincided with the demise of the British Raj but not before writing a small footnote in world history. During World War II, the company would become the talk of Calcutta's boxwallah society when one of its managers helped blow up three German ships sheltering in the harbour at Goa. The incident was later described in James Leasor's book *The Boarding Party* and in a film, *The Sea Wolves.*

From its small beginnings in 1869 in modest offices at 3 Mangoe Lane in Calcutta's business district, Williamson Magor gradually expanded. A century later, it would manage forty tea estates spread over 35,100 acres and cultivating 14m kg of tea. In the interim, the company shifted next door to No 4, dubbed Hampton Court by expats homesick for rainy grey skies, the river Thames and the British monarchy. In its heyday, Williamson Magor was one of the top three tea managing agency firms in India. It came as no surprise, then, that after Independence, this 'Rolls Royce outfit' came under attack from predatory firms, mostly Indians flexing their new financial muscle. By the late '50s, only eighteen gardens survived.

To protect these, Pat Williamson and Richard Magor, the descendants of the founders, reorganized Williamson Magor's holding pattern, but the business was under-capitalized and until more cash could be found, it would remain vulnerable. According to Khaitan: 'The partners had not been prepared to invest further. The most powerful partners were back in England and were not interested in increasing their holdings in India. The staff they had accumulated was becoming too expensive, their overheads were mounting, the political atmosphere was anathema to them, and they wanted to carry out retrenchments but could not.'

The real crunch came with an attack on Bishnauth Tea, Williamson Magor's flagship. In 1961, B. Bajoria, a shrewd Marwari bania like Khaitan, acquired a threatening 25 per cent equity stake in Bishnauth, a mere 1 per cent short of Williamson Magor's 26 per cent controlling stake. 'This was a turning point,' says Khaitan. If the Brits had lost this estate, it would have had a devastating effect on their interests in Assam.

Richard Magor—who was now more involved in the family's Kenyan plantations—decided the company desperately needed a white knight to pump in funds and fight off Bajoria. Given the wave of Indianization sweeping through British managing agency firms, he felt they too should consider an Indian partner. Looking around him, he chose Khaitan, an earnest and upcoming trader who was supplying them with fertilizer.

FROM BURRA BAZAAR TO *BURRA SAHIB*
Mulling over the offer, the thirty-four-year-old Khaitan figured that a one-third share in Williamson Magor wasn't too bad a deal. Financially the managing agency firm was better off than many others. It was focused, unlike the famous but unwieldy firms such as Martin Burn and Jardines. Its fortunes were partially hedged against nature's vagaries by its wholly-owned warehouses which brought in extra revenue along with the regular agency income and insurance commission. There was also the little matter of prestige. **Many Marwaris were**

cornering British tea gardens and becoming *burra sahibs*. Khaitan accepted. There was one inconvenient fly in the honey pot: Ellermans, a British shipping company which held one-third of Williamson Magor's equity.

'They started verbal abuse and letters of the type that few companies would write—very scurrilous and objectionable letters, all addressed to Pat Williamson, insinuating all sorts of things. This went on for a year and in my mind, finished Williamson,' Khaitan recounted to Peter Pugh, author of *Williamson Magor Stuck to Tea*. Other men might have been discouraged but Khaitan had been bred in a harsher school, that of the Indian joint family. Stubbornly refusing to be cowed down, he hung around and succeeded in getting himself appointed Williamson Magor's managing director in 1964 despite the Ellermans' objections. Matters came to a head when Pat Williamson died a few months later. Khaitan bought out the Ellermans' stake and became chairman. At the time he didn't realize this would be his first step towards becoming the world's biggest individual tea planter.

A quiet man, soft-spoken in his speech, in many ways Khaitan resembles another global leader, the late Aditya Birla. Birla abhorred flamboyance. Khaitan's discreet style—not just his well-cut conservative suits—matched that of the colourless viscose tycoon. An old friend describes Khaitan as 'the kind of man who would cross the road quickly if he saw trouble coming towards him'. Despite his innate pacifism, he has a knack of attracting trouble. His ascension to Williamson Magor's chairmanship was no exception.

It would be a crowning by rays of fire for the ambitious trader. The Chinese invaded Assam in October 1962, retreating unilaterally on November 21 but not before gunshots and looting destroyed the tranquillity of the tea gardens. Labour unrest had been rare in the company's tea estates in the early

'60s, but it became more frequent later in the decade as the Naxalite movement gained momentum in Darjeeling and Siliguri.

Its leaders 'were involved in land-grabbing and caused chaos and disruption throughout the state,' says Gillen Sandys-Lumsdaine, a former Williamson Magor director who was a junior assistant posted in Assam at the time. In Calcutta too the law and order situation deteriorated as the communists tried to wrest control of the state government from the Congress.

Then, just as the law and order issue had begun to recede, the rupee was devalued by 40 per cent (in 1966). For British managers such as Sandys-Lumsdaine, the finance ministry's move, aimed at boosting Indian exports, came as a rude shock. Suddenly they could not afford to send their children to élite boarding schools or to maintain residences in both Britain and India. Sandys-Lumsdaine had come to Williamson Magor through family connections (his grandmother was a Magor) and remained with the company for some years, but he would find it increasingly difficult to make ends meet on his Indian salary alone. The exodus of British managers became a flood, and their places were taken over by Indians, professionals like Rajeshwar L. Rikhye, a dapper little manager of tremendous courage who in time would become Khaitan's most trusted lieutenant.

'All this was part of the winding-up of the British commercial raj. Indian nationals fitted in well in the resultant vacancies, and were here to stay,' says Khaitan. Because they were cheaper? Diplomatic as ever, Khaitan rearranges the suggestion: 'At Williamson Magor, expatriate managers did insist on keeping standards, and received respect. After 300 years of colonialism, they had authority and they have left their mark [but] by the '70s there was less inefficiency.'

Under Khaitan, leisurely Friday afternoon lunches after

the London mail day on Thursday disappeared. The easygoing, affable British colonial approach gave way to a more basic management culture. Profits were more important than style, and Khaitan quickly stamped this philosophy on Williamson Magor, starting with the head office. Walking through the nine-storied block at 4 Mangoe Lane, he explains why he rebuilt it. 'Earlier there used to be a large forecourt where the British would park their Rolls Royces and Bentleys. At the back there was a garden where the *malis* used to grow carnations round the year. One day I told the English manager that it would be cheaper to fly in a fresh carnation for his buttonhole every day than to grow them in the backyard.'

Though in his mind he knew Khaitan was being practical, and he did eventually sign the documents authorizing the construction, Pat Williamson didn't like the idea. His father had lived like a maharaja in Hampton Court. The old building symbolized an era; its demolition, the end of an idyllic life. Khaitan empathized with the feeling. He too has a need to be known as a pioneer. Standing in the parking lot outside the new building and looking up at it, Khaitan observes: 'At least I have built something in my life.' The off-the-cuff remark is telling: like the corporate empire of his close friend, Rama Prasad Goenka, Khaitan's Rs 16bn fiefdom of twenty-five companies has been cobbled together almost entirely through buy-outs. Both Rama Babu and Briju Babu yearn to be greenfield promoters. RP once came close to realizing his dream and promised to include Briju in it but after Darbari Seth of Tata Tea hijacked the Haldia Petrochemicals project, the dream would become a nightmare from which both were happy to escape.

When the plans for the building were being drawn up, Khaitan earmarked the most attractive room for himself. It's a corner office on the top floor with a stunning view of the

Victoria Memorial rising above the tree tops. Behind Khaitan's kidney shaped marquetry table are six watercolours of galleons in full sail. On one side table is a glass ship inside a clear bottle. A heavy brass maritime-style clock gleams next to an onyx desk set. The room's decoration is strictly stereotype tycoon, with maroon leather chesterfields, a rich cream carpet and expensive floor-to-ceiling wood panelling. To get to his office, Khaitan avoids the bank of modern lifts, preferring an older one located unobtrusively to the side of the main entrance. Originally a goods lift, it's now reserved for the chairman's exclusive use. Its floor sparkles, as does the white uniform of the liftman. The biggest drawback to the building is its shabby approach, through a narrow, congested lane that branches off Surendra Mohan Ghosh Sarani in Dalhousie, Calcutta's business district.

As a full-time working chairman, Khaitan pruned flab wherever he found it. Recruitment procedures were among the first to be overhauled. 'No discrimination against Indians was allowed and an education overseas was not necessarily seen as a great advantage,' recalls BM. According to Michael Rome, a hefty giant who served Williamson Magor from 1949 to '89, its London office used to 'look for recruits who had served in the army, and they particularly favoured people who were over six foot tall.'

Standing 5'6¾" in his socks though his ramrod-straight back makes him look taller, had Khaitan not owned the company, he wouldn't have made the grade. His round face shines with good humour, and a stubby grey moustache lightly sprinkles his upper lip. The sparse graying hair is trimly combed. Behind old fashioned gold-and-horn rimmed glasses, his dark brown eyes glow with a zest for life. Khaitan is a finicky dresser, as dainty as his pale, effeminate hands. In summer, he concedes to Calcutta's humid heat with light coloured half-sleeved safari suits in finely spun cloth but normally he prefers dark formal suits and discreet ties.

His three-decade-long association with the British has Westernized Briju Babu. Fluent in Hindi, Bengali, Marwari and English, a Mayfair accent sometimes creeps into his light voice. His language as diplomatic as a Buckingham Palace spokesman, Khaitan prefaces sensitive topics with conciliatory phrases—'If you don't mind my saying', 'If I may use the word'—but there's no trace of humility. He is not a Peter Sellers playing the bumbling Indian in the '70s hit, *The Party,* but a corporate general, confident of himself and his worth.

According to BM's younger son, Aditya, his father enjoys typical British pastimes such as fancy dress balls and polo. But the colour of his skin is brown, and the thin band of red *mouli* on his right wrist identifies him as a Hindu. Like the Birlas, the Goenkas and the Bajajs, Khaitan is a Marwari from a trading caste. The community is widely regarded as being more prudish than a nun, but Khaitan relishes his reputation as a *bon viveur* who enjoys his weekend golf and likes the occasional brandy.

Another penchant he picked up from the British is a love for horse racing. During his younger days, he loved to ride in the park. Published photographs of Khaitan are rare except for those taken at racecourses. Earlier ones show a natty figure with binoculars at the ready. His glossy two-tone correspondents would make Stephen Fry's look dowdy. Khaitan was for several years steward of the Royal Calcutta Turf Club and his hold on its inner politics even today is awesome. Local gossip has it that he blackballed Russi Mody at the request of Ratan Tata and J.J. Irani, after the boardroom tussle at TISCO. Be that as it may, only after much closed-door activity could Mody become a member. Deepak, BM's eldest son, inherited his father's love for racing and built up the family stables. In 1994, they owned over 300 horses.

'Of all the people in your book, only B.M. Khaitan knows how to live like a maharaja,' says Harsh Goenka, Rama Babu's son and chairman of RPG Enterprises. 'And he doesn't do it for show. He is like that. Even if he is on his own, he will be properly dressed in silk pyjamas and a Sulka dressing gown. Don't phone him after 10 p.m. It's not done.'

Perhaps Khaitan is so *pukka* because he wasn't born to a gracious lifestyle. He earned it and learnt it. 'Briju Babu made his money in the early '80s,' says an acknowledged leader of Calcutta's 'high' society. 'I remember attending the wedding of J.P. Goenka's daughter with Deepak. The Khaitans were new money then and did not quite know how to spend it. All that changed after the wedding. The Goenkas have a lot of style, and BM and Shanti were quick to learn.'

BM's childhood in the narrow lanes of Burra Bazaar is straight out of Dominique Lapierre's *City of Joy*, and would appear as outlandish to a Sloane Ranger as Harrods would be to a *mourdi* seller on Russell Street. Khaitan's grandfather was a jail superintendent in Rajasthan who left the service of the British Raj in the 1880s, moved to Bihar, and later drifted to Calcutta. He had seven sons, three of whom were solicitors. One became a barrister who practised at one stage in England, the first from Bihar to do so. The most famous of the seven was Devi Prasad, a consultant to the Birlas and a member of the Constituent Assembly which drafted the constitution. Though not seriously wealthy, the Khaitans were more than comfortably well off and enjoyed tremendous prestige.

The misfit in this family of intellectuals was Brij Mohan's father, Gouri Prasad. He was the only one without a brief and appears to have been shunted around by the family whenever they needed someone to oversee projects outside Calcutta. When the Birlas wanted someone to oversee the erection of

Bharat Sugar, Devi Prasad packed off his brother Gouri Prasad to the cane fields of north Bihar. In 1932, another client, the Baglas, were building a factory in Kanpur, so Gouri Prasad and his wife Parmeshwari Devi were sent there. By the time this factory was running, the Chagarias, another Khaitan client, wanted a sugar mill. Once again Gouri Prasad had to represent the family at another god-forsaken place. And so it went on.

In between these trips, Brij Mohan was born on August 14, 1927. Rather than bring him and his five siblings up in the wilderness, his parents left him in Calcutta to be looked after by two aunts. BM saw his mother for brief periods during school holidays. The only person to give the youngster any guidance, attention or real affection appears to have been his uncle, Durga Prasad. 'He used to talk to me about politics, and I would get up at five every morning to read the newspaper before the others grabbed it so that we could discuss what was happening,' recalls BM. By the time he was nine or ten, he felt lost and abandoned in the rambling family house. 'I had a very unhappy life as a child,' says BM matter-of-factly. 'When your father is the weakest in the family, you are someone of no importance, someone who doesn't matter, who is quietly tucked away in the corner when important people come to the house.'

Durga Prasad's death at forty-two—'the biggest shock of my life'—would deprive BM of a godfather. Like the other Khaitan children, he studied at the reputed St. Xavier's School, but his education more or less ended there. His cousins went to fancy colleges and acquired impressive legal degrees. BM's higher education was limited to a two-hour course at a morning college. He sailed through his Bachelor's degree but, like Dhirubhai Ambani, a matriculate, Khaitan regrets the absence of a string of abbreviations after his name. 'Because everyone else in the family was so well educated, you felt yourself rather a Charlie. I suppose it would be very unusual if I didn't have a complex. In my case, I fought back. I felt I must catch up with the others. Now, I have no regrets because if I didn't feel the need to push myself, I wouldn't have tied up with the Williamsons. From the '60s, business-wise, I moved fast.'

If there was not much happening at college, there was certainly more than enough action at home. During his college days, the riots which marked the pre-Independence period were becoming more frequent. 'Where we lived, it was really bad. But, you know, when you are living in a place, you get used to it. You adjust yourself. It wasn't really comfortable because our house in Burra Bazaar was surrounded by Muslims. Oddly enough, on August 13, the chief minister was dining in the house. And he told us that on the next day there would be problems and we should get out, but we did not take him seriously. Luckily Devi Babu knew the British governor very well. Immediately he rang him up, and the army went in and moved the entire family out,' recounts Khaitan.

For the next three years, the clan lived in temporary apartments in Somani Park. It was here that one of BM's uncles arranged a match for his nephew with Shanti Aggarwal. They were married on January 17, 1947. He was twenty, she, fifteen. Neither had had a say in the matter, but it has proved to be an enduring match. They have three children: Deepak born in 1955, married to Yashodhara Goenka; Divya born in 1966, married to Sandeep Jalan; and Aditya born two years later, married to Kavita Ruia.

By the '50s, BM's various business schemes were beginning to generate profits. The biggest money-spinner was the supplying of fertilizers and plywood packaging crates to the tea industry. Soon he had made enough to contribute significantly towards the purchase of a new family home at 5 Queen's Park. He was no longer the downtrodden son of the weakest member of the family. According to Pratibha Chamaria, his niece, his wealth has not altered Khaitan's generous nature. 'He is always helping out less well-off members of the family. He does not have to do that. So many rich people don't bother, but he cares,' she says. In the '60s, he started work on a house of his own, a bit further down the road at No.10, in the shadow of the Birla temple.

'After it was built, I took Shanti to see it. She took one look at it and said it was terrible. I can't live here. If you want to live here, you can, but I won't. I kept asking her what was wrong, but all she would say was that it was bad. So we broke it down and rebuilt it,' says Khaitan wryly. It took them seven years to build a new home, but a welcome spin-off was the chance to stay in Lord Inchcape's beautiful home at 22 Camac Street.

When asked for a comment, Shanti tossed her head and refused imperiously. 'This time, you have come to interview my husband. I will give you my comments later.' A small, plump woman described by one of BM's executives as the group's Laxmi, she appears to be a major influence on her husband. Friends hint that a good part of his success should be attributed to her down-to-earth shrewdness. She certainly seems to be more ambitious than him, but her aspirations are discreet, like the elegant emerald-and-diamond bangles on nut-brown wrists peeping from under the decorous *pallu* of her crisply starched cotton saree.

The strong rapport between husband and wife, their loyalty towards each other, is obvious, charming, and somewhat unusual. Rupa Bajaj is Rahul's close confidante and Sarala Birla is BK's constant companion, but these women play unusual roles in a society of arranged marriages, particularly one belonging to a generation where child marriages were *de rigeur*. Perhaps the closeness between his parents, according to Aditya, is because his father 'is a loner with few friends'.

Or it could be that the bonds between BM and Shanti were strengthened by their banishment from Marwari society as Khaitan became more intimate with his British partners. 'You see, in Calcutta, the tea industry was dominated by Europeans. So naturally when you start associating with one, you start associating with others. And I don't mind admitting that I became slightly less mixable, that I was a misfit in my community. But the Williamsons and the Magors were my supporters, and once a big house supports you, you get an *entrée*,' says Khaitan.

A DISPLAY OF INITIATIVE

According to Alan Carmichael, a tall, fresh-faced tea supervisor in George Williamson (UK) who flies down periodically to check the health of the tea bushes, after Khaitan joined Williamson Magor, he initiated a far-ranging investment programme. Old bushes were replaced by new ones, one garden being taken up each year. New factories for cutting and drying tea were built on the estates. 'Today we have the youngest and latest machinery in the business in India. Nothing is over fifteen years old which is quite remarkable in comparison with the other gardens,' says Carmichael. Without Khaitan's initiatives, Williamson Magor almost surely would have gone under.

Within a decade, the number of tea gardens under Williamson Magor's control rose from eighteen to thirty-seven, and Khaitan's shrewd management of them brought him to the notice of Kenneth Peter Lyle Mackay, the Earl of Inchcape.

A doughty businessman who had fought in World War II as a Royal Lancer, Lord Inchcape spent several years in India, building up powerful managing agency firms and quarrelling with Walchand Hirachand and the Scindia Steam Navigation Company. In the UK, the Inchcape Group is today a big, profitable concern; but in the India of the '70s, it was a severely troubled business house. At the age of sixty, Inchcape was faced with the unpleasant task of presiding over the group's last rites in India. One member company badly in need of succour was Macneill & Barry (M&B), a Calcutta-based tea, jute and engineering agency in which the Tatas and the Nizam of Hyderabad held significant minority stakes.

Like Williamson Magor, M&B was a pillar of the British Raj. According to one of its former managers, Newman Baldcock, 'This was not just because of the Inchcape connection, but the people we had. The No.1 of Macneill's just before the war has often been described as the best *burra sahib* of all. This was W.L. Gordon, a great character and a great disciplinarian, but the most popular man I have ever known. His standing was very, very high in Calcutta. I felt I was in a first-class outfit.'

M&B came into play on March 14, 1954, the day the Tatas informed Inchcape that they wanted to pull out. They had an offer of Rs 100 each for their 21,000 M&B shares which they were inclined to accept considering the ccmpany's changed circumstances and poor returns. The news 'came as a considerable shock', writes Stephanie Jones, a business historian and author of *Merchants of the Raj*. Inchcape persuaded the Tatas to reject the offer and allow him to find a buyer for their shares. They agreed but on a stiff condition: they now wanted Rs 150 per share. The market price was Rs 52. The Tata walkout left Inchcape in a greater bind.

By 1974, Inchcape's need for a saviour increased in direct proportion to M&B's deteriorating position. There was an immediate cash shortfall that quarter of Rs 2m and suppliers were refusing to provide raw materials unless they were paid.

The first person with whom M&B directors began discussing a possible partnership was S.K. Birla, a member of the energetic Marwari business house headed by G.D. Birla. The talks broke down because Inchcape felt that SK was 'too much part of the Birla culture, and it would be undesirable for Macneill & Barry to be sucked into the Birla machine'. Shortly before the negotiations had begun, a desperate Inchcape had announced that he was prepared to 'welcome an Indian partner from outside who could play an active part in management'. The collapse of the Birla talks indicated quite the opposite: he wanted money, not the man.

In early June 1974, a dialogue began with Khaitan. By this time, Inchcape's worries had multiplied. Apart from the constant hunt for money to staunch M&B's financial bleeding, the imminent introduction of stringent foreign exchange (FERA) regulations suggested potential loss of control over the Inchcape group's Indian holdings. Inchcape was determined to avoid reducing the group's equity in M&B to 40 per cent. On the surface, a tie-up with Williamson Magor appeared to be the ideal solution. In the UK, Inchcape was on nodding terms with Richard Magor, and considered him a 'friendly rival'. His directors in India informed Inchcape that Khaitan was an influential Marwari and that under his management, Williamson Magor had made a remarkable turnaround. Additionally, Williamson Magor reportedly had substantial underutilized borrowing power.

Khaitan was flattered at being called to the same negotiating table as a Birla. At this early point of time, he didn't know how Inchcape's mind worked, nor was he in a position to appreciate the finer points on which the Birla talks had floundered.

The first round of deliberations resulted in a complicated deal involving mergers and restructuring of holding companies and managing agency agreements in the UK and in India. Simply put, Williamson Magor would be merged in M&B; M&B's capital would be increased to Rs 25m; the Inchcape group would hold 32 per cent, Khaitan's stake would be 28.3 per cent, and the rest would be held by the public.

From Khaitan's point of view, though he would lose his personal identity through the merger, the deal was satisfactory because for a Rs 6m cash payout, he would receive Rs 10m worth of shares in return. Inchcape liked the arrangement because the management's block was over 60 per cent. However, the Indian government refused to allow the merger to take place until the Inchcape holding had been diluted to 40 per cent. In effect this would reduce the Inchcape holding to 27 per cent, which dramatically changed the balance between Inchcape and Khaitan in the merged group, especially as he had acquired the Nizam's shares. Thus a fundamental intention of the merger as far as Inchcape was concerned—that of avoiding the reduction of shares to 40 per cent—was frustrated.

Khaitan and Inchcape huddled together again, this time in London. The government shot down the amended proposal also. Apparently the Department of Economic Affairs and the finance ministry viewed it as a way of circumventing FERA. By this time Inchcape had 'warmed' to Khaitan and both sides felt they had come so far with the deal that they didn't want to abandon it. Nonetheless, a final scheme eluded them. Inchcape began to suspect that someone was working against the merger because of the Department of Economic Affairs' continuous stalling and the adverse press comments. Eventually an agreement satisfying everybody was hammered out. Champagne corks popped on January 29, 1975 when the high court order granting the merger was finally received.

A new rupee company called Macneill & Magor was created with sixty tea gardens under its control. However, these were not tightly knit in terms of ownership. About a quarter were wholly-owned subsidiaries. A second quarter were subsidiary rupee companies with public shareholders. Williamson Tea Holdings held the third quarter, and the remainder was held by Assam Investments. Williamson was a partnership between Magor and Khaitan, and Assam was an Inchcape company. Khaitan became Macneill & Magor's first chairman.

Within three years, the partners fell out. Khaitan blames Sir Michael Parson and his 'cronies' Harnam Wahi and Charles Will. 'Will and Wahi were my No.2 and No.3 men. But Parson literally started making me feel as if he were the owner rather than a professional CEO. Differences of opinion started arising in the management of the tea companies. We were known for our tea expertise. We know what tea is. And for some chap who was running a jute mill to be telling us what to do in tea is slightly asking too much.'

Khaitan shrugs off Parson's actions, but not Wahi's. 'I took him in and I trusted him. I gave him the respect which nobody else in India would have given him. When Deepak was getting married, the only outsider at the *parhani* was Wahi. And eventually I came to know that he was stabbing me in the back. Not that it made any difference to me because there was nothing hanky-panky, no financial irregularity or anything of the kind in the running of Macneill & Magor. Nothing. But Wahi and Charles Will kept feeding Kenneth about things which I did not know, all wrong things about how I was running this company.'

Parson was Inchcape's eyes and ears in India. If Parson felt that Khaitan was becoming more powerful and dominant at the Inchcape Group's expense, Inchcape would naturally accept his reading of the situation. At the heart of the discord was control of the Assam Company, the biggest of Macneill & Magor's tea estates. Parson was convinced that Khaitan was trying to bring it into his sphere of influence. Khaitan doesn't deny the charge. 'Of course, I accept this. We merged with Inchcape in 1974 with Assam Company in mind because we were a tea company, and when we merged, we became India's largest tea group. But I paid a heavy price for the merger. Williamson Magor's Rs 100 share was being quoted at over Rs 120, while that of Macneill & Barry was Rs 44, and the ratio was 4:1.'

In London, Khaitan's lively interest in the Assam Company infuriated some British directors, who warned him against encroaching on Inchcape turf. Khaitan decided to confront Parson, asking him to call a board meeting to resolve the conflict. Parson refused, saying 'No, I can't call a board meeting because nobody will tell anything against you.' 'That's the time I realized things couldn't go on the way they had. That turned the table,' said Khaitan, who by now was fed up with Parson's needling. Break-point came when Parson demanded that the Assam Company be run the 'the way we want'. 'Certainly you can run the company the way you want to, but then I don't want to be your chairman,' Khaitan retorted angrily.

Flouncing out of the Inchcape Group's office, the adrenaline pumping fast inside him, Khaitan dashed off a letter tendering his resignation. Pintu remonstrated—Khaitan's 4.57 per cent of Assam Company's equity was worth Rs 1.6m—but BM's mind was made up. 'I kept thinking I have been double-crossed. I didn't want to be thrown to the vultures after Kenneth went out. Parson asked me not to tell anyone about this letter because this should be kept confidential, but I walked straight to Kenneth and told him that I have just resigned. I told him he has got enough East India men who will look after his interests better. Assam Company is your affair. I don't need anything and that it is best if we demerge.'

Had he wanted to, Khaitan could have launched an internal hostile takeover bid to oust Parson and company. After FERA, the Inchcape Group's holding in Macneill & Magor had declined to 26 per cent while Khaitan's had climbed to 32 per cent. There are hundreds of cases where takeover sharks have succeeded in swallowing large companies with far smaller stakes, but it appears that Khaitan hadn't as yet quite acquired the confidence such an attack would need, nor perhaps the funds.

Khaitan phoned Richard Magor, giving him less than ten minutes notice. Together they went back to Inchcape's office and presented him with a cheque subject to Reserve Bank permissions. The demerger was completed by 1982. Khaitan kept Macneill & Magor's engineering divisions and the tea gardens minus those belonging to the Assam Company. At the Inchcape head office, it was felt that Wahi's role in wresting the Assam Company from Khaitan's orbit should be rewarded: he became its managing director.

In the autumn of his life, Khaitan maintains, but not convincingly, that he has no regrets about the way things turned out. 'I believe that when God takes away something with one hand, he gives back double with the other. That's why I don't have a complex about it. Assam Company was lost [but] I got compensated in a bigger way. Over there, I was like a *kinari babu.* Today, I am an owner.' The 'compensation' was McLeod Russel India.

After the Inchcape experience, Khaitan resolved that if ever he took over another company, he would first have to be invited, thereby earning the title 'Gentleman Raider'. And what could be more upper crust than negotiating a deal over a sumptuous lunch at the Savoy in London. Among those who shook hands over cut crystal and petit fours were Philip Magor, Colin·Montgomery (CEO of McLeod Russel India), Nigel Openshaw, John Guthrie, BM and of course, Pintu.

Openshaw, an aspiring professional, then headed McLeod Russel plc, which held the controlling interest in McLeod Russel India. He saw the £18m UK company as not just a plantations group but a larger holding company with interests in surface coatings, air filtration, environmental engineering, textiles and property investment. To raise funds for his ambitious plans, he decided to hawk off 80 per cent of its Indian tea interests. In 1987, he offered for sale as one package a group of three companies, McLeod Russel India, Namdung Tea and Makum Tea (India), which between them consisted of twelve tea gardens.

John Guthrie, seated across from Khaitan in the high-ceilinged dining room, also held a substantial stake in McLeod Russel India. The Guthries are as prominent a tea family in the UK as the Williamsons and the Magors. They already had a joint venture with Khaitan, a small plywood company, Assam Railways and Trading, and it was this connection which helped Khaitan get in on the ground floor. Other potential buyers did not even know that a buy-out was being offered, and McLeod Russel India never even came on the market. Within days of the offer, BM formed a three-member consortium called Mendip Ltd., led by Philip Magor. By April 1987 they had sewn up the deal. As a totally offshore transaction, the £18.4m (then Rs 370m) acquisition didn't need any government of India permissions.

For Khaitan, the McLeod Russel India acquisition was a delicious feather in his cap. Many tea majors had wanted it, it was one of the most coveted deals in recent years, and to walk off with the prize brought a wide smile to his face. Its twelve gardens were widely recognized as producers of some of the finest teas in the world. The takeover added 10,138 hectares of matured tea area producing 21.5m kg to Khaitan's burgeoning tea empire. Its working for the financial year ended June 30, 1987 was excellent, with Rs 279m in cash reserves, sales of Rs 408m, pre-tax profits of Rs 121m and a net worth of Rs 393m.

The McLeod Russel acquisition made Khaitan the world's largest private tea producer, controlling fifty-four gardens. Tata Tea claims it is the single biggest tea company in the world but Khaitan produces more: 65m kg vis-à-vis Tata Tea's 50m kg, or roughly 10 per cent of all Indian tea and just under 5 per cent of all the tea produced in the world. There are four gardens each in the Dooars (near Bhutan) and Darjeeling (tucked between Bhutan and Nepal) but the majority of Khaitan's gardens are in Assam.

GARDENS OF FEAR

Visitors who have seen the tea gardens marvel at their tranquil beauty. Nestled in a valley below the Himalayas, on the banks of the river Brahmaputra, hundreds of terraced tea bushes soak up the sun and mists of Assam. It's often rainy here and the atmosphere is redolent with the fragrance of the hardy plants and the smell of wet earth.

It's peaceful in the valley, there are few buses and fewer cars. The streets and markets of Guwahati, like all state capitals, are full of bustle, but in the tea gardens, life is predictable. Every morning, hundreds of women fan out to pick monotonously and endlessly the tender leaves which blenders such as Brooke Bond and Tetley use to produce brews less sweet-smelling than the teas of Darjeeling but with a stronger, more aromatic body.

On Tuesday, February 11, 1991 at Lahowal, a small

village, gunshots shattered the peace. Three gangsters burst into the office of D.K. Chowdhury, pumped nine bullets into him and escaped on scooters before they could be caught. Chowdhury died on the way to the Assam Medical College in nearby Dibrugarh, the largest town after Guwahati. The assailants were members of ULFA (United Liberation Front of Asom), a terrorist organization. Their victim was the chairman of the Dibrugarh Unit of the Indian Tea Association, manager of the Romai Tea Estate, and one of Khaitan's key executives.

This wasn't the first time ULFA had shed blood. It's a seasoned group with hundreds of murders to its name. With forty-six tea gardens spread right through Upper and Lower Assam, Khaitan is a soft target.

Two days after the murder, a meeting of the Indian Tea Association was hurriedly called in Calcutta to discuss the murder. It was attended by nearly all the heads of firms with tea gardens in north India. Despite heated discussions, the planters failed to agree on initiatives to tackle the militants.

The ULFA was formed on April 7, 1979 at Rang Ghar in Sibsagar district under the leadership of Arvind Rajkhowa, Golap Barua, Paresh Barua, Samiran Gogoi and Hemanta Phukan. As students, they had participated in the anti-foreigners agitation launched by the All Assam Students' Union. Initially they kept a low profile. The first priority was to acquire sophisticated weapons and training. In 1981, Phukan negotiated a deal with the China-backed National Socialist Council of Nagaland (NSCN). In return for funds and shelter for its activists in Assam, NSCN would help train and arm ULFA cadres.

Over the next ten years, ULFA gained a Robin Hood-like reputation among the local population. Alongside its political agenda of 'freeing Assam from Delhi's colonial rule' and driving out the non-Assamese 'aliens', it introduced a number of social welfare measures and followed it up with a ruthless drive against anti-social elements. It banned the hooch business, gambling and eve-teasing, sentencing offenders in its 'people's courts'. It distributed free textbooks and uniforms to needy students, built village roads and helped poor farmers in harvesting operations.

For several years, tea planters like Khaitan and the Tatas ignored ULFA, despite the parallel government it had established. 'Donations' were frequently extorted from managers living in far-flung and isolated tea estates, but the amounts were small. Rajeshwar L. Rikhye, Khaitan's seniormost executive, admitted that ULFA would often 'borrow' tractors and other implements from the gardens to help poor cultivators. This sometimes caused hiccups if the equipment was urgently needed for the gardens' own use, but planters generally looked the other way. Living in Calcutta, the savage events in the Brahmaputra valley of Upper Assam seemed so far away. Buying peace was so much easier than losing production or picking a fight.

The murder of Surendra Paul on April 9, 1990 shattered the planters' complacency.

Paul, fifty-four, was a prominent Calcutta industrialist, chairman of the Apeejay Group and younger brother of Swraj Paul, head of the London-based Caparo Group, a businessman richer than the Queen of England, according to the *Sunday Times Magazine's* annual compilation of Britain's richest 500 in 1996. Surendra was ambushed by ULFA men during a visit to the group's tea gardens at Tinsukhia in Dibrugarh district.

The planters suddenly woke up to the uneasy fact that they were not immune from ULFA's enforcers. Though ULFA had murdered nearly a hundred people during 1985-90, these were mainly politicians and traders. Frightened by the violence, they offered silent sympathy to Paul's family but refrained from publicly condemning the killing. Only Viren Shah, then president of Assocham, and Raunaq Singh, president of FICCI, issued press statements denouncing the attack. The planters 'reacted to the murder with stoic silence. Every word spoken against the murder would be a word against ULFA. Every such word would be a death sentence against oneself,' said a commentator cuttingly.

The ULFA singled out planters because it was an easy way to finance their political agenda. It paid special attention to Marwari planters like Khaitan, the Birlas and the Goenkas because it felt that they were bleeding Assam, siphoning out profits from tea and investing these in other states. Hysteria built up against non-Assamese labourers in the tea gardens and the lack of local white collar jobs as the headquarters of most tea companies were in Calcutta and not Guwahati.

The planters responded by pointing to heavy taxes which the local government—elected by the Assamese—used to build roads, provide education and medical services. Only Darbari Seth, the head of Tata Tea, expressed remorse. 'Yes, we are guilty of everything they have said. We owe a debt of gratitude. From there we take away so much and give back so little. Everybody does it. It has been one of my consistent pleas with my colleagues to let us find something worthwhile in Assam,' he told reporters soon after Paul's murder. Unfortunately, his pious words didn't win Tata Tea the partial reprieve and chance to negotiate privately for which he was hoping.

On the contrary, when ULFA drew up its next hit list of tea majors, Tata Tea's name was there alongside Macneill & Magor (Khaitan's flagship), Warren Tea, Assam Frontier, Doom Dooma, Stewart Holl (India) and Jokai India. Executives of the seven companies were called to meet the ULFA high command in Dibrugarh on June 11, 1990. The ominous invitation, typed on ULFA's infamous letterhead embellished on the side with a cheery stamp of a rising sun inside a circle, was to the point:

> Sir
>
> The undersigned on behalf of the central committee request your presence immediately to discuss regarding the active participation of the tea industry in the economic development of Asom.
>
> Failing to honour our request will bound us to take action according to our constitution. Anticipating your active cooperation.
>
> Yours sincerely,   T.C. Dutta
> S. C. Gogoi   ULFA
> Commander, ULFA   Dist.committee, Dibrugarh

By 'the active participation of the tea industry in the economic development of Asom', ULFA meant a contribution of Rs 0.5m in cash from each company's gardens in Upper Assam. Collectively, the seven companies owned seventy-seven tea gardens. *Business Standard* calculated that if Macneill & Magor's subsidiaries were taken into account, Khaitan alone would have to shell out Rs 23.5m to buy peace. The demand had an unintended element of black humour: the money had to be deposited in Hotel Sonargaon in Karwan bazaar in Dhaka. Said one senior executive: 'It is absurd to think we will be heading for Dhaka with suitcases full of cash.'

At first the planters prevaricated. A day before ULFA's Thursday, June 21 deadline, they let it be known that they would not pay Rs 0.5m per garden, but would continue the earlier ad hoc payments system. As one planter said: 'We hoped that ULFA would not be so greedy as to kill the goose that lays the golden eggs.'

That wish was speedily demolished. To make sure everyone understood it meant business, four ULFA members, two of whom carried light weapons, barged into Jokai India's Panitola office on June 23. Written undertakings were extracted and non-Assamese managers present warned to leave. Panitola is just eight kilometres from where Paul was shot. Four managers left the next day, and the last one left on June 30. In public, Jokai India insisted that it 'had never received any demand for money from ULFA', but in Dibrugarh, on June 27, it quietly informed the district police of the incident after most executives had reached the safety of Calcutta.

Meanwhile, fourteen or fifteen managers flew into Dibrugarh from Calcutta on June 28. Shortly after dusk, they drove in three cars to a dilapidated bungalow on the town's outskirts belonging to a leading tea owner, guided by 'link men' under summons by ULFA. Among them were the Khaitan Group's Rikhye and his colleague, Gautam P. Barua, corporate vice-president of Williamson Magor; officials of the Indian Tea Board; and an Assamese politician. The meeting lasted three hours. Each executive was called separately by the ULFA leaders to a room at the secret rendezvous. The first to be called in were the Khaitan executives. They came out visibly shaken.

In Guwahati, the state government under chief minister Prafulla Kumar Mahanta tried to turn a blind eye to the blackmail, claiming that no tea company had lodged an official complaint. Once news leaked out to the press that several members of his Asom Gana Parishad Party knew about the June 28 meeting, Mahanta's office was badly embarrassed. In Calcutta the India Tea Association fared little better. In several closed door meetings, it wrung its hands and exchanged notes on who had been ordered to pay, and how much. It also kept tripping over its own feet. Initially it denied that such a meeting had taken place, but was subsequently forced to confirm it. It also tried to say that no demands or threats were made but retreated a second time after Unilever took a hard line.

From London, the Anglo-Dutch conglomerate announced that neither Doom Dooma nor Brooke Bond would give in to threats, and lodged a formal complaint against ULFA with the Indian high commissioner in London, Kuldip Nayar, the well-known journalist. Nayar immediately cabled the Assam chief minister. This was followed by a visit to Guwahati by a British official based in Delhi. With his back to the wall, Mahanta promised state action.

In New Delhi, the V.P. Singh administration was as worried by events in Assam as the planters. The coffers were empty, declared the prime minister, and India was on the verge of defaulting on her international loans. Exports were vital, and Assam tea was expected to bring in Rs 7bn. Unilever was exerting pressure through the British High Commission. And by kidnapping the head of Indian Oil Corporation's Guwahati refinery on July 15, ULFA extended its threats beyond the tea industry to the even more vital oil sector.

The planters found a sympathetic ear in Arun Nehru, Singh's Union commerce minister. The ULFA's financial demands were always nicely balanced with their victim's ability to pay. How could it have access to copies of their profit and loss accounts, income tax returns and bank balances, they asked. There had to be collusion between the Asom Gana Parishad and the terrorists, they told Nehru. Their managers often faced difficulties in getting FIRs (First Information Reports) registered with the local police, and even in the case of Paul's murder, the state government had shied away from accusing ULFA, they said. Its members walked in and out of Assam House, in the middle of Calcutta without fear of apprehension. Why didn't the state government ban ULFA?

Ruling out the possibility of outlawing ULFA, Mahanta threw the ball right back into the planters' court. 'Multinationals and big business houses themselves aided and abetted the growth of ULFA by pandering to their extortions as long as it was within manageable limits. Having whetted ULFA's appetite for money, they got into a self-created tangle by not informing the state government at the initial stage. It was only when the ULFA's demands grew that they started crying hoarse and blaming the state government,' he said. The planters' policy of appeasement had backfired as ULFA bought more and better guns with money extorted by kidnapping managers.

There was little value to these accusations and counter-accusations: the state government's ineffectiveness and the tea planters' money had created a Frankenstein's monster. No one really knew how to destroy it. ULFA hiked its demand on the tea majors to include a cess of Rs 1 per kg. As the kidnappings and killings increased, the Chandra Shekhar administration finally reacted. On the morning of November 28, 1990, it dismissed Mahanta and imposed President's rule. That night the army launched Operation Bajrang in the Brahmaputra valley. Operation Rhino followed some months later, after state elections. In all 3,500 ULFA members 'surrendered', but core leaders like Rajkhowa and Paresh Barua remain at large. In between, Hiteshwar Saikia of the Congress Party won the elections and took over as chief minister for the second time.

From this relative position of strength, Saikia began talks with ULFA, but these had to be abandoned by March 1991. Four months later, on July 1, ULFA demonstrated its muscle by kidnapping thirteen senior government officials and a Soviet mining engineer, Sergei Gretchenko. Two weeks later, Saikia was forced to offer to free 400 ULFA detainees. Overjoyed by its success, ULFA went on a mad spree. During 1992-94, it gunned down police officers, Congress and BJP politicians, and five of Saikia's relatives. It also killed an ONGC engineer, kidnapped the head of Prag Bosimi Synthetics, murdered a manager of the Paul-run Assam Frontier, and drove out a French team of scientists. The toll rose rapidly to 400 'executions'.

ULFA's victories became a role model to a motley collection of terrorist organizations such as the Boro Security Force (BSF). Like the ULFA, the BSF tapped tea managers for funds. One of its bigger successes was an attack on Subhir Roy, a manager of the Khaitan-owned Dimakusi garden. On March 18, 1992, they stopped his car and abducted Roy and his driver. Khaitan was asked to pay a 'land tax' at the rate of Rs 20,000 per hectare to obtain his manager's release. During the negotiations, on April 3, the BSF gunned down a manager of the Kanoi-owned Panbari garden. Roy was released after twenty days of captivity. Like others before him, Khaitan vehemently denied that any ransom had been paid. Journalists who regularly cover this beat are convinced, however, that Khaitan did pay off the BSF to save the lives of Roy and his driver. D.K. Chowdhury's murder would have been fresh in Khaitan's mind.

Today the gardens are guarded night and day by Khaitan's private army. Two thousand armed guards, forty per garden, patrol its perimeters constantly. No manager is allowed to go outside the garden without some protection. If he does, and he is kidnapped, it is his funeral. The management is not responsible for his ransom.

I asked Khaitan why he followed this policy of

appeasement. Wasn't there some truth in Mahanta's accusation that tea planters like Khaitan had created this situation?

Khaitan is unrepentant: 'Tell me one thing. If a man walks into this room just now with an AK47 and says "Do you mind parting with your file", what will you do? Be honest. Be honest. Yes, people accuse me that I am the largest planter and have paid money. But you tell me what I should do. If I take a view that I won't pay money and a manager is shot, the family and everybody will say that Mr Khaitan loves his money and he allowed the man to die. If you were in my position, what would . you do? What would you say to his family? I would much rather accept that I paid money than to be accused that you killed my husband.'

But why didn't the tea planters band together? 'Yes we tried that. We tried very hard. I was the last person to pay and I was the softest target in the whole of Assam. I've gone through nights of literally torture in my mind, putting my head on the pillow and not knowing who will be the person to be killed tomorrow morning. That was the time that I decided to build a good school in Assam. I have put in Rs 22 crores into the project, brought in the finest faculty—the principal of London's Westminster School.'

Can a mere school buy peace with ULFA? 'No. I want to prove that a good school will produce a good student, and that a good student will produce a good citizen, and a good citizen will produce a good country. I have gone out of my way to put money back into Assam, and people will realize it some day.'

Khaitan's protective attitude towards his executives has earned him their unflinching loyalty. Says Gautam Barua, 'All through the bad times, not a single manager left the group. Sir has looked after the murdered man's wife and children. He has paid for their education and offered them jobs in the organization.' Barua, an Assamese, had along with Rikhye faced ULFA commanders at the June 28, 1990 meeting outside Dibrugarh. Knowing that his wife and children would be looked after well should anything happen to him had made it easier for him to catch the flight, he says.

In Calcutta, the last stranglehold of communism, Khaitan is something of a super-boss in the eyes of his executives, and they jump to his defence at the slightest hint of criticism. P. Bajaj, the managing director of India Foils, one of the upcoming companies in the Williamson Magor group, is a typical example. 'I could have got a job in an engineering company eight times bigger and doing far better but I didn't because I felt Mr Khaitan had a commitment to his companies and he gave me the freedom to manage as I think I should.' It's rare to find a corporate star for whom everyone has a nice word, and even rarer when it comes from subordinates, but though his attitude towards ULFA won him brownie points in his tea and engineering companies, Khaitan couldn't crack the workers of Metal Box.

'I'M NOT AN ASSET STRIPPER'

In its heyday in the '70s, Metal Box was India's largest packaging unit, a premier company with a string of small plants spread across the country. As its name suggests, it produced metal boxes which it supplied to a number of blue-chips. By the early '80s, however, a series of miscalculations had run up heavy losses. Worried about their jobs, its workers had become querulous and militant. The impressive marble façade of Barlow House, Metal Box's head office in Calcutta, was constantly being disfigured by untidily stuck messages from various trade unions. Unable to control its troublesome subsidiary, UK's Metal Box plc—which held just under 40 per cent of its equity—tried on several occasions to sell it off. At least eight businessmen, including Russi Mody and Manu Chhabria, came to look but declined to buy.

Knowing its problems, why did Khaitan want its headaches? 'Today, I agree with you that it was a mistake. At the time, it appeared to be a good deal,' he says. 'It was a most publicly galling experience, and I misjudged the reality on the ground.'

Apparently Deepak had begun discussions with Metal Box some time in 1983 to acquire its plastic flexible packaging unit at Taratula in West Bengal. The talks dragged on for about a year and a half, and the price climbed slowly to Rs 120m. 'At this point, we started wondering whether it might be cheaper to build a new plant rather than acquire the old Metal Box unit. Then, one evening, Deepak and Rama Babu were chatting about it and it occurred to them that for Rs 500m, we might be able to get the full company.'

Khaitan was convinced that a packaging boom was round the corner. He already had an aluminium packaging company (India Foils), and felt that with Metal Box he would have the entire gamut of packaging forms 'under one roof'. Talking excitedly to reporters after the takeover, he told them: 'Packaging in India is still in its infancy. We have not touched even a fringe of it. For a company like Metal Box, a turnover of Rs 200 crores is nothing. Adulteration is creating havoc. More and more consumers prefer goods in packaged and sealed containers. The tin can business has its own utility. Plastic containers, for example, are not for fizzy items.'

Meanwhile, a modest recovery in Metal Box seemed to herald a better future. A bearings unit at Kharagpur which had been draining profits was sold to Tisco in October 1983. Though accumulated losses were Rs 150m, the bleeding was becoming sluggish. Losses for the eighteen-month period ended March 31, 1985 were Rs 56.3m compared to Rs 97.7m for the preceding twelve months ended September 30, 1983. Khaitan felt it could be turned round with a fresh injection of funds. Overjoyed, Metal Box plc jumped at his offer. At a board meeting on December 4, 1985, Deepak, Richard Magor and he joined the Metal Box India board. To Khaitan's immense satisfaction, its share price jumped up on news of the board changes.

Initially, the company's working moved according to Khaitan's plans. 'We pumped in Rs 20 crores and brought the company into the sound position of [having] three months of raw materials. All the backlog of banking limits were levelled. The debtors were under control.' But not the workers, of whom there were at least 2,000 too many. At the first board meeting after the Metal Box takeover, in January 1986, there had been a lot of back-slapping and camaraderie—'together we will meet the challenge of the future'. Two years down the road, much of this optimism had evaporated.

On the morning of March 17, 1988, Khaitan was particularly peeved. He was sitting at home, seething. His managers at Barlow House had sent a message that Metal Box workers were planning to stage an unruly demonstration outside 4 Mangoe Lane. Khaitan's presence could further inflame tempers, they warned. It would be best if he stayed away.

For Khaitan, the message was the proverbial last straw that breaks the camel's back. A month earlier, workers had marched from Barlow House to 4 Mangoe Lane in order to present him with a memorandum. There had been a series of strikes by the 4,000 workers of the West Bengal units almost from the day he had taken over. The endless labour conflicts were wearing him down.

Khaitan approached the hurdle in his usual pragmatic style. He wanted to sell Metal Box's valuable real estate at

Worli in Bombay and use the money to formulate a compensation package to retrench workers. 'But Metal Box plc (UK), who were my partners, suggested instead that we should reduce the wages by 20 per cent. 'Reduce' was the word, but the West Bengal chief minister changed it to 'deferred'. 'I agreed,' says Khaitan. When he took this watered-down proposal to the unions, the Bombay unit agreed, but not the Calcutta one.

Khaitan saw red. Before leaving for Bombay, he had held informal discussions with the Calcutta union leaders, who had then accepted his proposals. When they changed their mind, he put his foot down. 'I told them that if you don't agree, then I am sorry to tell you that the factory cannot run. I am not going to get involved. It's been accepted in Bombay, and you are saying I am a liar. I am not prepared to accept this. If you don't accept this proposal, then I'll leave this company and walk out.' Six months later, he carried out his threat.

Khaitan is not easily aroused, but once he is, he can be unforgivingly, stubbornly and mulishly adamant. After his fight with the Inchcape Group over the Assam Company, he had declared he would never talk to them again. He kept his word, rejecting every single olive branch. So it was with Metal Box. Walking out of Barlow House, Khaitan swore he would never step into it again. He never has. A board meeting had been called on Monday, April 18. The other directors were shocked when BM and Deepak handed over their resignations.

'The whole revival hinged on the labour agreement—and that started floundering. The banks also sat on the fence. In the meantime, the company became sicker. We felt we couldn't do more,' said Deepak. Talking to the press shortly after the board meeting, an angry Deepak told reporters: 'Till Monday, 3 o'clock, my father was a professional beggar. The time has come to stop treading the banks' corridors.'

Back at 4 Mangoe Lane, BM called his broker. 'I told him, do what you want with these shares. Dump them in the river Hooghly. Do anything,' says BM. As Metal Box floundered deeper and deeper into a morass of debts and lock-outs, Mamta Banerjee, the peppery INTUC leader, came to visit .Khaitan 'She asked me why I am taking this attitude, and why don't I open the plant. And I said, you open it. I've left the plant. The plant belongs to you, madam. You run it. You do it. It's yours.'

Annoyed by Khaitan's attitude, bankers at Grindlays and the State Bank of India criticized him volubly in the press. Politicians raised questions in the state assemblies of Maharashtra and West Bengal, editors wrote learned but indecipherable editorials. Minority shareholders refused to pass the Metal Box accounts at stormy annual general meetings. Two managing directors left, and its long-suffering chairman, Bhaskar Mitter, finally bailed out towards the end of 1988. Eventually a buyer was found for the jinxed company, but by then, Metal Box had become a hollow shell.

According to his detractors, it had been reduced to a shell because Khaitan had stripped Metal Box of its best assets. He was accused of having surreptitiously squirrelled away valuable flats, offices and even factories out of Metal Box for the benefit of his group companies. Khaitan quivers with indignation at the slur. 'I am not an asset stripper—I lost Rs 18 crores in Metal Box!' he exclaims.

The meanest allegations revolve round the plastic flexible packaging unit at Taratala, two flats in prime residential localities and Barlow House, the head office. 'We approached Metal Box because of Taratala, and India Foil concluded the deal before we acquired Metal Box,' claims Khaitan. 'As for the two flats, India Foil took them over as a part of the payment which they were advancing to Metal Box against the working capital. Now Ross Deas had also given money towards Metal

Box's rehabilitation—about Rs 2 crores to Rs 2.5 crores. So three floors of Barlow House were given to him as a mortgage. In the event Metal Box did not repay him, these three floors would belong to him. These are the only transactions I have done. How can anybody say I have made money? And what about the financial institutions? I kept borrowing from the banks and the institutions. Three institutional directors from ICICI, IDBI and LIC were on the board. There was no way you could even think of a single transaction without going to the board.'

Nonetheless, there's no hiding the fact that the Taratala factory is a flourishing cog in the Khaitan wheel while Metal Box remains mired in court cases, debts and disputes with several of its factories having had to be closed down. According to a Khaitan-watcher, the unpleasant episode 'still seems to pinch him. Because of this, he is being extraordinarily careful not to be seen as asset stripper in Union Carbide India'.

The Metal Box and Union Carbide India buyouts beamed a spotlight on a man loath to shine. S. K. Khaitan (no relation), a local fan manufacturer, grabs more headlines than the global tea baron. Few outside the Royal Calcutta Turf Club recognize, let alone know, BM, and that's the way he likes it. A hunt for background information through media archives over the past two decades spewed plenty of dry financial facts on group companies but just two profiles. The Who's Who is similarly unhelpful, merely providing a list of companies and an office address. It doesn't even mention his date of birth.

Khaitan's takeover of Union Carbide India in particular forced change. It lifted Khaitan out of the Calcutta backwaters and dropped him willy-nilly onto the national stage.

Famous for its red Eveready batteries and its 'Gimme Red' advertising campaign, Union Carbide India came up for sale in February 1994. Its American parent, Union Carbide

Corporation (UCC) had been trying to get rid of its unwanted child ever since the December 2, 1984 Bhopal tragedy in which 4,000 died and half a million were affected, but the Indian government froze ownership changes until a compensation package had been hammered out. A compromise was reached a decade later, in January 1994, in which it was agreed that UCC could sell its 50.90 per cent holding in Union Carbide India if it used Rs 650m of the proceeds to build a hospital. Anything UCC could manage to get on top of that, it could keep.

When merchant bankers from CreditCapital Finance Corporation and the State Bank of India approached him, Khaitan's reaction was lukewarm. Shanti, on the other hand, was keen as mustard. The boys needed more work, she felt. Aditya was doing well, looking after the tea business, and Sandeep, their son-in-law, was well settled in Kilburn Reprographics, but Deepak needed to buckle down a bit more. In 1994, *Business Standard* had front-paged a report on an imminent split in the group, hinting at competitive rivalry between the siblings. The report was inaccurate about several facts and BM maintained his usual frosty silence when it was published, but it goaded Shanti into some introspection.

Mad about racing, Deepak was more absorbed in his stable of 300 horses and his stud farm than in his garage of engineering companies. Instead of trying to improve the lacklustre performance of the divisions under 'his' charge, Deepak was always flying off for the day to racing centres like Bangalore, Bombay, or Pune whenever the racecourse at home was closed. 'The ecstacy that one experiences while watching one's horse win on home turf is unsurpassable,' Deepak was quoted as having said. What about when a company made profits, asked his sensible mother. A big Rs 3bn company like Union Carbide India would help pin down Deepak, make him more interested in business, she thought.

To convince her husband, she secretly phoned a man whom she knew BM would have to listen to: Rama Babu.

R.P. Goenka's opinions carry much weight in the Khaitan household. After the Harrods bomb blast, he was one of the first to reach BM's bedside. When he wanted help for his last-ditch Haldia Petrochemicals salvage operation, BM pitched in unblinkingly. Goenka's niece, Yashodhara, is Deepak's wife. And Khaitan credits his rehabilitation into Marwari society to Goenka. Their friendship is so well known that when income tax officials came to visit Goenka in March 1988, news flashed around Calcutta's business community that Khaitan was being interrogated as well. RP caught the first available flight the next morning after Shanti's call came through.

All through the day and deep into the night Shanti, RP and the boys reasoned with BM, pointing out the pros of acquiring Union Carbide India.

Over the past five years, whereas the near stagnant dry cells market grew by just 1.6 per cent per annum in volume terms, Union Carbide India's sales had surged by an average of 10 per cent per annum. Its pre-tax profits had grown to Rs 320m in 1993-94 against Rs 60m four years earlier. Debt, at Rs 110m, was a comfortable 13 per cent of its net worth of Rs 840m, which meant that it had tremendous borrowing capacity and could easily raise up to Rs 2bn, if necessary. Its fixed assets were substantially undervalued. Most important of all, its strong brand had been carefully shielded from besmirchment by the Bhopal stigma. Lastly, the Khaitans were already in the battery business (Standard Batteries) and this would be a good expansion opportunity. Persuaded by the combined strength of the forces working on him, Khaitan caved in.

At first, it was believed that a controlling interest in Union

Carbide India would cost Rs 800m. This was based on a share price of Rs 60. With the criminal liability of the Bhopal tragedy hanging like a sword of Damocles over it, the corporate pariah's share price had languished around Rs 55 through most of 1993-94 on Calcutta's Lyons Range. At Rs 800m, there were plenty of buyers. In mid-1994, CreditCapital and SBI Caps announced a shortlist of seven: R.P. Goenka, B.M. Khaitan, Nusli Wadia of Bombay Dyeing, T.P.G. Nambiar of the BPL Group, A.C. Muthiah of Spic, K.K. Jajodia of Assam Company and Arun Bajoria, the jute baron. The scrip began its inevitable climb upwards as speculators started kicking it around. Eventually Khaitan paid Rs 2.9bn or Rs 175 per share.

Though Goenka's name was first on the list, he was an even less serious contender than Nambiar or Bajoria. K.K. Jajodia, on the other hand, was keen to buy but 'could not put money on the table', says one of the bidders. The race quickly narrowed down to Muthiah, Wadia and Khaitan. Muthiah, often called the Ambani of the south, made a joint bid with Henkel, a German chemical company. They had a vested interest in that Union Carbide India was an existing distributor of SPIC's detergent powders and bars. But as the price moved up, the combine withdrew, leaving Khaitan and Wadia to slug it out.

Wadia, a canny battle-scarred samurai, at this point of time was rolling on a high. Bombay Dyeing's March 1994 results were excellent and he had recently swiped Britannia Industries, India's biggest bread and biscuit company, into his group from under the nose of Rajan Pillai, an old friend-turned-foe. In an expansive mood, Wadia wanted to beef up his group, and Union Carbide India's strong brands fitted in perfectly with his strategy for the future. To strengthen his bid, Wadia tied up with Ralston Purina, the American transnational which in 1986 had acquired UCC's battery business globally except in India.

Through the spring of 1994, the Union Carbide India scrip climbed steadily from Rs 55 to Rs 95 on news of serious bidding, but UCC wanted at least $70m (Rs 2.1bn at the then rates) or Rs 125 per share. According to a former Union Carbide India executive, this was a more than fair price. Ralston Purina's internal calculations, based on a meticulous due diligence assessment, pegged Union Carbide's market value at Rs 2.5bn. By August 1994, the press was trumpeting that Wadia looked to be the winner, but on September 9 the State Bank of India announced to several red faces the sale of UCC's Indian battery company to Khaitan.

'Price was the sole determining factor,' the Union Carbide India executive continued. 'The logic behind BM's thinking was quite simple. By any valuation, the price should not have been more than Rs 150. He knew that Wadia was a keen buyer. So he was willing to pay 10-12 per cent more or an extra Rs 25 to make sure of the result.' In the event, B.M. Khaitan offered Rs 2.9bn or Rs 400m more than Wadia.

At $96.5m, the sale was the biggest buy-out deal in Indian corporate history. Before this, H.J. Heinz had paid $67.5m (Rs 2bn) through its local subsidiary for the purchase of Glaxo India's family products division, and Atlanta's Coca-Cola Inc had reportedly paid $60m (Rs 1.8bn) for Ramesh Chauhan's soft drink brand, Thums Up.

Khaitan had won the race but there were few participants in the victory march. In 1985, news of his acquisition of Metal Box had caused its stock to rise. In 1994, on the contrary, the Union Carbide scrip fell from Rs 146 to Rs 122. Hurt by this public show of no-confidence in his management and some acidic comments in the media, BM went deeper into purdah, while a contrite Shanti repented. 'I wish I had not forced him to take over Union Carbide,' she confessed to me in private.

Some of the adverse comments were undoubtedly valid. In 1978, Khaitan had objected to a jute manager (Parson) teaching him the tea business. In 1994, the tables were turned with the media asking how a tea planter would run a consumer goods company at a time when the Indian battery market was passing through a turbulent phase. Analysts wondered how Khaitan would tackle increased competition from tightly focused global players such as Duracell and Matsushita who are making strong bids to carve out leadership positions in the newly liberalized economy.

In a bid to counter salacious gossip, Khaitan used a two-pronged strategy. He insisted that he would make no changes to the existing strong management structure of Union Carbide India (now renamed Eveready Industries). And he shook hands with ex-rival Ralston to jointly manufacture alkaline batteries in India. In addition, the contract allowed Khaitan to access state-of-the-art technology and Ralston would be able to share the Eveready brand.

The negative reports eased up after these announcements but Khaitan's dull reputation is a constant source of discomfort at 4 Mangoe Lane. Among Calcutta's corporate elite, Khaitan is considered to be at best an average businessman. He took a bad hit during the Metal Box episode, but even before that, he'd been accused of buying blue-chips and making them sick. During the Eveready Industries auction, a prominent local businessman had cuttingly wondered out loud why Khaitan wanted more companies when the group already had so many lines and wasn't growing in any of them. On the stock exchanges, shareholders don't consider him investor-friendly, and analysts dislike the low profitability of his non-tea companies.

Khaitan's poor public image is at odd variance with his very real achievements and unusual rags-to-riches background. He may not be a Dhirubhai Ambani, but then neither is he a Ratan Tata or Kumar Mangalam Birla, both heirs to mammoth empires. In a span of two decades, BM aggressively assembled a Rs 16bn empire from scratch through some shrewd manoeuvring. Apart from the Assam Company and possibly Warren Tea (where he made a lukewarm offer but later stepped aside in favour of his friend, Govind Ruia), Khaitan hasn't yet lost a deal for which he has hungered.

In 1995, his group consisted of twenty-five companies with interests apart from tea in batteries (Eveready Industries, Standard Batteries); engineering (Macneill Engineering, McNally Bharat, Kilburn Engineering, Worthington Pumps, Deutsche Babcock); packaging (India Foils); and financial services (Williamson Financial Service). Five of his companies make it to *Business Today's* 1995 list of India's 500 most valuable companies: McLeod Russel (at 141), George Williamson (275), Standard Batteries (314), Eveready (320) and Williamson Magor (384). How can a man who single-handedly built up such a substantial empire be viewed as a mediocre manager?

In most of his companies, Khaitan's personal holdings tend to be substantial, i.e., from 40 to 74 per cent, leading some analysts to regard him as one of India's richest men. A September 1994 report pegged the group's market cap at Rs 22bn and valued Khaitan's holdings at Rs 13.2bn. Oddly enough, instead of being perceived as a source of strength, these large holdings cause investors to shy away. Almost as a rule, fund managers, who tend to be more jittery than a flock of sparrows, prefer scrips with steady and high volumes of trading so that they can get in and get out easily. Khaitan's extensive holdings act as roadblocks.

'This disappointment over Khaitan scrips has become a mindset among punters on Lyons Range,' says a fund manager. 'It was because of this that the market reacted so negatively as soon as news of Khaitan's clinching the Union Carbide deal was announced.' His investor-unfriendly image was reinforced when Khaitan refrained from making an open offer to Union Carbide's minority shareholders at the time of its takeover. Later, the finance ministry would force him to overturn this decision.

The lacklustre performance of his numerous engineering companies has equally contributed to Khaitan's reputation as a middling manager. Mostly acquired between 1975 and 1985, the small, scattered and largely unprofitable companies manufacture a host of products, none of which stand out. Some, like Standard Batteries which manufactures car batteries and competes against the well-run Chloride Industries, are rich in real estate but poor in their production processes. Others, like India Foils, are poised to make a recovery, but the long time span taken by the restructuring has reduced public confidence in eventual success.

GIMME RED

One of his friends defends BM: 'Compared to some of the other businessmen in your book, Khaitan may not be all that dynamic, but he is a nice human being.' 'Too gentlemanly to lose his temper,' agrees another. Following his successful bid for Union Carbide India, boorish cocktail circuit speculation about his ability to pay for his purchase ruffled Khaitan's sensibilities, but he swallowed his pride, kept a tight rein on his temper and refused to be provoked.

Deepak and Aditya aren't cast in the same mould. As the day neared when Rs 2.9bn had to be handed over to the banks, and journalists went overboard calculating the pieces of family silver the Khaitans would have to sell in order to meet their obligation, Aditya was stung into issuing a challenge. 'Anyone who has any doubts can be my guest when we hand over the cheque to the State Bank of India,' he told *Business Today.*

Typically, Khaitan senior kept mum, worked out his options, did his sums, and boarded the evening Calcutta-Bombay flight. The next morning, under a blazing October sun—May and October are Bombay's hottest months—he was spotted entering The Oberoi for a meeting with a senior American Express executive. Before lunch, a consortium of three banks had been formed to provide the Khaitans with the bridge loan they needed. By evening, a queue had formed outside his door with banks competing against each other for the business. The cheque for Union Carbide India was due on December 5, 1994, three days after the tenth anniversary of the Bhopal gas disaster, but Briju Babu coolly pre-paid his bill two weeks earlier.

The story didn't end there, however. Business journalists, who had enjoyed the sport of Khaitan-baiting through the winter of 1994, had a field day during the summer of 1995. The AmEx loan was due for repayment six months later, in May. Khaitan was a rich man, but his wealth was tied up in the shares through which he controlled his empire. Some companies, especially the tea ones, were rich and commonly paid out generous dividends of between 45 and 55 per cent every year, but the group's net profit in 1994 was just Rs 380m. Khaitan didn't have Rs 2.9bn plus Rs 190m as interest charges in liquid cash. So he went to the market.

In October 1994, he announced that McLeod Russel India would shortly be making a Rs 2.7bn rights issue at a premium of Rs 210. At the time, the pricing seemed stiff but not overly greedy. McLeod was a blue-chip company quoting at Rs 310, and no tea major had made a public offering in several years. Unfortunately, by the time Khaitan could gather the requisite legal permissions, the arithmetic on which the pricing had been based went completely haywire. In early 1995, the bottom fell out of the primary market with the eruption of the MS Shoes scandal in which a promoter was arrested for possibly the first time in memory for misinforming the public in his prospectus, and the secondary market collapsed on the back of the primary market.

In keeping with the domino effect, McLeod's share price plummeted, hitting a low of Rs 205, making the scaled down price tag of Rs 190 for the new shares totally unappetising. Besides, in the prospectus, Khaitan had clearly stated that the issue was being made to fund the Eveready acquisition. If one wanted an exposure in Eveready, why pick up McLeod shares when the battery company's scrip was cheaper at Rs 150? Unhappily for the underwriters and Khaitan's reputation, there was no way of holding back the issue until the index picked up. The dynamics of the situation and the Reserve Bank of India's refusal to roll over the AmEx loan left Khaitan with no choice but to go ahead with the McLeod issue in a dangerously bearish market. The issue opened on May 25.

Prior to this, Khaitan had rolled up his sleeves as he had done once not so long ago, and begun meticulously exploring his options. Not surprisingly, backstage, wheels began to grind. A discreet support campaign pushed up the McLeod scrip to Rs 215, that of Eveready to Rs 175. More importantly, the tough heads of large institutional investment firms in Bombay and New Delhi took his long-distance calls, listened to his story, and promised him their support in case the retail market didn't bite.

Having taken all the precautions he could, Khaitan waited by the telephone, outwardly relaxed. 'He's cool, methodical, and calculating,' admires Nantoo Banerjee, a reporter with *Business Standard* who has been tracking Khaitan's progress for over a decade. 'Even under fire, he keeps a cool head.' During the tense weeks which his top executives spent fanning out across the country drumming up support for the McLeod issue, Briju Babu stuck to his routine. At the close of every working day, at 5 o'clock sharp, he closes his files and appointment book, whooshes down to the ground floor in his private lift and leaves for a brisk forty-five-minute walk before returning home.

This month of May was no different. His quiet faith in himself was justified. On the evening of June 2, after the counting was over, tired money merchants slumped with relief. The McLeod's issue was oversubscribed—by a bare 3 per cent, it is true, but oversubscribed nonetheless—and the Cassandras silenced.

Another person who had complete faith in Briju Babu's ability to pull it off was Aditya. 'As I was growing up, I found people had a lot of respect for Dad. People would talk about how he would never hurt anyone, about his code of behaviour. He would often help people and they would remember it. That's why the chairman of ICICI and American Express went out of their way to help us with Union Carbide. And Dad is a very particular person with strong likes and dislikes about the way things should be done. It taught me discipline. When I was a child and getting ready for school, I knew that every morning at a quarter to eight he would ask the servant for a cup of tea, and I would look at my watch and it would be a quarter to eight. For forty years he has followed the same routine; get up at 6.30 a.m., do yoga with an old guy who has been coming to our house for years, have a cup of tea and a light breakfast, read the papers, leave for work by ten. He's back home after his walk between 6.30 and 7 and likes to sleep early.'

His physical fitness probably saved his life after the Harrods bomb blast. According to the doctors, regular walks and yoga had strengthened Khaitan's constitution, enabling him to survive the lacerations caused by flying shrapnel, shredded car metal and splintered glass.

The Harrods incident was a bizarre case of poor timing from Khaitan's point of view. It was pure mischance that he happened to be where he was when the IRA struck. Had he decided to pick up a hamper from Fortnum & Mason on Piccadilly, he would have been safe and sound. Like most businessmen, Khaitan is not the sort of man who goes out of his way to meet trouble head-on. On the contrary, 'BM is the kind of man who will walk a mile out of his way to avoid trouble. If there is a dispute over Rs 10 lakhs, and someone threatens to take him to court, his first reaction will be to give in, to pay off the Rs 10 lakhs and end the chapter,' says a fellow industrialist.

He would much rather work through the entire span of his career peacefully, without sight or sound of a gun. Unlike Mr T of the old American television series, the *A-Team*, the Indian tea baron is a pacifist by nature, yet his is a life splattered by violence and bloodshed. As a child growing up in the tense locality of Burra Bazaar during the pre-Partition days, the young Khaitan would try to block out the screams wafting through his window. He would succeed only after the army helped the family flee to a safer locality. In his thirties, he concentrated on his work as best he could during the Naxalite movement which drove so many Marwari families out of Calcutta to the more orderly cities of Bombay and New Delhi. 'Where would we have gone? Our base is and always will be Calcutta,' says Shanti phlegmatically. Normally businessmen don't feel the need to own a private army, but BM maintains a 2,000-strong trained and armed militia to protect his managers from ULFA and other terrorists.

Murder, mayhem and other such horrors have no place in Khaitan's peaceful wood panelled study, with its charming vista, through delicate curtains, of lush green lawns stretching into the horizon. Sipping tea with Shanti and BM in fine bone china cups and chatting about the future of tea exports, it's easy to forget that ULFA's gun-smoke continues to out-reek the aroma of green tea buds ripening under Assam's mellow sun. But behind BM's genial smiles and the impish gleam in his eyes is a steely determination not to let the long nights of the past and the present affect the future. 'We're going to build good citizens in Assam, you'll see. Let things quieten down a little and then we'll go together to the gardens. They're lovely. Until then, come again to my humble little tea shop at 4 Mangoe Lane.'

Chapter 6

Bharat and Vijay Shah

THE SHAH FAMILY TREE

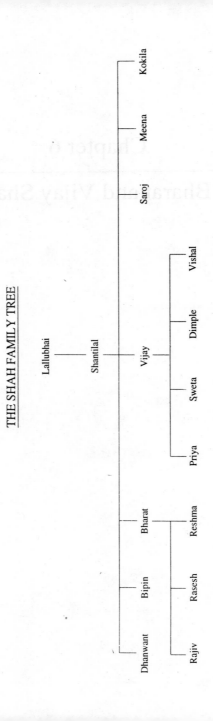

Wankhede Stadium, Bombay
December 21, 1989

Over a thousand lucky invitees received the much-sought-after card with the snappy Aston Martin cover on top. Inside, the inscription read:

> Dear Moneypenny, I'm on my way from assignment in Afghanistan to holiday in Bombay and I heard that Rajiv and Reshma; Rajesh and Bela are partying at the Regal Room, Hotel Oberoi Towers on December 22 1989 at 2100 hours, a black tie affair, naturally.
>
> Tell 'M' that I've picked up a lead on the diamond business out here and as the theme for the party is James Bond 007, I should fit in quite easily. You might ask 'Q' to send my Aston Martin to fetch _____ to accompany me to the party.
>
> Sweetheart, take messages till I return. Meanwhile, I'll look for a Maharajah for you from India. Love and kisses, James.

Reshma, Bharat Shah's 18-year-old daughter, was about

to be married. Traditionally, among Gujaratis, the bride's father makes all the wedding arrangements. Unlike Steve Martin in *The Father of the Bride*, Shah wanted to make sure the wedding would eclipse anything his friends, relatives and business associates had ever experienced. This would be a wedding to remember. The James Bond black tie party was just one of a dozen exotic parties planned for the nuptial arranged between two of Bombay's leading diamantaire families: Shah's B. Vijaykumar and Kishore Mehta's Beautiful Diamonds.

Fifteen thousand people were invited to the wedding on Thursday, December 21, 1989. To accommodate them, Shah hired Bombay's Wankhede Stadium, the venue of some of the fiercest cricket battles in Test history. A month before the wedding, 200 artisans descended upon its grounds. Beggars and neighbours gawked as they created a plaster-of-paris Rajasthani fantasy. Reshma's *mandap* was a fairy-tale palace with heavily encrusted pillars entwined with tulips from Holland and orchids from Thailand. Fireworks and laser shows, *mehndi* for the ladies, music and *dandiya raas,* an Indiana Jones party, complimentary Indian wedding attire for international guests—the entire office staff of B. Vijaykumar went into overdrive to ensure that everything went off smoothly.

In another part of Bombay, others were making their own plans. A motley collection of activists from groups such as the Bombay Sarvodaya Mandal, the Janmukti Sangharsha Vahini, the Chhatra Yuva Sangharsha Vahini, and the Stree Mukti Sanghatana were aghast at the millions being poured into the extravaganza. The do-gooders held angry demonstrations outside the stadium. Their chants of '*Yeh shaadi nahin, yeh tamasha hai. Band karo, band karo*' drowned the sweet notes of the shehnai playing the wedding ragas.

Pleading for a boycott of the 'wasteful show', on the evening of the reception, about eighty activists handed out leaflets asking guests to remember that millions of Indians had no food or clothing. 'We are ashamed. We protest', read one. Dressed in silks and jewels, invitees stepping out of chauffeured limousines were taken aback by the hostile reception committee at the stadium's entrance. Khadi-clad demonstrators booed and heckled them, provoking some to leave in a huff. Emotions ran high. Twenty-six women were arrested, and there was a police lathi-charge when the demonstrators became uncontrollable.

Such intense public interest in what should, after all, have been a private affair rattled the entire diamantaire community. Rallying behind Bharat Shah, the Diamond Industry Defence Association was born to educate the public.

Its hastily elected chairman, M. Mehta, wrote a strongly worded letter of protest to the *Times of India*. 'The diamond trade donated crores of rupees in three years of drought in Gujarat and distributed about 1,700 crores of rupees as wages to the diamond cutters there. Bharat Shah donates huge amounts for charities. Mr Kishore Mehta has donated crores of rupees for a big hospital in Bombay. The diamond industry gives employment to nearly ten lakh people in India. How many people have been employed or helped by the organizations who protested about the marriage reception?' he asked indignantly.

Gradually the media glare died down. The hard feelings have not. A silent class war lingers. The diamond merchants have a valid point of view: don't they have the right to spend their hard-earned money as they please? Ordinary people cannot understand how a handful of families, all belonging to one small community—Palanpuri Jains—have become so rich, so quickly.

PALANPUR

Palanpur, a parched, dusty village founded in AD 746, lies on the Gujarat-Rajasthan border, 350 km north of Surat, a town which would hit world headlines in 1994 for a suspected outbreak of plague. Traditionally, the Jains of Palanpur—whose surnames seem to start and end with Mehta with a handful of Shahs thrown in for good measure—served as accountants and administrators to the nawabs of the village. As it developed into a diamond trading centre, the experienced money-managers seized control of the lucrative business. In the '80s a combination of luck and hard work enabled the tiny community to snatch a significant portion of the global diamond trade from a group of powerful Hasidic Jews.

The tentacles of this trade reach from De Beers' legendary diamond mines in South Africa, to London, Antwerp, Tel Aviv, Hong Kong, New York and Surat. Though London and Antwerp remain the leading diamond cities, today seven out of ten diamonds pass through Bombay. First entering the city as roughs, these diamonds wind their way into the pockets of faceless *angadias* (couriers) travelling second class to cutting and polishing factories in Surat, Navsari and Palanpur. Returning to Bombay, the value-added diamonds are re-exported.

'It all started about twenty-five years ago,' recalls Bharat Shah. 'We went to the bottom end of the market, buying and cutting diamonds which the Jews had rejected.' Israeli and Belgium cutters sneered at the thought of carving stones under ten points or one-tenth of a carat (the Koh-i-noor, incidentally, is 109 carats), but Indians were not so fussy. Purchasing modest quantities of small industrial quality roughs, Bharat and other Palanpuris handed them over to the master craftsmen of their village who turned them into sparkling gems, some so small that few can handle them without a tweezer.

Buyers liked the products, but Jewish wholesalers were prejudiced against Indians. According to one of the first Jains to set up shop in the USA in 1966, 'We simply weren't liked. Since the Indian government loudly supported the Palestinian cause, this aroused a lot of emotions in the Jewish community. Initially few Jews liked to do business with me. But the fact that I had a good, cheap product to sell, the fact that I delivered on time—this made the difference.'

By the late '70s, De Beers woke up to the fact that Indians could create something out of nothing. The brown rough stones which were being thrown away could now be usefully cut and polished into marketable diamonds. The discovery coincided with inflation, and an emerging trend in fashion jewellery for diamonds the size of pinheads which only Indian artisans could deliver. Surat became a boom town as international buyers came running to Indian suppliers. Out of the grand total of 95 million carats of diamonds which were cut and polished all over the world last year, 59 million carats were processed in India. Big Jewish firms like Star Diamond continue to dominate the big stones market, but in dollar terms, Indians account for roughly 75 per cent—and growing—of De Beers' total sales.

The Oppenheimers, the Jewish family who founded and control De Beers, began wooing the Palanpuri merchants ardently. During the monthly auctions in London (known as sights), kosher beef and bagels are swept off the dining table to make way for the simple vegetarian food dictated by Jainism. And to keep the competitive spirit alive, the Oppenheimers shower high performers with rewards and awards, special privileges, and glamorous and exclusive invitations. Lavish parties and exclusive tête-à-têtes are arranged for the biggest and the best when Anthony Oppenheimer and his important cousin, Nicholas Oppenheimer, come to Bombay.

The growing closeness between the Palanpuris and white South Africans smacked of hypocrisy. Politically and officially, India and South Africa weren't on talking terms for much of this period. Like the United States, Britain and most of Europe, India protested against South Africa's apartheid policy by imposing sanctions. These were officially lifted after the April 1994 South African elections which brought Nelson Mandela to power. All through the preceding decade, as diamond exports climbed, the Indian government looked the other way. In a single decade, exports of polished diamonds surged from Rs 5.5bn (in 1979-80) to Rs 49.72bn (in 1989-90). Indians wrested 62 per cent of the global trade.

In one short decade, merchants like Bharat and Vijay, college dropouts, became the world's carat czars, founding and heading India's largest private empire, a Rs 35bn conglomerate known as B. Vijaykumar (in India) and Vijaydimon (in Belgium), with interests in diamonds, construction and films. They have cutting and polishing factories in Bangkok, Antwerp, Tel Aviv, Bombay, Surat and Palanpur, employing over 22,000 workers. The head office is in Bombay, under Bharat, while the Antwerp office is looked after by Vijay.

Nothing in Bharat's Bombay office suggests this accomplishment. The building itself, Mehta Bhawan, at Charni Road, is dingy and dusty. B. Vijaykumar owns three floors, or roughly half the nondescript building. Bharat's office is on the sixth floor, small but bright and sunny, with a well-used feel to it. The scarred, solid and workmanlike wooden table behind which Bharat sits (and Vijay, when in town), is littered with slips of paper and packets of diamonds. Three phones ring continuously, and staff saunter in and out without knocking. Unlike the offices of other Bombay diamond merchants, there are no video cameras or armed guards, nor heavily barred doors with peepholes.

Some security is offered by the miniature and smelly lift. It can carry just four including the bored liftman. Visitors—and the Shah brothers themselves—are served sweet, milky tea brewed Gujarati style. The cups are chipped china; the spoon, a 50 paisa metal strip of the kind used by wayside foodstalls. The furnishings are tacky. White Formica, yellow with age and dust, is used for panels on the walls and doors. The pocket-size reception area holds a couple of worn rexine sofas with holes along the sides.

The international corporate headquarters of this giant, extremely profitable, firm could as well belong to a middle-class yarn broker or a small-time plastic processor. Except for three giveaways. The first is a showy three-foot diameter lapis lazuli circle embedded in white marble in the sixth floor entrance lobby, with the initials B and V entwined in brass. The second, located opposite the blase receptionist-cum-telephone operator, is a glass cabinet stuffed with gleaming export awards from a grateful government. The third is a massive cement-and-steel walk-in vault concealed inside Bharat's office. It was built on-site when the Shahs acquired the Mehta Bhavan office in the mid-'70s. Nothing has changed except for the size of their operations.

To cope with increasing volumes, a huge new walk-in strongroom is under construction in Vijay's office on Pelikaanstraat in Antwerp. It's impossible to estimate how many dollars worth of diamonds such a vault can hold, but it would almost certainly be in nine-digit figures. Unlike the Bombay office, security in Antwerp is tight. Doors to every cubicle are kept locked and the entrance is manned by security officers. There are at least fifteen video cameras in operation, and Vijay keeps a wary eye on each cubicle and passageway through a hi-tech monitor in the corner of his grey silk and Italian marble office.

There's a video camera mounted in his cabin ceiling also. It's a small room, 16' by 12' at most, and dwarfed by its tall, well-built occupier. There's barely enough space for the five chairs surrounding the white and green desk piled high with packets of diamonds waiting to be checked before being forwarded to buyers. Every so often someone walks in with a cheap red plastic bowl stuffed with white paper packets of polished diamonds or small cream cloth sacks of roughs tied with bright *rani* pink ribbons. Seated opposite Vijay is an accountant whose job it is to tally what comes in with what goes out, mechanically and unremittingly.

The lingua franca in the office is Gujarati. From the view of concrete office blocks, to the brown skinned executives, to the distinct smell of curry in the kitchen and the framed portrait of the goddess Laxmi, the office could easily be in Nariman Point. Only the blonde long-legged and micro-minied secretaries with their heavily accented English remind you that this is not Bombay but the heart of Europe.

In the block next to Vijaydimon is the Beurs voor Diamanthandel, one of Antwerp's four diamond bourses. Its director is Peter Meeus, an energetic and dapper Belgian with sharp eyes and a quick warm smile, whose responsibility it is to uphold ethical trade practices among the diamantaires and keep them on a tight leash. He has known Vijay for the past twenty years. Are the Shahs the world's carat czars, I asked. His smile thinned. 'This is not something I can answer. The most I can tell you is that they are definitely among the top five, and I am including here companies from all over the world. Vijaydimon is one of our very very important members,' Meeus says warily.

What makes them so special? As with the entire Palanpuri diamantaire community, the Shahs' basic fortune lay in being in the right business at the right time and at the right place.

Over the course of the past twenty years, however, seven families have outstripped the rest. Today, Arun Mehta of B. Arunkumar, Madhu Mehta of Jayam, Dilip Mehta of Rosy Blue, Rashmi Mehta of Gembel, Jatin Mehta of Su-Raj, the Shahs and their in-laws, Kishore Mehta of Beautiful Diamonds, dominate the trade. Jatin Mehta is supposed to be the modern face of the Indian diamond business, Arun Kumar once held the title of being the world's biggest diamantaire, but what separates the men from the boys? What special skills do Bharat and Vijay possess? How did B. Vijaykumar become the number one?

According to Francois Van Looveren, a broker with Bonas-Couzyn, a large brokering firm, 'to be a successful diamantaire, you need to be intelligent—that goes without saying. But you need to have the right combination of the abilities of a banker, a manufacturer, a marketer and to have a good judgement of people. If there is a misjudgement in any one of these qualities, the combination goes wrong. It goes without saying that both Bharat and Vijay have the right combination of these qualities.'

Meeus is more candid. 'Vijay can take risks. I remember when they were thinking of setting up a factory in Bangkok—many were going to Thailand at the time—but everybody went in for small sizes, Jewish and Indians, but not Vijay. He thought they should be polishing medium stones. Everybody thought he would fail, but that factory is doing very well.' Contemplation of his success pushes Vijay into a reflective mood. 'I wish father had lived just five years more and could have seen our success. I always wanted to prove to my father that I could be somebody.'

Tall, fair and charismatic, Shantilal Lallubhai Shah was a jeweller, as was his father and grandfather before him. In 1957, under the Replenishment Scheme, the government permitted the limited import of diamonds so long as they were re-exported. Shantilal, who had just separated from his two brothers, spotted an opportunity. He spent the rest of his life shuttling between London and Antwerp, returning to Bombay every six weeks for a fortnight.

Living more or less on their own in a small bungalow, at 56 Ridge Road in the Malabar Hill area, a stone's throw away from Aditya Birla's home in Il Palazzo, it was a lonely life for Shantilal's family, wife Bhiki and their seven children: Dhanwant, Bipin, Bharat (b. August 5, 1944), Vijay (b. March 25, 1950), Saroj, Meena and Kokila. The children studied at various schools nearby such as Hill Grange, Campion and Bharda, leading a comfortable upper middle-class Gujarati lifestyle. However, the constant separation from a father whom they adored appears to have left a deep mark on his children and particularly Vijay, the youngest of the seven.

In the '60s, Shantilal settled in London, in a small house in Golders Green, at 38 Gainsborough Gardens (which he bought), and operated out of a small office in Hatton Gardens (which he rented). The Shahs still own the house, though of late Vijay prefers to stay at the Dorchester. 'It was not like he was staying there [abroad] all the time. At least he must be coming four-five times a year to Bombay,' says Vijay, curiously defensive.

During one of these trips, in 1969, Shantilal decided to take his daughters to Palanpur. He wanted to show them their roots. Soon after they arrived there, he suffered a paralytic stroke and died a few days later. Vijay, then nineteen and studying at the London School of Economics, was on a diamond-buying visit to Gibraltar. Twenty-five years later, he still hasn't accepted his father's death. 'For two or three years, whenever I heard a knock on the door, I thought of father. He used to have a special kind of knock. I kept thinking father would come back. I couldn't believe this could happen. He was just fifty-four and such a fine man. People used to call him "Guru". If only it hadn't happened in Palanpur and he had been able to get proper medical treatment . . . .'

Fortunately, all four boys had acquired some business experience by this time. Financially, their father's death was not as big a blow for the Shahs as, say, Nand Kishore Ruia's death would be for Shashi and Ravi of the Essar Group, or that of Aditya Birla for Kumar Mangalam. Dhanwant, Bharat and Bipin were all working in the family firm, a partnership with H. Patel, a friend of Shantilal's and fellow diamantaire. Nonetheless, like the Ruia brothers, Vijay dropped out of the London School of Economics to help out.

On his return to Bombay, Vijay found his family in turmoil. Bharat was about to get married to Bina H. Modi. Dhanwant, the eldest and since their father's death the head of the family, was losing interest in the diamond trade and wanted to risk the bread-and-butter business for the more glamorous world of movies. Bipin, fed up with all of them, wanted to opt out completely and set up his own diamond trading firm. Unwilling to fight with Bipin, the rest of the family moved out, leaving him with the original firm (SS Diamond Company) and the house at Ridge Road. Shifting to Atlas Apartments on Narayan Dhabholkar Road, they immediately scouted around for a new office.

AT FIRST SIGHT

In a city of mean streets, Zaveri Bazaar stands out as one of Bombay's most shattering experiences for a newcomer. Stretching beyond the Juma Masjid on the Crawford Market side towards the Mumbadevi Temple, it's the heart of the retail jewellery and silverware trade. A long line of narrow shops decorated with glittering mirrors, bright halogen lights, and tawdry gold jewellery stretches from one end of the noisy, congested bazaar to the other. Behind the counters are fast-talking, Gujarati-speaking, paan-spitting businessmen.

It was to this throbbing market that Bharat and Vijay gravitated after separating from Bipin. Vijay was ambitious: 'When you start something and if you would like to do it in a big way or you think it has big potential, when sky is the limit, you must do on your own. If you really want to achieve in business, it has to be your very own business.' So the Shahs ended their partnership with H. Patel and bought their own office, just off the main market at 32-34 Dhanji Street. The brothers also bought a plot of land at Andheri where they set up a diamond cutting and polishing unit with 400 workers. 'It was about 5,000 sq.ft. and cost around Rs 50-Rs 60 per sq. ft.,' says Bharat. Bipin had inherited the family company name, so they named their first firm after themselves, B. Vijaykumar.

While Dhanwant busied himself in film-making, Bharat and Vijay concentrated on building up the diamond business, slipping into an easy division of labour. 'I started handling the manufacturing activity in Bombay and meeting the buyers,' says Bharat. 'Vijay kept sending foreigners, the roughs and also the clients to me.'

To feed the Andheri factory, Vijay roamed markets off the beaten tracks, ones which would give better margins than the common diamond centres. 'I used to go to Africa, buying quite a lot of rough diamonds. I am not talking about huge volumes, those were not the days, you know, but still during that time we were buying quite a lot. I was never based in one place.' B Vijaykumar's first year's sales were Rs 5m-6m.

Vijay's aggressive purchases caught the eye of Monty Charles, a director of the London-based Diamond Trading Company (DTC), De Beers's main marketing arm. 'He was always looking for a dynamic firm, you know, which I can't call myself but at least he must have found something in us,' smiles Vijay. Charles asked Bonas-Couzyn, one of DTC's many brokers, to check out B. Vijaykumar. In 1973, they were appointed sight-holders. 'It was a big deal,' says Bharat. At the time, there were fewer than fifteen Indian sight-holders, and there was a long waiting list.

Once he had gotten over his awe of the international giant, Vijay cocked a snook at the DTC. 'In those days, people used to run for DTC whereas I didn't bother much. We were taking sights, we were buying. But those who don't understand roughs and those who don't have the confidence, they are depending on DTC and their closed boxes. Where I never had any fun.' Bharat explains: 'Only if you don't understand roughs, then you must go to DTC. Because there it is a standard price. But suppose if you know the rough, then you can buy from the open market directly, you know. Like my brother used to buy from Africa. Other people, they did not even visit at that time Africa.'

'Going to Africa during those times was not easy,' says Vijay. 'But I am a strong believer of self-confidence. I used to see with my own eyes. Also you have got to fight for prices. It was the most difficult thing because the African people are such that they won't believe in serious prices. If the goods are worth $10, they ask you for $100. Then if you understand the goods, you will start with $5, you know, but if you don't understand, what are you going to offer him? If I was lucky, sometimes I finished it at $6 or $7.'

His next stop was Tel Aviv where he established a tiny office and a state-of-the-art factory at Saphadz. In 1981, he received the Israeli government's highest export award. Sales surged from $2m to $21m in twelve months. Vijay—who speaks fluent Hebrew—wanted to settle there with his wife,

Dipti Jayantibhai Mehta, but Bhiki protested. 'My mother used to hear about bomb scares and all those things on television. So we thought we had better settle down in Antwerp,' says Vijay. Others had the same idea. Almost fifty Palanpuri families migrated to Antwerp bringing their *chakkis* for grinding wheat into *chappati*-flour with them. Around seventy or eighty new Indian diamond firms were established during 1980-82.

'Bharatbhai took over everything in Bombay, all the controls,' says Vijay. For the next three years, the two brothers scarcely saw each other, rarely were both in the same place at the same time. While Dipti created a Gujarati nook in an Antwerp flat and brought up their four children (Dimple, Vishal, Sweta and Priya), airline cabins became Vijay's real home and office. 'From 1974, I was travelling, I think, four times a month to Tel Aviv. I was there for two days, coming back again to Antwerp, flying back to London. And then to Bombay. You will find it very difficult to believe that till now I must have travelled more than a million miles, much more, far ahead. When you have to hold a market, you have to travel a lot.'

In most sagas of empire-building, there is usually one deal or one incident which acts as a springboard. For Bharat and Vijay, the turning point came in 1974-76 when the diamond trade passed through a major shakeout. Many Indian diamantaires went bust. Vijaydimon and B. Vijaykumar came out of it stronger. As others slowed down their manufacturing, Bharat began acquiring their factories. Located in Surat and Navsari, these small units were often owned by the workers themselves. According to Bharat, 'The market was very bad at that time. All top business people, they were afraid. They didn't go for business and they closed down their factories. All the workers, they approached our company and we always supplied raw material. Our company grew very fast.'

'The time was difficult for everyone, but we did not find it difficult. We were always keeping in our mind that do the business, wherever you can, but only to your capacity. That is always our policy. When many people just jumped around, they did big business and all, we did it in our capacity. And when the times came bad, always the people became panicky. Which is in every business. And they started selling. They could not sell much polished. They could not buy rough. You have to have the cycle running. You can't just stop at that place,' says Vijay. The cost of roughs accounts for 70 per cent of total revenues.

The mid-'70s was a difficult period for the entire diamond trade. A global recession forced down prices. Indian companies, operating at the lower end of the market, were as badly affected as the Jewish firms at the top end. In Antwerp, the trading floors were crowded with brokers, wholesalers and manufacturers, but few deals were being cut. The lacklustre atmosphere was most apparent at the Antwerpsche Diamantkring, generally the busiest of Antwerp's four main dealing rooms because of the large number of bit players who throng there.

These rooms look more like down-at-heel cafeterias than bourses where millions of dollars worth of diamonds change hands every minute. Rows of plain wood tables with cheap chairs on either side run through the long high-ceilinged rooms. Most have huge windows in one wall, allowing in as much light as possible. The tables start by touching the windows and stretch across two-thirds of the room, leaving space for a wide aisle. High-powered lamps dot the tables at regular intervals. Buyers and sellers face each other across the tables. There's no privacy but none is needed. Prices can be overheard but even the most inquisitive cannot make out for which quality. Trading starts by about 9 a.m. and peters out by 4 p.m., when chessboards and cards replace briefcases stuffed with white paper packets. Jewish traders like to unwind by playing a few friendly games with fellow brokers over a couple of beers before going home to their families. The Jains go home to their families.

As a small fish in a big pond, Vijay gravitated to the Kring. During the crisis of the '70s, however, there were more games than deals on the trading floor. Remembering those days, Vijay who was then in his twenties, describes the scene: 'The brokers used to sit there with numbers in front of them. Many Indians used to come, but the brokers used to tell them, please get up [and go]. There were more of sellers than buyers, and Indians used to hang around for watching, rather than doing any business, which nobody likes. So I used to sit there but I had one principle, if I give a offer, any offer, whatever I offer, the brokers have to take. Because I know diamonds. The brokers, they don't have to dictate their terms, that now he is asking so much, then I will take only this much.'

For the youngsters, this was a period of fast growth. 'The whole market used to sit around and just talk: What Vijay is doing? What is he up to? When everybody is going down, what is he doing? What is the magic?' recalls Vijay gleefully. The secret was simple: buy cheap, sell cheap, build up volume, even a rupee's profit is good profit. This minimalist philosophy went against the grain of most Indian diamantaires. 'People forget altogether that when the market is bad, you can ask for rough at much lower price. In a bad time, nobody wanted to hold roughs, even in the open market. You don't have to stick to old prices. So if the market is $20 cash, and if you can get the same roughs at $14, what's bad in it? You are talking about 30 per cent [reduction]. Some are very strong. They would not sell it for a month or two months. And they would come to their senses, and start selling it at less.'

Buying the roughs cheaper meant that B. Vijaykumar sold the polished cheaper. Because of that 'people were thinking that we are undercutting the market. But if you sell the polished 10 per cent cheaper and still are making good profits from the lower [priced] roughs, what's wrong with that? This is the tricks of the business,' says Vijay.

His confidence stemmed from the fact that the market for polished diamonds was buoyant at particular levels. He feels others didn't have confidence in themselves to go for that market and those prices. 'Like I said in the beginning, the raw material—the rough diamonds—is very important. You have to know the business and you also have to have guts and full confidence. I see my buying. I know processing costs. I used to tell my brother on the phone, "Just throw it in the manufacturing. Don't worry about anything, just keep on selling."'

According to Bharat, their profit margins increased though those of others were squeezed. 'That time we were dealing with very low quality, where the added value is more and we are converting in hard currency. So the profit increased. Also, in good period, everyone can run and the profit margin is very low. In bad periods, suppose you can do more business, naturally you have more profits and you have more chances. That is why whenever the market is weak, that time our business is double. Others are closing down their business because they are afraid. They don't have the guts, you know,' he shrugs. Vijay is more circumspect: 'We never went above our capacity but we made many turnovers. This is very important. You can make many turnovers if you are fast enough. We never stopped buying and on the contrary we bought bargains during that time because there were no buyers.'

It is said that the Palanpuri's ability to drive a hard bargain would make Shylock blush. Nor does the Shahs' tendency to count every paisa's interest on a daily basis endear them to other businessmen.

Such accusations cut Bharat and Vijay to the quick. 'In any business, there are not all good people and the same is true for diamonds. But if you ask for our company, you would not find any complaints whatsoever in the market because I believe in paying one day before, not one day later,' says Vijay. 'The first thing you need in business is prestige, you know, and this is not easy. The money comes last in my diary.' Normally laconic, Bharat is moved to protest: 'The Jewish people, you know, they take advantage up to the last. There are some Indians also who take advantage about the interest and other things. But you cannot cheat. We pay in time. In business, suppose you have a reputation, you don't waste [it] '

BOLLYWOOD

In December 1989, Shashi Kapoor, the heart-throb of the '70s as an actor and now a serious film director, was shooting his latest movie, *Ajuba*. For one crucial sequence, he needed a fantasy palace in the Rajasthani style. Bharat Shah graciously offered Reshma's Rs 1m discarded wedding *mandap*, the one which had caused such a furore less than a week back. From the PR point of view, the tie-up with Kapoor was a godsend. The lavish Rajasthani plaster-of-paris palace built at the Wankhede Stadium could now be termed a legitimate business deal for VIP Enterprises, a Shah group company. Similarly, six years later, when Reshma's brother Rafees got married, the palatial set at the NSCI Club custom built for an Asha Bhonsle performance would be used in director Pramod Chakravarty's *Barood* starring Akshay Kumar.

A part of the Shah group and closely held as most of their

companies are, VIP Enterprises is one of Bollywood's largest distributors. Bharat considers the film division to be 'not a big thing, not even 5 per cent of our total turnover. But for the film industry, it is a big chunk. There, for them, we are playing very big role.' If it's so insignificant a business, why do they continue? Is it business mixed with pleasure? 'No, no,' says Vijay quickly. 'We hardly go for a trial [preview], maybe once-twice. We don't have the time. Who will sit three hours there? We are always thinking about some other business.'

Glamorous Bollywood parties are another question altogether. There Bharat is a familiar sight, rubbing shoulders with his favourite directors, Gulshan Rai and Subhash Ghai, or snapping the *muhurat* take clapboard for the film debut of Sushmita Sen, Ms Universe. In a business notorious for its failures, VIP Enterprises has an impressive list of hits such as *Paapi, Ram Teri Ganga Maili, Ram Lakhan* and *Dil Hai Ki Manta Nahin.*

According to Vijay, the secret of their success is to stay away from the sets, use the best, and think big. 'We believe that if you are going to die, [then] better to die with the big doctor, good doctor,' he says. 'If you have big budget film, you never lose anything,' agrees Bharat. Vijay explains: 'People go first for word-of-mouth publicity. In big budget films, once they put the banner, immediately the people run to buy the film.'

Enter the Shahs with their territory rights. Reportedly, the Shahs average 100 per cent returns in this business. Bharat chuckles contentedly, but makes no comment. Vijay answers for him: 'We can't complain. It's a good, paying business.'

According to Bharat, movie distribution is a high-risk proposition as so many movies flop. India makes more movies than Hollywood, nearly 3,000 (in all languages) annually but less than 800 get released and barely a dozen can be called hits.

For VIP Enterprises, 1991 proved to be a bonanza as one after another of its movies hit the big time: *Henna, Saudagar, Dil Hai Ki Manta Nahin* and *Sadak*. But if VIP is neither a producer nor a financier, where is the downside if a movie flops?

Simple. VIP loses money, says Bharat, explaining the structure of the movie distribution business. Generally VIP buys the movie rights from the producer for Maharashtra and Gujarat, the two territories they control. If they can't sell the movie to theatre owners, they don't recover the purchase cost. Or if the movie moves slowly, they may break even. Sometimes, if a movie is really hot, they're able to sell it to theatres in advance under a minimum guarantee scheme, which could cover VIP's investments. So, to make profits, they need to sell a big budget movie made by a well-known producer under the minimum guarantee scheme which will move fast.

Real money can only be made when there's an 'overflow', i.e., the money made over the cost of the film plus the cost of publicity, print and commissions. 'Earlier a movie was declared a hit only after it reached the silver jubilee. Now things have changed and it depends on the overflow,' says Bharat. 'It's a risky business, particularly with cable and video but in VIP we have devised a foolproof system.

'We have the best directors, producers, the best men in the business. This way we have our investment covered because I feel that a movie should be distributed on the strength of the director. I am a firm believer in this. These are the men with the Midas touch and one cannot go wrong following this concept.' It's certainly a smart line-up with practically every Bollywood big gun present in it: Subhash Ghai, Yash Chopra, the RK banner, Rakesh Roshan, and Mahesh Bhatt. What about Amitabh Bachchan? 'In the '80s, we distributed practically every Amitabh Bachchan starrer.' Today, however, VIP no longer distributes the Big B's films 'because of the long gestation period', he says.

Oddly enough, it was Dhanwant who introduced them to movie-making and it was Bollywood which drove a wedge between the brothers, culminating in a family split in 1978-79.

Unlike Bharat or Vijay who immerse themselves totally in their work, Dhanwant could never generate a real interest in the diamond business. All Indians are movie-mad to some extent, and youths in their twenties even more so. Dhanwant went a little further. In the early '60s, while still in college, he started moving around Bollywood's fringes, picking up contacts with film-makers and starlets. He kept his interest hidden from his family, knowing that his father would disapprove. The secret tumbled out with the release of *Jeevan Saathi* around 1965 which he helped produce. Fortunately, the film made money. Unfortunately, the next one didn't.

Though Shantilal objected to Dhanwant's sideline, Bharat and Vijay profess to have supported their elder brother. 'Whatever he wanted to do, even in films, we were supporting him because he liked the film business. When he had his bad time, he stopped it and again we brought him back. Like I say, never say die. You have to show again in the same field what you can do,' says Vijay.

'When he lost a lot of money, we told him that he can start his distribution office. It is a better business than the production, you know. And he agreed but in two years he said he wants to again start production. We said sorry. We don't want to be in the field,' says Bharat. 'He likes to involve in film production. We have got different opinion, you know, because film line is most risky business. That is why when he said "I want to start movie, I want to go for production", we said no. We don't mind distributing, but he wanted production. We remained in distributing.'

In the circumstances, the separation was inevitable and once again the family would uproot itself. For the third time

Bharat moved house. In the first separation, the bungalow at 56 Ridge Road had gone to Bipin. From there, the family had moved to Atlas Apartments on Narayan Dhabholkar Road. In 1978, Bharat bought a flat in Swapnalok on Napean Sea Road, then the most prestigious building in Bombay, designed by the award-winning architect I. Kadri.

Twenty years after the event, the brothers are still uncomfortable about the family breach. 'It's not that we split, or this, or that, you know. It was his idea. We have got the finest relation. Always we were a support to him. Though he is a elder brother he would always think that we are elder than him. This was the thing,' says Vijay. A separation from Bipin had taken place ten or fifteen years before the split with Dhanwant. Analysing what went wrong, Bharat muses: 'They [i.e., Bipin and Dhanwant] had different nature and temperament, you know. Short-tempered, you know.'

At the time, the break with two of their brothers would be a big blow for the young company. Palanpuris don't employ professional executives for key positions, preferring instead family members. Kaushik Mehta, a former head of the diamond association, once lamented: 'In this business, you need personal attention. And you need trust. Only your family can give both. I have remained small because I do not have any brothers.' The international nature of the diamond business lends itself to large families. Most of the bigger firms have brothers and cousins manning offices in Hong Kong, New York, Antwerp and Bombay. The Shahs felt the loss acutely as they started expanding and building factories all over the world.

THE RED CARPET
The biggest of these is a factory in Bangkok. There are several Jewish plants in Thailand, but to date only two Indian ones,

though others are on the anvil. Madhu Mehta of Jayam beat the Shahs to it, but the latter's BV Diamond Polishing Works is reportedly the world's largest diamond cutting and polishing factory under one roof, employing some 1,200 workers, and spread over 40,000 sq.ft.

How much did it cost? Vijay hedges: 'The amount I don't like to discuss but we are definitely not talking about peanuts. We are talking about several million dollars. It is, I think, the best factory in the world. This was a very good decision.' The *Business Post,* Bangkok's local financial daily, was rather less coy: US$5m (about 125m baht). Above an article dated August 9, 1991, there's a grainy black-and-white photo of a dapper Vijay with his hair tousled, wearing a cream embroidered Nehru jacket, standing nervously next to the Thai governor and Alex Bardour, a CSO director, at the factory's opening.

If the details provided in the paper's front page report are true, Bharat and Vijay appear to be extremely conservative businessmen. Quoting one Milind Kothari, BV Diamond Polishing Works' managing director, the paper reported that BV Diamond was established in 1989 with a registered capital of 150m baht—or twenty-five million more than the entire project cost. No debt. And since not all the money was needed upfront—the factory opened in 1991, stage by stage, employing batches of 50 or so workers every month—the money must have fattened on interest.

To build in quality right from the beginning, the Shahs flew in experts from Vijaydimon's Belgium plants to train the Thai workers. In Antwerp, their cutters handle roughs valued at $700-7,000 per carat. In Surat, the range varies from $15 to $100. The Bangkok factory handles roughs of $200 per carat, pushing up sales turnover. 'In Bangkok, its production is more than $100m. In India, we are talking about 25,000 workers and Rs 500 crores,' says Bharat.

Among other details provided in the *Business Post* about the plant is the tidbit that the Shahs had wrung some key 'promotional privileges' out of the Thai Board of Investment. Vijay clearly enjoyed the manoeuvring. 'I told them, I have come here because you have sent for me. You yourself told me that you need me very badly; that you have heard [about me] from many firms, Diamond Trading Company, and everyone, that these people [i.e., the Shahs] can change many things.'

When the Thais were reluctant to give Vijay the concessions he wanted, he played tough. 'I told them I don't need a penny from here. I will not take away my factory. Whatever the investments, it is going to remain. If the economy needs changing, you know, it is your business how to put it right. So I told the ministers who were there, do me a favour. Get me the first available flight. Book me a first available flight back. I am wasting my time as well as yours. So nothing doing. He said Mr, Sir, the lunch is served. I said I am very strictly vegetarian. I like our *desi* food. I don't like anything else. Not even Italian food. Nothing except our food. So they insisted. Vegetables, you can have? I said, yes. I said, I will have a toast and bread and butter and all that. We had lunch.'

'Finally they told me, "Mr Shah, we won't let you go just like this." So I said, you have to pay for it, if you want. I never insisted on doing anything over here. I can do it in my country. There also I can see people. And they told me, Mr Shah, we want you very much. At 5.30, I got everything open. It is not like here [India], you know, like all these bureaucrats. It was a straight talk. They signed the papers. Everything.'

Vijay learnt to play hard ball from Nepalese bureaucrats. Invited to Nepal by its king, Vijay promised to build a diamond cutting factory there. Relying on an assurance of tax breaks by its bureaucrats, he spent Rs 3m on machinery. By 1974, the plant was up but not running. 'In order to be profitable, import duty on the roughs had to be 2 per cent. At the time it was over 20 per cent. Everywhere in the world, there is no duty on the roughs. They kept promising me that the duty would be reduced once the factory starts. Each day they said it would go down the next day. How can this be? I gave the plant away as a gift to the Nepalese. It was a good lesson to me.'

At the end of the negotiations with the Thais, Vijay promised that in return for the incentives and tax havens, the factory would be ready in ten months. The fact that it was built on schedule is a matter of pride, 'no matter the market went down, up, down, you know, because I am confident of selling my product'. Construction began in 1989 with a grand opening in 1991. 'Everyone, from Diamond Trading Company, and many people from all over the world, came.' Vijay's satisfaction is evident.

Red carpet treatment such as that laid out by the Thais is easy to get used to, and the Shahs, particularly Vijay, now take it for granted. Talking about a 'a very very huge project' in Jakarta, Indonesia, Vijay feels confident that he will be able to wrest significant concessions from its politicians also. 'The government in Indonesia, they are very good friends. Suharto, I have direct access to him,' he claims. 'Our name is worldwide, you know, whenever you are talking about diamond or anything. They know about our expansions, so we get many things.'

In India, on the other hand, they feel they get no recognition. They have won awards from the Israeli government and from the King of Belgium who conferred the Knight of the Order of Leopold on Vijay in March 1994. Here, though the government has showered export promotion awards on them, the equation with those who head the country is missing. On the contrary, they are made to feel like cheats in India.

'Every few months, there is harassment which affects our business. They check books, stocks, ask funny questions,' complains Bharat. Ham-handed investigations by government officials from various tax departments are even more embarrassing if foreign clients happen to be present. 'Earlier, they would ask them to turn out their pockets, open their bags. If you were in America and they asked you to do that, how would you feel? You would be insulted! But that is what used to happen.'

Stung once too often, Vijay swore all new investments would be outside India. 'Why did I start in Bangkok?' he asks rhetorically. 'I would have preferred my people, Indian people. But who needs this headache? Who needs the tension? This is the only thing in life you don't need!' Their investments abroad appear to be substantial. Apart from the Bangkok factory, there are two in Belgium (Antwerp, 110 workers, started in 1976; Campaign, 110 workers, 1981) and one in Israel (Saphadz, 140 workers, established in 1979). India's loss is their gain.

Bharat's ire with Indian tax officials reached its limit on April 7, 1989. He took to the streets in protest, along with 30,000 other diamond traders. It was a surreal procession. Hundreds of air-conditioned chauffeur-driven limousines lined up on the kerb in front of Bombay's Wilson College. While the drivers watched the fun, their employers—all in white except for black armbands—led by Jatin Mehta crossed the road to gather on Chowpatty beach, sweating under the mid-day sun. Slowly the procession wound its orderly way to Azad Maidan, a few kilometres away, where politicians from both the ruling Congress Party and the opposition Bharatiya Janata Party were waiting to accompany the *morcha* to Ayakar Bhavan, headquarters of the income tax department. After submitting a memorandum of protest to S.N. Deshmukh, the director general of income tax, the traders dispersed.

The immediate provocation for the *morcha* was an income tax raid on some *angadias*. A centuries old organization renowned for its reliability, *angadias* are licensed couriers used by the diamond trade to carry roughs and polished stones to and from Bombay and the cutting centres. 'We've lost packets of diamonds in the US postal system but never through *angadias*,' says Vijay. On March 6, 1989, officials believed to be from the income tax (IT) department and the Central Bureau of Investigation (CBI) detained twenty-seven *angadias* at Dadar and seized nearly 2,000 packets of diamonds worth Rs 300m from them. The *angadias* immediately protested that under the Indian postal laws and international convention they couldn't hand over goods to anyone other than the owner or the addressee.

The diamantaires considered this the last straw. Just a few days earlier, on February 22, five *angadias* had been relieved of Rs 120m worth of diamonds. The IT and CBI officials had overreached themselves this time. Rival associations temporarily buried differences and rallied together to take on the government. All import and export activity ground to a halt and with it customs revenues. Rajiv Gandhi was telexed, a delegation left for Delhi to meet S.B. Chavan, the finance minister, and Nitish Sengupta, the revenue secretary. In Bombay, Murli Deora, the suave president of the Bombay Regional Congress Committee, jumped to the diamond merchants' defence.

After several rounds of discussion between the antagonists, Deora issued a press release in which Deshmukh reportedly stated that it was not the IT department's 'intention to cause any harassment to the diamond trade and that the seizure of diamonds from *angadias* last week was on the basis of disinformation, and assured that such actions will not be taken again.' Aghast at his superior's assumed perfidy,

Deshmukh's deputy, S.K. Mitra, instantly issued another press release, denying that the IT department had bungled. 'To put the record straight,' he told the *Indian Express,* 'the selective search operation on five *angadias* was neither bizarre nor based on unfounded facts. On the contrary, the action was authorized on the basis of accurate, reliable and specific information which was discreetly verified.'

It was open war with both sides hurling accusations at each other. Neither could claim to be the good guys. Both have too many 'black sheep' in their ranks, as they admitted to journalists under promises of strict anonymity. Though the diamond trade enjoys incredible tax concessions, over- and under-invoicing of diamond imports and exports is common. On the other hand, they allege that income tax officers are not above board either and take advantage of their situation.

The face-off turned into black comedy on the afternoon of April 3 during a 'survey' operation by an income tax team at the office of a diamond merchant at Panchratna Building. Hundreds of tiny offices belonging to small diamond companies cram the decrepit office block located in the crowded Opera House area. In the evenings, street urchins sweep the dust off the pavement searching for stray diamonds which may have dropped out of their owners' pockets. The building's corridors are riddled with peepholes and security cameras. Any untoward incident flashes through the offices like wildfire.

A few hours before the income tax officers' visit to Panchratna, the diamond merchants' action committee had been assured that no raids would take place until earlier issues had been sorted out. So when the raiders came, the stage was set for an ugly showdown. A mob gathered outside the office being raided, shouting anti-income tax slogans. The tax officials were forced to sign a statement saying that they had 'harassed' the assessee and that their visit was 'illegal'. According to the diamond merchants, the tax officials high-handedly cut off the telephone lines and even prevented assessees from going to the toilet. The tax officials recounted how they had been *gheraoed* and detained until 9 in the evening when the action committee managed to free the officials. Later that night, the officials lodged a complaint at the local police station.

The next morning, a crowd of diamond merchants gathered outside Ayakar Bhavan. Inside, the action committee demanded that the department withdraw the police complaint. When the chief commissioner agreed to this, the crowd disbursed. Its place was quickly taken by the entire tax department, angry at the response of their superiors. Protesting against the assault and illegal confinement of tax officers while on official duty, and the lack of police action against the diamond traders, they demanded police protection while they were on 'search and seizure' duty. Three days later, the entire diamond trade downed shutters, met at Chowpatty beach, staged a *morcha* at Ayakar Bhavan and pulled its political strings.

The unusual show of solidarity shook the income tax department. It caved in. The revenue secretary, Nitish Sengupta, flew to Bombay to meet the action committee. He promised revisions to the Customs Act and fresh guidelines for income tax searches. It was a clear victory for the diamond trade.

Frustrated but determined, the tax department waited for an opportunity to strike back. Their patience was soon rewarded. Reshma's wedding celebrations a few months later, at Wankhede Stadium, barely a toss away from Ayakar Bhavan, provided its hawks with the perfect opportunity to hover over the raid-me-not diamond dealer. A family spokesman claimed that the whole show cost Rs 20m. Rumour placed it at Rs 80m-300m. After all, there was a Rs 1m fireworks display ordered from the Moranis, India's most famous fireworks designers. Enamor Tailors at Breach Candy worked round the clock to stitch rich silks for the 300 international invitees, including the governor of Belgium. As many as 15,000 guests ate a lunch catered by the Taj Mahal Hotel at Rs 110 a plate. Miscellaneous expenses add up.

As the sleuths prepared their dossiers, bystanders watched with bated breath, wondering if the antagonism between the IT department and the diamond lobby would flare up again. Those looking for excitement were disappointed. A compromise was reached the details of which were not publicized. For the future, the Shahs know that the department's watchful eyes will never blink where they are concerned, but shrug off the surveillance. All the three businesses they are in—diamonds, films and construction—are areas which attract black money like nails are drawn to a magnet. How much sleep can one waste on worry?

Under-the-table deals are especially common in a city like Bombay which is starved of decent housing because of poorly conceived rent control laws. Shantistar Constructions has built over 1,000 residential blocks in and around Bombay. According to Bharat, almost a third of group sales and roughly half of profits come from the construction division. It is manned by Ramesh Shah and Nathubhai Desai, two trusted executives who have been with the group from the last twenty-five years. Most of the group's early developments were built as one-off projects by private companies under different names.

The brothers started dabbling in real estate in the mid-'70s, building a couple of residential blocks with Dhanwant before the family divorce took place. The turning point was 1982 when Bharat and Vijay bagged a contract to build a new township at Mira Road, in Thane district, forty kilometres from the Gateway. They renamed it Shanti Nagar, after their father.

'Many people were after it [i.e., the contract] but we got the chance. But it was also risky. It was like a barren land. It was a very lonely area at that time. We weren't sure whether people would come or not. We built 400 buildings before people applied for flats,' says Vijay. To promote the complex, the Shahs painted huge advertisements on the outside of local trains, promising ample water supply. Today Shanti Nagar has 500 buildings spread over 200 acres and a population of 80,000 inhabitants. A similar complex is coming up next door called Shanti Park.

Many of Shanti Nagar's residents come from weaker sections of society, driven north of the city by high property rates. Ten years later, a yuppie middle class was taking over the area's brand new townships, pushing up demand and encouraging several large construction companies to jump onto the bandwagon. Unfortunately, the municipality's water supply couldn't cope with the sudden increase in demand.

Fed up with constant shortages of this basic amenity, Shanti Nagar's residents finally revolted. On a scorching October day in 1995—and in Bombay, October is the hottest month after May—a group of freedom fighters, an eighty-year-old lady, and a couple of well-known municipal corporators banded together to stage a *dharna* outside the Bhayandar municipal office. They would go on an indefinite fast until the colony received an assurance of regular water supply from Shantistar and the municipality.

By the second day of the fast, horror stories started appearing in the tabloid press. Residents were collecting water from gutters outside their homes to clean their toilets. A mother of two infants had to borrow water from her neighbour to wash nappies. A family went to stay with their relatives in another part of town to beat the water shortage. How could students prepare for exams without drinking water in the house! A beleaguered company spokesman tried to explain that Shantistar had simply built the buildings, that according to the agreement between the developer and the MIDC (Maharashtra Industrial Development Corporation), the latter was responsible for supplying water to the colony.

'The shortage is not because of any fault of ours,' he insisted. 'It is entirely the MIDC's problem. During the September crisis, we wrote to the MIDC complaining about the shortage. What more can we do?'

'Do the builders think that their responsibility ends with just complaining?' retorted the harassed residents. 'When it came to selling the flats, they promised a regular supply of potable water.'

The crisis blew over, but not the problem. Even so, people continue to pour into the suburb. And despite hectic building activity by several developers, demand hasn't kept pace with supply, leaving the Shahs with a second major image problem. As prices doubled and tripled, dissatisfied customers began to complain that the Shahs had no ethics. One buyer who bought an office in a block developed by them in Bombay's congested Opera House area claims that 'after they built the block, they are not giving the offices to those who had bought them earlier because prices have gone up. They don't care. Other builders are not like that. Even if prices go up from Rs 10,000 to Rs 12,000, the Makers and the Rahejas, they still keep their word. But not the Shahs.'

Vijay objects vehemently. 'In construction, we are not money minded at all. At Mira Road, we make a policy that so many flats go at this [fixed] price. No matter whatever the premiums are, we don't go for that. We see to it that it does not go to the hand of people who want to invest and then to make profits. We want the flats to go to real genuine people, you know, who are in need of it, at proper prices. We want that the prices should remain stable, you know, that it should not rise straight away, because this should be in the benefit of middle-class people and the lower class people rather than anybody who wants to make money. We sold flats at Rs 250-Rs 300 per sq. ft. when others were selling at Rs 1,200.' To control flat prices, Bharat says he holds a monthly meeting with Shah and Desai where prices are frozen 'so that no one can change it and there is no manipulation, nothing'.

Apropos the Opera House office block, Vijay admits that the deals haven't been as clean but asserts that the problems are due to two brothers who own the land. 'After the building was built, the brothers started fighting, and we had no control. We built the building but they sold the offices. Even we suffered for we wanted to shift from Mehta Bhavan to it,' he says. The incident has given him a distinct distaste for dealing with Marwaris. 'In order to save a paisa, they lose the rupee,' he says.

Be that as it may, the brothers appear to have made phenomenal profits from construction. Some of it is being poured into more real estate. Says one Shah associate jealously: 'We were driving near Jogeshwari when Bharatbhai pointed out a hill. I've bought that hill, he told me. It must be acres and acres! And unoccupied! Which industrialist has that kind of money? It must have cost a bomb.' Invitations for designs were recently issued. The Shahs plan to build a country house for themselves on the hill, complete with a winding road surfaced to look like a red carpet. Will they give it out for shootings? No way, says Vijay. 'This is private.'

In India, there cannot be total privacy and particularly

where the heera bazaar people (as they are better known) are concerned. Bharat is hurt by this intense interest. 'There is an image in India, you know, that diamond people make easy money. People in our country, lower people, they don't understand. You cannot change this impression. It takes time. Compared to all other industries, diamond business is very hard. Because it is a personalized business. We work from morning to late evening. In other industry, they attend office around 9 o'clock. They go exact at 6 o'clock. Here, we start work at 10, we are working till midnight, which we can't help.'

Nobody denies they work hard. What rubs people the wrong way is the ingrained Palanpuri attitude to thrift. Getting in touch with the Shahs is tougher than getting through to the PMO. At Vijaydimon in Antwerp, one Mr Kottary is curt and to the point: 'Mr Vijay Shah does not return calls, especially international ones.' Yes, well, it's important to take care of the paisas in order to save the rupees. It is well known that the Queen of England walks round Buckingham Palace in the evenings, switching off lights to save a few pounds annually.

The Shahs are probably among the five richest families in India in personal terms. Groups such as the Birlas and the Tatas run larger corporate empires with greater financial clout but their personal wealth is limited by tax laws. In the '70s, these laws were so severe that J.R.D. Tata once complained that he couldn't even serve a cup of tea in London to a potential client without infringing stiff foreign exchange regulations. Diamond merchants, however, enjoy tax free earnings in India. Even in Belgium, Israel, and Thailand, they have a special status and tax advantages. Moreover, as most of their companies are closely held, the Shahs don't have to share profits with outside shareholders.

Vijay, the more flamboyant of the two brothers, likes to spend some of this new affluence on himself. His residence,

Shanti, is the 'most fabulous house in Antwerp', fit for a James Bond setting. He spent four and a half years building it, moving into it in 1983. Ancient Roman statues and gracious fountains dot its manicured gardens and lush shrubbery. Inside are nine bedrooms, two elevators, a discotheque with psychedelic lights, a swimming pool, a health club, a movie theatre, marbled bathrooms, several drawing rooms and a gold-plated dining table, glittering enough for diners to require optical protection. Tourist buses stop outside the dark smoked glass façade for a few minutes while city guides describe the fabled interior.

There is something incongruous between the Shahs' way of living and working. It is difficult to reconcile Bharat's down-at-heel office with his dream flat in Swapnalok at Napean Sea Road; or Vijay's glamorous James Bond villa with his office's parsimony; or Reshma's wedding celebrations with the austerity of Jain philosophy. Vegetarians and teetotalers, given to holding *pujas*, the brothers are confirmed workaholics who don't have time to enjoy the good things of life, as Vishal, Vijay's son, admits.

'We tell him sometimes, that there is a point where you have to be satisfied,' says Vishaal, who is studying for a diploma in business management. But Vijay's mind is always working. 'I do make time for recreation, but after some time, I am always thinking about how to expand more and more,' Vijay confesses. 'I do see that our children are very well looked after. They need papa and mama, you know, both together.'

Father and son try to make time to swim together in their private pool and Vijay enjoys walks with Dipti whenever he is in Antwerp. Of late, he has given up reading books (biographies). He tried to keep up the habit, packing a couple for the endless hours of flying, but 'today, we don't get so much time. As soon as I am on the flight, I go to sleep quickly'. Even newspapers are becoming too much to handle, though he makes it a point to glance through the *International Herald Tribune* and the *Wall Street Journal* when in Antwerp, and the *Times of India,* the *Indian Express,* and the *Bombay Samachar* when in Bombay.

Do the brothers like to watch movies? 'Sure. Any business that we have, we have to take interest in it!' Vijay ripostes, but it took him four months to complete a video of *Sangam.* 'I cannot see a whole movie. Sometimes I have to go the next morning abroad. But I like the old movies very much.' As does Bharat. They also share a taste for Hindi film music. Vijay's favourite artistes are Mukesh and Mohammed Rafi, while Bharat's tastes are more catholic. 'I enjoy listening when I am in the bathroom, late in the evenings, and in the car,' says Bharat, a car enthusiast whose fleet includes a Lotus, a Mercedes, and a BMW besides a couple of Maruti 1000s. Shortly after the Scam broke out (May 1992), he sold off his maroon Lexus. It was too similar to Harshad Mehta's for comfort.

Though they appear to spend money lavishly, they have not entirely lost the habit of thrift. If he is on his own for one of the DTC's monthly auctions, Vijay stays at the Dorchester. But *en famille,* the Shahs patronize the more down-market apartments of the Tata-run St. James' Court Hotel. Both brothers seem to vacillate periodically between a 'if you have it, why not spend it' attitude and the austere Jain tenets of their childhood. They are not the only ones; the entire Palanpuri clan suffers from this dilemma.

To be a true Jain is difficult. Orthodox believers are so opposed to killing in any form, they will not swat flies. Some wear white gauze masks so that they won't inhale and kill bacteria. Others sweep the ground before them as they walk so that they don't trample a living creature by mistake. Ascetism is a virtue, renunciation the highest achievement. But when you deal with diamonds all the time and you're making money by the bucketful, it's tedious to be austere.

Much of the *nouveau riche* Palanpuris' wealth-flaunting is directed towards Bombay's industrial élite. Having made it good, the Palanpuris want recognition from the blue bloods of society. It was probably this hunger which made Arun Mehta of B. Arunkumar peel off Rs 1m for an M.F. Husain at a swanky society auction organized by Sotheby. The very next day, a *Times of India* reporter knocked on his door for an interview. A few days later the income tax official called.

Already well known in Bombay, the Shahs operate on a bigger, international, canvas. For Vijay, the thrill lay in being recognized in Thailand. 'When I went to Bangkok, they knew me,' he recounted gleefully. 'Everybody in the BOI (Board of Investment)! Though I did not know them, but everybody knew me. They had seen my photos in many magazines, many newspapers, everything.'

Entwined in the hunger for recognition is a strong spirit of one-upmanship, a sort of keeping-up-with-the Jhaveris mania. If Bharat Shah could spend a reported Rs 80m on his daughter's wedding, could the Mehtas be far behind? The sky was the limit for the jewels of their fond parents' eyes. Or was it? In December 1994, Laxman Popley, a Dubai-based jeweller, chartered an Air India airbus for a marriage made in heaven. Compared to these flights of fancy, Kumar Mangalam Birla's wedding was just too black-tie. The jealousy behind the cream silk *achkans* and the scarlet *gharcholas* is almost tangible in its intensity, fanned by the suffocating closeness within the Palanpuri community.

It's an inevitable fallout of their business. Dealing in small packages of great value and under constant threat from thieves, the world's diamantaires have over the years learnt to trust only themselves, their kinsmen, and their clansmen. Like the Russian Jews before Stalin, or the Hasidic Jews of Antwerp, the heera bazaar people keep themselves to themselves. Everyone knows everybody, and the energetic grapevine between London, Hong Kong, Tel Aviv, New York, Antwerp, Bombay and Palanpur constantly sizzles with news and scraps of trivia, greedily feeding invidious rivalry and heartburn.

According to Murli Deora, the frequent income tax raids on the diamond trade are a direct result of the envy rampant among the Palanpuris. 'They only organize the raids by giving out information about their rivals to the income tax authorities,' he says. 'It is rumoured that during the 1989 raids, the commissioner got most of his information from the trade itself. And during Bharatbhai's daughter's wedding, most of the details which appeared in all the newspapers came from jealous competitors. I don't think the Shahs spoke to the press at all.'

THE 1000 CARAT CASE

Apart from envy, their fabulous wealth has made the Shahs targets also of hundreds of appeals and some curious invitations. Bharat came across one of the latter while rifling through his mail one drizzly monsoon morning. It was a letter from one R. Choudhry, introducing himself as the new local representative of a well-known Italian firm, Ferruzzi Finanziaria. Dated August 20, 1991, the letter invited him to Delhi. Uninterested, Bharat says he didn't reply. 'I threw it straight into the wastepaper basket.'

A month later, a sensational kidnapping gripped the nation's imagination. People gasped over the huge ransom. The police were defeated by the kidnappers' audacity and modus operandi. It was then that Bharat remembered the letter, for the mastermind behind the kidnapping was suspected to be one Ravi (alias Rehman) Choudhry. It was a narrow escape.

At first glance, the letter appeared quite genuine. After introducing himself and Ferruzzi Finanziaria, Choudhry went on to say that his 'Chief Executive is visiting Delhi next month to officially inaugurate the opening of our Buying Office here'. He invited top exporters 'to discuss long term business relations and to place our first sizable order'. As an added inducement, he asked diamantaires to 'please quote your best F.O.B. prices based on Sight L/C for Diamonds in sizes up to -11 in grades Super Collection, Super Deluxe and Deluxe, Quantity 1000 Carats, Shipment October, 1991.'

Bharat was not taken in. 'Diamonds should be sold in offices, not hotels. And foreign buyers come to our offices. We do not go to hotels. But small people were attracted. For us what difference one 1000 carats polished order? I knew it was bogus. It looked it, you know. Because in a letter, no one can mention very big amount and other things, you know.'

Other diamond merchants were not so savvy. Choudhry had written to twenty-eight diamantaires in Surat, Ahmedabad and Bombay, inviting them to Delhi's Taj Hotel. He caught four in his net, besides a hapless export manager and a chauffeur. Surprisingly, they all belonged not to the smaller firms, but the larger ones. One of the four was Rajesh Mehta, the twin brother of Bharat's son-in-law, Rajiv. The other three were Gautam Mehta of Goenka Trading, Milan Parikh of Mahindra Brothers and his cousin Saunak. None of them checked out the simple fact that Ferruzzi Finanziaria existed but that it was a chemical, not a diamond, company. In the aftermath, other mistakes were discovered, but at the time it seemed the perfect crime. After nineteen days of captivity in the basement of an upper middle-class house in a New Delhi suburb, and a rumoured $1m ransom paid offshore, the victims returned unharmed to their families. A year later, the CBI reported to the Lok Sabha that Choudhry was believed to be a Pakistani national.

The 1000 carat case is not an isolated event. There have been several kidnappings, many robberies and murder cases involving diamantaires. One Romi Choksi went missing on January 17, 1987. On July 6, 1989, a leading Indian jeweller in New York, Hemant Zaveri, disappeared without trace, while three Jaipur jewellers were murdered in Bangkok in April 1994. More recently, on March 21, 1995, Bombayites were shocked by the brutal way a Dahisar-based diamantaire, Devraj Patel, and his wife were murdered. A few weeks earlier, a 24-year-old diamantaire had been found murdered in Taipei (Taiwan). These incidents are the tip of an iceberg. Hundreds of incidents go unreported as dealers are afraid of the underworld. Naturally enough, the kidnappings have made the diamond merchants close ranks and suspicious of outsiders.

Ironically, the kidnappings are increasing at a time when the days of super profits are ending. Margins are under pressure, partly because of foreign exchange regulations introduced by Manmohan Singh, Narasimha Rao's popular finance minister, and partly because of saturation and oversupply.

According to analysts, the diamantaires' sensational profits of the '80s were largely based on manipulation of India's tight foreign exchange regulations rather than true industrial value addition. Concessions like full income tax exemption on export profits and freedom from Maharashtrian sales taxes also contributed significantly. But lately, the outlook is no longer as rosy as it used to be.

The rupee's behaviour in recent years has been worrying diamantaires. It was devalued in 1991. The next year, it became partially convertible. Its steadiness towards the dollar since

1993 makes financial engineering difficult, and tax concessions no longer have the same impact. Profits are also being squeezed because competition, both local and international, has never been fiercer. To make matters worse, rough prices in the open market are volatile and polished prices low because of a global depression which looks as if it's going to take its own sweet time to revive. 'From the last few years, it is very tough. Today in diamond industry, though turnover is huge, profit margin is very low compared to other industry, I think,' agrees Bharat.

His solution? Integrate vertically into jewellery where there is 'very big scope'.

Currently, India does not even have 0.5 per cent of the world's $50bn jewellery market, but given the quality of Indian craftsmanship, Palanpuris predict they could corner at least 10 per cent of it. Along with a dozen others, the Shah brothers began producing jewellery around the turn of the decade. It was a timid effort and they spread the risk by joining hands in a 50-50 partnership with Suresh K. Mehta, a small-time jeweller. Together they set up a modest export factory for fashion pieces. It immediately proved its potential. 'When I entered into jewellery export, I had set a target of Rs 2 crores. I ended the year with Rs 8 crores of business,' recalls Bharat. The Shahs also set up a small factory in New York whose turnover is increasing every year.

The abolishing of the draconian Gold (Control) Act in the 1990 budget gave the business an extra fillip. 'We were always a little afraid of the Gold Act. Its provisions were very strict and we did not want to lose our prestige because of some minor carelessness. Now that fear is not there,' explains Bharat.

The experiment's success encouraged Mehta and the Shahs to build a state-of-the-art factory in the SEEPZ, an export-only industrial estate near Bombay's international airport. When fully operational—just now it is operating at one-third its capacity—BV Jewels will produce Rs 7bn worth of diamond-studded gold jewellery for the West. Mehta brims with confidence. 'The world buys from Italy, but Italy buys from us,' he says.

Designed by an Antwerp architect, the hi-tech six storey unit stands out conspicuously from the other buildings in the industrial estate. Its meticulously landscaped gardens include a lake. The corporate end of the factory is elaborately decorated with exquisite imported marbles and burl veneers. Most of the time it is empty, used only to impress foreign clients. The bosses generally sit at one end of a long room facing workers lined up in narrow aisles like stock brokers in a busy international equities firm.

The other floors are not much different, except for the gold refinery, the ovens where dies are cast, and the rhodium plating units. One area is devoted to trainees. For centuries, jewellery-making has been dominated by Bengali craftsmen, but at this factory anyone can get training. Local Maharashtrians appear to be picking up the requisite skills quite rapidly. The silence—the only noise is the gentle hum of air-conditioners needed to reduce gold dust loss—is odd for a factory. It is spotless with no oil, grease or untidiness anywhere. Good housekeeping is evident everywhere. 'The chairs the workers sit on, I imported them from Germany,' says Mehta. 'I did not want them to get tired after eight hours of working in one posture.' His own chair is Indian.

If BV Jewels takes off, it may usher in a mini-revolution in the international fashion jewellery business. For decades, De Beers have promoted the concept of 'a diamond for every woman'. The Shah-Mehta combine stretches it further. 'Our motto is that every janitor should wear our rings,' says Mehta excitedly.

To achieve this target, the cost of manufacture has been cleaved by at least one-third. Further cost reductions are being achieved by cutting wholesalers out of the chain. The Shahs are wooing retailers such as Wal-Mart and other large American discount stores to stock Indian machine-made jewellery. At the Andheri factory, rings which retail in the United States for $350 are sold for under $65.

Focusing on the American market has had its ups and downs. In 1992, the US government clamped a 6.5 per cent import duty on Indian jewellery. BV Jewels, with virtually 100 per cent of their output headed for the US market, was badly hit. 'Our exports fell by 50 per cent. We don't have the kind of margins to accommodate this tax,' said Suresh Mehta. The industry's immediate reaction was to lobby the Indian government for concessions, but gradually they became used to the tax. As Suken (Suresh's son) says, 'Our American customers toured the Far Eastern manufacturers and concluded that India still had a strong cost advantage.'

By slashing prices so dramatically, isn't there a danger of debasing diamonds? After all, De Beers has poured billions of dollars over many decades into glamorizing the image of diamonds. The principal job of the DTC and the Central Selling Organization is to keep diamond prices high and stable. Mountains of roughs are stashed in underground vaults below London's pavements and in South Africa so that diamonds remain expensive and De Beers' profit margins are protected. If BV Jewels sells real diamonds set in real gold at costume jewellery prices, won't they be in danger of turning diamonds into a commodity?

'No,' says Bharat confidently. 'We are just providing choice. There will always be people, you know, who want to buy a $1m necklace. And those who want just a small diamond ring. Some people will want both for different occasions.'

Meeus, who got to know the Shahs when he was working for Bonas-Couzn, before he became director of Antwerp's diamond bourse, agrees. 'It's a new market that the Shahs are opening up,' he says. With a little help from De Beers, of course. In June 1994, the Indo Argyle Diamond Council sponsored a series of trade fairs in the US to give Indian diamantaires a taste of the West. 'We paid a nominal $25,000 as membership fees. The total contribution could not have been more than $400,000, but Argyle spent in the region of $4m on the project,' says Suresh Mehta.

A new market is essential if the diamond trade is to sparkle again. Rough prices have been falling steadily with cheap Russian goods flooding the open market. From De Beers' point of view, the turbulence and volatility is unhealthy and could wipe out the entire trade. For decades they have built up the myth of diamonds as an expensive and trustworthy investment. Billions of dollars have been poured into creating the legend of the diamond as the woman's best friend. The reality is that the world is full of the glittering carbon chunks and only a fragile cartel keeps prices at levels profitable for miners, cutters, polishers, jewellers and shopkeepers. If the Russians successfully challenge the DTC's monopoly—and they have the resources to do so—the entire charade may fall about the industrial sector's ears.

The Shahs, who buy as much from the open market as they do from the DTC, have so far ignored Russian blandishments. 'We had a great chance in January 1994 from the Russians. They offered us special deals, large quantity as well as big stones, and a factory in Russia. But it is not good for anyone if prices crash, and if Russians sell in the open market and there is no single channel system. One channel keeps stability, and we have been enjoying that all these years. I have to support the DTC,' says Vijay.

Coincidentally, a moment later, the telephone rings. It is a senior DTC director. A sight is due to take place the following week, and he has heard that Vijay is unhappy about the sizes, quantities and prices of the roughs that the CSO are going to offer to him. As they haggle for the next half-hour, Vijay's voice gentles, becoming smoother than the Taj Hotel's rich vanilla ice-cream. 'Yes, give me a few millions of six grainers and a few millions of ten. But what about the bigger sizes? Yes, give a few millions of those. But what about the prices? I don't want any concessions, you know that, but what about the prices? Should I pay a penalty for sticking to the DTC? I turned away from the Russians for this? Be fair, old friend.' The message goes home. Four hours later, a broker comes over with a revised list for the sight. Not even a hint of a triumphant smile cracks Vijay's deadpan expression. It surfaces only in the evening, at home, while relaxing with his wife Dipti.

This little skirmish probably earned Vijay an extra few millions in profit but both Bharat and he are aware that the golden days are over. The diamond business will never again see the bumper profits of the '80s and the future is uncertain. To hedge their bets, they must diversify, but in which sectors?

For years, the brothers have acted as venture capitalists in a spectrum of enterprises ranging from electric batteries for cars and piped gas for Goa's towns to office chairs, roses, pens and ship-breaking. In most cases, the Shahs provide the money and hold the entire equity while the working partners rake in a 15 per cent share on profits. What about losses? 'We choose capable partners,' Vijay smiles.

Most of these enterprises are small to mid-size. To maintain the leadership position they have got used to, the Shahs need to plan bigger, invest in larger projects. As the government opens more doors to the private sector, the choice widens. How will they choose which projects?

Vijay's answer is enigmatic. 'You have to run around. You should have your own confidence. Your own expertise. Because always you will not have the same opinion about the business from everyone. Otherwise there is no secret left. Everything is open. But always there are some hidden cards. Whoever believes everything is open is not correct. You always have to leave some cards under your sleeves, you know. This is where you can really make your business grow.'

Bharat is less enigmatic. 'Earlier we would enter if we felt that we could get money on our investment in two to three years. But now, if you have certain size of capital, you must go for huge projects, otherwise you have to remain with small small things.' Vijay agrees. 'I tell you one thing, people should not have the same thinking always. For short term investment and quick money, you know, there are businesses. You have to see some big projects, very big projects, coming to your hand and this cannot be short term investment. Even if it is a long term investment, you see the future and the result at five years, at seven years, at ten years.'

One of the projects on the Shahs' drawing board is a Rs 2.5bn all weather port at Pipavav, a huge new Hazira-like industrial complex coming up on Gujarat's seaboard. L&T is planning a cement unit there, the London-based Bagris of Metdist plan to build a copper smelter, and the Ambanis hope to service the complex's energy needs through a power plant. A massive report on the project's feasibility is typed up and ready, waiting for the government's nod. Maintaining their usual purdah, the Shahs barely figure in the massive report. Instead it is littered with commodores, vice-admirals and other notables. But when it comes to the investors, a simple line states that the joint sector project is being promoted by Nikhil Gandhi and Bharat Shah through Sea King Engineers, a closely held company. The Shahs are also bidding for large telecommunications contracts in direct competition with powerful groups such as the Ambanis, the Birlas and the Tatas.

Apart from the big bucks they hope to earn, the Shahs are keen to invest in core infrastructural projects in order to earn recognition, both at home and abroad. 'We are on the top in diamond and in construction. In industry also suppose if we get some name, definitely we go for name,' says Bharat candidly. 'Definitely. For industry if there is a huge project, then we have a name internationally. Suppose the power project, it clicks, I think there will be international image, you know. The Gujarat port project, I think, if it clicks, then there is international image.'

If their application is approved, almost certainly the Shahs will have to go public, a step for which they are not yet mentally prepared. Other heera bazaar people are becoming a part of corporate India as more and more diamond companies go public, but B. Vijaykumar has so far resisted the lure of capitalizing on its name.

'So far there has not been need,' says Bharat. 'If we can get finance from the bank, why should we go to the public? For export units, banks give at 7.5 to 8 per cent. Besides, we have our own capital. And since the late '80s, we have not had to pay tax on profits, so it has built up. But today we are at the top. We cannot go any further, so we have to diversify. If there are four sons, one could be in industry. We want to get into industry and if we do, then those companies may be public limited companies. We are still thinking.'

Won't the public expect a professional management structure? 'We are professional,' protests Vijay. 'There would be at least two to three MBAs in the organization. But in the diamond business or in the construction business, it's different. But if once we get into industry, we will look for the top people.' It's unlikely however that there would be delegation of any real power. As Vijay had pointed out in the context of

the Bangkok factory, its top management is with the family.
'We have two people from our family. My uncle's sons—my
cousin brothers—because always I like to have the key with
our own people.' Unless they are open to handing over
responsibility, they may find it difficult to attract the calibre of
managers they will need for the mega projects on the drawing
boards. But all this is in the future. Today, there's optimism in
the air. Vijay sums it up: 'We had expanded much but sky is
the limit. I am quite big believer of this.'

Chapter 7

Ratan Tata

THE TATA FAMILY TREE

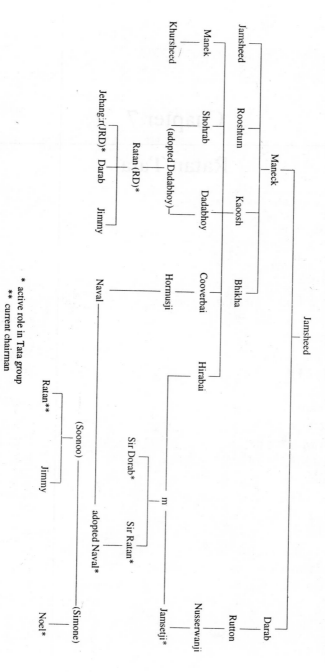

* active role in Tata group
** current chairman

Bombay House
March 22, 1991

'**D**olly, is that you? Is Mr Palkhivala in town on Monday? You're not sure? Will you check up and let me know?'

'Sheila? Can you tell me whether Mr Ratan Tata is in Bombay on the coming Monday? Mr Tata would like to prepone Wednesday's board meeting by two days.'

'Mr Pallonji? I'm calling on behalf of Mr J.R.D. Tata. He would like to bring forward the Tata Sons meeting from the 27th to the 25th. Is the new date convenient?'

Many such calls later, the elegant Parsi tiredly called her assistant, 'Get me Jamshedpur on the line please.' 'Is that Mr Russi Mody's office? Can you please check if Mr Mody can come to Bombay on Monday? The agenda? I believe Mr Tata will discuss that privately with Mr Mody.'

On Friday, March 22, 1991, there was a flurry of telephone calls and faxes as eighteen secretaries tried to rearrange the schedules of their busy bosses. JRD wanted to advance by two days a meeting of Tata Sons scheduled for March 27. The agenda was a well-kept secret between him and the directors.

On Monday, March 25, the group met in the boardroom on the fourth floor of Bombay House. There are at least two other boardrooms in the unobtrusive brownstone building, but the one on the fourth floor is the most attractive, with its panelled walls the colour of dark honey and high cream ceiling. On one end is a white marble bust of Sir Jamsetji Tata, the group's founder. On the walls are oils of three generations of Tatas and the sole non-Tata chairman, Sir Nowroji Saklatvala. Eighteen chairs, upholstered in crimson tapestry, surround a massive oval mahogany table. In the centre of the table sits an ivory and wood cigar box, probably placed there at the turn of the century, now empty. The atmosphere is hushed, redolent with memories.

Facing the nine-foot double doors is the chairman's chair, slightly taller than the rest. In the '30s, the chair seemed too small for the dapper young man JRD used to be, as he fidgeted with restless energy. In the '90s, the chair seemed to have grown bigger. Or JRD had shrunk. Never tall and born with a slight build, ill health and old age had caught up with the grand old man of steel.

The lithe middle-aged man sitting next to him appeared positively brawny compared to him. Ratan is tall—six feet at least—and broad shouldered. The craggy face is fair and clean shaven with light grey-green eyes above a large Parsi nose. His dark hair is liberally peppered but he looks younger than his age. His light but gravelly voice has an American twang, a hangover from his college days, but on that Monday, he preferred to listen rather than talk.

JRD, group chairman since July 1938 of India's biggest business house, opened the meeting by speaking about his sixty years in Tatas and his experiences. It was a moving occasion. 'I wish we had had a tape-recorder,' one of the directors regretted later. JRD told his colleagues that the time had come for him to hand over charge and proposed Ratan, sitting quietly on his right.

Pallonji Shapoorji Mistry, a construction magnate who owns more stock in Tata Sons than the Tatas themselves, seconded the proposal. The directors were conscious that they were witnessing the end of an era. JRD rose. With courtly dignity, he offered his chair to his successor. JRD became chairman emeritus. Significantly, Russi Mody chose not to attend the meeting, allowing Ratan's appointment to be termed unanimous.

The Tata Sons board meeting laid at rest two decades of speculation about the heir to JRD's throne. From the mid-'80s, several senior Tata directors had been jostling for the coveted position.

It was no secret that Russi Mody, the head of Tata Steel (Tisco), was among JRD's blue-eyed boys, but JRD stopped short of naming Mody his successor. In the '80s, Darbari Seth, the chairman of Tata Tea and Tata Chemicals, had been one of his favourites. So had Nani Palkhivala, the group's legal adviser and head of ACC, India's biggest cement company. Brilliant men, any of them could have easily stepped into JRD's boots. As could have Nusli Wadia, chairman of Bombay Dyeing and JRD's godson. Like the Birlas, the Tatas are not a fecund family. JRD didn't have children, nor did the generation before him. The blood relationship between JRD and Ratan was tenuous. Ratan was seen as the apparent heir, never the heir apparent.

His declining health forced JRD to step down from his throne. Throughout this decade of uncertainty, Ratan behaved with immense dignity, not surprising in a man once voted India's most perfect gentleman. Unlike his rivals, he tried to keep himself to himself—no dropped hints or leaked information. He refused to react to the whispering around him, but the campaign left its scars on him. In 1989, *Business World* had featured a smiling Ratan on its cover as the 'Man of the '90s'. A 1993 cover showed a man who in four short years had aged considerably. Grim new lines were carved around the mouth and there were marks of strain near the eyes. Innocence and a bashful smile had been replaced by a stern, out-thrust jaw.

JRD bequeathed on Ratan eighty-four companies of which thirty-nine are listed, a corporate empire whose sales topped Rs 240 bn with pre-tax profit of Rs 21.2 bn. The group claims to contribute three per cent to the national GDP and annually pays out Rs 35 bn in taxes; that is, approximately 3.2 per cent of total government revenues come from the Tatas. The group has 2.6 million shareholders or about 16 per cent of the investing public and constitutes about eight per cent of national stockmarket capitalization. Of its sales turnover, 16 per cent comes from chemicals, 23 per cent from steel and 30 per cent from trucks. Crudely stencilled behind every truck made by Telco is the legend: Horn OK Please! Tata! The jaunty message on seven out of every ten trucks which bump and grind their way along India's potholed highways gives fair warning to other motorists. The overloaded giants are often dangerously driven and the unlucky ones lie scattered along every national highway.

Since he became its chairman in 1991, Ratan has been trying to push the group into a higher gear. He knows that the group is at a watershed in its 125-year history. Equally, he is intensely aware that as head of an amazingly diversified conglomerate producing just about everything from steel to lipsticks and employing 270,000 people, he cannot afford to take a wrong step.

Harry C. Stonecipher, president and CEO of USA's McDonnell Douglas, a Fortune 500 company, once described the Tatas as 'the one company in the world that combines the attributes of old-line industrial giants like US Steel, Dow Chemicals and Ford, leading lights in the service sector like Hilton Hotels, major utilities like Commonwealth Edison and highly innovative newcomers like Microsoft and Compaq.' Of course, the eulogy had nothing to do with the fact that Stonecipher at the time was trying to sell McDonnell Douglas aircraft to Tata for his proposed airline. Had the Tatas possessed all these attributes, there wouldn't be a consensus on the need for change within the group. How this should be brought about is another matter.

Ratan wants the group to shed its lethargy and become an aggressive player in India's increasingly competitive climate. He wants to make it more agile, more modern, both in terms of technology and management systems, more consumer-oriented—and more united. His concept of what the Tata Group should be is clear. He enunciated it through a formal document, the 1983 Strategic Plan, and lately has been describing his Vision 2000 informally through interviews and chairman's statements. To implement it, however, will be a tough challenge.

It didn't help that Ratan took over the reins from Jehangir Ratanji Dadabhoy, 'J. R. D. Tata' (1904-1993), Jeh to friends. It was a difficult act to follow. The half-French, half-Indian was the only industrialist to be awarded the Bharat Ratna. The Tatas have always been India's biggest business house, but over a legendary fifty years, he consolidated this position and established unrivalled standards of probity and professionalism in management.

At the same time, JRD left Ratan a tangled legacy with more rough edges than smooth planes. The aura hanging over JRD shone so brightly that it cast into the shadow some of his failings. India was changing, and changing rapidly, and outsiders had begun to describe the House of Tatas as a dinosaur.

CLOSE BONDS

Ratan was born in Bombay to Soonoo and Naval Hormusji Tata on December 28, 1937. He was their first child, Jimmy following two years later. An old family with old wealth, as a kid, Ratan squirmed when their British driver dropped him off at the all-boys Campion School in the family Rolls Royce. From childhood, he was uneasy with the ostentatious display of wealth. Even now, he prefers a simple lifestyle with walks on the beach to cocktails at the Taj.

Naval was born with a famous surname and not much else. Distantly related to India's richest and most powerful business family, his parents died early, leaving Naval to be raised in an orphanage. He was thirteen when he was suddenly plucked out of it by the childless and widowed Lady Navajbai Tata, whose husband, Sir Ratan Tata, had promoted some of the group's biggest enterprises.

Lady Navajbai took Naval to live with her in Tata House, near the Bombay Gymkhana, close to the printing presses of the *Times of India*. Better known as Tata Palace, it was a residence of epic proportions. Naval's children grew up in splendid rooms of monstrous ostentation with plush velvet drapes, gilt-and-silk sofas and high ceilings embellished with intricate plaster of paris mouldings.

By all accounts, Ratan's childhood was troubled as Naval and Soonoo did not get along with each other. They finally separated in the mid-'40s when Ratan was about seven and Jimmy was five. The divorce must have left its mark on young minds. Soonoo moved out. Ratan and Jimmy continued to live at Tata Palace, brought up by Lady Navajbai. 'She was like a Dresden doll, always perfectly turned out, often in an exquisitely embroidered *ghara* (a traditional Parsi sari),' says K.A. Divecha, the group's public relations consultant, producing a black and white photograph of Lady Navajbai taken late in life. The grainy texture of the old print can't quite hide the delicate features and flawless complexion. Ratan remembers her affectionately. 'She was a wonderful, wonderful person, of the old world, from whom one learnt a lot, with a very rich experience of life in England and in India. I owe her an enormous amount of gratitude for what she did for me throughout my life. My whole life with her was full of endearment. She had a great influence on my life. She taught me the values which I consider very important in myself.'

From his grandmother, the young Ratan imbibed the importance of dignity, keeping promises and being dependable. Apparently, Lady Navajbai was not only a strong and competent woman, she was also a proud hausfrau, running Tata Palace efficiently and bossing over its retinue of servants. His fondness for his grandmother grew as she made up for the absence of Soonoo in the house. Almost ten years after his divorce from Soonoo, Naval married a Swiss, Simone in 1955. The next year, Ratan and Jimmy acquired a stepbrother, Noel.

Meanwhile Soonoo had married Sir Jamsetji Jejeebhoy and had three daughters: Shireen, Deanna and Geeta. Whenever he could, Ratan would spend time with them. On returning from Cornell (he graduated with a B.Sc. degree in architecture with structural engineering in 1962) Ratan moved to Jamshedpur on his first assignment with Tatas. Six years later when he came back to Bombay, he stayed with Naval and Simone at Tata Palace but moved soon into a bachelor's pad at Colaba. It was small, but it was his own.

The only really close family bonds Ratan had were with his mother and grandmother. Towards Soonoo, he was a devoted son, spending hours at her bedside when she contracted cancer. He was with her when she died in 1982 at New York's Sloan Kettering, a specialist hospital.

Thinking about Soonoo brings a warm glow into Tata's

normally shuttered eyes. 'Apart from being my mother, she was a friend. As I grew up, and I was in my late teens, and then early twenties, and going through a lot of soul-searching, she really became a person I could talk to. We shared a lot of our troubles together. We shared a lot of our joys together. We were just very very good friends. When her house was being rebuilt, she and her daughters came to stay in my flat at my invitation. It was very uncomfortable because it was very overcrowded but for a year they were there. Despite the close quarters and the inconvenience, there was no conflict. It was a very compatible thing and I think that is a very good indication of the fact that if you can do that and not have conflict, you are doing okay.' Ratan designed and oversaw the building of Soonoo's house at Bombay's Peddar Road. It is perhaps the only occasion when his Cornell architectural training was put to use.

After his graduation, Ratan was inclined to stay on in the US. There's wasn't much to draw him back to India. Ratan was happily installed in a flat in an apartment complex with a swimming pool in Los Angeles. His Cornell degree easily helped land a job. He could look forward to furthering a career there. Lady Navajbai thought differently and he couldn't say no to her pleadings. He left Los Angeles with an American girlfriend to follow him but she apparently didn't come to India finally.

Tata has never married. In Bombay, he would date on and off, more off than on, and once even got engaged, but broke it off before the cards could be printed. Without a family and children, what motivates him? 'I have asked myself this quite often. I don't have a monetary ownership in the company in which I work and I am not given to propagating the position I am in. I ask myself why am I doing this and I think it is perhaps the challenge. If I had an ideological choice, I would probably want to do something more for the uplift of the people of India. I have a strong desire not to make money but to see happiness created in a place where there isn't.'

A formal invitation from JRD to join the Tatas arrived. Ratan's acceptance letter was becomingly proper: 'Words could never adequately express my sincere gratitude and appreciation for your decision—I shall attempt to express my thanks by serving the firm as best as I can, and to do all I can to make sure that you will not regret your decision.'At this point of time, there was no question of Ratan rising to the top of the Tata tree.

Ratan's first posting was in Bihar and the experience must have been a major challenge after a college lifestyle in the US. In all Ratan would spend six years in the Telco and Tisco Jamshedpur complexes. 'Beginning in 1962, I spent six months in Telco, then was moved to Tisco where I spent two years on the shop floor, then in the engineering division, with projects and finally as technical assistant to Mr Nanavati, director-in-charge. In those managing agency days that is what the chief executive used to be called,' he recollects.

Ratan's immediate bosses must have sent JRD a good performance report, for Ratan was called to Bombay. He was sent on a short-term assignment to Australia and returned to Bombay a year later. From steel-making, he would later plunge into Bombay's textile industry where he rubbed shoulders with aristocratic mill-owners such as Nusli Wadia and upcoming ones such as Dhirubhai Ambani. The move was a logical transition as Naval was involved in the group's mills, but for Ratan the experience was traumatic.'I was given two sick companies supposedly to train me. First Nelco and then I had also to take over the ailing Central India Textiles,' Ratan said. 'Central India was turned around, its accumulated losses were wiped out and it paid dividends for several years. Then came the recession in the textile industry and Tata Sons decided not to support the company financially. It was taken into voluntary liquidation.'

The winding up of the group's textile interests didn't dent Tata's reputation as badly as did Nelco's troubled history. 'My first directorship was that of Nelco and the status of that company has forever been held against me,' he says. 'But people forget it is a Rs 200cr company today.'

The radio and television manufacturer might shine in comparison with R.P. Goenka's troubled Murphy but flickers dully before the tremendous success of newcomers like Venugopal Dhoot's Videocon or Gulu Mirchandani's Onida. According to Tata, this view represents only one side of the picture. 'It's unfair. No one wanted to see that Nelco did become profitable, that it went from a 2 per cent market share to a 25 per cent market share. Those issues have been forgotten.'

Analysing Nelco's performance in 1982, Ratan had said: 'For three years, from 1972 to 1975, Nelco made a profit and wiped out some of its past losses. Then, in 1975, the Emergency came and demand for consumer goods just disappeared, not just for Nelco, but for everybody. At that time the company was poised for growth and we were pumping money into non-consumer goods, which were sucking in a lot of money. This was followed by an industrial relations problem in 1977. So, while demand improved, there was low production. Finally we confronted the unions and, following a strike, we imposed a lock-out for seven months.'

Soon after Ratan's appointment, the subject of Nelco's heavy losses came up at a Tata Sons meeting. The criticism naturally upset Ratan. He had nothing to do with the past performance of the company and he was being penalized for it. 'Jeh came to my rescue,' Ratan recalled, 'and slowly turned round the whole conversation. If you are confident, he will question you and grill you, but if you are fighting with your back to the wall, he will come and duel beside you.'

It was in Nelco that JRD perhaps saw Ratan's determination and supported his plans for the company's growth against the views of many other seniors within the group. When he was put in charge of Nelco in 1971, sales were Rs 30m, by 1992 they rose to Rs 2bn with a pre-tax profit of Rs 13.5m, and in 1995, sales were halved to Rs 1.13 bn though profits were higher at Rs 32 m.

Nelco stiffened Tata's spine. 'I learnt a lot. I don't think I could have learnt as much the hard way as I did in Nelco. I'm most grateful to the powers that be that they gave me Nelco and that they made me fight for three years, wondering where my next payroll was coming from, and to [fight] in a very competitive market place. In fact Telco is the first company in which I could actually do something. In other companies, I was always put in a fire-fighting situation.'

A STRATEGIC PLAN

Ratan had been beavering away anonymously when, in October 1981, the spotlight suddenly swung towards him. He took over the chairmanship of Tata Industries from JRD (then seventy-eight). The move immediately established Ratan as a possible successor to JRD, on par with Nusli Wadia, Russi Mody, Sumant Moolgaokar, Nani Palkhivala, Darbari Seth and a host of others. The announcement sparked wild speculation inside and outside Bombay House. Journalists clambered over each other to interview him. The phone rang itself off the hook. Calmly, Ratan refused to be taken in by the hype. 'The chairmanship of Tata Industries was a titular one,' he says. 'Tata Industries had a great aura about it but it was only a Rs 60 lakh company with no business activity. I had no plan at the start. It was a soul-searching time to begin with.'

Ratan's personal life was in greater turmoil. Soonoo was found to have cancer a few months later. They flew to New York. In the four months in the hospital with her, Ratan wrote out a new agenda for the group called the 1983 Tata Strategic Plan. Later, S.K. Bhattacharya, a leading management consultant, fleshed it out.

It was a plan alien to the then Tata culture. During and after the '70s, the group had become somnolent, its spirit crushed by restrictive government regulations. It couldn't expand. Whatever it produced sold. There was little inclination to improve. Sitting in New York, Ratan worried that too much was being taken for granted: 'There was a need to look into the future and plan for it more than [we had] in the past, and to look at new business areas in a different kind of way.'

He foresaw that India would one day stop being a seller's market and unless the group began a process of strategic planning immediately, it would suffer. While unfolding his plan, Tata explained his philosophy: 'I believe that a lack of strategic planning has a profound effect on the position of a business organization in the market place and most of the problems of an organization can usually be traced to lack of planning.'

Keen to change the passive image of the Tata Group, Ratan wanted to propel it to the cutting edge of technology. His argument was that the Tatas have all along been pioneers, taking up frontier industries. Jamsetji Tata set up steel and power plants in the last century when they were unheard of in India. Why should they restrain themselves in the '70s?

'You must remember there was an explosion of new emerging technologies in the West in the late '70s: the super mini and personal computers, driven by microprocessor advances, artificial intelligence, the convergence of computing and communications into information technology and biotechnology. So I thought that the Tatas should be in these areas. We were among the few who would be willing and able to invest in these areas without expecting quick returns, I argued. Why shouldn't Tatas enter those fields of recent technological advancement which have application potential in India?'

JRD agreed. As he said at the time: 'It would be ideal for the Tatas to get the opportunities to enter high technology, high risk industries. In fact, it is almost a duty since only large groups can afford to take risks . . . . All industries are eventually going to be high-tech eventually and India cannot afford to miss out on it.' This was all the encouragement Ratan needed to plough ahead.

The hi-tech areas Ratan wanted to concentrate on were telecommunications, oil exploration services, computers and its associated businesses; advanced materials like special alloys and composites; and biotechnology and energy storage systems. Most of these areas were then closed to the private sector. 'However, I felt convinced that these were the areas Tatas must enter as they were the businesses of the future for India. My point was, why should Tatas not be first. As it happened, with the first round of liberalization under Rajiv Gandhi, these were precisely some of the areas that were encouraged. Suddenly our success rate in getting licences was 100 per cent! So next we were running around trying to organize the necessary management and finance.'

The plan, however, failed to win acceptance among some of the senior influential directors for the other business areas, who saw their own interests being subordinated if it were to be implemented. On an academic level, the reasoning made sense. Outlining his viewpoint at the time, Ratan had said: 'Tata Industries, being a collection of chief executives of the Tata companies, offers a chance to be innovative in terms of where the Tatas should be. There is need for strategic planning, looking at opportunities. Such opportunities are available to various companies and there is need to focus them in a central place.'

In practice, however, the directors who had learnt to thrive in a laissez-faire environment within the group, found it difficult to subordinate to the slightest extent their companies' interests for that of the group. Individual companies had done well on their own and any measure which would apparently affect their independence of operations was not one which found ready acceptance.

Recovering from the initial setback, Ratan re-sized the plan to fit his pocket. Nelco's surpluses were minuscule, and Tata Industries' ability to raise funds severely curtailed. He was forced to look at areas requiring little capital investment. Using innovative means, somehow he managed to establish five new enterprises under the Tata Industries umbrella: Tata Honeywell, Tata Telecom, Hitech Drilling, Tata Keltron and Tata Finance. Another four were added later and six more are under implementation. Collectively, these generated Rs 5.87 bn in sales in 1995. Tata Industries thus became the focal point of the group's foray into areas of technology and other emerging businesses.

One of the key features of Ratan's futuristic plan was the division of the group's businesses into eight. These were: metals and associated industries (headed by S.A. Sabavala), engineering (J.E. Talaulicar), chemicals and agrobased industries (Darbari Seth), utilities (K.M. Chinnappa), consumer products (Minoo Mody), services (Fredie Mehta), and hi-tech industries and international business (both under Ratan's charge).

Ratan could not have foreseen that way out in the future

he would be in a position to implement most of what he had been unable to do in his earlier years. It started with his appointment as deputy chairman of Telco, a post which fell into his lap by chance.

Some months before Ratan's appointment as the deputy chairman of Telco, in July 1988, JRD had finally made up his mind over the succession issue, and his choice fell on Mody. To ensure a smooth transition, JRD drew up an elaborate plan. He was already Tisco chairman. Mody would become Telco's chairman, taking over from Moolgaokar, its ailing chairman. This would make Mody head of·the two biggest companies in the Tata group, with a combined sales muscle of Rs 30bn, or a little more than half the group's total sales at the time, and would put him in a strong position to stake a claim to the group chairmanship after JRD retired. In JRD's gameplan, once Mody was Telco's chairman, Ratan would become his deputy.

When JRD played the first move in this grand game of chess, Mody was overjoyed. Had he but restrained his glee, he could have had it all. Instead, Mody allowed himself to prematurely gloat in an interview to the *Business Standard*. His supporters went one step further by crowing about how easily Mody would sort out Telco's problems. Telco was then passing through a rough patch with a dip in profits due to its ambitious expansion programme (in March 1987, Telco made a meagre profit of Rs 29.3m on sales of Rs 12bn). Mody's gung-ho attitude alarmed several Telco executives who began to fear a putsch once he took over.

On hearing the whispers, an incensed Moolgaokar refused to step down. He would carry on in the saddle. He insisted that Ratan should be immediately inducted into Telco as executive deputy chairman giving him the portfolio of Telco's day-to-day operations. Palkhivala, then deputy chairman, voluntarily resigned but continued as a director. Mody tried to wriggle out of the tight situation by blaming the faux pas on 'speculative' and 'mischievous' reporting but the damage had been done.

Both Mody and JRD tried to persuade Ratan to resign and publicly state that he would only accept the position under Mody's chairmanship, but he refused to do so. Among the values he had learnt from his grandmother was the sanctity of promises. He would not denigrate Moolgaokar, who had built Telco over the years.

Mody tried to put a good face on a sticky situation but inside he was seething. News of a strike at Telco, therefore, may have acted as a soothing balm to his sore spirit.

CORPORATE SPURS

Trouble at the truck manufacturer's Pune plant had started brewing even before Ratan Tata entered the scene. It gradually developed into one of the bloodiest strikes in recent history. On April 7, 1988, the day Tata was appointed Telco's deputy chairman, everything appeared normal. By December 1988, when he formally took over the chairmanship from the fragile eighty-two-year-old Sumant Moolgaokar (1906-1989), the tension was palpable.

Nonetheless, few expected the situation to snowball as it did. Most people had their eyes on Russi Mody, wondering how he would react to Ratan's stepping up the ladder leading to JRD's throne. Nobody anticipated that an assault on Ratan's position would come not from an autocratic Tata executive but an unknown trade union leader.

His name was Krishnan Pushparajan Nair, better known as Rajan Nair. The son of a trade union leader and the eldest in a family of eight, Nair worked in Philips before joining Telco as a machine miller in September 1976. Six years later he became the general secretary of the Telco Kamgar Sanghatana

(TKS). Though a Keralite, Nair was fluent in Marathi and has been described as a 'first rate demagogue with a penchant for drama'. In March 1988 he was suspended for allegedly threatening to murder a security guard and sacked a few months later.

The day Nair was sacked, he left Telco vowing 'to bring the Telco management to its knees'. He tried his best to keep to his word. The unresolved wage agreement became his rallying point with the management. Nair insisted on Tata's recognition of his status as the workers' leader as a starting point for any negotiation. The management's view was that a dismissed worker with a criminal record could not be accepted as the leader, and while it was willing to talk with other members of the TKS on Telco rolls, Nair had no locus standi. At the time, there were 8,525 blue-collar workers at the Pune plant and two major unions. From November 1988, antagonism between workers and management worsened. Rumours of a lock-out fuelled the tension. Tata was not new to tackling labour problems, having warded off a sticky situation in his Nelco days. But this was hardly the sort of welcome he needed in Telco. As a strong believer in the principles of transparency and fairness, he was willing to negotiate, but Nair's ego had the better of him and he thought he could put it across to the new, amiable looking chairman of the company. He was mistaken. Behind the soft exterior of Tata was a determination toughened by many years of hard experience in the corporate world.

Matters reached a flashpoint on January 31, 1989. Tata's visit to the Pune plant was greeted on the shop floor with a tool-down strike. On the same day, the local authorities saw fit to take Nair into preventive custody. On hearing this, the second shift workers hijacked buses which were supposed to take them to the plant at Pimpri (just outside Pune), and diverted them to the city where they besieged the district court. Nair was released. Tata says that he was unaware of what was happening in the city as he was huddled in a meeting at the plant with Powar, one of Nair's closest aides, and others. 'Nair chose to make out that he was arrested because I said so [but] I didn't get him arrested. It happened totally independently. If there was an issue of getting him arrested, I wouldn't be meeting his people. But that was the last time I met with them because when they went out, they misrepresented the meeting.'

All through the summer and monsoon, the situation inched inexorably towards a strike despite mediation attempts by Sharad Pawar, Maharashtra's chief minister, and others. Nair was not interested in parleying for peace. On March 15, Nair's men selected about twenty-two managerial personnel and rival unionists and assaulted and stabbed them in various parts of the city. Asked about this, Nair said 'the provocation was from the management because the previous day one of the TKS members was slapped on the shop floor'.

This was as much as Tata could take. From then on his resolve hardened and he refused to give in to any intimidatory tactics of Nair and his men. Meanwhile, Ratan launched measures to build bridges between the management and the workforce. Telco had been contributing silently to the development of the Pimpri-Chinchwad belt. Now, at the time of its worst industrial crisis, it needed the support of the local community most to correct the impression of the image of the exploitative corporation which Rajan Nair's campaign had sought to project. Telco shed its conservative image for the first time and utilized the media to create a public opinion; the managers initiated a one-to-one contact with the workforce to convince them of the management's intentions and slowly the tide began to turn.

On September 19, in a shrewd move to woo away support

from Nair, the management signed a three-year retrospective agreement with TKS's rival, the Telco Employees Union (TEC), offering a wage hike of Rs 585 and a lumpsum arrears of Rs 7,000. There was a stick attached to the tempting carrot. Tata wrote to every Telco employee in the Pimpri and Chinchwad units, warning that 'the company would have to reconsider its plans for further investments in Pune if the trend of labour unrest continued'. The management claimed that 1,570 workers had accepted the offer and more were expected to follow. Seriously worried, Nair mulled over his options.

Two days later, Nair announced that he and his supporters would go on an indefinite fast at the Shaniwarwada fort. With red bandannas tied round their foreheads, 3,000 or so workers trooped into the fort to begin their fast. Significantly the initials RNP (for Rajan Nair Panel) and not TKS were printed on the bandannas. Clearly this was not just a management-union issue, but one involving a personal agenda. A one-day bandh was organized in the Pimpri-Chinchwad areas as a display of strength as also to convey the impression of Nair's growing influence in the region. From Bombay, Datta Samant rushed to Pune to express his support.

By the third day, workers were fainting from hunger. At the end of a week, there was a real fear that a fatality could trigger off uncontrollable violence. Pawar stepped up the pressure on both sides to break the deadlock and meet. They agreed.

On the morning of Wednesday, September 27, Tata flew into Bombay from the USA. Nair had arrived from Pune the previous evening. A tripartite meeting between Tata, Nair and Pawar was arranged for the afternoon at Varsha, the chief minister's official residence. Before that, Samant led a morcha to Bombay House while Nair held rallies and press conferences. These vitiated the already charged atmosphere.

In an obvious bid to slight Tata, Nair and his team deliberately arrived very late. Scheduled for 4 p.m., the meeting finally opened at 5.30 p.m. It proved to be inconclusive. Nair was unwilling to concede ground.

Meanwhile, Pawar was becoming increasingly worried about the strike's political repercussions. The Pimpri-Chinchwad area was a crucial vote bank, home to over 2,000 industrial units with an annual turnover of Rs 35bn and nearly a quarter million workers. Opportunistic politicians of every hue had jumped onto Nair's bandwagon. The Janata Dal leader, Sambhajirao Kakade, was backing Nair. George Fernandes and Madhu Dandavate, socialist leaders, were in constant touch with the strikers. And in the shadow of the Lok Sabha elections scheduled for November 24, Pawar was getting flak from Delhi politicians and Pune industrialists for the state government's kid-glove treatment of Nair. Moreover, Telco was the largest company in the region and any prolonged dispute would have a tremendous economic fall-out. He had to do something.

Under cover of darkness, at 2.30 a.m. on September 29, the State Reserve and Pune city police launched Operation Crackdown. Eighty buses stopped outside the Shaniwarwada fort's quadrangle. Pouring out of the buses, the police cordoned off the fort, stormed inside, and rounded up the workers.

The evacuation went on in batches until 4 p.m. While the workers were taken to police stations in Pune, a separate vehicle took Nair and his lieutenants to the nearby Ratnagiri jail where they were charged with attempting to commit suicide and defying prohibitory orders. Nair was released on bail the next day but it was clear to everybody that the strike had been effectively smashed.

For Tata, the Telco crisis became a test of his managerial abilities. Because Nair so obviously lost, the media trumpeted

Tata's victory. Tata believed it was a vindication of the principles and values which the group had so zealously protected and propagated all along.

In hindsight, he takes heart from a new spirit of teamwork which emerged during the strike. 'Intimidation led to a hunger strike [but] workers came back to work during the strike. Fearing intimidation, they stayed in the plant. Office staff were manning machines and people in the accounts department were moving materials. Some people were fed up and they came back as an "enough is enough" kind of situation emerged. We started producing vehicles with about 800 people. I think that the kind of spirit that was created in Pune then would never have been created were it not for that conflict. So there were winners. They were caused by circumstances which were, ironically, created by Rajan Nair.

'Today there is a sense of friendliness. I can walk around the shop floor and talk to people. They come and talk to me. We smile and shake hands. I think the union has become a very productive and constructive organ of the company. Perhaps, we took our workers for granted. We assumed that we were doing all that we could for them when probably we were not. We gave a Rajan Nair—or any name—a chance to come and do what he did.'

In Jamshedpur, Russi Mody brooded over the Rajan Nair crisis. Mody was the acknowledged labour expert of the Tata group. Under his helm, there hadn't been a single tremor of labour unrest at Tisco for almost half a century. The media's portrayal of Tata as a tough manager capable of handling difficult labour situations posed a subtle threat to the ageing baron.

Indifferent or unaware of the forces around him, Tata concentrated on patching up the shredded labour relations and building up trust between management and workers. March 31,

1991 was a red letter day. Despite the strike, Telco overtook Tisco to become India's biggest company in the private sector by sales. Telco's sales shot up by almost a third to Rs 26bn and profit before tax grew by 58 per cent to Rs 2.35bn. Vehicle production rose by 26 per cent to 81,931 units. Tisco's sales were Rs 23.3bn. Telco's excellent results established Tata's credentials as a top-notch manager. Reason enough for Mody to feel even more threatened.

RUSSI MODY

At Tisco, Mody took every opportunity to declare he would leave only when the board kicked him out. Which it summarily did on April 19, 1993, closing a mordant chapter in the group's history. As an outstanding man-manager in his heyday with a hands-on style which earned him a Padma Bhushan, Mody had set many precedents. His last was not particularly illustrious. Before this, no Tata chairman had ever been fired, let alone been forced to resign. The sacking came bare days before he was to officially retire on May 21. It was a pathetic comedown for a rare man who was once the 'toast' of industry.

The bespectacled *bon vivant* was appointed Tisco's managing director in 1974 and became the chairman in 1984 of India's biggest company in the private sector. His large ego often prompted him to say 'There are only three great men who have come out of Harrow in this century—Jawaharlal Nehru, Winston Churchill and Russi Mody.'

So why did JRD sack a man who once was thought to be one of India's most astute managers? He didn't have a choice: Mody forced it upon himself. He displayed a singular lack of finesse during his last few years with Tatas. Had he behaved with greater decorum, he could have had a much more graceful exit and assured himself pride of place in Tata history.

The last straw was an interview published in the *Hindu* in

which Mody accused Ratan (Tisco's then deputy chairman) and Jamshed J. Irani (its managing director) of mismanaging Tisco's affairs and causing its share prices to crash. He also threatened to launch a campaign to mobilize support for himself from shareholders and financial institutions.

At an emergency meeting on April 19, 1993, there was a great deal of anger and resentment at Mody's statements. As Ratan pointed out, 'The main issue is that a chairman either agrees with his management's policies, or he leaves the board.' Coming as it did after a series of Mody misdemeanours and with tempers running high, it was a foregone conclusion that the board would fire Mody. And when the resolution was put to the vote, it was unanimously passed. Ratan Tata would be 'chairman of the company as from today'.

Earlier, Mody had avoided the March 25, 1991 Tata Sons board meeting which appointed Ratan as chairman of Tata Sons, but the day JRD handed over his crown to Ratan, Mody began to worry in earnest. Tata had become Tisco's deputy chairman on January 31, 1985, and as group chairman would undoubtedly take over Tisco's chairmanship from Mody whenever Mody chose to retire. However his term as managing director was due to expire on June 14, 1993. Mody was anxious that his protégé, Aditya Kashyap, should succeed him. The only hitch was that there was already a number two—Irani.

On the afternoon of November 26, 1991, a circular signed by Mody quietly announced sweeping managerial changes. Tisco would now have four managing directors. In the new pecking order, Irani was demoted from being the joint MD to additional MD, Kashyap moved up from executive director (corporate) to Irani's former position as joint MD, and Ishaat Hussain, the executive director in charge of finance, was designated a deputy MD. Mody continued as chairman and MD. Despite the intentional fuzziness of the designations,

Mody's strategy was transparent. He wanted to move up Kashyap and Hussain, both in their mid-forties, and position Kashyap as Tisco's future chairman with Hussain as his number two.

Mody was so confident that his diktat would be obeyed that he flew off to Europe with Kashyap for a month-long holiday the next evening.

In designing his coup, Mody had totally neglected to take Ratan's reaction into account. And Tata was upset. 'In the largest professionally managed corporation in the private sector, when changes in the senior management structure at the board level and/or succession plans are drawn up, then surely it should be a subject for collective decision-making rather than the decision of any single individual,' he stressed.

Pointing out that neither at or after Tisco's November 27 board meeting did Mody make an attempt to get the board's approval or leave room for discussion, Ratan reiterated his stand that 'the board of directors constitute a collection of independent individuals and each one has the right to express his independent judgement without being accused of being pro or anti'.

There were other arguments stacked against Mody. A professionally-run company had to take more than ordinary care not to show favouritism. It was true that the divorced Mody had never hidden the fact that Kashyap was his constant companion and legal heir, yet others on the Tata Steel board were perturbed by the impropriety of the methods adopted to suddenly elevate Kashyap. Mody had overreached himself and had to be curbed. Furthermore, it was not as if Irani lacked experience or was incompetent. On the contrary, the government had once sounded him out for the chairmanship of the Steel Authority of India. Palkhivala and Nusli Wadia endorsed Ratan's hard line. Palkhivala, the group's legal expert, discovered that Mody had violated Tisco's articles of association by not informing the board of the changes prior to sending out the circular.

Mody's friends lost no time in updating him in London, but he failed to fully appreciate the vigour of the forces building up against him in his absence. On December 29, he flew into Delhi from London where he tried unsuccessfully to meet Narasimha Rao, the prime minister, and Manmohan Singh, the finance minister. On the afternoon of December 31, Mody arrived in Bombay and drove straight to Bombay House for a private meeting with JRD. Mody also began hectic lobbying of the outside directors, but it was apparent to him that he did not have a case to be backed.

By 2.30 p.m. on January 1, a compromise had been hammered out. Mody would apologize to the board, Irani would be clearly number two, there would be only two managing directors—Mody and Irani. The rest would be executive directors. The expected discord at the Tisco meeting did not materialize. By 4.55 p.m., the show was over. It was a clear victory for Ratan.

Heroically, Mody wrapped a few tattered shreds of black humour around him. At Tisco's EGM the next day, when a shareholder asked what award Mody should get when *Business India* had named Ratan Businessman of the Year and Irani was Steelman of the Year, Mody promptly quipped: 'I got the Bamboo of the Year.'

From this moment, Mody's star began to set. At about the same time Ratan pushed through with his retirement policy which called for Tata directors to give up their executive powers at sixty-five years and for non-executive chairmen to retire at seventy-five. Framed in the larger interests of the Tata Group to promote succession planning, it affected Mody directly as he was on the verge of turning seventy-five.

Mody started to feel insecure and sounded out whether he would be allowed another five-year term as executive chairman if he resigned as managing director. The response from Bombay House was a firm 'No'.

Mody accepted the no with considerable ill grace and was forced to change his position only after Nusli Wadia told him during the lunch recess that if he did not fall in line, he (Wadia) would personally move a resolution at the board's post-lunch session to sack Mody as managing director. Mody then caved in and a formula was quickly hammered out. Wadia woke up JRD who had been taking a post-lunch nap, and an agreement was reached. When the board reconvened at 2.45 p.m., Mody began by calling for champagne.

According to the agreement, Mody was offered two concessions in view of his past contributions as also his long association with the group. He would remain chairman until June 1993 and he would retain charge of Tisco's international operations. And Tisco would hold off the Tata Sons policy on the retirement age of Tata chairmen and managing directors for the time being. But far from ending the feud the compromise prolonged the uneasiness within the company. The feuding grew into a low-intensity warfare and, predictably, the company's operations suffered. Mody accepted the compromise unwillingly and continued to create problems for Irani in the discharge of his responsibilities as the new managing director.

In March 1993, at the Founder's Day celebrations in Jamshedpur, JRD and Ratan once again brought up the issue of Tisco's acceptance of Tata Sons' retirement policy with Mody. Mody had crossed seventy-five on January 17, 1993. Instead of taking the hint, Mody suggested that the policy, if introduced in Tisco, should exempt present incumbents. His predecessor, JRD, had had a long innings. Why should Mody be deprived of his?

Ratan pointed out that JRD's was a special case when the retirement policy was not in place. It was now important to depersonalize structures and remove subjective elements, such as the granting of extensions, in the tenure of the group's directors. Mody asked for the details of his retirement package in case he agreed to step down. Once he had them, he said, he would finalize things.

By all accounts the severance package was very generous but Mody kept hedging the question of his retirement. During the March 11 board meeting JRD eventually introduced the retirement policy, at which point Mody rose, picked up his papers and walked off saying, 'I declare the meeting closed.' The meeting continued after a few moments of silence, this time presided over by the deputy chairman, Ratan. Badly upset by Mody's walkout, some directors strongly objected to Mody's behaviour. The retirement policy was adopted unanimously. The next issue was, when? The board agreed Mody should retire before the next AGM (which would be held in July) but that he should be allowed to choose and announce the actual date. Mody was lucky to be allowed the choice. Later, when JRD phoned him to communicate the board's decision, Mody preferred to have his severance package approved before he announced the date.

At the next meeting, on April 13, which Mody avoided by going to Delhi, the protests grew shriller. Mody had taken to vociferously bad-mouthing Tisco's performance in the press and on Doordarshan. The board retaliated by passing a resolution that Mody would have to go by May 1 and not July 17. It took two and a half hours of debate to come to this decision. When JRD phoned Mody to convey the board's decision, he requested time till May 21 as it was an auspicious day for him. Then came the fatal *Hindu* interview. And the sacking. Ratan's perseverance and commitment to principles had managed to bring down Mody from the high pedestal that he had assumed for himself.

FROM CONFEDERATION TO UNION

For historical reasons, the Tata shareholdings in their companies have declined. By the '80s, Tatas held, for example, 2.4 per cent in Tisco, 3 per cent in Telco, 12 per cent in Indian Hotels, 18 per cent in Voltas, 19 per cent in Tomco, and 19 per cent in Tata Chemicals. As for Tata Sons itself, 81 per cent of it was owned by trusts, 17.5 per cent by Pallonji S. Mistry and a scant 1.5 per cent by the Tatas. Ironically, in Tisco, the Birlas, through Pilani Investments, owned 6 per cent or double Tata Sons' stake in their flagship. In ACC, Mistry's stake was higher than that of the Tatas. Only in Tata Tea and Tata Chemicals did the Tatas hold significant stakes, and this was more a result of Darbari Seth's foresight than any group directive. In very few companies do the Tatas hold 26 per cent—the level required to block critical resolutions.

In contrast to the Tatas' weak position, the government is a majority shareholder in several Tata companies, and particularly the important ones. This in itself is not unusual. Over the years, financial institutions such as UTI, LIC, ICICI, IDBI and GIC have acquired large and valuable stakes in many of India's biggest companies. Managements had to borrow low-cost funds for their projects from the FIs and the FIs' habit of taking equity and board positions in return has turned them into powerful partners. Worried by this, industrialists such as Aditya Birla lobbied hard with the finance ministry to find an alternative to this practice and restore privateness to the private sector, but to date no finance minister has been receptive.

This issue didn't unduly bother JRD. Above all, the protected Indian economy provided no impetus to build any safeguards for possible corporate takeovers. He was convinced that the Tata reputation was so impeccable that neither the government nor small investors would ever throw out the Tatas from any of the companies under their management.

JRD was equally convinced that in the event of a hostile takeover bid, once again neither the government nor the small shareholder would permit the raid to succeed. For a brief moment, after Swraj Paul's abortive bid for Escorts and DCM, Tata had second thoughts and the group hiked its stake in Tisco from 2.4 per cent to 8 per cent (in 1989), but the trepidation evaporated almost immediately afterwards.

Ratan disagreed. Questioning the propriety of running large companies through small stakes, especially in a much more liberalized economy, Ratan felt the group should shore up its holdings as quickly as possible. Secondly, looking into the future, he saw these small stakes becoming dangerously microscopic. Several Tata companies were planning to tap the stock markets to fund their new investment programmes, and the group's control looked to be further diluted. 'While we are all proud of the trusteeship management concept that J.R.D. Tata propounded, if we are managing a company, our holding should be more than symbolic,' said Ratan.

Bringing this issue to the directors' notice in his 1983 Strategic Plan, Ratan suggested that not only should the group hike its holdings in the companies under its management, but it should also encourage crossholdings between companies, including Tata Sons. The Birlas had done this very successfully, making it almost impossible for a takeover shark to swallow any of their companies. Also, this would help knit together an empire which was showing increasing signs of fission.

Without JRD's clear support, Ratan's idea had to be buried. Thirteen months after his appointment as chairman of

Tata Sons, however, Ratan initiated serious moves to shore up the group's control over the companies it managed. His 1992 proposal was basically a revival of the 1983 plan with some minor modifications.

At an April 1992 board meeting of Tata Sons, JRD proposed a Rs 220m rights issue. The trusts and Mistry would renounce their rights in favour of other Tata companies such as Tisco, Telco, Tata Chemicals, Tata Electric Companies, Indian Hotels, Tata Oil, Forbes Forbes Campbell and Voltas. Ratan's plan raised questions from some board members.

One of the directors leaked details to the *Economic Times*, and its stiff editorial of May 8, 1992 was equally blunt. 'The new game plan of Messrs JRD and Ratan Tata to convert the Tata group from a loosely-held confederacy to a centralized family business affects lakhs of small shareholders and government institutions. . . . Given that Tata Sons has a real value of at least Rs 1,500 crores, a reasonably-priced rights issue could require the various Tata companies to invest Rs 500 crores, a very big sum. Is it fair for shareholders' money to be used to prop up Mr Ratan Tata's position rather than invest in new plant and equipment? . . . The question also arises what Tata Sons will do with the hundreds of crores it collects . . . . The deal also aims to reduce the limited clout of Mr Mistry, and indeed the Tata family is keen to buy him out altogether . . . . What is important is that the money of shareholders of various Tata companies should not be used to pay Mr Mistry inflated sums for his shares . . . . The Tata case will set a precedent, and it should be a good one.'

The editorial stung Ratan to the quick. 'Over the past decades, the Chairman and Directors of Tata Companies have always acted in the best interests of their shareholders and there has never been an abuse of shareholders' funds to acquire or gain control of Tata companies through Tata Sons. I take very strong exception to such motives being ascribed to Mr J.R.D. Tata and myself. I also take exception to the statement in the editorial that there is a move to convert the Tata Group "from a loosely-held confederacy to a centralized family business". Tata Sons has been, and continues to be, professionally managed by a Board of Directors and not by "family members" as alleged by you. The allegations and insinuations being made by you appear to be an effort to discredit the values and the philosophy on which the House of Tatas has been built. It shall always be my endeavour to uphold the Tata values and philosophy,' he wrote in an impassioned letter to the editor.

Finally, in November 1995, Tata Sons made a rights issue which closed a month later. All the major Tata companies such as Tisco, Telco, Tata Tea and Indian Hotels contributed. It was another victory for Ratan. Earlier, in July 1994, he had successfully launched Tisco's preferential allotment issue to double the Tata stake to 16 per cent.

Since then, several Tata companies have been tapping the capital market. A steady stream of rights issues, convertible debentures, Euro-issues, floating rate bonds, and warrants are being offered to old and new investors. While most of the money is earmarked for fresh capital investment in new projects, Ratan has managed to utilize some of it for increasing crossholdings and generally strengthening the group's holdings.

Ratan made a modest but encouraging beginning but the bill to raise the group's stakes to anything like 26 per cent in each of the major companies will be huge. As Darbari Seth pointed out during the Tata Sons 1993 rights issue furore, 'The capitalization of the five or six biggest companies works out to about Rs 20,000 crores. And even 1 per cent of that works out to Rs 200 crores.'

From where is Tata going to get the money? Wait and see is his only answer.

CABBAGES, KINGS AND RATAN

The flight attendants of Indian Airlines once got together to choose their favourite executive passenger. The awardee of the unofficial 1992 poll was not Rahul Bajaj or the jocular Dhirubhai Ambani or even the courteous half-French JRD but Ratan Tata. When flying Indian Airlines, Ratan uses the VIP seats but generally has no personal assistants or other staff accompanying him. Most of the time he buries his head in paperwork. He doesn't bother with food but has coffee, strong, brewed directly with the milk and without sugar. 'Though even if it is not served as he likes it, he doesn't complain,' said an air hostess.

The crews serving the Bombay-Delhi sector have ample opportunity to notice Ratan's little habits. It's the route Ratan flies most frequently, though not by choice. An experienced pilot, a love for flying was one of the few common bonds between JRD and Ratan. If he could, the easy-to-please executive would far rather take the controls of one of the group's many private aircraft and take off for Pune or any of the group's plants around the country. Instead Ratan has to travel often on business to Delhi.

Despite the Narasimha Rao administration's attempts to loosen the Licence Raj, the government's various ministries continue to exert stifling control over business, especially in the core and infrastructure related sectors. In the past, JRD had refused to pay under the table for licences. Ratan upholds the tradition—and to an extent is paying the price for his commitment to the Tata group's values. During his long chairmanship, JRD stood on the sidelines watching helplessly as other business houses got licences denied to Tatas. Other entrepreneurs built huge factories, the Tatas couldn't. That has not daunted the spirit of Tatas who, despite the constraints, have remained India's premier industrial house. 'Jamsetji Tata took a national view and so inevitably we were in basic industries and infrastructure,' explains Ratan. 'After Independence, these became the natural domain of the public sector. Through the '60s and '70s, excessive government controls and the MRTP restrictions deprived Tatas of growth. Our passenger car proposals were rejected. Tisco was not allowed to expand in the manner that was needed and its entry into special steels was thwarted.'

In the mid-'80s, Telco tied up with Honda, but the government dilly-dallied until Honda lost patience. Darbari Seth wanted to build a refinery, petrochemical complex and fertilizer plant. The Tata power companies badly needed to expand. The only new business activity of any significance in the '80s was the group's entry into watches (Titan). Indira Gandhi's administration turned down virtually every major application, which is why Rajiv Gandhi's attitude towards the group came as a welcome surprise when he became prime minister after her assassination in 1984. 'I considered him [Rajiv Gandhi] as a friend even though there was no close friendship between us,' Ratan would write in a touching obituary after Rajiv Gandhi's assassination in May 1991. 'We did not have frequent meetings or even much direct interaction even though I was appointed by his government on the boards of a number of government organizations such as CSIR and Semiconductors Ltd or oversaw the preparation of some committee reports such as the one on project implementation.'

There had been coolness between Indira Gandhi and JRD but the relationship between her son and Ratan was warmer. This could have been because Rajiv and Ratan spoke the same language in many ways. Both were westernized and technically minded and they loved flying, and neither was particularly enamoured of his job. They could tinker with sophisticated computer programmes but found themselves operating hopelessly out of their depth in the cut and thrust of today's India. All too often, they found that they'd been too open, too trusting, taking people at face value, and then been disappointed.

'I first met Rajiv Gandhi with his mother at Jamshedpur shortly after the death of his brother Sanjay Gandhi in a plane crash in 1980,' said Tata. 'We had dinner together and I was struck by the man's politeness and sincerity. After that we did not meet for a few years. When he took over as prime minister, I was very much excited by the things he was saying, the freshness with which he was looking at economic and political issues. I felt here was a prime minister who was a man of our times. I then met him not to ask for anything but just to express my happiness and excitement at the new direction he was charting out for the country. I was once again struck by his decency, sincerity and forthrightness.'

Their friendship and mutual admiration brought about a major change in the group's attitude towards the government and vice versa. Indicative of the new approach was the Air India chairmanship—'I read about my appointment in the papers!'—and Ratan's close advisory relationship with Gandhi. 'One task which I liked a great deal was working for the science and technology ministry,' recalled Tata. 'I was part of a technology mission to the US, where the effort was to set up a venture capital company in that country which could buy into hi-tech companies. The model would roughly be what the Tatas did with Elxsi.'

Many Tata project applications, which had been buried under mountains of paper, were approved during this period. In his 1983 Strategic Plan, Tata had pleaded to be allowed into hi-tech industries of strategic importance. 'With the first round of liberalization under Rajiv Gandhi, these were precisely some of the areas that were thrown open [to the private sector]. Suddenly our success rate in getting licences was 100 per cent!'

said a pleased Tata with some surprise. Darbari Seth had been lobbying for the group's entry into the petrochemical and petroleum sectors for decades without making much headway. According to Darbari's son, Manu Seth: 'When Ratan Tata heard that the government was looking for a private partner for the Karnal refinery, he sent me to Delhi in November 1986 to look at the project.' Shell was a 'top contender' but the Tatas bagged it.

Tata's ability to pull off these coups had JRD acknowledge his achievements: 'The government has at least started acting on proposals which were not being approved for two years.'

The new understanding which Tatas had with the government did not survive Rajiv Gandhi's assassination. Be it under V.P Singh or Narasimha Rao, it was back to status quo, or near enough. Try as he might, Ratan has not yet been able to clear an airline venture with Singapore Airlines and his attempts to renew Tisco's mining rights in Orissa illustrate his difficulties. Instead of the lease being extended, the Tatas lost ground.

QUESTIONING THE UNQUESTIONABLE

Stepping across the threshold of Bombay House is like walking through a time warp. Tea for afternoon visitors arrives on little wooden trays covered by crisp white napery. Burnished steel teapots, buried under thick cosies, accompany plates of dainty pastries. As many little old ladies hobble in and out of the marble portals of Bombay House as dashing young money managers clutching important company statements.

The head office's air of old-fashioned courtliness is far removed from the rough and tumble atmosphere of the Bombay Stock Exchange, a stone's throw away. The ladies room on the ground floor is an oasis of quiet, a refuge from the stress of modern life, much like the ladies room at the Bombay Gymkhana. Tables and benches are provided for those who want to eat their lunch in privacy, there is a comfortable chair to rest tired feet, and a small vanity area to refresh war paint.

There's been some attempt to bring the headquarters of a Rs 240bn business house in line with the rest of the world. Last year, Ratan's computer boys installed a state-of-the-art security system complete with swipe cards and computerized identification codes. But the eggheads forgot to teach the peons manning the lifts and strategic doors to cope with the system. Unfamiliar with the hi-tech gizmos, the instructions and codes for the entry points, the peons appear frustrated, demoralized and afraid of becoming useless after decades of service. Also, there's no completely secure security system, old or new, in operation.

The play of the old and the new overlapping and clashing against each other is repeated on the fourth floor, the executive floor. The passage is thickly carpeted and richly panelled. Open the door to Ratan's office suite, and its starkness hits you in the face.

Yet Tata's office is as self-effacing as the man. Located a few steps down from the main boardroom where he was appointed group chairman, the suite was allotted to Ratan when he became head of Tata Industries in 1982. Neither after JRD's retirement or his death has Ratan made any move to occupy his famous corner office. Currently the room is unused but dusted meticulously. The only occupant in the silent anteroom is JRD's secretary. A building to house the Tata archives is coming up in Pune where JRD's room will be recreated. Until then the clock on the table ticks forlornly.

Conversely, Ratan's office is a beehive of activity. It was renovated about three years ago when the 800 to 1,000 sq. ft. space was partitioned into several cubicles. Apart from the reception area, there's a handkerchief size cabin for his executive assistant, Rajiv Dube and two cubbyholes for Sheila Shastri and K.D. Skandan (Tata's two secretaries) besides a conference room to seat eight which is used by Ratan as a functional working area. Tata's own office facing the entrance is slightly—but not much—larger than the reception area and dominated by a picture of a jet cockpit.

On the coffee table in the reception area is an eclectic range of reading material. Copies of *Tata Sphere* and the *Tisco News* are in the company of *Forbes, Fortune,* the *Economist* and the *Far Eastern Economic Review.* Sandwiched between them are thumbed issues of *Computerworld, Semiconductor, Le Figaro,* and the *International Herald Tribune.*

The decor is purely functional. Not even the gentle Bendre landscape behind the receptionist's desk can soften the harshness of the white laminated partitions, the inexpensive black cloth sofas, the slate-grey short-pile carpet. The mandatory potted plants look cowed down by the clinical atmosphere with its harsh white lighting. There are no *objets d'art*, no ashtrays, no bits of paper and fewer frills than in a dentist's waiting room. In the conference room, however, Tata's passion for aviation is very visible in the aircraft memorabilia which adorn the wall unit.

The Tata group is at a watershed in its 125-year history, and there are hard decisions waiting for its group chairman. It needs a leader who can bridge the past and the future. Is Ratan the right man for the right job at the right time? Even though he has brought to heel some of the brightest and best brains in management proving that he has the ruthlessness and doggedness of a leader, some peers still question his acceptability. Like a nagging stepmother, they keep finding faults with the stepchild.

One reason for this could be Ratan's aloofness.

Circumstances and personality have combined to make Tata a loner. The boardroom battles carved deep scars and he's shed his trustful nature. Reticent to a fault, few know his secrets, hopes and desires. He doesn't share confidences with anyone, not even Nusli Wadia, Ambani's *bête noire* and Tata's childhood friend. Today, his closest companion is Tito, an Alsatian dog.

But in India, chairmen—especially aggressive ones—are expected to be within hearing distance of the mobile's shrill ring. Anytime. Anywhere. Networking outside the office is equally important. However, Tata has a habit of disappearing which even his supporters find trying. Considered remote and inaccessible, he is out of his office up to fifteen days a month. He leaves office at 6:30 and doesn't like to be disturbed at home. Saturdays and Sundays are equally sacrosanct although 'he finds it difficult to keep work away from weekends and often reads reports late into the night', says a close friend. According to his office, 'Given Tata's hectic schedule, it is difficult at short notice to get a time in his diary. However, often at his own inconvenience, he goes out of his way to accommodate a meeting to resolve a mundane grievance of an employee or a shareholder. Despite his trying to be as accessible as possible, there are some who still find him remote.'

Brushing aside the censure, Tata says: 'It's probably true in some cases, probably not in others. I think more often the people who make those complaints have to ask themselves what they push into this office that they shouldn't—and how much of the buck they pass, they can keep with themselves. Yes, there are only twenty-four hours in the day, and there are great pressures on me. Sitting here with you is depriving someone of their time with me and unfortunately the worst complaints about my time are from people from outside and not so much from within.'

Isn't that part of the chairman's role?'Not necessarily. While I don't mind the occasional meeting with a visiting delegation from overseas who want to know more about India and Tatas, people have to realize that it is not the only role that I have to play. Although I can't do anything about it, that's a role I don't enjoy and one that I find somewhat wasteful!'

Aware of the criticism and whispering going on behind his back, Ratan understands the challenges that face him. He knows that the decisions he takes today will decide the future. It's hard to read tea leaves but he has to get it right if he wants to stop analysts from calling the group a dinosaur. Ratan wants to radically change the Tata culture, make it more competitive and agile.

Does he consider himself a risk taker? 'There have been occasions when I have been a risk taker. Perhaps more than some, and less so than certain others. It is a question of where you view that from. I have never been speculative. I have never been a real gambler in the sense that some successful businessmen have been.'

Asked once to comment on Ratan Tata and the future of the Tata Group, the late Aditya Birla hedged: 'If you don't have systems, any individual will fail, and if you have systems but don't have a leader to lead the system, it will fail. Both factors are very important. There has to be a man at the helm who can provide the motivation, the dynamism, the force, the leadership to make the system work. I'm sure that the Tatas have very good systems.'

Ratan feels many of these systems need fine-tuning. How will he force change? 'Change is not going to come by merely making that a mandate. Change is not going to come by writing letters to various group companies. Change is going to come from the competition that the environment provides. It's going to come from people who for the first time are fighting to survive. It's going to come from—if I am to portray my role—it's going to come from my being harsh on those who don't meet their tasks. It's going to come from forcing companies to set tasks and perform against those tasks,' said Tata. 'To give an example, Tata Steel never had to concern itself about profit. Profit was a plug number. All it needed to do was to produce and if the production levels were high, any increase in cost became a price increase because there was a government formula for price increase and the profit was a plugged number. Suddenly you had competition, you had a very aggressive public sector steel company, and for the first time Tata Steel had to fight for its profit. The spirit of a company and the spirit of the people just blossomed. We averted what could have been a disaster with our own efforts. They just went ahead and did it. But that was short-lived. An attitudinal change has to be more permanent, and it will come from this environment where somebody is constantly pushing them to be more aggressive and I think that's my role. This is why I keep saying, question the unquestionable. To stop people from saying this is how we've dealt [with matters] for the last twenty-five years.'

Many within the group feel that what Tata is doing is not only questionable, but downright painful. Such as the pruning exercise he is contemplating. 'We have approximately eighty companies in so many different businesses. As we began to move into an era of free markets and competition, it was clear that the Tatas need to re-focus,' says Tata. 'I think we were in many more areas than we should have been in and we were perhaps not concerned about our market position in each of those businesses. I think the needs today are that we define our businesses much more articulately, if you like, and that we remain focused rather than diffused, and that we become much more aggressive than we used to be, much more market driven, much more concerned about consumer satisfaction.'

Within the Tata monolith is a small team called the Tata Strategic Management Group headed by Raju Bhinge, whose office is on the ground floor next to Reception. Bhinge, a pleasant young man in his thirties, is often entrusted by Ratan with the sensitive job of analysing the strengths and weaknesses of group companies and coming up with their restructuring programme. In the 1983 plan, Ratan had suggested that the Tatas get out of soap-making. Once in the saddle, Ratan promptly sold off Tomco to the Unilever group. Who will be next in line?

Ironically, even as Tata huddled with S.M. Datta of Hindustan Lever, Darbari Seth announced plans to get into detergents through Tata Chemicals. Meanwhile three different Tata companies applied to build cement plants. There were several other instances of group companies acting independently and in competition with each other. Synergy is not something the Tatas apparently rely on. Ratan is convinced that this attitude has to change.

For the moment, Tata has put these and other such knotty issues on the backburner and is focusing on Tisco and Telco 'because they constitute 50 per cent of our turnover. In many ways they have been role models for other companies. If these more visible companies can be converted from being production-driven in a seller's market to more responsive companies in a buyer's market, the message will spread faster within the group.'

If other group companies want to match the recent outstanding performance of these two companies, they'll have to sprint to catch up. Ratan would appear to be on the right track, and though pleased, 'they are not running at the speed they should be,' he qualifies.

Ratan's management philosophy is most evident in Telco. 'In fact Telco is the first company in which I could actually do something,' he says. 'In other companies, I was always put in a fire-fighting situation, but as I said, in Nelco I learnt a lot.' For the past decade, Ratan has been working on making the truck manufacturer more responsive to consumer needs. Under Moolgaokar, Telco was a single product, virtually a single model company. Today, the product profile has changed. Now there are medium commercial vehicles, light commercial vehicles and cars. 'I helped conceptualize the Sierra which, along with the Estate, are the bridge, so to speak, between commercial vehicles and passenger cars,' explains Tata. 'The emphasis in commercial vehicles is on durability and reliability, not on comfort and finish. In passenger cars people look for a different kind of reliability and also for things like good finish, tight fits, high-gloss finishes and good handling. Telco had to choose between two market segments—a low priced, high volume car [or an upper range product]. We chose to produce a large, upmarket car to international standards. This route is harder as the consumer here is paying more and is therefore more demanding. If a cheap car fails, one can say that the model failed, whereas if an expensive car fails, the company's image is on the block.'

There were no dearth of people to predict its failure. Tata was flying against conventional wisdom, his people said. Customers won't pay over the top for these extras, they said, but Tata insisted. He put in central locking, electric windows and other features. Buyers queued up.

The strategy had the additional benefit of raising the engineering standards in Telco's plants. Moolgaokar had laid the foundation but Tata wanted to bring 'about an attitudinal change in acceptance levels in the company. It should lead to an entirely different concept of dimensional tolerances in design.'\Telco always had been slow off the mark. Now it's looking more streamlined, revved up.

Similarly, there's been a major turnaround at Tisco. The biggest steel producer in the private sector has always been regarded as an excellent company, but under Ratan's management, its profits have risen phenomenally. These achievements combined with his skilful handling of the controversies bubbling within the group, have finally earned Tata his corporate spurs. Five years ago, other Tata executives used to be lionized as 'powerhouses', 'leading lights', or 'great man managers', whereas Ratan Tata, at best, was described as merely a 'decent human being'. Today, not only has he cast aside the shadow of Nelco and Central India Mills, but proven himself in several corporate areas. He has outmanoeuvred and vanquished some of India's most brilliant strategists in bitter battles inside and outside the boardroom. He has pioneered the design and manufacture of a completely Indian multi-usage car. And he has earned acceptance from labour leaders after one of the bloodiest management-worker showdowns in recent times.

Ratan finds it easier to hold his ground against the experts and stand up for what he believes is the right strategy. A few years ago, he would have never said: 'I think today there has to be a little more than guidance—it has to be to provide some degree of stated direction even if it is not dictated. I think there is need to take some hard decisions which doesn't come from guidance alone.'

Success is knocking confidence into Ratan . . . .

Appendix

Dhirubhai Ambani

Group sales for year ended March 1995: Rs 80bn
Core interests: Petrochemicals, synthetic yarns and textiles, financial services, oil (on the anvil)
Major companies:
Reliance Industries, Reliance Capital, Mudra Communications, Reliance Petroleum*, Reliance Polypropylene*~, Reliance Polyethylene*~

* start up concerns
~ joint venture with C Itochu, Japan

Rahul Kumar Bajaj

Group sales for year ended March 1995: Rs 40bn
Core interests: Two-wheelers, three-wheelers, sugar, small electricals, and special steels
Major companies:
Bajaj Auto, Bajaj Auto Finance, Bajaj Electricals, Bajaj Hindustan, Mukand*

*in partnership with Viren Shah

Aditya Vikram Birla

Group sales for year ended March 1995: Rs 150bn (including Rs 50bn from companies overseas)
Core interests: Viscose staple fibre, palm oil, insulators, carbon black, cement, aluminium, rayon filament yarn, flax, caustic soda and financial services

Major companies in India:
Grasim, Hindalco, Indo-Gulf Fertilizers & Chemicals, Indian Rayon & Industries, Century Textiles, Century Enka, Bharat Commerce, Jayshree Tea, Kesoram Industries, Mangalam Cement, Renusagar Power, Mangalore Refinery & Petrochemicals, Birla Growth Fund, Tanfac Industries, Bihar Caustic & Chemicals

Main companies in Thailand:
Thai Rayon, Thai Carbon Black, Indo-Thai Synthetics Century Textiles, Thai Polyphosphate & Chemicals, Thai Peroxide, Thai Acrylic Fibre

Main companies in Indonesia:
PT Indo-Bharat Rayon, PT Elegant Textile, PT Indo Liberty Textile

Company in Philippines:
Indo-Phil Textiles

Companies in Malaysia:
Pan Century Edible Oils, Pan Century Oleo Chemicals

Company in Egypt:
Alexandria Carbon Black

Rama Prasad Goenka

Group sales for year ended March 1995: Rs 45bn
Core interests: Tyres, power, agribusiness, and telecommunications
Major companies:
CEAT, Calcutta Electric Supply Corporation, Phillips Carbon Black, KEC International, ICIM, Harrisons Malayalam Spencer & Company, HMV (The Gramophone Company of India)
Company in Sri Lanka:
Associated Ceat

Brij Mohan Khaitan

Group sales for year ended March 1995: Rs 16bn
Core interests: Tea, batteries, engineering
Major companies:
Deutsche Babcock, Dewrance Macneill & Company, Flender Macneill Gears, George Williamson, India Foils,. Kilburn Chemicals, Kilburn Engineering, Kilburn Reprographics, Makun

Tea, McLeod Russel, McNally Bharat Engineering, Namdang Tea, Bishnauth Tea, Eveready Industries (Union Carbide), Standard Batteries, Williamson Magor

Bharat and Vijay Shah

Group sales for year ended March 1995: Rs 35bn.
Core interests: Diamonds, real estate and construction, movies.
Major companies in India:
BV Jewels, B Vijaykumar & Company, Bharat Associates, Donyipolo Petrochemicals, Gujarat Pipavav Port, Horizon Battery Technologies, Revlon Pen, Shanti Star Builders, Shantilal Lallubhai & Sons, Vijay Star, VIP Enterprises, Vishal Chairs
Major company in Belgium:
Vijaydimon
Major company in Thailand:
BV Diamond Polishing Works

Ratan Tata

Group sales for year ended March 1995: Rs 240bn.
Core interests: Steel, automobiles, power, chemicals, tea, hotels, textiles, engineering, information services, financial services, cement, and watches
Major companies:
TISCO, TELCO, ACC, Tata Electric Companies (Andhra Valley Power, Tata Hydro-Electric Power, Tata Power), Indian Hotels and the Taj Group of Hotels, Lakmé and Lakmé Exports, Forbes Forbes Campbell & Company, Gokak Patel Volkart, Tata Chemicals, Tata Tea, Nelco, Svadeshi Mills, Tata Consultancy Services, Tata Exports, Tata Press, Tata Housing, Tata Finance, Tata Sons, Tata Industries, Tata Unisys, Tata Honeywell, Tata Telecom, Tata IBM, Tata Advance Materials, Investment Corporation, Hi-tech Drilling, Titan, Rallis, Voltas

A Note on Sources

While the bibliography lists all the sources used in the writing of this book, I would like here to acknowledge separately the many people who helped me get a better insight and understanding of the business maharajas and to single out some of the published sources which form the backbone of individual chapters.

1. AMBANI

B.N. Uniyal, an old and close friend of the Ambani family, provided privileged information about aspects of many controversial events which I would not have otherwise known. Professors Sumantra Ghoshal and J. Ramachandran's excellent study of Reliance's headlong growth during the '80s and '90s is another key input. The articles published in the *Indian Express* by Arun Shourie and S. Gurumurthy were invaluable, as was a profile of Dhirubhai Ambani written by the late Madhu Valluri published in *Society* in July 1985, and H. Mehta's profile on Mukesh and Anil Ambani which appeared in *Gentleman* in July 1986.

2. BAJAJ

Few families are as open and frank as the Bajaj family, especially Rahul Bajaj who very kindly let me wander at will through his Akurdi plant and chat with senior executives, many of whom know him from the '60s. Most of this chapter is based on two such factory visits. Uday Kotak, head of the merchant bank Kotak Mahindra, Viren Shah, head of Mukand Ltd and a political activist, and Pradip Shah, the former head of CRISIL and now George Soros's man in India, helped me acquire another perspective. Additionally, I would be remiss in not acknowledging the interview of N.K. Firodia published in the *Sunday Observer* of October 9, 1988, and Nitin Belle's elegant profile of Rahul Bajaj which appeared in *Gentleman,* March 1988.

3. BIRLA

Ironically and quite by chance, I spoke to the late Aditya Birla the day before he left for Baltimore. At the time, I didn't realize this would be my last conversation with him. As a free-lance writer, I covered his business career for over fifteen years, and every time I requested information, he was extraordinarily kind and supportive, always agreeing to an interview within a day of the request reaching him. This chapter therefore is an amalgam of many interviews spread over a number of years. I have also relied heavily on B.K. Birla's autobiography, *A Rare Legacy,* T.N. Ninan's perceptive account of the tensions in the Birla clan which appeared as a series of articles in *India Today* between 1983 and 1988; and on interviews with Rajashree Birla and Kumar Mangalam Birla.

4. GOENKA

More than any other chapter, with perhaps the exception of the Khaitan one, this chapter owes itself wholly to its maharaja. A born story-teller, Rama Babu can't keep secrets and I have to admit that I unabashedly egged him on, to the consternation of both Harsh and Sanjiv. Others who spoke candidly to me were

Paresh Vaish of McKinsey; S. Venkitramanan, former head of the Reserve Bank of India; Vinod Doshi, head of Premier Auto; and Chander Dhanuka, who put together the CESC deal. Among the plethora of published sources on the group—on any given day, RPG Enterprises is mentioned at least three dozen times in the press—Chander Uday Singh's profile of the Goenka brothers published in *India Today* of August 31, 1986 remains outstanding.

5. KHAITAN

Initially I didn't have a clue about how to gain the confidence of the elusive B.M. Khaitan—and I knew that unless I obtained it, I would not be able to write this chapter. At the same time I was determined to write about a man for whom everyone has a pleasant word, about a man who has to deal with terrorists on a daily basis, about a unique business of global size. After some dubious arm-twisting, I managed to get a toehold. I would like to thank Harsh Goenka for obtaining my *entrée* into Briju Babu's domain—and to stress that all the mistakes are entirely mine. Eventually, I spent two days shadowing the reticent billionaire, interviewing his family and executives, and was overwhelmed by his frank description about his childhood and his life so far. I also relied on Sanjoy Hazarika's *Strangers of the Mist* for information on ULFA, and on Stephanie Jones' account of Khaitan's dealings with Lord Inchcape published in *Merchants of the Raj*. When I stumbled, Nantoo Banerjee of *Business Standard* pointed out the correct track to tread.

6. SHAH

Very little is known about the world of the diamantaires and almost all the material used in the chapter was provided by the Shah brothers themselves. Murli Deora chipped in with some insights, and Professor Pankaj Ghemwat of the Harvard Business School kindly allowed me to see the proofs of a forthcoming study on the Indian diamond trade.

7. TATA

The Tata group is perhaps the best documented of all Indian business houses. Pick up any copy of *Business India* and you will be spoiled for choice by the stories on the group. However, 'Ratan Tata: Living in Today's World' by Nazneen Karmali and A.B. Ravi which appeared in *Business India,* June 19, 1995 is perhaps the most comprehensive account of Tata's corporate philosophy. Given the sheer volume of information available on the Tatas, the list provided in the bibliography at the back of this book is limited to those works actually drawn upon in the text. Apart from these published sources, I could not have written this chapter without Sailesh Kottary's invaluable aid, data provided by the Tata Group's media relations department and interviews with two Tata executives, Homi Sethna and Raju Bhinge.

Select Bibliography

AMBANI

Books

Gates, B. *The Way Ahead*. London: Viking, 1995.

Herdeck, M & Piramal, G. *India's Industrialists*. Washington: Three Continents Press, 1985.

Salve, N.K.P. *The Story of the Reliance Cup*. New Delhi: Vikas Publishing House Pvt Ltd, 1987.

Articles

Ambani, D. 'I do not consider myself clever than my colleagues', *Business India,* April 28, 1990, p48;

'Business is my hobby', *Business India,* December 20, 1993, p58;

'I will salaam anyone in the government', *India Today,* June 30, 1985, p89;

'Nothing less than the best', *Business India,* June 17, 1985, p89;

'Success is my worst enemy', *India Today,* October, 1989, p118;

Baweja, H. 'Umesh Khatre—I don't know any of the Ambanis', *India Today*, September 30, 1989, p58.

Belle, N. 'Battle of the barons', *Bombay*, December 7, 1985, pp29-30.

Bhagat, Dhiren. 'Why Dubey left *Express*', *Sunday Observer*, February 21, 1988.

Bhagat, M. 'L&T, the Reliance alliance', *Business India,* October 17, 1988, p49.

'Reliance Loan Mela—Ambani does it again', *Business India,* June 2, 1986, p23.

Bhanu, T. 'Mukesh Ambani next L&T chairman?', *Financial Express,* February 17, 1991.

Bombay, 'Ambani again', April 22, 1984, p98.

Business Standard, 'Bond holders' interest to be protected: Ambani', June 12, 1986;
  'Reliance may convert bonds to equity again', June 7, 1986;
  'D. N. Ghosh eased out of L&T', February 16, 1991;
  'Fund holding abroad by *Express* alleged', September 4, 1987;
  'R. N. Goenka explains $200,000 payment', September 5, 1987;
  'Saroj Goenka granted bail', September 8, 1987;
  'Ramnath Goenka interrogated', September 18, 1987;
  'Readings and readings', January 4, 1991.
Business Today, 'Tisco: No more the blue-eyed boy', February 22, 1993, p125.
Business World, 'Another Ambani wins his spurs', August 15, 1993, p43.
Chakravarti, S. & Taneja, S. 'Reliance Industries—Grand gamble', *India Today*, September 20, 1991, pp98-103.
Chandra, P. 'Reliance: The man behind the legend', *Business India*, June 17, 1985, p88.
Das, I. 'Ghosh wins first round', *Sunday Mail,* January 20, 1991.
Deora, M. 'Bridging the chasm', *Sunday*, November 3, 1991, p42.
Dhar, R. N. 'Reliance Industries—Fresh offensive', *India Today*, May 31, 1990, p113.
Director Digest Portfolio, 'Reliance Textiles—How multiple strategies led to phenomenal growth',1983 annual, p99f.
Dubashi, J. 'Larsen & Toubro—Aiming high', *India Today*, January 31, 1985, p120.
Economic Times, 'Massive raids launched on Express offices', September 2, 1987;
  'Express Group: Rs 33.5 lakh duty evasion, says DRI', September 3, 1987;
  'DRI charge dishonest: Goenka', September 5, 1987;
  'RIL defers conversion move', June 15, 1986;
  'Reliance shares decline further', June 13, 1986;
  'Debenture issue under reveiw', June 13, 1986;
  'Reliance to offer conversion option to bondholders', June 7, 1986.
Fortune, reprinted in *Business Today,* 'Windows on Microsoft', November 7, 1995, p97.
Gangadhar, V. '*Express* problems', *Sunday,* June 23, 1991, pp72-3;
  'Goenka, warts and all', *Sunday,* November 3, 1991, pp84-5;
  'Khaki chaddi investigators', *Sunday*, March 10, 1991, p14f.
George, T.J.S. 'A life of courage and conviction', *The Week,* October 13, 1991, pp28-32.
Ghani, A. H. 'Advantage Wadia', *Business World*, October 9, 1991, pp63-70.

Ghosh, D. N. 'Family firms have no vision', *India Today*, August 31, 1990, p132.

Ghoshal, S. & Ramchandran, J. 'Reliance Industries Ltd: A case study', European Foundation for Management Development, 1995, p2.

Goenka, Ramnath. 'It's scandalous', *Indian Express,* September 5, 1987.

Gurumurthy, S. 'Debenture conversion: Sub-rule or subversive rule', *Indian Express,* March 22, 1986.

Illustrated Weekly of India, 'The empire strikes back—Raid on *Indian Express'*, September 20, 1987, p8f.

Imprint, 'Reliance: A success story', January 1984, p27.

Indian Express, 'DRI's allegations a tissue of lies', September 3, 1987;
'PM seeks file on rent deal with *Express'*, September 6, 1987;
'Mysterious power failure at *Express'*, September 11, 1987;
'Government forces Ambanis to shelve L&T takeover plans', April 14, 1994;
'Kulkarni selected new chief of L&T', April 21, 1994;
'The strike in Delhi: Film nails lies', November 10, 1987.

Jha, Prem Shankar. 'The Reliance Example', *India Today,* September 15, 1986, p99.

Joglekar, S. 'L&T: Room to manoeuvre', *Business India,* September 12, 1994, pp174-5.

Kamath, V. 'Shyam Kothari: Thinking big', *Business World,* May 18, 1994, pp62-3.

Karmali, N. 'Dhirubhai Ambani—Top gun,' *Business India,* December 20, 1993, p57.

Khaitan, Vivek. 'On advance information', *Indian Express,* September 15, 1987.

Kottary, S. 'Guilty? Or is Nusli Wadia being framed in the controversial Fairfax inquiry?', *Illustrated Weekly of India,* August 23, 1987, p11;
'Super sleuth—S. Gurumurthy', *Illustrated Weekly of India,* April 22, 1990, p11f.

Krishnakumar, B. 'The Ambani Allure', *The Week,* October 17, 1993, p50.

Malkan, Deven. 'L&T gearing up for new era', *Indian Express,* November 25, 1991.

Mathai, P. 'Reliance-L&T', *India Today,* November 15, 1988, pp116-7.

Mehta, A. 'Conversion into shares banned', *Economic Times,* June 11, 1986.

Mehta, H. 'Reliance: Heirs apparent', *Gentleman,* July, 1986, p42.

Merchant, M. 'Dhirubhai Ambani—The empire-builder', *Gentleman,* June, 1981.

Mitra, S. 'The Old Fox', *Sunday,* April 16, 1989, pp28-33.

Mulgaonkar, S. 'The magnificent rebel', *Indian Express,* October 6, 1991.

Nair, M. 'L&T may get 3-month extension', *Economic Times,* April 15, 1994.

Narayan, R. 'Reliance: A story of astonishing growth', *Business India,* April 28, 1980, p41.

Narayan, Sanjoy. 'Nusli Wadia: Corporate samurai', *Business World,* July 28, 1993, pp19-25.

Ninan, T. N., and Singh, C.U. 'The Reliance mystery: Non-resident investment', *India Today,* December 31, 1983, pp101-2

Ninan, T. N., and Chawla, P. '*Express* case—Pandora's box', *India Today,* April 15, 1987, p32f.

Ninan, T. N. 'Reliance roulette', *India Today,* May 31, 1982;
'Reliance—Sudden stumble', *India Today,* October 31, 1985, p122;
'Reliance—Under pressure', *India Today,* August 15, 1986, p94;
'Reliance Industries—Embattled giant', *India Today,* June 30, 1986, p102;
'Dhirubhai Ambani—The super tycoon', *India Today,* June 30, 1985, p86;
'Reliance Industries—Spinning out of trouble', *India Today,* August 31, 1987, p89;
'Reliance Textile—The investment maze', *India Today,* January 15, 1984, pp129-131;
'Polyester industry—Hard times', *India Today,* February 15, 1988, p111;
'Reliance Industries—Back in battle', *India Today,* December 31, 1986, pp114-6.

Noorani, A. G. 'Thakkar-S. Natarajan Commission: The sound and the fury', *Illustrated Weekly of India,* January 3, 1988, p20f.

Pachauri, P. 'CBI—Playing politics', *India Today,* September 15, 1989, p32f.

Pania, T. 'GDR—The road show goes on', *Business India,* July 19, 1993, p93.

Parbat, K. 'Decks cleared for Ambani bid to control L&T', *Economic Times,* April 12, 1994.

Pednekar, V. 'How many times can the finance minister lie?', *Illustrated Weekly of India,* January 29, 1984, pp58-9.

Pillai, S. 'Reliance and L&T—A grand alliance', *India Today,* November 15, 1988, p116.

Piramal, G. 'A Gujarati renaissance', *Sunday,* November 13, 1988, pp65-9;

'India's global leaders', *Sunday,* September 25, 1988, p57;

'Political pendulum now favours Nusli Wadia', *Financial Times,* December 21, 1989;

'Executive held on plot to kill charge', *Financial Times,* August 5, 1989;

'Ambanis—A tough climb up India's corporate ladder', *Financial Times,* January 30, 1990;

'Reliance Petrochemicals—Making a mark', *Economic Times Corporate Dossier,* January 25, 1991;

'Madhu Dandavate, finance minister—The pragmatic socialist', *Illustrated Weekly of India,* January 28, 1990, pp22-5;

'Leadership in the '90s', *Gentleman,* Anniversary Issue 1991, pp49-51;

'The turning point', *Gentleman,* Anniversary Issue 1994, pp30-3.

Radhakrishnan, N. 'The way of the manipulators', *Bombay,* June 22, 1982, pp45-8.

Rahman, M. 'Reliance petrochemicals—Runaway success', *India Today,* September 30, 1988, p96.

Rahman, M., *et al.*'Ambani-Wadia war: Crime, money and politics', *India Today,* August 31, 1989, p22f.

Rahman, M. & Dhar, R.N. 'Khatre-Reliance: A tangled web', *India Today,* September 15, 1989, p35f.

Raman, A. 'Reliance—Just like old times', *India Today,* August 31, 1988, pp102-3.

Ravi, A. B. 'L&T: Entering new fields', *Business India,* February 14, 1994, p21;

'L&T: Takeover drama—Scene IV', *Business India,* March 28, 1994, pp70-1.

Sanghvi, V. 'Conversations with Goenka', *Sunday,* October 13, 1991, p36.

Seshadri, C. P. 'Over half a century of association with RNG', *Indian Express,* October 6, 1991.

Shankar, R. 'Reliance's debenture debacle', *Sunday Observer,* June 15, 1986.

Shankar, V. 'The future news at *Express*', *Island,* September, 1989, pp51-3.

Shourie, Arun. 'Tomorrow will be too late', *Indian Express,* November 20, 1987.

Sidhu, W.P.S. 'Ambani-Wadia clash: Paper wars', *India Today,* September 15, 1991, pp62-3.

Singh, C. U. 'Reliance Roulette', *India Today,* May 31, 1982, pp91-3.

Singh, R. 'R.H. Goenka: A man who did not bend', *Independent,* October 7, 1991.

Skaria, G. 'Team Reliance', *Business Today,* September 7, 1995, pp66-75;
   'Reliance runs into a roadblock', *Business Today,* October 7, 1994,
   pp56-7.
Srinivasan, R. 'Ad blitzkrieg to make a winner of Only Vimal', *Times of
   India,* November 24, 1991.
Sunday Observer, 'Ambani leaves for the US', March 16, 1986.
Swami, P. 'Reliance Industries—Badly bruised', *India Today,* November
   15, 1986, p144.
Swaminathan, S. 'Reliance CP: Money at six per cent?', *Business India,*
   August 30, 1993, p104.
Tak, D. 'Mudra: Sprinting to the top', *Business India,* July 18, 1994, p113.
Tellis, O. 'On the takeover trail', *Sunday,* October 30, 1988, p55.
Tellis, O. & Sanghvi, V. 'Can he take on the Raja', *Sunday,* April 15,
   1990, p28.
Thakurta, P. G. 'Larsen & Toubro—Tacky game', *India Today,* March
   15, 1991, p121;
   'Reliance Industries—Taken to account', *India Today,* May 31, 1989,
   p110f.
Times of India, '*Express* evaded tax: DRI', September 2, 1987;
   '*Express* has "foreign accounts"', September 4, 1987;
   'Spell out Briner deal, Goenka told', September 6, 1987;
   'Bail for *Express* MD, 2 others', September 8, 1987;
   '*Express* denies prior knowledge', September 15, 1987;
   'DRI calls Goenka for questioning', September 18, 1987;
   'Market reels under debenture rule', June 12, 1986;
   'RIL meet a tame affair', October 19, 1991;
   'RIL-RPL merger shortly: Ambani', August 30, 1991;
   'To lock out or not wonders *Express*', November 10, 1987;
   'Letter to editor', November 10, 1987.
Thomas, E. 'Reliance: A low-key affair', *Business India,* October 28,
   1991, p17.
Valluri, M. 'Dhirubhai Ambani, the bucks never stop coming', *Society,*
   July, 1985.
Vasuki, S.N. 'Reliance Industries—The big push', *India Today,* October
   31, 1989, pp112-8;
   'Larsen & Toubro', *India Today,* December 31, 1989, p104;
   'L&T Debentures—Contentious issue', *India Today,* September 31,
   1989, p97;
   'The Ambanis—On the firing lines', *India Today,* April 30, 1990, p92f;
   'Larsen & Toubro—A tame ending', *India Today,* May 15, 1990, p104.
Vasuki, S. & Thakurta, P. G. 'Reliance-Bombay Dyeing—Corporate

clash', *India Today,* March 15, 1990, p121.

Vidyadharan, Aravind. 'A rejoinder to Vandana Pednekar: Much ado about nothing', *Illustrated Weekly of India,* February 26, 1984.

Vijayraghavan, R. 'PM's image builder', *Business Standard,* August 23, 1987.

Other Literature
Company brochures, press releases, pamphlets and annual reports.

Koffend, J. *Bombay Dyeing: The First Hundred Years.* Bombay: The Perennial Press, 1980.

BAJAJ

Books
Anand, Dr Mulk Raj. *Homage to Jamnalal Bajaj.* Bombay: Allied Publishers Pvt Ltd

Bajaj, Jankidevi. *Meri Jeevan Yatra* (Hindi).

Bajaj, Kamalnayan. *Kakaji-Bapu-Vinoba* (Hindi).

Bajaj, Ramkrishna. *Indian Economy.* Bombay: Allied Publishers Pvt Ltd, 1986.

Consumer View-point. Bombay: Council of Fair Business Practices, 1991.

Atlantic ke Uspar (Hindi). New Delhi: Sasta Sahitya Mandal, 1981.

Challenges to Trade. Bombay: Popular Prakashan Pvt Ltd, 1982.

Rusi Yuvakon ke Beech (Hindi). New Delhi: Sasta Sahitya Mandal, 1982.

Social Role of Business. Pune: Maharashtra Chamber of Commerce, 1970.

Young Russia. Bombay: Popular Book Depot, 1980.

Bajaj, Savitri. *God's Plan Works—An Autobiography.* Bombay: Sevak Prakashan, 1991.

Birla, G.D. *Jamnalalji* (Hindi, Gujarathi). New Delhi: n.d.

Jain, Yashpal & Upadhya, M. (eds.) *Kamalnayan Bajaj—Vyakti aur Vichar* (Hindi). New Delhi: Sasta Sahitya Mandal, 1977.

Kalelkar, Kakasaheb. *Bapu ke Patra* (Hindi). Benares: Jamnalal Bajaj Seva Trust, 1957;

To a Gandhian Capitalist. Bombay: Sevak Prakashan, 1946.

Kamath, M.V. *Gandhi's Coolie—Life and Times of Ramkrishna Bajaj.* Bombay: Allied Publishers Pvt Ltd, 1988.

Kamath, M.V. & Pingle, S. (eds.) *Ramkrishna Bajaj, Felicitations*

Volume. Pune: Maharashtra Chamber of Commerce, 1983. There is also a Hindi edition.

Kulkarni, V. *A Family of Patriots*, Bombay: Hind Kitabs Ltd, 1951.

Lomax, David. *The Money Makers: Six Portraits of Boardroom Power in Industry*. London: BBC Publications, 1986.

Nanda, B. R. *In Gandhi's Footsteps—The Life and Times of Jamnalal Bajaj*. Delhi: Oxford University Press, 1990.

Narayan, Shriman. *Jamnalal Bajaj* (Hindi, English). Publications Division, Ministry of Information and Broadcasting, Government of India, 1976;
Vyakti aur Vichar (Hindi). Bombay: Jamnalal Bajaj Seva Trust.

Oza, Suresh Dutt. *Jamnalal Bajaj aur unka Rashtriya Jeewan me Yogdaan* (Hindi). Unpublished Ph.D. diss., Lucknow University, 1982.

Parvate, T. V. *Jamnalal Bajaj*. Ahmedabad: Nav Jeevan Gujerathi, n.d.

Tripathi, R. *Seth Jamnalal Bajaj* (Hindi). Prayag: Hindi Mandir, 1932.

Upadhya, Haribhau. *Shreyarthi Jamnalalji* (Hindi, in two editions, one complete, one abridged). New Delhi: Sasta Sahitya Mandal, 1951.

Upadhya, Mukul. *Jamnalal Bajaj Kathni Karni Eksi*. Bombay: Bajaj Group, n.d.
Jamnalal Bajaj—Making Words into Deeds. Bombay: Bajaj Group, n.d.

Articles

Abraham, S. 'Bajaj Electricals: Stepping into the light', *Business India,* April 25, 1994, p82.

Aiyar, S.S.A. 'Whatever happened to Bombay Club?', *Economic Times,* December 8, 1994.

Ambani, D. 'Business is my hobby', *Business India,* December 20, 1993, p58.

Asiaweek. 'India's scooter tycoon goes global', October 5, 1990, p62.

Bajaj, Rahul: 'The Raj and Me', *India Today*, August 15, 1991;
'Bajaj Auto's major objective in the 1990s is to increase exports', *Independent,* January 22, 1990;
'Bumpy road ahead for two-wheeler king', *Independent,* October 3, 1992;
'Change came with Rajiv Gandhi', *Sunday Observer,* May 26, 1991;
'We will not diversify except into cars', *Economic Times,* May 10, 1994;
'We're not worried by the competition', *Sunday Observer,* August 7, 1988;
'Top priority to customer service', *Sunday Mid-day,* November 9, 1986;
Speech, Kleinwort Benson road show, October 21, 1994.

Balachandran, Chhaya: 'Rahul Bajaj—On wheels of success', *Business*

World, September 11, 1991, p62.

Baru, S. 'The Bombay Pleas—Modest ambitions of big business', *Times of India,* November 12, 1993.

Belle, Nitin. 'Rahul Bajaj: A passion for excellence', *Gentleman*, March, 1988.

Business India. 'Viren Shah: The businessman politician,' March 13, 1978, pp23-9.

Business Standard, 'LML bid to scuttle fresh Piaggio-Bajaj tie-up', December 26, 1989;

'Bajaj bid for Leyland rebuffed', March 12, 1987;

'Private misgivings', March 23, 1987;

'Strike ends at Bajaj Auto unit', July 7, 1988;

'Bajaj Auto unit reopened but workers keep away', May 6, 1988;

'Bajaj Hindustan invites bids for cement unit', October 13, 1992;

'FIs opposed to Bombay Club divestment plan', September 21, 1993.

Carvalho, Brian. 'Bajaj beats the slump', *Business World*, June 2-15, 1993, p24.

Chawla, P. 'The business blacklist', *India Today,* July 31, 1986, pp94-5.

Dalmia, Gaurav. 'Reforms and Indian businessmen', *Economic Times,* November 10, 1993.

Dass, Basudev. 'Ashok Leyland: Enter the Hindujas', *Business India,* November 2, 1987, p41.

Dubashi, Jagannath. 'Bajaj Auto—At a premium', *India Today,* January 15, 1986, p73.

Economic Times, 'LML settles row with Piaggio', March 31, 1994;

'Piaggio, Bajaj Auto plan tie-up', October 11, 1989;

'Singhanias put spanner in Piaggio-Escorts venture', December 17, 1993;

'Sawhney denies buying Ashok Leyland shares', August 25, 1987;

'Ramkrishna Bajaj dead', September 22, 1994;

'Ramkrishna Bajaj—A conscientious industrialist', September 22, 1994;

'Ficci endorses Bombay Club's plea for level playing field', November 7, 1993;

'Govt committed to provide level playing field : FM', November 12, 1993;

'Bombay Club—Centre's approval', November 11, 1993.

Economic Times editorial, 'The 14th point', November 12, 1993.

Ethiraj, G. 'The coming investment boom', *Business World,* August 10, 1994, pp20-7.

Firodia, N.K. 'Squeezed out of Bajaj Auto', *Sunday Observer*, October 9,

1988.

Ganguli, B. 'Mukand: IISCO takeover', *Business India,* May 9, 1994, p92.

Ganguly, S. 'Testing time for the king of the road,' *Business World,* October 11, 1982, pp40-57.

Gaya, Javed. 'Raids, black money and politics', *Business India*, January 13-26, 1986, p.48;

'Privatising the private sector—Bajaj Tempo vs Bajaj Auto', *Business India,* October 28, 1991, p102.

Gupta, Surajeet. 'LML-Piaggio, revving up', *India Today,* October 31, 1990, p133.

Hindustan Times, 'How Bajaj Group was hounded', November 17, 1977.

Indian Express, 'Escorts may snap ties with Piaggio', April 10, 1994;

'3 workers killed in firing', June 18, 1979;

'Big haul from Bajaj dealers in first phase', December 24, 1985;

'Bombay Club submits charter of demands to FM', November 11, 1993;

'Pranab justifies "level playing field" demand', April 19, 1994.

Karnani, R. 'Kinetic Honda—Who is in control?', *Business India,* June 7, 1993, p81.

Kasbekar, Kiron. 'Bajaj Auto vs Piaggio', *Business-India,* August 30-September 12, 1982, p77.

Mehta, F. A. 'The Economics of Aditya Birla', *Sunday Observer,* October 8, 1995.

Mukherjee, S. 'Industrialists demand level playing field', *Economic Times,* March 23, 1995.

Nadkarni, Shirish. 'We're not worried by the competition', *Sunday Observer,* August 7, 1988.

Nair, Shila. 'Executive lifestyle—Rahul Bajaj', *Afternoon on Sunday,* April 25, 1993.

Ninan, T. N. & Chandran, R. 'The Hindujas—A prize acquisition', *India Today,* November 15, 1987, pp106-7.

Panchal, S. 'Bajaj Auto market share to fall: Crosby', *Business Standard,* May 13, 1995.

Piramal, Gita. 'Indian Airlines surveys a catalogue of mishaps', *Financial Times,* January 5, 1989;

'Mukand', *Financial Times,* March 31, 1992;

'Rahul Bajaj appointed as new chairman of Zenith', *Financial Times,* March 16, 1990;

'Bajaj Auto—Indian auto industry shows the strains of recession', *Financial Times,* February 22, 1991;

'The Rise of the Marwari', *Bombay,* August 22, 1990, pp42-53;

'To the manor born', *Times of India,* October 7, 1989;

'India's global leaders', *Sunday,* September 25, 1986, pp56-8;

'Bajaj Auto—Stepping up the pace', *Economic Times Corporate Dossier,* August 5, 1989;

'Bajaj Auto GDR oversubscribed', *Economic Times,* October 29, 1994.

Poona Digest, 'Rahul Bajaj', May, 1987

Radhakrishnan, N: 'Hamara Bajaj', *Business India*, October 11, 1993, p58;

'Bombay Club', *Business India*, November 22, 1993, pp56-7.

Rao, Kala: 'Saffron flag over Pimpri', *Business World*, May 19, 1993, pp115-7.

Senthil, Chengalvarayan, 'Piaggio, Bajaj deal falls through', *Business Standard*, November 23, 1993.

Shah, Viren. 'Ramkrishna Bajaj, RIP', *Business Today*, October 7, 1994, pp14-5.

Shekar, M. 'Firing on all cylinders', *Business World*, August 11, 1993, pp72-3.

Shekhar, S. 'The top-notchers', *Business World*, March 27, 1991, p57.

Sunday, 'Exit Tata and Bajaj', January 29, 1989.

Sunday Times, 'Britain's richest 500, 1996', April 14, 1996.

Taneja, S. 'Bajaj Auto—Trying to accelerate', *India Today,* January 15, 1991, pp106-111.

Thakore, Dilip. 'The house of Bajaj and ethics in business', *Business India,* January 22, 1979, pp26-9;

'The Firodias move to prove a point,' *Business World,* September 12, 1983, pp36-53.

Times of India, '31 Bajaj workers fined Rs 1 lakh each', September 7, 1993;

'Raids an act of political vendetta: Bajaj', November 17, 1977;

'Join battle against MNCs, workers urged', April 25, 1995;

'Leading industrialists to meet Manmohan Singh soon', October 4, 1993;

'Industrialists press Singh for reforms', December 14, 1993;

'Level playing field demand backed', February 7, 1994;

'Bombay Club to meet Manmohan', November 10, 1993;

'Industrialists meet Manmohan—Plea to remove constraints', November 11, 1993;

'Bombay group poses "corrective" agenda', November 12, 1993;

'Meeting with city industrialists—Reform or perish', November 28, 1993.

Times of India editorial, 'Sticking it out', November 18, 1993.

Vasuki, S. N. 'Aurangabad—Boom blues', *India Today,* July 15, 1990, pp102-7.

Wagstyl, Stefan: 'Bajaj Auto aims to maintain its dominance', *Financial Times*, May 13, 1994.

Watts, H. 'Opportune time for more reforms: Rahul Bajaj', *Economic Times*, February 24, 1994.

Other Literature

Company brochures, press releases, pamphlets and annual reports.

Brochure on Hindustan Sugar, 1932-1982. Published by Bajaj Group, Bombay: n.d. Anon.

'The House of Bajaj—A Profile,' published by Bajaj Auto Ltd, Bombay, 1982.

'I had Him in Mind', published by Bajaj Auto Group Ltd, Bombay, 1982.

BIRLA

Books

Anand, Mulk Raj. *Mr & Mrs B.M. Birla—A Profile in Pictures.* Calcutta: Birla Group, n.d.

Anon. *The Path to Prosperity: A Collection of Speeches and Writings of G.D. Birla.* Bombay: A Birla Group Publication, n.d.

Anon. *Modern India—Heritage and Achievement: Shri G.D. Birla's 80th Birthday Commemoration.* New Delhi: Hindustan Times Press, 1977.

Anon. *Nehru Family and Ghanshyam Das Birla.* New Delhi: Vision Books, 1986.

Barua, Rishi Jamini Kaushik. *Raja Baldevdas Birla.* Calcutta, n.d.

Basu, D. & Dalal, S. *The Scam: Who Won, Who Lost and Who Got Away.* New Delhi: UBS Publishers' Distributors Ltd, 1993.

Birla, B.K. *A Rare Legacy.* Bombay: Image Inc., 1994. Originally published in Hindi as *Swantah Sukhaya.*

Birla, G.D. *Atulananda Chatterjee.* Calcutta, 1956;

'Bapu'. Speech delivered at Sangit Kala Mandir, Calcutta, December 24, 1981;

Bapu—A Unique Association (4 volumes). Bombay: Bharatiya Vidya Bhavan, 1977;

Bikhere Vicharon ki Bharoti. New Delhi: Sasta Sahitya Mandal, 1957;

Diary kee Panee (Hindi). New Delhi: Sasta Sahitya Mandal, 1957;

India's March Towards Freedom, 1935-1947. New Delhi: privately published, 1981;

In the Shadow of the Mahatma. London: 1953 and Bombay: Orient Longman, 1955;
Krishnam Vande Jagadguru (Hindi). Bombay: Bharatiya Vidya Bhavan, n.d;
Kuch Dekha, Kuch Suna (Hindi). New Delhi: privately published, 1966;
Rup aur Swarup (Hindi). New Delhi: privately published, n.d.
Shri Jamnalal Bajaj. New Delhi: n.d

Birla, K.K. *Indira Gandhi Reminiscences.* New Delhi: Vikas, 1987.

Burman, Debajyoti. *The Mystery of Birla House.* Calcutta, 1957; *TTK and Birla House.* Calcutta, 1957.

Chopra, Dr P. N. *Quit India Movement: British Secret Documents.* Delhi: Interprint, 1987.

Jaju, Ram Niwas. *G. D. Birla—A Biography.* New Delhi: Vikas Publishing House, 1985.

Juneja, M. M. *The Mahatma and the Millionaire.* Modern Publishers, 1993.

Khanolkar, G. D. *Walchand Hirachand.* Bombay: Walchand & Company Pvt Ltd, 1969.

Lakhotia, R. N. *Towards Better Living.* New Delhi: Asha Publishing House, 1992.

Parekh, Kishore. *G.D. Birla—His Deeds and Dreams.* New Delhi: Arnold Heinemann, 1983.

Rao, P. Chentsal. *B.M. Birla—His Deeds & Dreams.* New Delhi: Arnold-Heinemann (India) Pvt. Ltd

Piramal, G. & Herdeck, M. *India's Industrialists.* Washington DC: Three Continents Press, 1985.

Ramachandran, K. S. *Scanning the Scam.* New Delhi: Neo Publishing Company, 1993.

Ramanujam, K. S. *Glimpses of a Prince among Patriots.* Sundara Prachuralayam, 1993.

Ross, Alan. *The Emissary, G.D. Birla, Gandhi and Independence.* London: Collins Harvill, 1986.

Shankar, Gauri. *To man, to Country and to God—Biography of M. P. Birla.* New Delhi: Har-Anand Publications, 1993.

Singh, Badri N. *Role of G. D. Birla in Indian National Movement.* Delhi: Anupam Publications, 1991.

Articles

Almeida, M. 'Century Rayon—The drain of death', *Business India*, March 29, 1993, pp125-7.

Arkay. 'Aditya Birla's brush with the masters', *Afternoon Despatch &*

Courier, September 28, 1990.

Bajaj, R. 'Aditya, my friend', *Business Today,* October 7, 1995, p10.

Banerjea, Sumita. 'G. D. Birla: I'm trying to be a good guy,' *Society,* July, 1983.

Banerjee, N. 'Birlas lead scramble for Vizag Steel', *Business Standard,* August 13, 1991;
'Birlas win accolades from Thai PM', *Business Standard,* November 22, 1994.

Banerjee, I. 'Kesoram Rayon factory: The invisible menace,' *India Today,* June 30, 1984.

Basu, B. 'A.V. Birla to revive Eastern Spinning', *Economic Times,* May 15, 1994.

Behara, Meenakshi. 'The quiet rise of Aditya Birla,' *Business India,* May 7, 1984, pp52-62;
'Aditya Birla: Big plans', *Business World,* April 8, 1992, p27;
'Grasim's big plans', *Business World,* April 8, 1992, p28.

Bhandari G. & Kedai, A. 'Spinning a good yarn', *Business Today,* February 22, 1992, p107.

Bhanu, T. 'Birlas overtaking ACC in cement', *Financial Express,* April 20, 1990.

Bhargava, A. 'India's most cash-rich companies', *Business World,* May 5, 1993, pp14-23.

Bhaskar, R. N. 'Aditya Birla trips?', *Financial Express,* April 6, 1990.

Birla, Aditya. Speech delivered on March 22, 1994 at Euromoney Conference in New Delhi;
'We will get more aggressive', *Business World,* April 4, 1993, p26;
'We are not a company without a soul', *Business World,* April 8, 1992, pp26-27;
'One has to be realistic', *Sunday,* December 23, 1990, pp51-2;
'My experience of Indian management and present business environment', S. Anantharamkrishnan lecture, Bombay, October, 1990;
'Needed: A truly private sector', *Sunday Times of India,* December 29, 1991;
'Pre-budget meeting with the finance minister', memo, March, 1990;
'The government is destroying this wealth', *Independent,* May 5, 1990;
'Globalising Indian industry for the next century', *Dateline,* December 15, 1994;
'Potholes on the road to globalisation', *Sunday Observer,* September 18, 1994.

Birla, B.K. 'I am keen to expand', *Sunday,* June 17, 1990, pp57-60;
'Backroom Birla', *Business World,* October 24, 1990, pp81-87.

Bombay, 'Indian Masters badminton bonanza', December 7, 1983, p46;
'Making a scene', June 22, 1989, pp24-9.

Bose, A. 'B.K. Birla—The doyen turns 70', *Business Standard*, January 12, 1991.

Bose, J. 'B.K.'Birla plans steel plant at Kharagpur', *Telegraph*, December 17, 1991.

Bose, K. 'Basant Kumar Birla—Rites of passage', *Economic Times*, April 20, 1990.

Bose, M. 'Birla Tyres—On a disaster road', *Business India*, August 16, 1993, pp89-91;
'K. K. Birla's Texmaco—Derailed', *Business India*, October 24, 1994, pp74-6.

Business & Political Observer, 'US Exim Bank loan for Grasim sponge iron unit', November 9, 1990.

Business India, 'Egyptian Venture', September 2, 1991, p16;
'G.D. Birla: A patriarch passes away', June 20, 1983, pp50-1;
'Century—The bluest of the blue-chips', May 15, 1978, p22-31;
'HRD—Time for a turnabout', October 28, 1991, p172;
'Aditya Birla's new venture', July 18, 1990, p112;
'Egyptian Venture', September 2, 1991, p16;
'Into the black?', February 28, 1994, p12;

Business Standard, 'Aditya Birla group revives plan to enter steel sector', October 21, 1994;
'A.V. Birla one up on family rival', July 1, 1988;
'Birla co among top 10 exporters in Malaysia', August 30, 1986;
'Birlas take the lead in cement production', September 3, 1991;
'Birla settlement comes apart', January 31, 1987;
'Birla family accord on Grasim, Hindalco', August 27, 1987;
'Birlas make new bid for division of family empire', May 5, 1987;
'Cement industry price war hots up', April 15, 1986;
'Sarala Birla: Centenary Star', November 14, 1994;
'Cos. put Euro-issues on hold', July 8, 1992;
'Four firms short-listed for Mangalore refinery', November 20, 1986;
'Gas price uncertainty stalls sponge iron units', January 18, 1985;
'Grasim in focus for steadiness', May 28, 1987;
'Gwalior Rayon unit in Kerala to reopen', September 16, 1988;
'Gwalior Rayon unit not to be nationalised', March 23, 1988;
'Indian Rayon gets LI for hydrogen peroxide unit', October 8, 1988;
'L. N. Birla dies in London', August 30, 1994;
'Reopening of Ashok Paper bogged down', August 29, 1986;
'Indian Rayon offers to buy Hanuman Cotton Mills', January 23, 1990;

'Kankaria group buys Hanuman Cotton Mills', February 7, 1990;

'Malaysian credit refused for palm oil purchases', August 19, 1992;

'Mangalore refinery decision by February', December 28, 1989;

'Shares of Birla cos. flare', July 18, 1987;

'Widespread buying in equities of Birla cos.', July 10, 1987;

'Birlas take the lead in cement production', September 3, 1991;

Business Today, 'The BT 500—India's most valuable companies', August 22, 1995, p122.

Business World, 'The king is keen', March 24, 1993, p12;

'Birla's petro-plans', March 8, 1995, p208;

'Aditya Birla's new venture—Pulp plant in Haryana', July 18, 1990, p112;

'MBAs need prior work experience—Panel discussion', October 19, 1994, p42f.

Capital, 'The empire that GD built', April 16, 1984, pp19-55.

Chatterjee, D. 'Kumar Mangalam Birla: His father's son', *Times of India,* October 14, 1995.

Chawla, Prabhu. 'Indo-Gulf—A soured dream', *India Today,* January 11, 1986, pp74-6.

Corporate Finance (UK), 'Grasim's market reopener', December 1994, p38.

Dagli, Vadilal. 'A maker of modern industrial India,' *Commerce,* June 25, 1983, pp1044-52.

Dasgupta, S. 'B.K. Birla—A new spirit is abroad', *Business Standard,* August 4, 1985.

Dass, B. 'Kesoram's new lease of life', *Business Today,* March 7, 1995, p56f.

Datta, E. 'An evening in homage to an empire-builder', *Business Standard,* November 11, 1994.

Dewani, M. D. 'Birla group widening horizon', *Mid-day,* February 21, 1985;

'Gwalior Rayon to set up Rs 100cr sponge iron plant', *Financial Express,* March 28, 1984.

Dey, T. 'After GD what?', *Surya India,* July 1, 1983, pp35-9.

Dubashi, J. 'The buzzings of the corporate bazaar', *Sunday Observer,* October 4, 1987.

Dutta, P. 'Grasim: The tiger's choice', *Times of India,* November 24, 1995.

Dutta, S. 'Chloride Industries—Up the creek', *Business India,* August 16, 1993, pp66-8;

'Chloride India—Endgame', *Business India,* November 22, 1993, p71.

Economic Times, 'A mixed bag', May 27, 1991;
   'Aditya Birla recovering', June 10, 1995;
   'Birla shares in demand', July 18, 1987;
   'Birlas chosen for M'lore refinery', February 3, 1987;
   'Birla group acquires pulp project in Russia', December 14, 1994;
   'Birla likely to set up steel plant at Haldia', June 6, 1992;
   'Extensive damage to machinery', November 4, 1988;
   'Failure to reopen Gwalior Rayons—Nayanar govt flayed', February 13, 1988;
   'Grasim Ind seeks approval', September 21, 1989;
   'Grasim shelves Rs 225cr picture tube shell project', July 26, 1991;
   'Grasim launches HBI plant near Bombay', April 2, 1993;
   'Grasim signs MoU with Mexican firm', May 3, 1989;
   'Grasim, MP govt sign MoU for 1,000 MW plant', October 30, 1994;
   'HPC-Indian Rayon pact signed', June 27, 1987;
   'Indian Rayon float $125m Euro equity issue', January 4, 1994;
   'Indian Rayon GDR offering oversubscribed by 13 times', January 26, 1994;
   'Gwalior Rayon to revive Ashok Paper', February 23, 1985;
   'Mavoor Rayon workers on warpath', March 5, 1988;
   'Mangalore Refinery', February 9, 1987;
   'PIB clears Mangalore Refinery, 5 power projects', December 1, 1990;
   'Rs 30cr project in jeopardy', May 22, 1991;
   'Snags in partition of Birla assets', April 17, 1987;
   'Tidco signs MoU with Grasim for Rs 3,300 crore mega steel plant', March 22, 1995;
   '26-year-old son to take over from Aditya Birla', December 31, 1993;
   Economic Times editorial, 'Indian MNCs', November 26, 1994.
Financial Express, 'A.V. Birla buys 55 per cent stake in Russian rayon company', December 14, 1994;
   'Birla's 4th subsidiary in Philippines', December 6, 1991;
   'Century Textiles plans Rs 600cr pig iron plant', December 20, 1994;
   'Grasim Euroissue awaits govt approval', April 23, 1994;
   'Grasim sponge iron unit by mid-1992', September 21, 1989;
   'Mavoor pact', February 16, 1989;
   'Retrenchment in Mavoor Rayons hinted at', January 3, 1989;
   'Which Birla is the best?', April 10, 1989;
   'Kumar Mangalam: New captain for Century in making?', February 8, 1990.
Gabrani, K. 'BITS—Knowledge is power supreme', *Span,* October, 1988, p2f.

Ghani, A. H. 'Zenith—A fresh lease of life', *Business World*, January 27, 1993, pp579.

Gupta, M. 'Kumar Mangalam Birla—I've got very sharp ears and eyes', *Sunday*, January 27, 1991, pp64-6.

Gupta, S. D. 'GP-CK Birla Group—On a new road', *Business World*, November 4, 1992, pp50-5.

Gupta, S. 'Texmaco: Crash landing', *Business World*, September 9, 1992, pp 56-7.

Guru, S. & Maitra, D. 'Aditya Birla—The no-risk gambler', *Business Today*, July 22, 1992, p43f.

Illustrated Weekly of India, 'Jugal Kishore Birla (1883-1967)', March 28, 1971, pp11-13.

Indian Express, 'Birlas to invest $55m in Philippines', November 20, 1987;
'Birla's Thai mission', March 7, 1994.

India Today, 'Master copycat', October 31, 1990, p192.

Jack, Ian. 'The King is dead,' *Sunday*, June 26, 1983.

Jayakar, R. 'Managing Eurosuccess', *Business Today*, May 22, 1994, pp44-5.

Joshi, Anjali. 'A business tycoon takes up the brush', *Sunday Observer*, September 30, 1990.

Kamath, M. V. 'G.D. Birla—The business of freedom', *Times of India*, March 15, 1987.

Kartha, S. 'The idle chimneys of Mavoor', *Sunday*, March 27, 1988.

Katiyar, Arun. 'Making a scene', *Bombay*, June 22, 1989, pp24-29.

Karnani, R. 'Century Enka—The wages of parsimony', *Business India*, August 15, 1994, pp122-3.

Khairullah, H. 'Birlas' brightest star', *Illustrated Weekly of India*, March 20, 1983, p17.

Kumar, S. 'Kumar Mangalam taking over reins in Birla empire', *Economic Times*, December 31, 1993;
'Lavish wedding invites I-T men', *Times of India*, June 14, 1989.

Lakhotia, R. N. 'Working with the Birlas', *Business World*, June 17, 1992, p134.

Lala, A. R. 'Four projects in WB cleared—2 steel units', *Telegraph*, January 2, 1995.

Maitra, D. 'Euroissues—All in the family', *Business Today*, May 7, 1993, p14;
'S.K. Birla Group—Weighed down by heavy debt', *Business Today*, May 7, 1993, pp.54-61.

Marco. 'Is it patronage?', *Economic Times*, March 5, 1989.

Mathai, P. 'Birlas—High Honour', *India Today,* August 31, 1989, pp82-9.

Mathew, G. 'Son to rise on Birla group horizon', *Indian Express,* October 9, 1995.

Mathur, R. 'Aditya Birla planning $200m overseas ventures', *Financial Express,* March 23, 1994.

Mayur, A. K. 'Thailand—A rebuff to rayons', *Probe India,* July 82, pp72-3.

Mitra, K. 'Birla Tyres: A fresh lease', *Business India,* April 11, 1994, p21.

Mukherjee, S. 'Sanjiv Goenka—Born tough', *Sunday,* September 1, 1991, p45.

Nagarajan, U. 'Hindalco: Back on the road', *Business World,* August 11, 1993, p83.

Nair, G. V. 'Deadlock at Mavoor', *Business Standard,* November 9, 1986.

Narayan, S. & Ethiraj, G. 'Kumar Mangalam—The grooming of a young Birla', *Business World,* November 2, 1994, p34f.

Nikkei Weekly, quoted in the *Economic Times,* 'Aditya Birla group sees potential in Southeast Asia', May 5, 1995.

Ninan, T. N. 'Empire in transition', *India Today,* July 15, 1983, pp98-107; 'Slicing up the cake', *India Today,* September 30, 1986, pp127-9; 'The grand partition', *India Today,* September 30, 1987, pp104-5.

Pal, A. 'S.K. Birla—An alliance powered to win', *Business Standard,* February 21, 1988.

Parmanand, B. 'Indian Rayon in power venture', *Economic Times,* September 25, 1993.

Pillai, S. 'Grasim Industries—A disastrous closure', *India Today,* August 31, 1987, pp98-100.

Piramal, G: 'Indian multinationals: Girdling the globe, slowly', *Economic Times,* May 17, 1991;
'The Big Birla', *Business World,* February 28, 1990, pp58-67;
'Hindalco's bright sheen', *Business World,* May 24, 1989, p35;
'Fast food history—The Emissary, G.D. Birla, Gandhi and Independence by Alan Ross', *Business World,* October 26, 1986, p63;
'Grasim—Twists to the Rs 300 crore quickie', *Business World,* June 15, 1994, p122
'The rising stars of Indian business', *Bombay,* December 7, 1990, pp20-5;
'Ashok Birla—Back in business', *Bombay,* September 7, 1988, pp28-31;
'Birla family—Divided but prospering', *Forbes,* July 24, 1989, p210;
'India's young inheritors', *World Executive's Digest,* July, 1987, pp16-21;

'Ashok Birla—A man ahead of his time', *Times of India*, February 17, 1990;

'Speculation pushes Hindalco GDR price down', *Economic Times*, July 10, 1994;

'What comes down in the West goes up in India', *Financial Times*, September 13, 1989;

'Grasim Industries to tap market with Rs 650m issue', *Financial Times*, December 10, 1988;

'Grasim takes a quiet leap up the ranks', *Financial Times*, February 28, 1990;

'Rahul Bajaj appointed as new chairman of Zenith', *Financial Times*, March 16, 1990;

'Investing in India's economic future', *Financial Times*, November 28, 1990;

'Head of Rs 8bn Birla group dies', *Financial Times*, August 1, 1990;

'The warring business clans of India', *World Executive's Digest*, February 1989, pp28-30;

'India's young inheritors', *World Executive's Digest*, July, 1987, pp16-21;

'Century Textiles may discount GDR price', *Economic Times*, September 21, 1994;

'Grasim GDR may fetch premium', *Economic Times*, June 9, 1994.

Prasad, G. 'Dynasty', *Society*, August, 1994, pp43-9.

Roy, Abhijit. 'Chloride's battery of changes', *Business Today*, October 7, 1994, pp58-9.

Roy, Subir. 'The House that G.D. Birla Built,' *Telegraph*, June 26, 1983.

Roy, Subrata. 'The house that BK built', *Business World*, October 24, 1990, pp89-90;

'Backroom Birla', *Business World*, October 24, 1990, p86;

'Birlas: The reorganization', *Business India*, June 15, 1987, p59.

Sabharwal, J. 'Shobhana Bhartia—Pretty good', *Society*, August, 1988, p90f.

Sahjwala, D., *et al.* 'Aditya Birla, the man, his vision', *Dalal Street Journal*, September 5, 1994, p17f.

Sasankaran, R. 'Mangalore Refinery', *Economic Times*, February 9, 1987.

Satyanarayan, S. 'Birlas plan $400m expansion in Thailand', *Indian Express*, November 25, 1994;

'Big in Bangkok', *Mid-day*, November 25, 1994;

'Birlas to expand Thai business', *Telegraph*, February 16, 1995;

'Thailand may penalise Indian cos. for dumping', *Economic Times*, June 1, 1994.

Sen, S. 'Faces of the future', *Business India,* September 16, 1991, pp46-52.

Sharma, S. 'C.K. Birla—Shifting into higher gear', *Business World,* February 21, 1996, pp58-64.

Shekhar, S. 'The top-notchers', *Business World,* March 27, 1991, pp55-9.

Shenoy, M. 'Indian Rayon—Serving up cement', *Business India,* August 14, 1995, p149.

Sinha, D. 'GP-C.K. Birla: On a new road', *Business World,* November 4, 1992, pp50-3.

Singh, K. 'With Malice Towards One and All,' *Mid-day,* February 1, 1982.

Solitaire, 'Kirtilal Manilal Mehta—The boy who built an empire', May, 1988, p42.

Srinivasan, L. 'A portrait of the CEO as an artist', *Business World,* August 26, 1992, pp119-21.

Sunday Observer, 'Big sell-out by LDF govt', October 30, 1988.

Sunderesan, S. 'Kumar Mangalam Birla: On the threshold', *Times of India,* October 5, 1995.

Suri, S. 'Grasim's GDR issue success reaffirms faith in Indian paper', *Economic Times,* June 14, 1994.

Tellis, O. 'Wedded to wealth', *Sunday,* July 2, 1989, p75;
'Discovered, an artist in hiding', *Business Standard,* October 6, 1990.

Thakore, D. 'How Century plans to keep flying high,' *Business World,* March 26, 1984;
'G.D. Birla—A legend in his lifetime,' *Business World,* March 20, 1981, pp28-41;
'Ashok Birla—The rebel Birla makes good', *Business World,* October 28, 1985, p42f.

Thomas, E. 'Aditya Birla, building on a fortune', *Business India,* December 24, 1990, p58.

Times of India, 'Kumar Mangalam elected chairman of 4 key Birla firms', October 20, 1995;
'Kumar Mangalam Birla appointed chairman of MRPL', October 27, 1995;
'Malaysian palm oil losing charm', April 11, 1989.

Toshniwal, J. 'Grasim—On the threshold of growth', *Update,* October 31, 1986, pp29-31.

Zuzarte, J. 'Do great minds paint alike', *Society,* November, 1990, p39.

Other Literature

Company brochures, press releases, pamphlets and annual reports.

Birla Group, '25 years of Birla-Thai Economic Alliance', full page advertisement in the *Times of India,* December 13, 1994.

Century Textiles and Industries Ltd Preliminary Offering Circular, September 7, 1994;
Paribas Capital Markets, Company profile—Century Textiles, September, 1994

Essar Gujarat Offering Circular, July 29, 1993, pp27-8.

Grasim Industries Ltd, Prospectus, December 12, 1988;
Grasim Industries Ltd Offering Circular, June 9, 1994;
Grasim—*A Profile of Success*
Barclays de Goete Wedd, Company profile—Grasim Industries, May, 1994;
Barclays de Goete Wedd, Company profile—Grasim Industries, January, 1995.

Indo-Gulf Fertilizers and Chemicals Corporation Ltd, Offering Circular, January 18, 1994;
Indo-Gulf Fertilizers—*A profile*;
Indo-Gulf Fertilizers and Chemicals Corporation Ltd—*Golden Harvest*
Barclays de Goete Wedd, Company profile—Indo-Gulf Fertilizers.

Indian Rayon and Industries Ltd, GDR Preliminary Offering Circular, January 15, 1994.

We Keep the Wheel Moving Nationally and Internationally. Brochure of B.K. Birla Group, Bombay: n.d.

Words to Remember. Published by G.D. Birla Group, Bombay, 1983.

India Developing. Published by G.D. Birla Group, Bombay, 1983.

Partners in Progress. Published by Ashok Birla Group, Bombay, n.d.

Videos

Rajiv Mehrotra (director), 'G.D. Birla. Adventure of a Quest', produced by Birla Academy of Art and Culture, Calcutta.

Grasim Industries Ltd—*A Record of Sustained Progress.* June, 1994.

Century Textiles and Industries Ltd, September 7, 1994.

GOENKA

Books

Goenka, R. P. *Indira Priyadarshni.* Bombay: R.P. Goenka, 1985.

Kochanek, Stanley. *Business and Politics in India.* Berkeley: University of California Press, 1974.

Nanda, H.P. *The Days of My Years.* Viking: New Delhi, 1992.

Timberg, Thomas A. *The Marwaris*. New Delhi: Vikas Publishing House Pvt. Ltd, 1978.

Articles

Abdi, S.N.M. 'The great scramble', *Illustrated Weekly of India,* January 21, 1990, p42f.

Bamsai, S. 'RPG Group—Masters of their destiny', *Dalal Street Journal,* January 9, 1995, pp25-7.

Banerjie, Indranil. 'Dunlop India—Containing the coup', *India Today,* January 15, 1985, p137.

Basu, B. 'The Haldia Effect', *Business Standard,* January 14, 1990.

Basu, Debashish. 'Gramophone Co's new song', *Business World,* April 25, 1988, p68;

'Gramco—The Bose phenomenon', *Update,* April 4, 1986, pp52-3.

Bhagat, Mukarram, 'Dunlop India—Bumpy ride ahead', *Business India,* August 8, 1988, p46;

'RPG Enterprises—Back in the takeover game', *Business India,* October 3, 1988, pp60-1.

Bist, R. 'Ceat Ltd—Wheel deal', *Business India,* September 27, 1993, p21.

Bose, A. 'A raider in Victoria House', *Sunday,* April 16, 1989, pp63-5.

Bose, M. 'RPG Telecom—Right numbers', *Business India,* February 28, 1994, pp97-8;

'Remington Rand—A turn for the better?', *Business India,* February 4, 1991, p43;

'Gramophone Company—In good voice again', *Business India,* May 1, 1989, pp69-71;

'CESC—Powering ahead', *Business India,* April 1, 1991, pp60-2.

Business and Political Observer, 'Can RPG beat the heat at CESC?', February 13, 1991.

Business India, 'PAL—Up for grabs', May 23, 1983, pp54-55.

Business Standard, 'Basu announces lease of 2 gas turbines to CESC', January 6, 1991;

'The house that Goenka built,' May 10, 1981.

Business World, 'Asian Cables: Going strong', December 4, 1991, p81;

'Ceat—Enter Goenkas', December 7, 1981, pp52-3;

'Wooing an RPG man', September 13, 1989, p128;

'Dunlop—Higher stakes', February 18, 1985, p116;

'Bayer—Acquisition with a difference', February 18, 1985, p116;

'RPG's prize catch', August 26, 1992, p16;

'The front-line aspirations of G.P. Goenka,' March 15, 1982.

Chatterjee, Gouri. 'Talking to the takeover king', *Business Standard,* June 30, 1985.

Chatterjee, S.K. 'CESC—Power brokers', *Sunday,* April 12, 1992, pp92-3.

Chawla, P. 'The business blacklist', *India Today,* July 31, 1986, pp94-5.

Cherian, Dilip, 'The return of the raiders', *Business India,* April 4, 1988, p52;

'Tyres—Goenka spins ahead', *Business India,* January 14, 1985, pp63-9.

Datta, Ella. 'Sanjiv Goenka—A low-profile corporate czar', *Business Standard,* December 30, 1994.

Doshi, J. 'Ceat fund management: In whose interest?', June 11, 1990.

Dutt, D. & Sen, A. 'Let there be light', *Sunday,* July 28, 1991, pp51-3.

Dutta, S. 'CESC: Electricity in the air', *Business India,* July 18, 1994, pp83-9.

Economic Scene, 'Dunlop—Selling the family castle', November 1, 1983.

Financial Express, 'Murphy to be merged with Ceat', December 23, 1989;

'Murphy union for review of merger with Ceat', August 11, 1992;

'BIFR for Murphy, Ceat merger', June 12, 1990.

Fisher, M. 'Ceat finalises takeover of Murphy India', *Independent,* July 27, 1990.

Ghosh, A. 'ICIM: Back in form', *Business World,* February 12, 1992, pp71-3.

Ghosh, Shekhar. 'Searle India—Butachlor blocked', *Business India,* February 19, 1990, p150.

Goenka, R.P. 'Goenka's Haldia plan', *Update,* February 7, 1986, p50;

'FICCI—The year in retrospect', *Business Standard,* May, 19, 1987;

'Of raids and raiders', *India Today,* April 15, 1986, p99.

Goenka, Sanjiv. 'Looking beyond business', *Business World,* July 3, 1991, pp34-35;

'The Indian woman', *Society,* October, 1989, p89.

Guha, B. 'HMV—Songs of experience', *India Weekly (UK),* May 12, 1995.

Gupta, S.D. 'RPG Enterprises—Back in business', *India Today,* November 15, 1988, pp118-123.

Gupta, Sujoy. 'No pipedreams', *Business World,* May 20, 1992, pp25-30;

'Raid raj revisited', *Business World,* April 11, 1988, p78;

'ICIM: Looking for a white knight', *Business World,* September 10, 1988, p65;

'Harrisons Malayalam—Rise and shine', *Business World,* November 21, 1990, pp56-66;

'Dunlop—Changing equations', *Business World*, August 17, 1988, p28.

Independent, 'PM to meet Goenka in Calcutta', December 21, 1990.

Indian Express, 'Ceat: Subsidiaries liberally milk the cash cow', March 11, 1991.

Karmali, Nazneen. 'Searle India—A planned exit', *Business India*, February 15, 1993, p72.

Kasbekar, Kiron & Roy, Subrata. 'The Goenka split', *Business India*, January 18, 1982, pp40-55.

Katiyar, Arun. 'Kamani Engineering Corporation—The plot thickens,' *Bombay*, December 7, 1983.

Khan, S.H. 'S.S. Nadkarni—A model technocrat', *Business India*, February 13, 1995, p41.

Kottary, Sailesh. 'The Goenka connection: Ceat's turning point, *Business World*, May 9, 1983.

Kumar, Avi. 'Harrisons Malayalam—Profits up, vistas widen', *The Week*, November 4, 1990, p44.

Kumar, K.G. 'Harrisons Malayalam—Striving to be the best', *Business India*, February 18, 1991, p82;

'Harrisons Malayalam—Waking up', *Business India*, March 6, 1989, p80;

'Harrisons Malayalam—The Guinness connection', *Business India*, September, 19, 1988, pp77-8.

Kuttappan, L. 'RPG-Ricoh: Á fight to fax', *Business India*, October 25, 1993, p65.

Laha, Ashoke. 'GCI's muscial comeback', *Business World*, July 4, 1990, p12f.

Mathai, P.G. 'Tyres—Taking a spin', *India Today*, February 28, 1985, p116.

Maitra, D. 'Spencer & Co—Trading its past for its future', *Business Today*, February 7, 1994, pp38-40;

'Ceat Tyres—New directions', *Business India*, December 25, 1990, pp69-73;

'Murphy-Ceat: Munna moves house', *Business India*, October 29, 1990, p76.

Mitra, M. 'New takers for Haldia?', *Independent*, December 20, 1989.

Mittra, K. 'G.P. Goenka—Making of a megacorp', *Business India*, January 16, 1995, pp113-5.

Mukerjea, D.N. 'HMV—Mastering old times', *Business World*, April 22, 1992, pp43-4.

Mukerjee, Sourav. 'Sanjiv Goenka—Born tough', *Sunday*, September 1, 1991, pp45-47.

Murthy, R.C. 'Ceat set to take over Nirlon', *Business Standard,*
November 14, 1987.
Nadkarni, Shirish. 'ICIM—Not far-sighted enough?', *Sunday Observer,*
October 16, 1988.
Nair, Mohan. 'Ceat—Treading a new path', *Economic Times Corporate
Dossier,* December 7, 1990;
   'Murphy India to close down as staff accepts new VRS', April 27,
1994.
Narayan, Sanjoy. 'Nusli Wadia: Corporate samurai', *Business World,* July
28, 1993, pp19-25;
   'The restructuring of RPG Enterprises', *Business World,* October 6,
1993, pp26-35.
Newsday, 'Ceat gets a ticket to nowhere', June 25, 1993.
Ninan, T.N. 'Nirlon—Wary suitors', *India Today,* December 15, 1987,
p149;
   'FICCI—Unseemly quarrel', *India Today,* June 15, 1985, p123;
   'Tax raids—New fervour', *India Today,* April 15, 1988, pp105-6;
   'FICCI—Chambers of conflict', *India Today,* December 15, 1985,
pp89-91.
Padmanabhan, M. 'Spencer changes hands', *Sunday,* January 15, 1989,
pp60-1.
Pal, A. & Nandi, S. 'Remington Rand—A takeover true to type', *Business
Standard,* January 6, 1991.
Pal, A. & Dasgupta, S. 'HMV—Remarrying mammon and muse',
Business Standard, December 15, 1985.
Patherya, Mudar. 'Ceat: Good going', *Business World,* June 3, 1992, p103.
Piramal Gita. 'Top twenty business houses: Staying ahead', *Economic
Times,* September 29, 1989;
   'A pat on the back is important to me', *Economic Times,* January 24,
1989;
   'Harsh Vardhan Goenka: The boy with the silver spoon', *Bombay,*
November 22, 1987, pp18-23;
   'Indian tyre companies', *Financial Times,* March 27, 1992;
   'Cracker projects fuel competition', *Financial Times,* May 27, 1990;
   'Plain sailing for jinxed scheme—Haldia complex', *Financial Times,*
November 2, 1989;
   'W. Germans plan Indian naphtha plant', *Financial Times,* January 25,
1989;
   'Goenka—Powering into a window of opportunity', *Financial Times,*
July 19, 1990;
   'G.P. Goenka—Out of the shadows', *Economic Times Corporate*

Dossier, March 8, 1991.

Piramal, G., *et al.* 'The great company bazaar', *Sunday,* December 18, 1988, p32.

Raman, Anand. 'Dunlop—Crucial moves', *India Today,* August 15, 1988, p92.

Ramaswamy, J. 'Changing of the guards at Kamanis', *Sunday Obersver,* December 11, 1983.

Ravi, A.B. 'The reincarnation of Murphy', *Island,* October, 1990, pp60-1.

Roy, Abhijit. 'Changing course', *Business Today,* June 22, 1992, pp34-45; 'R.P. Goenka—Seeking new frontiers', *Economic Times Corporate Dossier,* October 27, 1989; 'Remington Rand', *Economic Times Corporate Dossier,* February 1, 1991; 'Gramophone Co—Finding its voice', *Economic Times Corporate Dossier,* April 13, 1990.

Roy, Subrata. 'Rama Prasad Goenka—A saga of empire building', *Business India,* January 11, 1988, pp38-48.

Sanandakumar, S. 'Murphy India in trouble again', *Sunday Observer,* October 4, 1992.

Sarkar, Aroon. 'ICIM—A full dimension', *Business India,* August 16, 1993, p.21

Sarkar, Avi. 'The big rush', *The Week,* January 7, 1990, p.46.

Sharma, Rahul. 'ICIM—Small is better', *Business India,* July 23, 1990, pp79-81.

Singh, Chander Uday. 'Premier Automobiles—A takeover drive', *India Today,* December 15, 1982, p130; 'The Goenkas, corporate raiders', *India Today,* August 15, 1984, p80f.

Srinivasan, T.S. 'What's in store for Spencer?', *Business Standard,* January 29, 1989.

Sunday Observer, 'RPG group set to make waves', July 27, 1987; 'Smart money—The business of making it big in Calcutta', November 17, 1991.

Telegraph, 'RPG vs Sen—Charges and challenges on power front', September 27, 1995.

Tellis, Olga. 'India Polyfibres: The bonanza that never was', *Sunday,* February 21, 1988, p60f.

Thakurta, Paranjoy Guha. 'The Dunlop Takeover', *Update,* January 22, 1985; 'West Bengal—Basu's perestroika', *India Today,* April 15 , 1990, pp82-4.

Thomas, C.P. 'BIFR rejects Ceat's plea for I-T certificate', *Economic Times,* April 8, 1993;
'Murphy India union moves court on Ceat's MoU with FGP', August 12, 1993;
'Murphy TU seeks action against Ceat', July 6, 1993.
Thomas, E. 'Aditya Birla, building on a fortune', *Business India,* December 24, 1990, p60.
Times of India, 'Murphy union to contest closure', August 11, 1992.
Vasuki, S.N. 'ICIM: Uncertain at the top', *Business India,* January 25, 1988, pp79-81.
Venkatesh, R.S. 'Privatisation in UP—A bold experiment', *Business India,* October 29, 1990, pp85-7.
Vijayraghavan, R. 'Enfield Electronics—RPG makes a bid', *Sunday,* July 9, 1989, pp57-8.

Other Literature
Company brochures, press releases, pamphlets, annual reports.
CESC GDR Offering Circular, 1994.
Duncan Group Profile (Pamphlet published by J.P. Goenka Group and Companies, anon, n.d.)
The Duncan World of Textiles. Published by Swan Mills, Ltd, n.d.
Khanna, T. 'RPG Enterprises', Harvard Business School, N9-796-111, January 12, 1996.
'Life Sketch of Rai Bahadur Sir Badridas Goenka.'
Romance of the Road—Ceat Tyres of India. Brochure published by Ceat Tyres.
Singh, Khushwant. *The Power and The Sword: Asian Cables—The First 25 Years: 1959-1984.*
'Write-up on the G.P. Goenka Group of Companies.'
'Write-up on the late K.P. Goenka.'

KHAITAN

Books
Birla, B.K. *A Rare Legacy* Bombay: Image Incorporated, 1994.
Hazarika, Sanjoy. *Strangers of the Mist.* New Delhi: Viking, 1994
Jones, Stephanie. *Merchants of the Raj.* London: Macmillan Press, 1992.
Pugh, Peter. *Williamson Magor Stuck to Tea.* Cambridge Business Publishing, 1991.

Articles

Ahmed, F. 'Assam losing business', *India Today,* July 31, 1993, pp78-9.

Bakshi S. & Ganguly, T. 'Dangerous designs', *The Week,* April 29, 1990.

Banerjee, N. 'A helping hand for Metal Box', *Business Standard,* January 12, 1986;

    'McLeod offload investments to protect projected EPS', *Business Standard,* May 24, 1995;

    'Perils of issue pricing in a depressed market', *Business Standard,* May 4, 1995;

    'Elecon Madras unit falls into Magor lap', *Business Standard,* September, 19, 1994;

    'Khaitan-Birla deal to benefit McNally Bharat', *Business Standard,* April 9, 1989.

Banerjee, N. & Dasgupta, S. 'Williamson Magor gears up to hike battery market share', *Business Standard,* February 14, 1995.

Banerjee, N. & Fernandes, S. 'McLeod issue mops up 103 per cent subscription', *Business Standard,* June 6, 1995.

Basu, B. & Pal, A. 'Winning bid for Union Carbide may be Rs 200-250cr', *Economic Times,* September 9, 1994;

    'McLeod Russel may drop Euroissue', *Economic Times,* September 13, 1994.

Basu, B. 'McLeod seeks bigwigs' helping hand in hour of need', *Economic Times,* May 26, 1995;

    'Khaitans seeking light aircraft for captive use', *Economic Times,* June 23, 1994;

    'Magor revamp to turn Makum, Namdang into investment firms', *Economic Times,* June 21, 1994;

    'Metal Box units to be sold', *Business Standard,* July 10, 1990.

Basu, D. 'Macneill & Magor', *Update,* May 9, 1986, pp44-9.

Bose, A. 'ULFA summons tea majors', *Business Standard,* June 15, 1990.

Bose, J. 'B.M. Khaitan acquiring 7 per cent stake in Nestle', *Economic Times,* August 29, 1992.

Bose, M. 'UCIL: Gaining brand equity', *Business India,* October 10, 1994, p21;

    'The Dooars of success', *Business India,* July 4, 1994, pp134-6;

    'A stronger brew', *Business India,* February 13, 1995, pp98-105.

Bose, R. 'Racing to get ahead of the pack', *Economic Times,* August 26, 1994.

Business and Political Observer, 'P.K. Mahanta', December 13, 1990.

Business Standard editorial, 'Reviving Metal Box', February 9, 1989.

Business Standard, 'Bankers blame MB for revamp plan deadlock' and

'MB defends action', July 21, 1988;

'2 bids for MB foreign stake', October 11, 1988;

'B.M. Khaitan bags UCIL in biggest corporate deal', September 9, 1994;

'B.M. Khaitan group set to take over Metal Box', December 5, 1985;

'Funding the Union Carbide takeover', May 18, 1995;

'Khaitans close Carbide deal ahead of schedule', November 24, 1994;

'MB unions plan jt strategy', February, 19, 1988;

'McLeod Russel benefits from FI-bank rate war', November 2, 1994;

'Metal Box MD resigns', March 17, 1987;

'Metal Box proposes three-year wage freeze', March 24, 1988;

'Ministry quizzes McLeod Russel on Carbide takeover', October 29, 1994;

'Politics by murder', April 11, 1990;

'Resolutions at Metal Box AGM passed amid uproar', December 31, 1988;

'Reduction in labour force vital for Metal Box revival', December 27, 1989;

'SC stays Calcutta HC on Metal Box revival', November 12, 1994;

'Tea majors playing foul, says Assam CM', July 13, 1990;

'Worli unit sale plan irks MB shareholders', August 24, 1987;

'Fear stalks industry in Assam', April 11, 1990;

'No plan to ban ULFA, says Mahanta', September 15, 1990;

'Tea cos. not to keep ULFA deadline', June 20, 1990;

'ULFA deadline to tea cos. ends on Thursday', June 18, 1990;

'ULFA makes Jokai a test case', June 27, 1990;

'Ultimatum to tea cos. to shift HO to Assam', June 21, 1990;

'Macneill & McLeod form formidable tea combine', April 24, 1987;

'Namdung merger with finance firm in a month', June 2, 1995;

'WB livid at Khaitan outburst', September 22, 1991;

'High tea at PM's', August 22, 1989;

'Workers resist change in Macneill unit identity', July 24, 1989.

Chatterjee, D. 'McLeod Russel fixes Rs 210 issue premium', *Business Standard,* October 28, 1994.

Choudhury, R. 'Back with a bang', *Sunday,* January 14, 1990, p58f.

Dasgupta, S. 'Banks compete to fund Carbide takeover', *Business Standard,* October 8, 1994;

'Union Carbide to offload imported long-life cells', *Business Standard,* October 18, 1994.

Dey, N. 'UCIL share soars close to Khaitan takeover price', *Business Standard,* November 2, 1994.

Dutta, S. 'Metal Box India—Alive and ticking?', *Business India,* March 28, 1994, p124.

Economic Times, 'Paul's murder still a mystery', April 25, 1990;
 'Bid to end Metal Box stalemate: New wage proposals', February 18, 1988;
 'High stress test for Carbide scrip', September 15, 1994;
 'Magor UK nominee on Mcleod Russel board', June 17, 1987;
 'Market bearish on McLeod Russel public issue', May 6, 1995;
 'MacNeill & Magor deal with MB', December 6, 1985;
 'Metal Box chalks out Rs 80cr revival plan', January 1, 1995;
 'Metal Box AGM held amidst noisy scenes', December 24, 1989;
 'Race for UCIL stake hots up', September 9, 1994;
 'Worli-Deonar units' merger recommended', September 3, 1988;
 'No clandestine operations: Metal Box', July 23, 1988;
 'Operations of all but one unit suspended: Metal Box', January 21, 1988;
 'Ralston Purina, Eveready Ind. launch joint venture', June 9, 1995;
 'Search for a buyer', July 18, 1988;
 'Surendra Paul's killing stuns Assam industry', April 11, 1990;
 'SPIC, Bombay Dyeing in race for UCIL unit,' July 14, 1994;
 'The great brew connection', December 12, 1987.

Fernandes, S. & Dey, N. 'McLeod issue open after earliest closing date', *Business Standard,* May 31, 1995.

Fernandes, S. 'B.M. Khaitan looks for foreign tie-up in financial services', *Business Standard,* May 5, 1995.

Financial Express, 'BIFR to decide on Metal Box takeover by Allied Deals', August 20, 1995;
 'New twist to Metal Box takeover game', May 21, 1989;
 'Saikia—Haunted but undaunted', January 17, 1993;
 'Metal Box AGM sans accounts', December 31, 1988.

Financial Times, 'McLeod Russel chairman dies suddenly aged 50', November 27, 1994.

Gupta, M. 'Wadia-Purina joint bid for Carbide', *Business Standard,* September 9, 1994.

Gupta, Sujoy. 'Raid raj revisited', *Business World,* April 11, 1988, p79;
 'The silent strides of B. M. Khaitan', *Business World,* March 14, 1990, p29;
 'The tea zamindar', *Business World,* March 14, 1990, p37;
 'New brew', *Business World,* September 23, 1992, p62.

Gupta, R. 'Assam—Killing business', *Business India,* April 30, 1990, pp60-2.

Hussain, Wasbir. 'Gardens tense as planters obey ULFA writ', *Telegraph*, July 2, 1990;
    'Talks with ULFA leave tea bosses shaken', *Telegraph*, July 9, 1990;
    'Assam police sound alert in 54 tea gardens', *Telegraph*, July 10, 1990.
Independent, 'Russi Mody blackballed by RCTC', March 3, 1994.
Indian Express, 'Metal Box AGM disrupted by irate shareholders', December 31, 1988;
    'Tea barons blame Assam violence on inequality', May 13, 1990;
    'ULFA had no statute', April 5, 1992;
    'ULFA rebels held', January 25, 1991;
    'McLeod Russel', July 20, 1987.
Iyengar, J. 'DCA punctures Khaitan stand on Eveready stake', *Business Standard*, July 28, 1995.
Jain, P. 'Metal Box sale plan opposed', *Financial Express*, July 25, 1990.
Kottary, S. 'Fresh wrinkle to Union Carbide acquisition', *Economic Times*, September 9, 1994.
Krishnan, J. 'UCIL's takeover helps US parent firm go scot-free', *Financial Express*, November 30, 1994.
Maitra, D. 'Nusli Wadia—I want to buy strong brands', *Business Today*, July 22, 1994, p66;
    'Recharging UCIL's Batteries', *Business Today*, August 7, 1994, pp48-9.
Majumdar, S. & Chatterjee, D. 'Keen contest likely for Union Carbide', *Business Standard*, September 6, 1994.
Mathai, P. 'Metal Box—Cutting links', *India Today*, May 15, 1988, p105;
    'Breaking into a canter', *India Today*, June 15, 1989, pp118-21.
Mehta, A. 'Exide to pick up stake in Standard Batteries', *Economic Times*, July 21, 1994.
Mitra, Kaveri. 'Making the network', *Business India*, April 10, 1995, p99.
Mookerjee, A. 'Assam—Tea and tragedy', *Business India*, December 10, 1990, pp113-9.
Mukherjea, D. N. 'Union Carbide: No more in charge', *Business World*, June 16, 1993, p44;
    'McNally Bharat: A long-term outlook', *Business World*, August 11, 1993, p57.
Munshi, D. 'False visions of peace', *Times of India*, February 7, 1993.
Nair, M. 'Standard Batteries to expand, diversify', *Economic Times*, September 25, 1989.
Nair-Ghaswalla, A. 'Firm develops battery for Russian sub', *Times of India*, April 14, 1994.
Narayan, S. 'Recharging a dead cell', *Business World*, September 9, 1992,

pp58-9.

Pal, A. 'EILL ties up with Ralston of US for new battery venture', *Economic Times,* March 27, 1995;

'McLeod Russel to pay for UCIL stake in November', *Economic Times,* October 21, 1994;

'Kilburn Reprographics may divorce unfaithful partner', *Business Standard,* December 22, 1994;

'Khaitans wash their hands of Assam cracker', *Business Standard,* August 20, 1990;

'Metal Box MD offered UK stake for a song', *Business Standard,* January 8, 1991;

'UCIL chairman quits after takeover', *Business Standard,* November 1, 1994;

'B.M. Khaitan-G.P. Birla joint foray into power sector', *Business Standard,* August 13, 1991;

'Macneill motel chain for Assam', *Business Standard,* February 14, 1990.

Panneerselvan, A. S. 'Tea—High-tech processing', *Business India,* August 16, 1993, p111.

Pioneer, 'Panic in tea gardens after killing', April 6, 1992.

Piramal, Gita. 'A pariah that recharged its batteries after gas disaster', *Financial Times,* January 15, 1992;

'Assam tea chiefs flee terrorists', *Financial Times,* November 10, 1990;

'Union Carbide India', *Financial Times,* May 6, 1992;

'Terrorism stalks Assam's tea gardens', *Financial Times,* July 6, 1990.

Rattan, K. 'Metal Box—Trimming fat', *India Today,* March 15, 1988, p116.

Ravi, A. B. 'Eveready to move on', *Business India,* August 30, 1993, p81f;

'Union Carbide—Which way will it go?', *Business India,* February 28, 1994, p21.

Roy, Abhijit. 'Bankrolling the UCIL buy-out', *Business Today,* September 22, 1994, p49;

'Chloride's battery of changes', *Business Today,* October 7, 1994, pp58-9;

'One good deal', *Business Today,* October 22, 1994, p18.

Roy, Subrata. 'Metal Box up for sale', *Business India,* September 12, 1983, p62f.

Roychowdhury, P. 'B. M. Khaitan emerges frontrunner in Carbide race', *Business Standard,* September, 1994.

Sen, A. 'ICICI formula to revive Metal Box', *Financial Express,* January

23, 1989.

Singhal, R. & Gupta, S. 'Wrapped in red', *Business Standard,* February 28, 1988.

Sinha, R. N. 'Assam gas cracker: Khaitans find terms difficult', *Economic Times,* May 5, 1991.

Srikant, P. S. 'McLeod issue marketed in Euro-style', *Economic Times,* December 7, 1994.

Subramanian, S. 'Khaitans—Aiming for the big times', *Economic Times Corporate Dossier,* February 4, 1989.

Sunday Times Magazine, 'Britain's richest 500, 1996', April 14, 1996.

Suri, S. 'Brooke Bond turns down ULFA demand', *Telegraph,* June 24, 1990.

Telegraph, 'Khaitan, Ralston firm up joint venture', June 8, 1995
    'Metal Box loss mounts to Rs 5.9 cr in 1994-95', July 11, 1995;
    'Tea manager shot in Assam', April 5, 1992;
    'Fear psychosis grips business community', April 11, 1990;
    'General amnesty for ULFA men', July 9, 1991;
    'Police hunting for Paul's killers in Tinsukhia', April 11, 1990.

Times of India, 'Two kidnapped in Assam', December 23, 1992;
    'Tea co GM shot dead by ULFA', February 16, 1994;
    'City firm issues lock-out notice', January 24, 1988;
    'Bodos strike terror in Assam', April 11, 1992;
    'Centre shelves talks with ULFA', March, 19, 1991;
    'ULFA blackmail routed through Dhaka', July 15, 1990.

Venkatachalam, K., MD, Jokai India Ltd, 'Letter to editor', *Business Standard,* July 12, 1990.

Other Literature

Company brochures, press releases, pamphlets, annual reports.

'Williamson Magor Group', n.d.

McLeod Russel (India) Ltd, Prospectus for rights issue, May 25, 1995.

SHAH

Articles

Afternoon Despatch & Courier, 'Traders protest triple murder', March 23, 1995;
    'The loudest wedding of the year?', December 18, 1989.

Almeida, M. 'SEEPZ—Cast for the world', *Business India,* August 16, 1993, pp106-110;

· 'Jewellery Exports—US tax hits industry', *Business India,* October 25, 1993, p33;
  'Jewellery·exports—Successful US pitch', *Business India,* August 15, 1994, pp35-6;
  'Jewellery EOUs—Pushing for change', *Business India,* April 11, 1994, p36.

Ashraf, S. F. 'Mira Road: Where east and west are poles apart', *Sunday Observer,* July 23, 1995.

Arora, De'epa. 'The diamond clan', *Society,* November, 1981, pp61-5.

Bamzai, S. 'Films are forever', *Sunday Observer,* March 1, 1992;
  'Kirtibhai Mehta—A gem of an entrepreneur', *Sunday Observer,* March 8, 1992.

Basu, R. 'Mira Road colony reels under water crisis', *Times of India,* October 10, 1995.

Bhanu, T. 'Taxmen bite diamond', *Business Standard,* April 2, 1989.

Bhargava, S. 'Diamonds, a cut above the rest', *India Today,* May 15, 1989, p111.

Business Post, 'BV Diamond set to expand output', Bangkok, August 9, 1991.

Business Standard, 'Diamond trade shutdown today', March 9, 1989.

Chinai, R. 'Meet Atul Shah, the millionaire turned environmental monk', *Sunday Observer,* June 3, 1991.

Choudhary, M. 'Surat—Ghost town', *Afternoon on Sunday,* September 25, 1994;
  'The diamond city is getting back some of its old glitter', *Afternoon Despatch & Courier,* October 25, 1994.

Engineer, S. 'Nirmal Zaveri—Jewel king', *Afternoon Despatch & Courier,* April 9, 1995.

Financial Express, 'Diamond trade bandh today', March 9, 1989.

Gupte, Pranay. 'The big money in cheap rock', *Forbes,* August 10, 1987, p64f.

Indian Express, 'Diamond trade all set to take to the streets', April 6, 1989;
  'IT officials deny bungling', March 15, 1989;
  'Diamond raid: IT admits bungling', March 14, 1989;
  'Indian jeweller in New York missing', July 6, 1989;
  'Forged letter sealed their fate', September 18, 1991.

Irani, Jeroo. 'The street of gold', *Signature,* April, 1987, pp26-30.

Island, 'For whom the bells toll', January, 1990, pp65-6.

Krishnamoorthi, J. 'Boom time at Mira Road', *Island,* September, 1994, pp76-7.

Koppikar, S. 'Atulkumar Shah—From riches to rags', *Independent,* June 6, 1991.

Malkan, D. 'Equity cult spreading fast to diamond sector', *Indian Express,* February 20, 1989.

Mahurkar, U. 'Diamonds are not forever', *India Today,* June 30, 1991, pp112-3.

Mehta, M. 'Letter to editor', *Times of India.* January 7, 1990.

Mehta, Mafatlal. 'You could put Kirtilal anywhere in the world', *Sunday Observer,* August 8, 1993.

Mid-day, 'Mira Road, Bhayander residents to intensify stir against water shortage', October 10, 1995.

Mishra, A. 'Demonstrations give jarring start to Mehta-Shah wedding', *Independent,* December 22, 1989;
'Grand wedding raises storm of protest', *Independent,* December 21, 1989.

Moos, M. H. 'Just married', *Afternoon Despatch & Courier,* October, 19, 1994.

Nadkarni, S. 'Diamonds—Behind the glitter', *Sunday Observer,* April 9, 1989.

Parekh, D. 'Diamond trade—Keeping the glitter', *India Today,* December 15, 1992, pp120-1.

Pathak, R. & Katiyar, A. 'A 24-carat crime', *India Today,* October 15, 1991, p138.

Pillai, A. 'It was not cricket', *The Week,* January 7, 1990, pp10-12.

Piramal, G. 'Jewels in the crown', *Economic Times,* June 22, 1990;
'Sparkle on Indian diamond market dims', *Financial Times,* June, 1990;
'S. African struggle hits Indian diamond merchants', *Economic Times,* March 29, 1994;
'Indian diamond firms fall to Russian miners' charm', *Economic Times,* December 14, 1993;
'De Beers polishing up its India act', *Economic Times,* October 14, 1993.

Rathore, M. 'Cutting Edge', *Mid-day,* February, 19, 1996.

Roy, S. G. 'Palanpur: Perennially under curfew', *Sunday Observer,* December 10, 1990.

Sharma, S. 'A gem of a family', *Family,* September, 1995, pp107-9.

Shor, Russell. 'Will India be a force as a high-end diamond supplier?', *Jewelers' Circular-Keystone,* July, 1988, pp308-314.

Singh, R. 'The mysterious carat club', *Indian Express,* September 29, 1991.

Solitaire, 'Indian impressions on Antwerp', March, 1988, pp7-12;

'Kirtilal Manilal Mehta—The boy who built an empire', May, 1988, pp42-6;
'In the world's eye—Selling the small diamond', June, 1988, pp10-12;
'Bangkok blinks in', June, 1988, pp28-9.
Subramanium, A. 'Plagued by doubts', *Business India,* October 10, 1994, pp54-9.
Sunday Mail, 'Bearing the Zaveri name proudly', December 21, 1991.
Tellis, Olga. 'The glitter is not real', *Sunday,* August 21, 1988;
'Gem merchants battle the taxman', *Sunday,* April 23, 1989, pp65-6;
'Diamonds and rust', *Sunday,* January 14, 1990, pp64-5.
Times of India Sunday Review, 'People', December 31, 1989.
Times of India, 'Public ire over lavish wedding', December 20, 1989;
'Wedding glitter amid protests', December 22, 1989;
'Diamond trade at standstill', March 9, 1989;
'Diamond traders call against harassment', March 22, 1989;
'Traders, I-T men clash', April 5, 1989;
'For whom the hammer came down', March 28, 1989.
Trivedi, M. 'Tax probe against millionaire monk angers Jains', *Sunday Observer,* August 4, 1991.

Other Literature
Company brochures, press releases, pamphlets, annual reports.
Gembel Group, full-page advertisement, *Indian Express*, August 7, 1991.
BV Jewels, *The Style of the Times.*

TATA

Books
Datta, S. B. *Capital Accumulation and Workers' Struggle—The Case of Tata Iron and Steel Company, 1910-1970.* Calcutta: K. P. Bagchi, 1990.
Elwin, Verrier. *The Story of Tata Steel.* Privately printed, 1958.
Etienne, G. *Asian Crucible—The Steel Industry in China and India.* New Delhi: Sage Publications, 1992.
Fyzee, Murad. *Aircraft and Engine Perfect.* New Delhi: Tata McGraw-Hill Publishing Co, 1991.
Harris, F. R. *Jamsetji Nusserwanji Tata.* Bombay: Blackie and Son (India) Ltd, 1958.
Karaka, D. F. *History of the Parsees,* Vols 1-11. London, 1884.
Keenan, John. *A Steelman in India.* New York, 1943.
Lala, R. M. *The Creation of Wealth: A Tata Story.* Bombay: IBH

Publishing Company, 1981;
The Heartbeat of a Trust. Bombay: Tata-McGraw Hill, 1984;
Beyond the 'Blue Mountain. New Delhi: Viking, 1992.

Menen, Aubrey. *Sixty Years: The Story of the Tatas*. Oxford: Oxford University Press, 1948.

Pandey, S. N. *Human Side of Tata Steel*. New Delhi: Tata-McGraw Hill Publishing Co., 1992.

Saklatvala, B.S. & Khosla, K. *Jamsetji Tata,* New Delhi: Publication Division, Ministry of Information and Broadcasting, Government of India, 1970.

Sen, A. *Five Golden Years of Indian Aviation—Tata's Memorable Years*. Bombay: Aeronautical Publications of India Pvt Ltd, 1978.

Tata, J.R.D. *Keynote.* Bombay: Tata Press Ltd, 1986.

Wacha, D. E. *The Life and Life-work of J.N. Tata*. Madras: Ganesh and Co, 1914.

Articles

Afternoon Despatch & Courier, 'Busybee's Round and About', April 22, 1993;
'Favourite VIP', June 30, 1992;
'The baton changes hands at Tatas', April, 19, 1991.

Ahmed, F. 'Tisco—Making peace', *India Today,* October 31, 1991, p122;
'Tisco—Under fire', *India Today,* August 15, 1990, p108.

Ambani, D. 'Nothing less than the best', *Business India,* June 17, 1985, p89.

Balakrishnan, S. 'A new militancy', *Illustrated Weekly of India,* October 15, 1989, p24;
'Militant messiah', *Illustrated Weekly of India,* June 18, 1989, p48.

Bana, S. 'Tisco finally pulls it off', *Blitz,* August 8, 1994;

Banerjee, G. 'Does Tata mean goodbye?', *Sunday,* May 16, 1992, p52-56.

Banerjee, N. 'Tisco board to discuss Russi decisions', *Business Standard,* December 25, 1991;
'Top-level changes in Tata Steel', *Business Standard*, November 8, 1991.

Basu, D. 'Is Tata a winner?', *Business Today,* January 7, 1992, pp38-48.

Belle, N. 'Tatas: The battle for succession', *Gentleman,* July, 1988, p32.

Bhagat, Mukarram. 'The Tata group cannot disintegrate—J.R.D. Tata', *Economic Times,* April 5, 1991;
'Minoo Mody—A sudden exit', *Business India,* July 24, 1989, pp65-66;
'The House of Tata—An era ends, another begins', *Economic Times Corporate Dossier,* April 5, 1991.

Bhanu, T. 'Telco on the test track', *Business Standard,* October 1, 1989.

Bist, R. 'CCL takeover—Tata Tea's unique bid', *Business India,* October 2, 1989, pp163-64;

'Rallis India—Seth's sorrow, *Business India,* October 1, 1990, p41.

Bombay, 'Rodabeh Sawhney—Daughter of R.D. Tata', July 7, 1983, p7.

Bose, J. 'Corporate battles—A year of boardroom brawls', *Economic Times Corporate Dossier,* January 1, 1993.

Bose, M. 'Haldia: An American in Calcutta', *Business India,* May 23, 1994, p73.

Business India, 'Businessmen in the news', July 8, 1991, p26;

'Chilka controversy: Prawn cocktail', July 4, 1994, p157;

'Tata's new interest', August 20, 1990, p16;

'Crisis averted', August 20, 1990, p16.

Business Standard, 'Group cos. to pay issue price for Tisco shares', February 28, 1989;

'Showdown at AGM likely', February 23, 1989;

'Hi-tech man with a mission', March 26, 1991;

'Ratan Tata tipped for Telco', April 14, 1988;

'Telco not sick, says Russi Mody', March 31, 1988;

'Mody plans to retire', April 9, 1988;

'Russi still packs enough punch', January 10, 1992;

'Tisco controversy a thing of the past, Russi', January 17, 1992.

Business World, 'Will the empire hold', May 20, 1992, pp21-24;

'Indian Hotels troubles', October 13, 1986, p104.

Business Today, 'Tisco: No more the blue-eyed boy', February 22, 1993, p125;

'A Requiem for JRD', December 7, 1993, pp18-21.

Carvalho, C. 'Voltas: Confounding the Cassandras', *Business Today,* April 22, 1993, pp36-7;

'Lakmé—A facelift for the beauty shop', *Business Today,* October 7, 1992, p76.

Chawla, P. 'The Business blacklist', *India Today,* July 31, 1986, pp94-5.

'Aviation—A New Order', *India Today,* October 15, 1986, p35.

Chiravuri, S. 'Voltas Ltd—No more the mere marketeer', *Economic Times Corporate Dossier,* August 15, 1992.

Choudhury, M. R. 'The Telco imbroglio', *Business World,* October 25, 1989, p56;

Contractor, A. 'ACC—At the crossroads', *Business India,* February 8, 1988, pp69-73;

'New Ahmedabad Advance Mills—Against all odds', *Business India,* May 9, 1989, p72;

'Obituary—Naval Tata', *Business India,* May 15, 1989, p43.

Daruwala, R. 'The other Tata', *Business India,* June 8, 1981, p44f.

Dé, Shobha. 'Ratan Naval Tata—The chosen one', *Afternoon on Sunday,* October 24, 1993.

Dhawan, R. 'Whose name is it anyway?', *Business Today,* March 22, 1994, pp98-102.

Dubashi, J. 'The Mody episode', *Sunday Observer,* January, 19, 1992;
'A Personnel Affair', *Probe India,* September 1986, pp66-67;
'ACC—Raising an issue', *India Today,* December 15, 1984, p138;
'Tax Raids—Tightening the Bonds', *India Today,* March 15, 1986, pp96-97;
'The Tatas—Changing of the Guard', *India Today,* December 31, 1981, pp96-105.

Dutta, S. 'Tata Refractories: Hot bricks', *Business India,* April 25, 1994, pp97-9.

Dutta, S. and Datt, N. 'Tisco's big comeback', *Business India,* June 3, 1996, p54.

Economic Times, 'JRD hands over reins to Ratan Tata', March 26, 1991;
'Mody's retirement package not discussed yet', April 14, 1993;
'Mody ousted from Tisco', April 4, 1993;
'Tata, Russi' (editorial), May 30, 1993;
'Not just a Tata affair' (editorial), May 8, 1992;
'Tata group plans massive hi-tech investments', February 11, 1985;
'Tisco's Rs 265 crore issue', December 21, 1988;
'Tisco crisis defused', January 3, 1992;
'Will Russi Mody hand up his gloves?', May 23, 1992;
'Top level shuffle at Tisco threatens row at Tata helm', December 24, 1991;
'Russi meets JRD to defuse crisis', January 2 , 1992.

Ethiraj, G. 'Indian Hotels: Growth, the last resort', *Business World,* September 8, 1993, pp40-2.

Financial Express, 'Enter JRD to clip Russi's wings', May 27, 1992;
'Russi Mody shown the door', April 20, 1993;
'Shareholders force changes in Tisco issue', January 4, 1992;
'Tisco resorts to window dressing', July 20, 1992;
'Tisco clarifies position', July 21, 1992;
'Transparency wanting' (editorial), July 23, 1992;
'Tatas to double holding in Tisco?', February 24, 1989;
'Russi beats a retreat', January 3, 1992;
'Telco stir may lead to lock-out', September 2, 1989;

Gangadhar, V. 'Cutting no ice', *Sunday,* April 21, 1991, p78.

Gentleman, 15th Anniversary Issue, quoted in *Mid-day,* 'Present perfect', March, 19, 1995.

Ghani, A. B. 'Merger mania', *Business World,* January 1, 1992, pp62-68.

Ghosh, A. 'Watch out for the action', *Business World,* December 16, 1992, pp90-1.

Ghosh, I. 'Tomco: Pushed to the sidelines', *Business World,* December 1, 1993, p57;
'Voltas-Pepsi: Bottled up grouses', *Business World,* August 11, 1993, p41.

Ghosh, S. 'Telco's cars—Technological triumph', *Business India,* August 20, 1990, p123.

Gupta, Sunil, 'We've changed the rules', *Business World,* May 6, 1992, p57.

Gupta, Sujoy. 'Russi Mody—If I were the prime minister', *Business World,* July 31, 1991, pp52-55.

Hariharan, C. 'The heir apparent in the house of Tatas', *Business India,* December 21, 1981, p53.

Housego, D. and Piramal G. 'Indian industry—A colossus poised to flex its muscles', *Financial Times,* July 23, 1990.

Independent, 'Tisco row resolved', January 3, 1992;
'Mr Mody bows out' (editorial), April 21, 1993.

India Today, 'Russi Mody—The Board was right to remove me', May 31, 1993, pp84-85.

Indian Express, 'BT refutes Tata's version', July 28, 1994;
'Russi Mody climbs down', January 3, 1992;
'Talks with Nair after verdict: Tata', September 29, 1989;
'The year when the Titan hung up his boots', March 28, 1991;
'Tisco preferential issue sails through', August 27, 1994.

Irani, M. J. 'Right on, Tata', *Afternoon Despatch & Courier,* August 7, 1994.

Jacob, V. M. 'Tata Chemicals—Searching for synergy', *Business Today,* November 7, 1993, p46.

Joglekar, S. 'Voltas', *Business India,* May 24, 1993;
'Voltas—Challenging change', *Business India,* June 7, 1993, p21.

Joseph, L. 'Merind: Tough times ahead', *Business India,* August 31, 1992, p71.

Joseph, L. & Dossani, R. 'Telco—Long term benefits', *Business India,* May 28, 1990, p129.

Kamath, V. & Raghavan, N. 'Titanic triumph', *Business World,* December 6, 1989, pp46-50.

Kar, S. 'Tifco-TFL merger: Who gains?', *Business India,* October 28,

1991, p100.

Karmali, N. 'Tata Chemicals: By mutual consent', *Business India,* April 11, 1994, pp70-1;
'Ratan Tata—Businessman of the year 1988', *Business India,* December 26 1988, pp50-6.

Karnani, R. 'Telco—Going flat out', *Business India,* April 2, 1990, p32.

Katiyar, A & Parikh, D. 'J.R.D. Tata—A Gentleman of Substance', *India Today,* December 15, 1993, p88.

Khairullah, H. 'Heir-apparent to the Tata throne', *Illustrated Weekly of India,* March 13, 1983, p26.

Khanna, S. 'IBM: Striking new roots in India', *Business Today,* February 22, 1993, pp99-107.

Kottary, Sailesh. 'The board that Russi Mody could not tame', *Economic Times,* April 26, 1993;
'Tata Sons enlarges capital stock', *Economic Times,* January 20, 1994.

Kumar K.R.M. 'Ratan Tata—The end of innocence', *Business Today,* December 23, 1991, pp54-60.

Kure, Mavin. 'Labour resurgence in Pune', *Times of India,* September 26, 1989.

Kuttappan, L. 'Tata Unisys—Towards total solutions', *Business India,* November 22, 1993, p100.

Maitra, D. 'ACC—Sprucing up', *Business India,* July 23, 1990, pp68-71.

Malhotra, J. 'Lakmé—A losing proposition', *Business World,* July 28, 1993, p140.

Malkan, D. 'Russi regret may end Tisco crisis', *Indian Express,* January 2, 1992;
'Will the House of Tatas collapse after JRD?', *Fortune India,* December 16, 1993, p8.

Marpakwar, M. 'Cong-I proxy war in Telco', *Indian Express,* October 6, 1989.

Mathai, P. G. 'Golden boy of steel', *India Today,* October 31, 1989, p123;
'ACC—A controversial issue', *India Today,* June 15, 1988, pp110-12;
'Airline boards—Troubled experiment', *India Today,* April 30, 1987, pp106-9.

Mathrani, S. 'Titan: Titanic times', *Business India,* July 4, 1994, p129.

Mehta, A. 'The dark horse of Bombay House', *Economic Times,* December 8, 1993;
'Tata Chemicals—Raid in the empire', *Economic Times Corporate Dossier,* June 3, 1989;
'Tata Tea—A refreshing brew', *Economic Times Corporate Dossier,* October 6, 1989.

Mehta, Fredie. 'Dealing with sick units', *India Today,* April 15, 1988, p106.

Mid-day, 'Ratan Tata—Life after JRD', December 5, 1993;
'Gentleman Jeh', December 5, 1993;
'The storm bloweth', August 1, 1994.

Mohan, N. C. 'Tisco—Rejuvenated', *Business India,* May 8, 1995, p141.

Mohorkar, S. H. 'Telco—Flickering flames', *Economic Times,* October 23, 1989;
'Telco—On a collision course', *Economic Times,* October 13, 1989;
'Telco—Trial of strength', *Economic Times,* July 29, 1989.

Moodbidri, D. & Nadkarni, S. 'Making room at the top', *The Week,* June 7, 1992, pp28-33.

Moskowitz, M. 'The Tata Group', *World Executive's Digest,* January 1989, pp32-35.

Mukerjea, D. N. 'Tata Steel pulls it off by a whisker', *Business World,* August 10, 1994, p48.

Nag, K. 'Tisco—Making concerted efforts', *Business India,* May 14, 1990, p94.

Nageswaran, N. 'Titan Watches—A clock-work success', *Economic Times Corporate Dossier,* June 10, 1989.

Nair, M. 'Peico Electronics & Electricals—Caught in a cleft stick', *Economic Times Corporate Dossier,* April 3, 1992;
'Telco—A troublesome transition', *Economic Times Corporate Dossier,* January 1, 1990.

Nanda, S. 'Privatisation—Steeling ahead', *Sunday,* October 19, 1991, p37.

Nandy, P. 'JRD—The Inheritors', *Illustrated Weekly of India,* August 31, 1986, pp8-17.

Narayan, S. 'Shoring up at Bombay House', *Business World,* July 13, 1994, p.50;
'Nusli Wadia: Corporate samurai', *Business World,* July 28, 1993, pp19-25;
'Telco's big ambitions ride on small cars', *Business World,* September 20, 1995, pp34-44;
'The Tatas after JRD', *Business World,* December 15, 1993, pp18-25;
'Titan Watches—Timing the attack', *Economic Times Corporate Dossier,* June 7, 1991.

Narayan, S. & Roy, M. G. 'Crowding the driveway', *Business World,* November 1, 1995, pp149-51.

Neri, Michael. 'Ratan Tata', *Sunday Observer,* April 7, 1991.

Nilekani, R. 'Elxsi—Taking on the Titans', *India Today,* August 15, 1985, pp108-9.

Ninan, T.N. 'ACC—A resignation, and some questions', *Economic Times Corporate Dossier,* August 8, 1988;
'J.R.D. Tata—I've been very frustrated', *India Today,* August 15, 1986, p140f;
'Telco—A company in transition', *Economic Times Corporate Dossier,* August 8, 1988;
'Voltas—Changes at the helm', *India Today,* September 13, 1985, pp113-14.

Pattajoshi, L. 'Wooing the Tatas', *The Week,* September 1, 1991, p22.

Pillai, A. 'Meek surrender', *The Week,* December 10, 1989, p8.

Parijat, P. 'Telco: Benz's Indian blueprint', *Business Today,* January 22, 1995, pp52-3.

Pinto, R. 'Voltas—A traumatic takeover', *Business India,* October 25, 1993, p21.

Piramal, G. 'Tata Tea posts record earnings', *Financial Times,* June 26, 1991;
'The Tata Group—The colossus awakens', *Economic Times,* August 31, 1990;
'ACC—Links behind a startling turnaround', *Financial Times,* September 19, 1990;
'Coming up trumps', *Illustrated Weekly Of India,* February 4, 1990, pp22-3;
'Darbari Seth, intrepid intrapreneur', *World Executive's Digest,* April 1990, pp68-71;
'House of Tatas—The rings of power', *Economic Times Corporate Dossier,* December 28, 1990;
'Tata Electric—Powerful plans', *Economic Times Corporate Dossier,* November 2, 1990;
'Man of steel', *Times of India,* February 2, 1992.

Radhakrishnan, N. 'J.R.D. Tata—An obituary', *Business India,* December 6, 1993, pp65-9.

Radhakrishnan, N. & Bhandarkar, G. 'Russi Mody—Five memorable decades', *Business India,* October 16, 1989, p173.

Rahman, M. 'The Tatas: Transfer of power', *India Today,* October 15, 1988, p107;
'NCPA—Jinxed plans', *India Today,* September 30, 1988, p58;
'Telco—New drive', *India Today,* August 31, 1988, p117.

Rahman, M. & Tripathi, S. 'Air India—A turbulent ride', *India Today,* July 31, 1988, pp90-92.

Rao, K. 'Telco: Unusual union', *Business World,* January 27, 1993, p89.

Rao, N. & Bist, R. 'Tata Aquatic—Caught in a bind', *Business India,*

October 15, 1990, p84.

Ravi, A. B. 'Tisco—A crack at the top', *India Today,* January 31, 1992, p129;
'The Tata Group—Consolidation capers', *India Today,* April 15, 1993, pp106-7.

Reddy, M. 'Tisco—Crack in the armour', *Business India,* January 6, 1992, p73;

Roy, A. 'The threat to Tisco', *Business Today,* July 7, 1994, p72f;
'Letters—L'affaire TISCO', *Business Today,* August 7, 1994, p1.

Roy, S. 'Tatas look at hi-tech areas', *Times of India,* April 25, 1993.

Roy, S. 'The Telco transition', *Business World,* September 14, 1988, p51;
'Tisco: Temporary truce', *Business World,* January 15, 1992, p57.

Roy, S. 'Ratan Tata—A man for the nineties', *Business World,* January 3, 1990, pp41-49.

Sanghvi, V. & Tellis, O. 'Palace intrigues', *Sunday,* July 17, 1988, pp21-31.

Sen, S. 'Lakmé—Touch of success', *Business India,* December 10, 1990, pp86-87.

Shah, S. 'ACC—Sheen doesn't wear off', *Economic Times Corporate Dossier,* December 3, 1993.

Shankar, P. 'Rallis India—Out of the doldrums, *Business India,* July 24, 1989, pp58-61.

Shankar, P. & Dass, B. 'Tata Chemicals-Tata Fertilisers merger—Seth to the rescue', *Business India,* June 12, 1989, pp50-63.

Sharma, R. 'Nelco—Seeking a focus', *Business India,* September 3, 1990, pp73-5.

Sharma, S. 'Is Bailadila being sold for a song?', *Business World,* August 23, 1995, p62f.

Shenoy, M. 'Tata Tea: A good brew', *Business India,* October 10, 1994, pp96-100;
'Hyderabad Allwyn—BPL, Voltas win race', *Business India,* December 21, 1992, pp84-89.

Shirali, R. 'Tisco—Tensions at the top', *Economic Times Corporate Dossier,* January 3, 1992.

Singh, C. U. 'J.R.D. Tata—Flight into history', *India Today,* November 15, 1982, pp26-28.

Sinha, Debjani. 'Sons and heirs: Under the looking glass', *Business World,* Aug 15, 1983, p48.

Sunday Observer, 'Historic Tata residence sold', August 26, 1990;
'Ratan Tata's vision now tempered with realism, say Tata managers', April 7, 1991.

Swami, P. 'Tatas—Twin trouble', *India Today*, July 31, 1986, p100.

Tak, D. 'ACC's RCD—Looking beyond the organisation', *Business India*, November 25, 1991, p.113.

Taneja, S. 'Telco—Hotting up', *India Today*, November 15, 1989, p118.

Taneja, S. & Ahmed, F. 'Tatas—Heady heights', *India Today*, February 28, 1990, pp117-20.

Tata, J.R.D. 'The Tata group cannot disintegrate', *Economic Times*, April 5, 1991.

Tata, Ratan. 'I can be my own person', *The Week*, June 7, 1992, p31;
  'Jeh was a man of today', *Economic Times*, December 1, 1993;
  'Letter to the Editor', *Business Standard*', January 18, 1991;
  'Tata Sons rights issue denied' (letter to the editor), May 9, 1992;
  'Tatas look at hi-tech areas', *Times of India*, April 1, 1993;
  'Man of our times', *Economic Times*, May 23, 1991.

Telegraph, '4 top Tisco officers resign', December 24, 1991;
  'Russi Mody apologises to Tisco board', January 3, 1992;

Tellis, Olga. 'Ratan Tata takes on JRD's mantle—A thinker turns manager', *Sunday Observer*, March 31, 1991;
  'Is Tisco takeover talk a ploy for sympathy', *Observer*, July 24, 1994;
  'Tisco succession raises a storm', *Sunday Observer*, December 8, 1991;

Times of India, 'Free hand for FIs at Tisco meeting', May 22, 1992;
  'J.R.D. Tata's retirement, end of era', March 27, 1991;
  'JRD held the group togther', November 11, 1993;
  'Dogged by controversy', July 31, 1994;
  'New Twist to Tisco Row', July 28, 1994;
  'Russi Mody apologises', January 3, 1992;
  'Russi Mody—Historical exit', April 20, 1993;
  'Ratan Tata takes over Tisco—Russi Mody sacked', April 20, 1993;
  'Ignominious exit' (editorial), April 23, 1993;
  'Tata's stand angers workers', September 30, 1989;
  'Tata unaware of takeover move', July 21, 1994;
  'Union leader's status doubtful', September 29, 1989;

Thakore, Dilip. 'Housing: Enter the Tatas', *Business World*, August 29, 1983, pp26-38.

Vasuki, S. N. 'Trade union leaders—A smart new breed', *India Today*, August 15, 1989, p70;
  'Tatas—Troubling departures', *India Today*, July 31, 1989, pp86-87.

Vaidya, Abhay. 'Phenomenal rise of Rajan Nair', *Times of India*, September 30, 1988.

Verma, S. 'Tata-SIA: A venture in jeopardy', *Business India*, May 8, 1995, pp42-3;

'Tata-SIA: On the wings of success', *Business India,* September 12, 1994, p160;

Viswanath, T. S. 'Tata Refractories Ltd—The heat is on', *Economic Times Corporate Dossier,* August 28, 1992.

Vora, S. 'Titan-Times—Timing it right', *Business India,* September 12, 1994, p122

Yadav, S. 'Letter—Skilful manoeuvring', *Illustrated Weekly of India,* August 23, 1987, p4.

Other Literature

Company brochures, press releases, pamphlets, annual reports.

'The Tata Iron and Steel Company,' pamphlet issued by TISCO, 1966.

The Empress Mills Golden Jubilee 1877-1927.

Kottary, S. *Jehangir Ratanji Dudabhoy Tata 1904-1993.* Bombay: Tata Press Ltd, n.d.

Index